HERE IS WHAT EXPERTS ARE SAYING A
WEALTHCOUNSEL® ESTATE PLANNING

"Estate planning today is a dauntingly complex challenge. The experts in this book cut through that complexity to offer useful insights into trusts, taxation, insurance, and many other estate-related topics."

— Kenneth Silber
  Senior Editor of *Research* magazine
  Hoboken, New Jersey

"WealthCounsel has brought together a collection of articles that should be read by both the professional adviser and the theoretician who wants to understand how the estate planning concepts discussed can be used in practical applications. This collection of articles is both timely and relevant and will prove to be a valuable resource for consumers, financial planners, and estate planning professionals."

— Robert J. Lindner, ChFC, CFP, AIF
  CEO of Lindner Capital Advisors, Inc.
  Marietta, Georgia

"This book is a great tool. It can help you gain an easy understanding of the many estate planning strategies available. The information discussed throughout this book is invaluable. It is a "must have" for advisors who work with high net worth clients."

— Jeffrey A. Carbone, CFP®
  Cornerstone Financial Partners
  Cornelius, North Carolina

"WealthCounsel's new book, *Estate Planning Strategies*, clearly shows the reader who has an interest in preserving and protecting his or her hard-earned wealth the procedures to make sure those dollars and benefits go to the ones they love. Written and edited by experienced estate planning experts, it flows, is easy to follow, and has good illustrations and flowcharts to boot."

— John J. Checki Jr., CPA, CFP®, CRC®
  Richardson, Texas

"This book is a treasury of wisdom, usable suggestions, and resource information that will be of great benefit to readers. Its broad coverage will appeal to the novice as well as the seasoned professional."

— Burk Rosenthal, CFP®, ChFC®, CRC®, CFS
  President of Rosenthal Retirement Planning, LP

"This is a state-of-the-art, best practices compendium of estate planning tools and thinking. Estate planning continues to be, if done properly, a priceless gift to the ones we care about and this publication can greatly enhance that gift."

— Gary L. Myers, J.D., LL. M. in estate planning
   Family Investment Center, Inc

"This book could create the 'new' state-of-the-art of estate planning, written at the intersection of a high level of expertise and practical client application. A critical reference tool for the client looking for unbiased planning tools based upon multiple lifetimes of experience (and 'written in English' for non-lawyers), this work contains a plethora of useful material for the practitioner in the financial planning, legal, and accounting fields as well. What makes this work so fascinating is its approach in the delivery of dozens of experts over multiple topics, complete with enough overlap to create an inherent second opinion."

— Andrew Samalin
   Samalin Investment Counsel, LLC
   Mount Kisco, New York

"A remarkably practical and useful book! Think of it as *Everything You Always Wanted to Know about Estate Planning, But Were Afraid to Ask*. Short and to-the-point chapters, clear definitions, abundant worksheets, and (best of all) many practical examples to help us get our heads around this arcane but vitally important field. I especially appreciate the inclusion of unexpected topics such as: transferring your values and ideals (and not just your stuff); nontraditional relationships and evolving definitions of marriage; "modest philanthropy" (i.e., expressing your values with small gifts); and pet trusts. *WealthCounsel® Estate Planning Strategies* lives up to the promise of its subtitle: "Collective Wisdom. Proven Techniques." A great reference for financial planners and their clients!"

— Ed Jacobson, Ph.D.
   Author of *Appreciative Moments: Stories and
   Practices for Living and Working Appreciatively*

"This book is an invaluable resource and "must-have" for both professionals and consumers who are interested in maximizing their wealth through estate planning. It makes complex estate planning strategies easy-to-read and comprehend for virtually anyone…which is quite an accomplishment!"

— Deborah Price
   CEO and Founder of The Money Coaching Institute
   Author of *Money Magic: Unleashing Your True Potential
   for Prosperity and Fulfillment*

"Fantastic! It's like a *Chicken Soup for the Wealth Advisor's (and their clients) Soul!* This book is smart, easy to read and full of great ideas. I love the variety of estate planning insights and the geographic diversity of the attorneys who present them. It's a "first step" resource I can use to help my clients understand what can often be challenging concepts."

— Lisa Dickholtz, CFP™
  President of Dickholtz Wealth Management
  Northbrook, Illinois

"This book is the perfect book for the lay person. Confusion melts away as the reader reviews the simple examples and clearly written chapters."

— John L. Jenkins, AEP, EA, CFP®
  Fellow, Esperti Peterson Institute
  President and CEO of Asset Preservation Strategies, Inc.
  San Diego, California

"By far, the best book on estate planning I've ever seen. It offers everything consumers and allied professionals need: it's comprehensive, authoritative, up-to-date and clearly written, answering all the common questions people ask about estate planning, and then some. I can't wait to give this book to my financial planning clients. They're going to love me!"

— Peter W. Johnson, Jr.
  Principal of PWJohnson Wealth Management
  Host of *Pro Money Talk*
  Founder of The Financial Literacy Project

"Estate planning is very technical and very personal; both aspects are equally important and subject to continuous change. When the experts package their knowledge to make it understandable and interesting to those outside of their profession they empower individuals and families with confidence, encouraging clients to partner with their attorneys to make the best possible plan for their loved ones. This book offers the information, knowledge, and wisdom needed to sort through the estate planning maze of confusion and create an estate plan that reflects values, minimizes taxes, and meets the specific requirements of the family."

— Susan Bradley, CFP®
  Founder, Sudden Money Institute
  Author of *Sudden Money — Managing a Financial Windfall*

"The *WealthCounsel Estate Planning Strategies* book will be one of those publications you keep within reach as a comprehensive, search-here-first resource for all of your estate planning questions. Nearly 100 estate planning attorneys and experts give you brief, to-the-point guidelines for every imaginable estate planning scenario, complete with worksheets and information tables. And this book isn't just for advisors' clients; with chapters like 'Business Succession Planning' and 'Limited Liability Companies,' you'll find it essential in running your own business too."

— David J. Drucker, MBA, CFP
    Columnist for *Morningstar Advisor* and frequent contributor to *Financial Planning, Research, Wealth Manager* and *Financial Advisor* magazines
    Author of three books including *Tools and Techniques of Practice Management* (National Underwriter Company, 2006)
    President of Drucker Knowledge Systems
    Principal of Virtual Office News, LLC

"In reading this book, I found several authors' ideas especially noteworthy, including: the importance of effective communication among all trusted advisors; how estate planning, business succession planning, and exit planning fit together; the value of relationship-centered planning; and keeping your estate planning updated. These are all exciting concepts that allow clients to be better served."

— Karl Bareither
    Founder of FBR System, Inc.
    Author of *Planning a Family & Business Legacy* and *Becoming a Wealth Transfer Specialist*

"This book does an impressive job of covering the estate planning gamut. There is a great deal of technical detail. Yet it is written for a consumer to understand. It is a must-have reference manual for any Estate Planner, Fiduciary, CPA or Financial Planner."

— Daniel G. Gensler, MS, RLP®, CFP®
    Co-author of *The Boomer's Guide to Multi-Generational Planning* (Financial Forum Publishing, 2009)
    Coronado, California

"What a great source of knowledge and strategies communicated in understandable terms and illustrations. This cornucopia of tips from top attorneys is a must-have reference book. Whether you are a financial advisor or a general reader, this book can help you understand how to best protect, preserve, and perpetuate your wealth and values for future generations."

— Devery "Rusty" Cagle, CFP®, CRPC®, CAP™
    President and Founder, ASE Wealth Advisors

WealthCounsel®
Estate Planning Strategies

Collective Wisdom
Proven Techniques

edited by
Randy Gardner, JD, LLM, MBA, CPA, CFP®
Leslie Daff, JD, MBA

Wealth Builders Press, LLC
800 West 47th Street, Suite 430
Kansas City, MO 64112

**Publisher's Cataloging-in-Publication
(Provided by Quality Books, Inc.)**

WealthCounsel estate planning strategies : collective
  wisdom, proven techniques / edited by Randy Gardner and
  Leslie Daff.
  p. cm.
  LCCN 2008939713
  ISBN-13: 978-0-9821779-0-7
  ISBN-10: 0-9821779-0-9

  1. Estate planning--United States--Popular works.
2. Tax planning--United States--Popular works. 3. Wills--
United States--Popular works.   I. Gardner, Randy.
II. Daff, Leslie. III. WealthCounsel.
IV. Title: WealthCounsel estate planning strategies.

  KF750.Z9W43 2008   346.7305'2
                            QBI08-600319

This book is a collection of general legal essays written and edited by attorneys from across the United States. In the preparation of this book, every effort has been made to offer the most current and correct information possible. Nonetheless, inadvertent errors can occur, federal tax and estate laws often change, and probate, estate, and property laws vary from state to state.

The information in the text is intended to afford general guidance to the public. The impact of estate and tax laws varies greatly based upon the unique facts of the individual. Accordingly, the information in this book is not intended to serve as legal, accounting, investment, or tax advice. The authors, editors, and publisher disclaim any responsibility for positions taken by taxpayers in their individual cases or for any misunderstanding on the part of the readers. The editors have reviewed the book for stylistic and grammatical consistency and disclaim any responsibility for the accuracy or originality of the authors' contributions.

The publisher is not engaged in rendering legal, accounting, or other professional service and disclaims any responsibility for the accuracy or originality of the author's contributions.

If legal, accounting, tax, investment, or other expert advice is required, readers are encouraged to consult with professional advisers. This book is sold with the understanding that the authors, editors, and publisher are not offering such advice in this publication.

Printed in the United States of America.

Cover design by Ted Stone.

Preface

From the Partners of WealthCounsel®

This book is designed to educate you about the importance of estate planning. More specifically, the purpose of this book is to help you avoid the common pitfalls that often occur without adequate planning so that you may fulfill your vision and family legacy in the disposition of your assets. In short, the proven strategies in this book will empower readers with knowledge about estate planning techniques that enable clients "to leave what they want, to whom they want, and in the manner they want."

The ideas in this first-of-its-kind book were drawn from the "mind meld" and collective wisdom of estate planning attorneys throughout the country who saw the need to compile a summary of the most effective estate planning strategies being used today. In addition to their commitment to sharing individual expertise for the benefit of many, these attorneys share another common genetic factor — they are all members of WealthCounsel®.

For more than ten years, WealthCounsel attorneys located in all 50 states have been helping clients "of all ages and at all stages" of life fulfill their estate planning objectives. As a membership-based organization of nearly 1,800 practitioners and users of the WealthDocs™ drafting platform, WealthCounsel and its member attorneys promote a client-centered approach to estate planning founded on the principles of legal competence, professional collaboration, and a commitment to excellence.

You, the reader, will discover that the 100 or so ideas and strategies showcased in this book derive not from simplistic legal theory, but from practical application in complex situations. The attorney-authors have carefully illustrated compelling scenarios drawn from estate planning solutions developed for hundreds of clients throughout the country. The techniques discussed span the full continuum of the estate planning process, from the goals of estate planning and the documents generated in the process to planning for incapacity, tax avoidance, charitable giving, retirement, and business succession.

One of our most interesting challenges in bringing this book project to fruition had less to do with its content than its title. The authors had many great suggestions for a title which included:

- *Your Assets. Your Future. Our Focus.*

- *101 Estate Planning Strategies*

- *You Can't Take It With You*

- *If the Attorney Who Drafted Your Estate Plan Also Handles Divorces or Criminal Cases, You Need This Book!*

- *Everything You Wanted To Know About Estate Planning but Were Afraid to Ask.*

But we all had our greatest moment of levity when one author suggested the title should be:

- *Just Because You Can't Take It With You Is No Excuse for Leaving It in Such a Mess!*

After much soul searching and many collaborative e-mail exchanges regarding the book's title, our team drew inspiration from the simple term "WYSIWYG" (pronounced wiz-e-wig), a computer technology acronym for "What You See Is What You Get" that describes a graphical interface system in which content visually displayed during the editing appears graphically similar to the "final output." Therefore, we decided the book's title should simply reflect its final output, i.e., proven estate planning strategies developed through the collective wisdom of WealthCounsel attorneys.

THE PARTNERS OF WEALTHCOUNSEL®

C. Dennis Brislawn, Jr., Esq.
Kirkland, Washington

Mr. Brislawn is a partner in Brislawn Lofton, PLLC, located in Kirkland, Washington. He has a multi-disciplinary practice that includes wealth planning, estate and gift tax planning, estate and gift tax audits, asset protection, business planning, operations and succession, and charitable planning. His law practice serves primarily mid-to-high net worth clients located in the states of Washington, Oregon, and Alaska. As a former member of the U. S. armed forces, Mr. Brislawn received numerous U.S. and foreign decorations and awards, including Airborne-Ranger and French Army Commando qualifications. He is host of the Real Wealth Network KI-570 AM talk radio in Seattle. He has an undergraduate degree with honors from Gonzaga University, and a law degree from the University of Washington.

William A. Conway, Esq.
McLean, Virginia

*As a tax attorney, investment banker, and legal educator practicing in McLean, Virginia, Mr. Conway serves his clients with both financial and legal counsel. A graduate of Georgetown University Law Center, he is a registered investment advisor and tax attorney included in **Who's Who in Finance and Industry**, and in **Who's Who in American Law**. As co-author of WealthCounsel's **Irrevocable Trust Compendium**, Mr. Conway annually teaches continuing education courses on estate planning and wealth preservation for attorneys, financial planners, and accountants. In addition to making guest appearances on television programs such as "The Money Makers" on PBS, Mr. Conway created and hosted the radio series, "Legacy," for many years on Washington Business Radio, and served as a co-host on*

"Money Talk – Family Fortunes." Mr. Conway is a member of the bars of the Commonwealth of Virginia, District of Columbia, and the State of Maryland. Bill was recently appointed to the editorial board of Wealth Management Business, a series of five regionally based magazines published by France Publications, Inc.

W. Edward Dean, Esq.
San Francisco, California

Mr. Dean is the principal of W. Edward Dean, P.C., located in San Francisco, California. He is a tax attorney who protects wealth through estate, income and charitable tax planning. Mr. Dean is a California Bar Association certified tax specialist and a member of the San Francisco Estate Planning Council and Northern California Planned Giving Council. He is a former editor of the **Virginia Law Review,** *the* **Virginia Journal of International Law,** *and the* **New York University Tax Law Review.** *Mr. Dean received a B.A. and M.B.A., magna cum laude, Phi Beta Kappa, from Dartmouth College, a J.D. from the University of Virginia, and an LL.M. in Taxation from New York University.*

Lewis W. Dymond, Jr., Esq.
Frisco, Colorado

Mr. Dymond is president and founder of Dymond Consulting, Inc. located in Frisco, Colorado, a WealthDocs™ consulting, auditing, and customized drafting solution for wealth planning professionals. In 2000, Mr. Dymond was asked by the principals of WealthCounsel, LLC to program the WealthDocs Family Limited Partnership system, and then in 2001, to design the Revocable Living Trust system. In that same year, he was hired on as CEO of WealthCounsel and tasked with the ongoing expansion of WealthDocs and the support of WealthCounsel members. Mr. Dymond became a principal of WealthCounsel in 2005 and resigned as CEO in 2007 to dedicate his full time and attention to Dymond Consulting. Mr. Dymond received his undergraduate degree in Managerial Economics in 1969 from the University of Colorado, and his J.D. in 1971 from the University of Denver.

Stan Miller, Esq.
Little Rock, Arkansas

Mr. Miller is the senior shareholder of Miller & Schrader, P.A., a national estate planning law firm based in Little Rock, Arkansas. He advises clients with respect to a wide range of issues relating to wills and trusts, estate planning, trust administration, corporate and partnership matters, charitable giving, private foundations, supporting organizations, life insurance, and taxation, family owned businesses, succession planning, and the significance of these issues to family relationships. A graduate of Vanderbilt Law School, Mr. Miller is licensed to practice before the United States Tax Court, Eighth Circuit Court of Appeals, and before all Arkansas Courts. Mr. Miller is co-author of WealthCounsel's Family Limited Partnership system, the Revocable Trust system, and the Irrevocable Trust system. A publisher's interview with Stan was featured in the November 2007 issue of **Southeast Wealth Management Business,** *one of a series of five regionally based publications by France Publications, Inc.*

Peter J. Parenti, Esq.
San Antonio, Texas

Mr. Parenti is a wealth strategies estate planning and tax attorney in San Antonio, Texas. In addition to advanced wealth strategies planning, estate planning, and probate and tax law, his practice specializes in real estate transactions, business entities planning, business buy-outs and sell-outs, charitable estate planning, living trusts, family limited partnership creation, and design and asset protection estate planning. Mr. Parenti received his J.D. degree from St. Mary's University School of Law, and his LL.M. degree in taxation from New York University School of Law. He is one of the few attorneys in the state of Texas who is Board Certified as a specialist in both tax law and estate planning and probate law by the State Bar of Texas Board of Legal Specialization.

Thomas J. Ray, Jr., Esq.
Arnold, Missouri

*Mr. Ray is an estate and tax attorney with offices in the Greater St. Louis metropolitan area, and the primary drafter of WealthDocs™ charitable components. Ray has lectured and written extensively in the charitable tax planning area, and he has conducted seminars and workshops for attorneys, accountants, financial advisors, development officers, and donors throughout the United States. He is the author of the ABA bestselling deskbook entitled **Charitable Gift Planning: A Practical Guide for the Estate Planner**, the second edition of which was published in April 2007. Mr. Ray has written two privately published technical training manuals for lawyers on remainder trusts, lead trusts, private foundations, and supporting organizations. He is a member of the Missouri and Oklahoma bars, and is admitted to practice before the United States Tax Court and the United States Supreme Court. In addition to his law practice, Mr. Ray is a principal in Planned Giving Concepts, Inc., a trust administration company that provides administrative support for charitable remainder trusts, lead trusts, and private foundations. Mr. Ray received his undergraduate and law degrees from Oklahoma City University.*

D. Scott Schrader, Esq.
Little Rock, Arkansas

Mr. Schrader is a principal of Miller & Schrader, P.A. in Little Rock, Arkansas and concentrates his practice in the areas of estate planning and post-death administration, as well as estate litigation and disputes. He advises clients with respect to a wide range of issues relating to wills and trusts, estate planning, trust administration, charitable giving, life insurance, and taxes. Mr. Schrader is licensed to practice before the Arkansas Supreme Court, the United States District Courts for the Eastern and Western Districts of Arkansas, the United States Appellate Court, Eighth Circuit, and the United States Tax Court. Mr. Schrader received his J.D. in 1996 from the University of Arkansas at Little Rock and his B.A. in Business Administration & Accounting from Ouachita Baptist University in 1993.

Roberta Trudeau
Portland, Oregon

As one of the founding principals, Ms. Trudeau leads WealthCounsel's member recruitment and retention team. She began her career as a securities broker for a family office in New York City in 1975. Since that time she has held sales and marketing executive positions in the financial services and legal education and technology industries and helped found five investment and legal support companies, the most recent being WealthCounsel, WealthCounsel Advisors Forum, and ElderCounsel.

Carl R. Waldman, Esq.
Westlake Village, California

*Mr. Waldman is a practicing attorney with offices in Westlake Village, California. He specializes in tax planning and estate planning for business owners and executives, and Trust and Estate Administration law. Mr. Waldman is a member of the State Bar of California, American Bar Association Section of Taxation, Beverly Hills Bar Association, and Los Angeles County Bar Association. In early 2006 he co-created and is a managing principal of the WealthCounsel Advisors Forum, a sister company of WealthCounsel, LLC. Mr. Waldman was a guest lecturer for the "Estate Planning for Practitioners" course at California State University at Northridge from 1985 through 1990. Mr. Waldman has taught "The Basics of Estate Planning" and "Beyond the Basics of Estate Planning" for the California Society of Certified Public Accountants, Mr. Waldman has served as an Adjunct Professor at National University, Los Angeles and as a consultant to The Richard M. Nixon Library and Birthplace. He is a member of the Legal Advisory Board of The Capital Trust Company of Delaware. He co-authored the **Family Limited Partnership Compendium** published by Wealth Enhancement Strategies, LLC in 1995, the new **Family Limited Partnership System** published by WealthCounsel, LLC in 2000, and the **Living Trust Practice System** published by WealthCounsel, LLC in 2001 Mr. Waldman received his undergraduate degree in History at Pomona College (Claremont, California), and received his law degree at the University of California, Los Angeles.*

If you are an attorney or a financial advisor with questions about WealthCounsel, Advisor's Forum, or ElderCounsel, please contact Roberta Trudeau at 888-659-4069, ext. 803 or visit our website at www.wealthcounsel.com.

EDITORS' ACKNOWLEDGEMENTS

This book is the product of many people's efforts. We would especially like to thank the authors who contributed to the book, Jessica Culpepper who prepared many of the charts, and our families.

We would also like to thank Laura Wilson; Marlene Frith; Lori Berry; Marie Swift; Alison Courtney; WealthCounsel, LLC's partners, members, employees, and clients; Estate Plan, Inc.'s employees and clients; Retirement Plus, Inc.'s employees and clients; Ted Stone; UMKC faculty and students; Keir Educational Resources; Kaplan Schweser; and all the other people who helped us. Without their help and support, this book would not have been possible.

This edition is specially dedicated to our children: Chuck Daff, Katie Daff, Bryn Gardner, Kara Gardner, Creyton Gardner, and Hope Gardner. Our children are the ones who have a wonderful future before them. Our estate, trust, and probate systems should work for us, our futures, and our children's futures.

— *Randy Gardner and Leslie Daff*

Table of Contents

Preface   vii

Editors' Acknowledgments   xii

INTRODUCTION TO ESTATE PLANNING

1. Goals of Estate Planning   Hannon Ford   2

2. Estate Planning Documents Overview   Leslie Daff   5

3. Estate Planning Team   Kimberly Lee   8

4. An Overview of the Estate, Gift, and   F. Moore McLaughlin IV   11
   Income Tax Rules Pertaining to Estates   and Jill Sugarman

PROPERTY OWNERSHIP

5. Real Property and Personal Property   Chris Mares   20

6. Joint Tenancy   Darlynn Morgan   23

7. Classification of Property Interests as   Brian Albee   29
   Present Interests, Contingent Future
   Interests, or Vested Future Interests

ESTATE PLANNING DOCUMENTS AND DRAFTING ISSUES

8. Intestate Law Overview   Ellen Gay Moser   34

9. Wills – Testamentary Capacity   Christopher Berry   36
   and Undue Influence

10. Types of Wills   Alexandra Gadzo   39

11. Who Are Your Descendants?   Richard F. Nevins   42

12. Designating Fiduciaries   Sheri Peters   44

13. Make Sure Your Property Is Distributed   Randy Gardner   47
    the Way You Want if One of Your Children   and Lewis W. Dymond
    Dies Before You

14. No-Contest Clauses in Wills and Trusts   Roland Achtel   50
                                                and Olga Álvarez

AVOIDING PROBATE (WHAT HAPPENS AFTER YOU DIE?)

15. The Pros and Cons of Probate   Diedre Dennis Wachbrit   54

16. Types of Probate Administration –   Richard Dayton   57
    Formal and Informal

17. Non-Probate vs. Probate Assets – Why You Should Care — Susan McMakin — 60

18. Trust Terminology and Types of Trusts — Arlyn J. Bossenbrook — 65

19. Overview of the Taxation of Trusts — David Allen Hiersekorn — 69

20. Generation-Skipping Transfer Tax and the Rule Against Perpetuities — Jimmie L. Joe — 73

21. Planning for Estates Worth Less Than the Generation-Skipping Tax Exemption — W. Edward Dean — 78

22. Health Care Durable Powers of Attorney and Durable General Powers of Attorney for Property Management — Richard Peterson — 82

23. Advance Health Care Directives — Peter S. Myers — 86

24. Long-Term Care and Disability Insurance — Peter J. Parenti — 90

25. Special Needs Trusts — Diedre Dennis Wachbrit — 92

ESTATE TAX PRINCIPLES

26. What Is Included in Your Estate? — Kristine Kyllander — 98

27. Estate Tax Deductions — Steven B. Spewak — 101

28. Marital Deduction — Joseph O'Brien — 104

29. Using Credit Shelter and Marital Trusts to Reduce Estate Taxes — Julie Garber — 109

30. A QTIP Trust Can Protect Your Children's Inheritance if You Remarry — Troy Wilson — 113

31. Use of Disclaimers — David Harowitz — 118

32. Non-Citizen Spouses and the Qualified Domestic Trust (QDOT) — Matthew T. McClintock — 122

33. Planning for Nontraditional Relationships and the Evolving Definition of Marriage — Jerry Chasen — 125

AVOIDING ESTATE TAX WITH LIFETIME TRANSFERS

34. Annual Exclusion Planning — Brian C. Layman — 130

35. Advantages and Disadvantages of Gifting — Jeffrey Roth and David Bacon — 133

36. Avoiding Estate Tax With Lifetime Transfers: Gift Splitting — Richard Redgrave — 136

37. Custodial Accounts for Minors — Nancy Kaupp Ewin — 140

38. Providing Education and/or Nest Egg Funding for Young Beneficiaries — Timothy M. Halligan — 144

39. Intra-Family Loans — Sean Kenney — 149

40. Sales, Installment Sales, and Self-Canceling Installment Notes — Henry Weatherby — 152

41. Private Annuities – a Simple Strategy for Estate Planning, Business Succession Planning, and Asset Protection — Ryland F. Mahathey — 155

CHARITABLE TRUSTS

42. Outright Gifts — Jackson Doggette — 162

43. Charitable Remainder Trusts (How to Benefit Yourself and Others) — Stephen J. Bailey — 165

44. The Charitable Lead Trust — Scott Gunderson — 170

45. Charitable Deductions and Contributions of Partial Interests in Property — David Straus — 175

46. Conservation Easements – How to Give Your Land Away but Still Use It — Matthew Brown — 178

47. Modest Philanthropy – Encouraging Modest Gifts Using "The Expression of Charitable Intentions" — Timothy Borchers — 182

48. Setting Up a Private Foundation in Your Will or Trust — Thomas J. Ray, Jr. — 185

REVOCABLE LIVING TRUSTS

49. Revocable Living Trusts, Pour Over Wills, and Probate Avoidance — Donna L. Wilson — 190

50. Revocable Living Trusts – Separate or Joint — Karen Reagler — 195

51. What Happens After the First Death — Brad Wiewel — 198

52. Revocable Living Trusts – Trustee Distribution Powers — William Carmines — 201

53. Choosing a Trustee for Your Living Trust — Glenn Price — 205

54. Revocable Living Trusts – Timing Distributions After the Second Death — Kevin Forbush — 208

55. Revocable Living Trusts – Independent Trustees and Trust Protectors — Dennis Sullivan — 211

56. "Funding" Your Trust — Chris Caswell — 215

57. Trust Administration to Reduce Estate Taxes — Craig R. Hersch — 220

LIFE INSURANCE

58. Who Has an Insurable Interest? — Marty Burbank — 230

59. Tax Issues Associated With Life Insurance — Dennis Cullen — 234

60. Irrevocable Life Insurance Trusts	Bruce G. Kaufmann	237
61. Avoiding Tax on Life Insurance Distributions Before Death – Life Settlements and Viatication	Neil Covert	241
62. Transfer for Value Rule	Christopher D. Soto	244
63. Can You Afford Your Buy-Sell Agreement?	Natalia Kabbe	247

RETIREMENT PLANS

64. The Tax on Income in Respect of a Decedent – an Estate Tax for Everyone	Natalia Kabbe	252
65. Planning Strategies to Avoid Income in Respect of Decedent (IRD)	Randy Gardner and Bob Keebler	254
66. Retirement Plans – Beneficiary Designations	Guy Garner	257
67. Required Minimum Distributions and Stretching	Patrick B. Casey	261
68. Using Standalone Retirement Distribution Trusts	Stephen T. O'Neill	269
69. The IRA Designated Beneficiary Trust – Saving Your Family Millions	Stuart Kalb	272

BUSINESS AND INVESTMENT INTERESTS

70. Business Succession Planning	John R. Windsor, Jr.	278
71. Estate Planning, Business Succession Planning, and Exit Planning – How Can (or Do) They Fit Together?	Daniel B. Capobianco	284
72. Valuation Discounts and Premiums on the Transfer of Business and Investment Entities	Ron Feinman	288
73. Family Limited Partnerships	Michael Burstein	292
74. Limited Liability Companies	James K. Burau	296
75. Grantor Retained Annuity Trusts	Henna Shah	299
76. Qualified Personal Residence Trusts	Erin Thrash	302
77. Corporate Recapitalization	Beth K. Rautiola	305
78. Using Section 6166 to Assist With Payment of Estate Taxes	Vanessa Gregor	309

ASSET PROTECTION

79. Asset Protection Case Studies	William R. Black and Joseph Strazzeri	314

80. Asset Protection Utilizing Asset Protection Trusts and Limited Liability Companies — Jeffrey R. Matsen — 319

81. Multiple Business Entities as an Asset Protection Tool — Robert Vaksman — 323

82. Alaska Asset Protection Trusts — Ellen Gay Moser — 326

83. Planning With Wyoming LLCs — Cecil Smith and Carol Gonnella — 329

84. Estate Planning for Physicians and Other Professionals — Theodore G. Gudorf — 335

OTHER CONSIDERATIONS IN ESTATE PLANNING

85. State Death Taxes – Potential Impact and Strategies — Jeffrey L. Knapp — 340

86. Pet Trusts – Can You Trust Your Pet? — Peggy Hoyt — 343

87. The Buildup Equity Retirement Trust or BERT! The Wonder Trust™ — Cecil Smith and Carol Gonnella — 346

88. Beneficiary-Controlled Descendants' Trusts — James N. Voeller — 352

89. Captive Insurance Companies — Marc Selden and Brian A. Eagle — 354

90. Elder Law Concepts — Brian Andrew Tully — 357

91. Medicaid/Medi-Cal Preplanning With Trusts — Russell C. Miller — 360

92. Anyone Can Leave Money Directly to Children, but It Is Better to Leave It in Trust – How Not to Make a $250,000 Mistake — Robert M. Goldberg — 364

93. Don't Let the Tax Tail Wag the Dog! Providing Flexibility During Life and After Death Through Disclaimer Planning — Patrick Shin and Michelle Lee — 367

93. When Should We Do Estate Planning? Make Sure You Plan for Your Disability and Death While You Still Can — Toni DeGasperin — 371

94. The Importance of Keeping Your Estate Plan Updated — Barry D. Siegel — 374

95. Relationship-Centered Planning — Heinz Brisske — 376

96. Ethics in Estate Planning — Marcella Downing and Robert Howk — 378

Index — 382

INTRODUCTION
TO
ESTATE PLANNING

CHAPTER 1

Goals of Estate Planning

HANNON FORD (Windom, Minnesota)

The true goals of estate planning are different for everybody. Some people enjoy living frugally and saving to leave assets to their loved ones, while others hope to spend their last dollar on their last day. Some want to leave their entire estate outright to their children, whereas others want to strictly control the manner and timing of distributions to their beneficiaries. Still others intend to leave most of their estate to charity.

Because the phrase "estate planning" is thrown around so much today, it is important to come up with a definition of estate planning. Basically, your estate consists of all the assets you have accumulated during your lifetime, including your real estate, bank and brokerage accounts, retirement plans, life insurance, other investments, and even your junk. Everything you own and value that can be passed on is your estate. Planning for your estate is best done while you are still alive and well because the purpose of planning is for the time when we are either no longer alive or no longer well. Thus, good estate planning should cover three potential time frames: the present, disability, and death.

Planning for the present consists of coming up with a plan that does not unduly complicate your life as well as one that enables you to stay in control of your estate as long as possible. You also need a plan that remains as flexible and changeable as possible in order to adapt to constantly changing rules, statutes, and laws. Planning for disability usually comes next. Although none of us wish to become incapacitated, the reality is that surveys suggest close to half of all seniors will become disabled at some point in their lives. Do you know who will take care of you, your spouse, and others who may be dependent on you if that should occur? Lastly, you plan for when you're gone. This time frame is where most of us focus when considering our estate planning. Again, everyone's goals will be different for post-death planning.

Many well-respected attorneys battle the myth that the only purpose of estate planning is to avoid probate and save on taxes at death. While both of these goals are important, they are but a small part of our true purpose for post-death estate planning. For some people, the primary goal is to pass on a family business or farm to a child who is active in the business, yet try to equalize assets going to another child. Others want to ensure inheritances going to family members are protected as much as possible from divorcing spouses, creditors, lawsuits, illness, or bankruptcy, and also want to protect heirs who may be too young or too immature from their own bad spending habits, possible addictions, and bad influences. Getting advice from a qualified estate planning attorney can offer many options with which to achieve these goals.

With the proper tools and advice you can accomplish almost any estate planning goal you have in mind. This book is a collection of estate planning tools used by some of the best estate planning attorneys in the country; all members of WealthCounsel, a national organization of estate planning attorneys. In contrast to some professionals who may prepare estate plans focused on little more than probate-avoidance and tax-minimization, or as the old saying goes, "If you only have a hammer, everything looks like a nail," the attorneys contributing to this book have assembled a hardware store's supply of tools to enable you to achieve your individual and varying estate planning goals in the best possible way for you and your loved ones.

Hannon T. Ford, The Ford Law Office, L.L.C., creates estate, medical assistance, and business succession plans. Through our unique counseling and design process our clients understand they have a plan which will work.

Estate Planning Goals Worksheet

X	GOALS
	Provide financial security to my spouse.
	Provide financial security for my children and/or grandchildren.
	Divide my estate equally among my children.
	Gift interests to family members.
	Transfer ownership of a business or other assets to loved ones, partners, or employees with a minimum amount of transfer tax.
	Provide adequate liquidity and ongoing cash flow for those responsible for administering the estate.
	Minimize current and future transfer and income taxes.
	Provide for a favorite charity.
	Fund educational expenses for children or grandchildren.
	Provide an adequate safety net for lifetime contingencies such as disability or death of a spouse.
	Avoid probate and other administrative costs.
	Avoid legal hassles or disputes with third parties, including taxing authorities.
	Maintain flexibility in the overall estate plan to adapt to changing circumstances.
	Maintain control over or ensure competent management of assets.
	Minimize exposure to liabilities that could consume one's assets.
	Ensure that assets ultimately pass to intended parties.
	Avoid disputes among family members or business owners.
	Avoid complexity in the overall estate plan and in the specific techniques used to implement the plan.
	Other:
	Other:
	Other:

CHAPTER 2

Estate Planning Documents Overview

LESLIE DAFF (Laguna Beach, California)

An estate plan benefits both you and your loved ones in the event of your incapacity and upon your death. Planning now, while you are healthy, enables you to choose appropriate fiduciaries to handle your affairs. Without such a plan in place, the court will appoint a conservator if you are incapacitated and will appoint an administrator upon your death. The court will also appoint guardians for your minor children.

By taking the time to plan now, you make these decisions yourself instead of leaving it up to the court. Moreover, you choose your beneficiaries instead of having the state determine them for you; you are able to plan the manner and timing of distributions to those beneficiaries; and you can avoid probate and minimize taxes. Thus estate planning has lasting benefits for both you and your loved ones. The documents most commonly used in estate planning, both basic and advanced, are described below.

BASIC ESTATE PLANNING

Generally, the documents comprising a basic estate plan are a revocable living trust, a pour over will, an advance health care directive or health care power of attorney and living will, a durable power of attorney for financial matters, and a Health Insurance Portability and Accountability Act authorization.

Revocable Living Trust

People often use a revocable living trust to avoid probate, for tax planning, and to control the manner and timing of distribution to beneficiaries. Unlike a will, which is a public document filed with the court, the trust is private. Property held in the name of the trust is not subject to probate proceedings.

You need to transfer your assets (e.g., real estate) into the trust, generally with the assistance of an attorney. You continue to control and manage the assets as you do now, but upon your incapacity, your named successor trustee manages the trust assets on your behalf without a court having to appoint a conservator. Upon your death, your successor trustee distributes the assets to your beneficiaries according to the terms of the trust.

Will

A "pour over" will is typically used in conjunction with a living trust, to catch any assets that may not have been transferred to the trust, so they can be distributed according to the trust's terms. You also nominate guardians for your minor children in the will.

Durable Power of Attorney for Property Management

A Durable Power of Attorney for property management enables a designated individual to handle your non-trust assets (e.g., pay your bills from a non-trust checking account, transfer assets to your living trust) in the event you are incapacitated.

Advance Health Care Directive, Power of Attorney for Health Care, and Living Will

An Advance Health Care Directive or Power of Attorney for Health Care allows you to designate an agent to make health care decisions for you in the event you are incapacitated. In addition to the release and execution of health care records and forms and consent to surgery and the like, it can be used to express your preferences regarding life-sustaining care. In some states, you express your directives to medical providers and medical institutions in a Living Will.

Health Insurance Portability and Accountability Act Authorization

A Health Insurance Portability and Accountability Act ("HIPAA") authorization permits your designated agent to obtain protected medical information about you in order to handle your medical affairs.

ADVANCED ESTATE PLANNING

Larger estates; those in excess of the federal estate tax credit amount or applicable exclusion amount ($2 million per person in 2008, and $3.5 million in 2009) may benefit from one or more of the following strategies and associated documents, which can be used alone or in conjunction with others.

Irrevocable Life Insurance Trust

There is a common misconception that life insurance proceeds are not subject to federal estate taxes. While the proceeds are free from income tax, they are countable as part of your taxable estate and therefore about half its value can be lost to estate taxes. An Irrevocable Life Insurance Trust (ILIT) is created specifically for the purpose of owning your life insurance policy. The ILIT holds the policy outside of your estate and keeps the proceeds from being taxable to your estate. The proceeds can then be used to provide your estate with the liquidity to pay estate taxes, pay off debts, pay final expenses, and provide income to a surviving spouse or children. You can use your annual gift tax exclusion to make cash gifts to your trust to pay the premium on the life insurance policy.

Qualified Personal Residence Trust

A Qualified Personal Residence Trust (QPRT) allows you to give away your house or vacation home at a discount, freeze its value for estate tax purposes, and still continue to live in it.

Family Limited Partnerships and Limited Liability Companies

Family Limited Partnerships (FLPs) and Limited Liability Companies (LLCs) are entities involving members of your family. The main advantages of forming and funding FLPs and LLCs involve estate and gift tax savings and asset protection.

Grantor Retained Trusts

A Grantor Retained Annuity Trust (GRAT) is an irrevocable trust to which you contribute assets. You retain the right to receive annuity payments for a specified period of time based on an assumed discount rate determined by the IRS. At the end of the term, assets in the trust pass to other beneficiaries. The GRAT provides gift and estate tax savings if the return on the assets placed in the GRAT exceeds the assumed discount rate. Grantor Retained Unitrusts (GRUTs), where distributions are based on a percentage of assets instead of an annuity, and Grantor Retained Interest Trusts (GRITs), where you retain an income interest, are similar techniques.

Intentionally Defective Grantor Trusts

Alternatively, you may want to sell assets to an Intentionally Defective Grantor Trust (IDGT), an irrevocable trust you establish that is excluded from your estate for federal estate tax purposes, yet owned by you for income tax purposes. The sale can be in exchange for a promissory note. Similar to a GRAT, the sale of the promissory note provides gift and estate tax savings if the return on the IDGT exceeds the interest rate on the note.

Charitable Planning Documents

If you are charitably inclined and seek to minimize taxes while enhancing the amounts going to your loved ones, you may want to consider charitable planning. Documents associated with charitable planning include Charitable Remainder Trusts (CRATs and CRUTs), Charitable Lead Trusts (CLATs and CLUTs), and Private Foundations.

In preparing any of the foregoing documents, it is important to work with a qualified attorney because the law in this area is very specialized, changes often, and involves complex tax matters. The ramifications for you and your loved ones can be far-reaching, both emotionally and financially.

Leslie Daff, JD, MBA, of Estate Plan, Inc. (www.estateplaninc.com) specializes in estate planning, trust, and probate law. She has offices in Laguna Beach and Irvine, California.

CHAPTER 3

Estate Planning Team

KIMBERLY LEE (Indian Wells, California)

In all of life's endeavors the importance of teamwork can not be overemphasized. Little can be accomplished by an individual working alone, because no one person can hope to equal the abilities of a dynamic team, each member of which contributes a set of unique abilities. However, working successfully as a team is not as easy as it may seem. Whether it is with an attorney's employees or among a group of diverse professionals, teamwork requires good leadership, clear communication, established roles, and a desire to work cooperatively.

A MULTI-DISCIPLINARY APPROACH

In estate planning, the most important technique is not the creative use of the "Alphabet Soup" — RLT, ILIT, IDGT, FLP, QPRT, and CRT — but rather using a synergistic team approach.

Transferring your values and ideals, in addition to your monetary wealth, is an important part of leaving a legacy. In other words, what your children and grandchildren inherit should be not only stocks and bonds, but also cherished goals and beliefs for which they should strive — for example, the value of hard work, recognition of one's heritage, respect for family traditions, and the need to contribute to the community and society at large. As Dr. Barry Baines wrote in *Ethical Wills: Putting Your Values on Paper*, "It's not just about valuables, but about values; not just about principal, but about principles."

To create an estate plan that serves your unique needs and reflects your beliefs and values is not an easy task. You are best served by a group of skilled advisors from a variety of disciplines. Sound estate planning is built upon a multidisciplinary approach.

A great football team is led by a quarterback who executes a game plan with the confidence of his coach and teammates. Similarly, a successful estate planning team is best led by an advisor who "quarterbacks" the estate planning process with the confidence of the client and the confidence of a team of financial, legal, and tax professionals.

This estate planning team should consist of, at the very least, the following professionals: certified public accountant (CPA), estate planning attorney, financial advisor, and may also include a professional trustee, insurance professional, and appraiser/valuation expert. Each advisor on the team should be able to form cooperative relationships with the others and work together to shape and implement the client's estate plan.

The attorney is the only person on the team licensed to create legal documents. Remember that no one attorney is an authority on all areas of the law. Be sure to work with an attorney who specializes in estate planning. The CPA is another integral part of this team. Federal estate tax laws have changed dramatically in recent years and the CPA can address potential tax issues and work with the attorney to minimize taxes and explore the advantages of tax-deferred investments.

Another important member of the team is the financial advisor. A qualified and experienced financial advisor takes a holistic approach to your overall financial health. He or she can recommend investments best suited to your estate plan while taking into consideration your current and future financial goals. Many financial advisors are also well versed in the insurance field and can help with matters involving life insurance and disability coverage.

Of course, one of the most important considerations when assembling this estate planning "dream team" is to make sure all the advisors communicate with each other and are "on the same page." When advisors act and advise independently of each other, they run the risk of working at cross-purposes or with different agendas. Looking at a single sliver of a client's circumstances with limited information may lead to a recommendation that is inappropriate when viewed from a broader perspective.

An advisor who has the skills to work effectively in a team environment should enjoy the powerful synergy that is created by other team members' strengths and perspectives, while contributing his or her own experience to the quality of the final result. This team approach not only adds tangible value to the planning process, but also makes the experience educational and enjoyable for you, and for all clients.

THE IN-HOUSE TEAM IS IMPORTANT TOO

In their book *The Experience Economy*, B. Joseph Pine II and James H. Gilmore declare "work is theater, and every business a stage." Their thesis is that the quality of the client experience is just as important to a successful client relationship as the goods and services being purchased.

This concept is especially true in a law firm where the "product" — legal services — is largely invisible. Additionally, quite often you deal as much or more with an attorney's staff, as with the attorney. That means the quality of the in-office estate planning team is crucial, not only their legal knowledge and competence, but their friendliness and willingness to serve you.

Estate planning attorneys build a great in-house team by, among other things, creating a positive and supportive work environment, helping team members reach and achieve their career and personal goals, maintaining focus on the firm's mission, conducting regular and efficient meetings to facilitate communication, continuously training, and creating a "client-centric" office culture.

In short, teamwork is essential to the estate planning process, both among the group of legal and financial professionals working with you and with the support staff and office personnel who often deal regularly with you.

Kimberly T. Lee has a successful estate planning practice near Palm Springs, California. She frequently lectures on estate planning topics and holds workshops for her clients and advisors.

CHAPTER 4

An Overview of the Estate, Gift, and Income Tax Rules Pertaining to Estates

F. MOORE MCLAUGHLIN IV and JILL SUGARMAN (Providence, Rhode Island)

Proper estate planning helps you accomplish many goals, including minimizing taxes. Even when considering your non-tax goals, the tax consequences of your choices should still be taken into account. You should focus on the wealth transfer taxes that could arise upon implementation of your estate plan. You must also anticipate the taxes that will be imposed upon your death. Lastly, income taxes may be assessed upon your estate during its administration. While estate planning certainly involves more than planning for these taxes, you do not want to overlook opportunities to pass on more wealth by reducing taxes whenever possible.

In any estate planning scenario, two basic federal taxes are involved: wealth transfer taxes and income taxes. Wealth transfer taxes consist of the gift tax and the estate tax. The gift tax is based on the value of assets transferred during your life. The estate tax is based on the value of assets transferred upon your death. In 2008, you are allowed to transfer up to $1 million in gifts tax-free during your life and up to $2 million (including gifts made during your life) upon your death. For deaths in 2009, the limit is $3.5 million. This amount is called the applicable exclusion amount. Additionally, you may generally transfer up to $12,000 ($13,000 in 2009) per year tax-free to any number of people. This amount is referred to as the annual gift tax exclusion.

Both the gift tax and the estate tax are based on the fair market value of the assets transferred; the determination of which has resulted in much litigation. The IRS has sanctioned several estate planning techniques based on determining the value of a present or future gift.

In many instances, especially if you have never undertaken any estate planning and depending upon the value and nature of your assets, your estate planning attorney may recommend making gifts, perhaps even in amounts exceeding the lifetime $1 million exemption amount. Gift tax returns must be filed when gifts exceed the annual gift tax exclusion amount.

You must also account for the income tax consequences of your current gifts. You are not allowed an income tax deduction for gifts (except to certain charities), and the recipient of your gift reports no income. For gifts of assets that have increased in value since you acquired them, the recipient of your gift will take over your tax basis and holding period. Tax basis consists of the original amount paid for the asset, plus capital expenditures you make to the asset, less any depreciation deductions you are allowed. Basis is used to determine any taxable gain from the sale of your assets. Gain is the amount you receive from the sale of your asset reduced by your basis.

If your estate plan includes family limited partnerships and trusts, the income tax ramifications associated with such estate planning tools must be considered. Shifting your income tax burden to your children or a trust may result in overall income tax savings which can provide you with benefits in addition to the gift and estate tax savings.

In most estate plans for married couples, no federal estate tax is due upon the death of the first spouse. These plans typically take advantage of the unlimited marital deduction — your ability to transfer an unlimited amount of assets to your spouse during your life or upon your death — often by utilizing special trusts. In such instances, upon the death of the second spouse, the estate tax will be imposed on the value of the assets the surviving spouse owns when he or she dies, including life insurance policies, joint accounts, and certain interests in trusts.

In contrast to gifts you make during your lifetime, your beneficiaries at death will inherit your assets with a "stepped-up" basis — the fair market value of the assets on the date of your death. This step up (or step down) in basis effectively eliminates any gain (or loss) if the assets are sold soon after your death. Under this scenario, enormous tax savings can result. An experienced estate planning attorney can help you make these calculations and determine the best course of action between making gifts during life or planning to transfer your assets upon death.

In addition to the Federal estate tax return for estates exceeding the applicable exclusion amount, a final income tax return, which includes all income received prior to death, must be filed on behalf of the decedent.

Upon death, a new taxpayer — the estate — is created. The estate may receive income and pay expenses prior to making final distributions. If so, then an income tax return will be required to be filed on behalf of the estate. The types of income received by the estate may include salary or wages during the final pay period, certain retirement accounts, accrued rents, interest, and dividends. The estate is also allowed certain deductions against the income, such as administrative expenses and fiduciary fees. Whether the estate is required to pay taxes, or whether the beneficiaries of the estate will bear this burden, is determined under a complex set of rules.

You must consider many taxes in the course of preparing and implementing your estate plan. While focusing on gift and estate taxes, you must not forget about income tax. Engaging an experienced estate planning team, including an attorney, CPA, and financial advisor, is your best avenue for avoiding or minimizing these taxes.

McLaughlin & Quinn, LLC (www.mclaughlinquinn.com) is a law firm focused on preserving wealth through estate planning, asset protection planning, income tax planning, IRS and state tax representation, and bankruptcy.

Gift Tax Formula

1. Total gifts in current year (fair market value of all gifts)		$_____
2. **LESS:**		
One-half of value of gifts split with spouse	$_____	
Annual exclusions ($12,000 per donee for present interests, and $13,000 in 2009)	$_____	
Marital deduction	$_____	
Charitable deduction	$_____	
Total Subtractions		($_____)
3. **EQUALS:** Taxable gifts in current year		$_____
4. **ADD:** Taxable gifts made in prior years		$_____
5. **EQUALS:** Total taxable gifts to date (tax base)		$_____
6. Tentative tax on total taxable gifts to date		$_____
7. **LESS:** Tax paid or deemed paid on prior taxable gifts		($_____)
8. **EQUALS:** Gift tax on current year taxable gifts before applicable credit amount		$_____
9. **LESS:** Applicable credit amount ($345,800)		($_____)
10. **EQUALS:** Gift tax due on current year taxable gifts		$_____

Estate Tax Formula

1. Gross Estate $_____

2. **LESS: EXPENSES, DEBTS, AND LOSSES**

    Funeral and administrative expenses $_____

    Debts of decedent, mortgages, losses $_____

    Medical expenses $_____

    Unpaid taxes $_____

    Total Expenses, Debts, and Losses   ($_____)

3. **EQUALS:** Adjusted Gross Estate (AGE) $_____

4. **LESS: TOTAL ALLOWABLE DEDUCTIONS**

    Charitable deduction $_____

    Marital deduction $_____

    State death taxes paid $_____

    Total Allowable Deductions   ($_____)

5. **EQUALS:** Taxable estate $_____

6. **ADD:** Adjusted taxable gifts (post-1976) $_____

7. **COMPUTE:** Tentative tax base   ($_____)

8. **COMPUTE:** Tentative tax $_____

9. **LESS:** Tax paid or deemed paid on prior taxable gifts   ($_____)

10. **EQUALS:** Estate tax before reduction for allowable credits $_____

11. **LESS:**

    Applicable credit amount $_____

    Other credits $_____

    Total Subtractions   ($_____)

12. **EQUALS:** Estate tax liability $_____

2008 Unified Federal Estate and Gift Tax Rate Schedule

IF THE TAXABLE AMOUNT IS:	THE TENTATIVE TAX IS:
Over $0 but not over $10,000	18%
Over $10,000 but not over $20,000	$1,800 plus 20% of the excess over $10,000
Over $20,000 but not over $40,000	$3,800 plus 22% of the excess over $20,000
Over $40,000 but not over $60,000	$8,200 plus 24% of the excess over $40,000
Over $60,000 but not over $80,000	$13,000 plus 26% of the excess over $60,000
Over $80,000 but not over $100,000	$18,200 plus 28% of the excess over $80,000
Over $100,000 but not over $150,000	$23,800 plus 30% of the excess over $100,000
Over $150,000 but not over $250,000	$38,800 plus 32% of the excess over $150,000
Over $250,000 but not over $500,000	$70,800 plus 34% of the excess over $250,000
Over $500,000 but not over $750,000	$155,800 plus 37% of the excess over $500,000
Over $750,000 but not over $1,000,000	$248,300 plus 39% of the excess over $750,000
Over $1,000,000 but not over $1,250,000	$345,800 plus 41% of the excess over $1,000,000
Over $1,250,000 but not over $1,500,000	$448,300 plus 43% of the excess over $1,250,000
Over $1,500,000	$555,800 plus 45% of the excess over $1,500,000

Estates and Gifts: Applicable Credit and Applicable Exclusion Amount

For Transfers Made in	ESTATES		GIFTS	
	The Credit is	Taxable Estate Exclusion	The Credit is	Taxable Gift Exclusion
1987-1997	$192,800	$600,000	$192,800	$600,000
1998	$202,050	$625,000	$202,050	$625,000
1999	$211,300	$650,000	$211,300	$650,000
2000-2001	$220,550	$675,000	$220,550	$675,000
2002-2003	$345,800	$1,000,000	$345,800	$1,000,000
2004-2005	$555,800	$1,500,000	$345,800	$1,000,000
2006-2008	$780,800	$2,000,000	$345,800	$1,000,000
2009	$1,455,800	$3,500,000	$345,800	$1,000,000
2010	Estate tax repealed	Estate tax repealed	$345,800	$1,000,000
2011	$345,800	$1,000,000	$345,800	$1,000,000

To illustrate the gift, estate, and income tax aspects of estate planning, consider the following sequence of examples.

EXAMPLE 1: Assume you, as a single person, purchase stock in 2004 for $300,000. In 2006, the stock value appreciates to $512,000 and you gift the stock to your daughter. The amount of gift tax you owe is zero, calculated as follows:

Fair market value of the gift	$512,000
Annual exclusion	(12,000)
Taxable gift	500,000
Tentative gift tax	$155,800
Unified credit ($345,800, limited to tentative tax)	(155,800)
Gift tax due for 2006	0

For income tax purposes, your daughter is deemed to have purchased the stock when you did in 2004, giving her a basis in the stock of $300,000 for determining long-term or short-term capital gain.

EXAMPLE 2: Continuing Example 1, assume you purchased other stock for $800,000 in 2003. By 2007, the value of the stock has decreased to $762,000 and you gift the stock to an irrevocable trust for the benefit of your son. The amount of gift tax you owe is calculated as follows:

Fair market value of the gift		$ 762,000
Less: Annual exclusion		(12,000)
Taxable gift for the current year		750,000
Add: prior taxable gifts	(gift to daughter in 2006)	500,000
Total taxable gifts		$1,250,000
Tentative gift tax		448,300
Less: deemed gift tax paid in 2006		(155,800)
Less: unused unified credit ($345,800 – 155,800)		(190,000)
Gift tax due on Form 709 for 2007		$102,500

Because the value of the stock is less than your purchase price, the trust's income tax basis is not adjusted for the gift tax paid and cannot be determined at the time of the gift. If the trust sells the stock shares for less than its fair market value at the time of the gift ($762,000 total), its basis for loss is the fair market value ($762,000 total) at the time of the gift and its holding period starts on the day of the gift. If it sells the stock for more than your basis ($800,000), the trust's basis for gain is your basis ($800,000) and its holding period includes the time you owned the stock. If it sells the stock for an amount between $762,000 and $800,000, the trust reports no gain or loss.

EXAMPLE 3: The trust funded in Example 2 will report its income from the trust assets (interest, dividend, rent, and gains from the sale of assets) on a separate trust tax return (Form 1041) unless the trust is taxable to the grantor because the grantor retained control over the trust. The trust tax rates are very high, reaching the 35% marginal tax rate bracket on income greater than $10,450. These rates can be avoided if the trust distributes its income to its beneficiaries (e.g., the son).

EXAMPLE 4: Building further on Examples 1 and 2, assume you die in 2008 with $3,000,000 in stocks and bonds. Your executor pays: outstanding debts of $100,000; administrative expenses, including burial expenses, of $50,000; state death taxes to your state of residence of $75,000; and $150,000 to your favorite charity. Your estate tax is calculated as follows:

Gross estate	$3,000,000
Add: gift taxes paid in 2007	
(included in the estate because paid within 3 years of death)	102,500
Less: debts	(100,000)
Less: administrative expenses	(50,000)
Less: state death taxes	(75,000)
Less: charitable contributions	(150,000)
Tentative gross estate	2,727,500
Add: post-1976 gifts	1,250,000
Taxable estate	3,977,500
Tentative tax	1,670,675
Less: gift tax paid since 1976	(102,500)
Less: unified credit	(780,800)
Estate tax due with Form 706	787,375

The income tax basis of the $2,625,000 ($3,000,000 – 100,000 – 50,000 – 75,000 – 150,000) in assets passing to the heirs after estate obligations will step up or step down to $2,625,000. Any sales of assets will be treated as long-term even if the holding period of the asset to the decedent and subsequent heirs is less than one year.

EXAMPLE 5: Continuing examples 1-4, unless the assets you own avoid probate because they were owned by a trust, jointly owned with rights of survivorship, or transferred by some other probate-avoidance mechanism, they will be administered by your personal representative. Any income earned by the assets, such as interest, dividends, rent, and gains from sale, during the time they are held by the representative before distribution to the eventual heirs will be subject to the same high tax rates as the trust described in Example 3. The personal representative will report this income on a separate return for the estate (Form 1041). Similar to a trust, the estate can avoid this income tax by distributing the income to beneficiaries.

PROPERTY OWNERSHIP

CHAPTER 5

Real Property and Personal Property

CHRIS MARES (Appleton, Wisconsin)

When you describe property in legal terms, there are two types of property. The two types of property are known as real property and personal property.

Real property is generally described as land and buildings. These are things that are immovable. You are not able to just pick them up and take them with you as you travel. The definition of real property includes the land, improvements on the land, the surface, whatever is beneath the surface, and the area above the surface. Improvements are such things as buildings, houses, and structures. These are more permanent things. The surface includes landscape, shrubs, trees, and plantings. Whatever is beneath the surface includes the soil, along with any minerals, oil, gas, and gold that may be in the soil. The area above the surface is the air and sky above the land. In short, the definition of real property includes the earth, sky, and the structures upon the land.

In addition, real property includes ownership or rights you may have for easements and right-of-ways. This may be for a driveway shared between you and your neighbor. It may be the right to travel over a part of another person's land to get to your property. Another example may be where you and your neighbor share a well to provide water to each of your individual homes.

Your real property has a formal title which represents and reflects your ownership of the real property. The title ownership may be in the form of a warranty deed, quit claim deed, title insurance policy, or an abstract of title.

Personal property describes everything that is not real property. The most significant difference between real property and personal property is that personal property is movable. You are able to pick up personal property and take it with you as you travel. Personal property includes such things as your household goods, investments, and motor vehicles.

Your personal property may have a formal title representing and reflecting your ownership. This title ownership includes titles for motor vehicles, boats, motor homes, travel trailers, etc. However your household goods will not have a title. Instead there will be receipt or bill of sale for the purchase of household goods.

TANGIBLE PROPERTY AND INTANGIBLE PROPERTY

There are two classifications for the personal property you own. These are tangible property and intangible property.

Tangible property is personal property that can be touched or felt. It includes the types of property you can hold and move. Examples of tangible personal property are your household goods and motor vehicles.

Intangible property refers to personal property you cannot touch, feel, or move. Although intangible personal property cannot be touched or felt, it has a value and there are documents showing value and ownership of the intangible personal property. Examples of intangible personal property are stocks, bonds, mutual funds, and securities. In addition, if a person owes you money, you may have a promissory note which describes the loan and amount of money the individual owes you. Although you can touch the promissory note, the actual value is in the underlying debt the individual owes to you and that is not touchable.

Some less common examples of intangible personal property include copyrights, patents, and trademarks. It may be that you hold a patent and have the right to receive payments of money from a person or company using the patent you own.

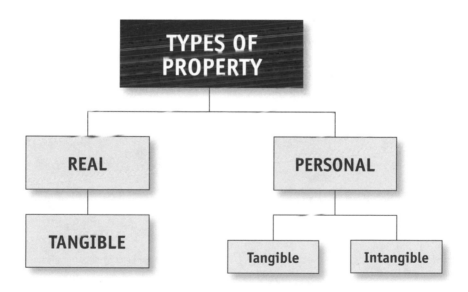

FEE SIMPLE

There are many different types of property ownership. The most common type of property ownership is fee simple.

Having the right to control, use, and transfer your property as you wish and when you desire is known as fee simple ownership. With fee simple ownership, you privately own your property with the full enjoyment of that property. Your ownership may be by yourself or with another person. For example, a husband and wife may own their house together, or two sisters may own a car together.

Fee simple is typically the way you own most of your property. However, there may be some restrictions on the property even if it is owned in fee simple. For your house, there may be restrictions for a mortgage loan you owe for the house, or the limitation may be by governmental agencies for such things as taxes, zoning laws, and subdivision rules.

Owning property in fee simple allows you the right to pass the ownership of the property, while you are alive or upon your death, to whomever you wish. During your lifetime you may gift the property you own as fee simple. Upon your death, you may pass the property through your Revocable Living Trust or Will. If you have no Revocable Living Trust or Will, upon your death, the transfer of the property will be by state laws of intestacy for the state in which you lived at your death.

Fee simple property will pass to the person or charity you designate. Unless directed otherwise, the property will pass to the person or charity with any restrictions existing upon the property. Restrictions include such things as mortgages or loans against the property.

Chris J. Mares has been an attorney since 1984. His practice concentration is Estate Planning and counseling clients in the areas of estate, tax, charitable, and business planning.

CHAPTER 6

Joint Tenancy

DARLYNN MORGAN (Newport Beach, California)

JOINT TENANCY

Joint tenancy is a type of ownership by two or more persons of the same property, real or personal. The individuals, called joint tenants, share equal ownership of the property and have the equal, undivided right to keep or dispose of the property. Joint tenancy with right of survivorship (JT/WROS) means that upon the death of one joint owner, title passes by "operation of law" to the surviving owner, who receives sole ownership of the asset, thus avoiding probate. Even if a joint tenant intends to have his or her share pass to loved ones, the property is not controlled by the instructions in the owner's will or trust Although fraught with problems, joint ownership remains a popular planning device used by many families. However, for most people, the disadvantages of joint tenancy exceed the advantages.

HUSBAND AND WIFE AS JOINT OWNERS: PROBATE POSTPONEMENT

If you are married, you may have already encountered joint tenancy. Many married couples own property as joint tenants, whether it be their family home, an investment account, or bank accounts. Let's take a look at a common scenario: Bob and Mary, husband and wife, own their family home as joint tenants. Why? Because that's what their real estate agent likely advised them to do. After Bob dies, Mary automatically becomes the sole owner of their home and there is no probate. That is the good news.

But what happens when Mary dies? At that point there will be a probate. There must be a court process to transfer Mary's ownership to her heirs. Why? Because Mary's signature is no longer available. We can't transfer real estate without someone with legal authority signing the deed to transfer the property.

So the first important lesson about joint tenancy is that it does not really avoid probate; it only postpones it. Sure, upon the death of the first joint tenant, title will automatically pass to the surviving joint tenant, and it does avoid probate at that time. However, upon the death of the surviving spouse, there will be a probate unless the surviving spouse creates a new joint tenancy or places his or her assets in a living trust.

An All Too Common Scenario

Here is an all too common scenario filled with traps for the unwary or ill-advised. Let's say that instead of dying as in our previous example, Mary lives. Now, as a widow, she owns the family home in her name alone. Holding the home in joint tenancy seemed to work well when she owned it with Bob because there was no probate at his death. So Mary decides to add her son Sam as a joint tenant on the family home. Debbie, her daughter-in-law is a paralegal and she confirms that holding the property in joint tenancy will avoid probate. Debbie will even prepare the deed, so there is no need to consult with an attorney or pay any legal fees.

What if Son Divorces?

What happens if son Sam gets into a nasty divorce? Unfortunately Mary's home could get dragged into the proceedings and the property will be tied up until things get sorted out.

What happens if Sam get into a car accident and someone then obtains a judgment against him? The property could be seized as settlement.

So our next important lesson about holding property jointly is that if the other joint owner ends up in a divorce or a lawsuit this will expose the asset to the other joint owner's debts.

What if Mary or Sam Become Incapacitated?

Let's turn to another scenario: Imagine that either Mary or Sam become incapacitated. Recall, that often when families do "joint tenancy" planning, they have not consulted with an attorney. This means they likely do not have certain legal documents, such as a living trust or a power of attorney for financial matters in place to assist them in handling legal and financial affairs for their loved one upon incapacity.

If Mary became incapacitated and Sam needed to sell the property in order to put her into a full-time nursing home, he wouldn't be able to do so without first going to court. The court would appoint a conservator (whomever the court thought was best for the job, not necessarily Sam), and then the conservator could decide if the property should be sold.

So if either joint tenant becomes incapacitated and the proper legal documents are not in place, the joint tenancy property may be tied up in a guardianship or conservatorship proceeding at a time when the family desperately needs the cash.

Mary Changes Her Mind: Trouble With the Other Joint Owner

Now let's look at a different scenario. What if, at some point after she has added Sam as a joint owner, Mary decides she wants to change her estate plan and provide shares for her three grandchildren in addition to her two children? Mary meets with an attorney and determines a revocable living trust will best meet her needs and that title to her property will need to be changed to the name of her new living trust.

When Mary asks Sam to sign over the deed, what happens if Sam refuses? Although he is provided for in the new trust, it still means his share is being reduced and he won't be getting the entire property. What can Mary do? If she cannot prevail upon Sam to sign the deed, she will need to initiate a court action against her son.

It's always easy to add a joint tenant onto a deed. However, getting him or her off the deed if you change your mind is not always as easy.

What if Mary Remarries Instead? Unintended Disinheritance

What happens if Mary remarries instead and wants to add her new husband Nate to the deed as her joint tenant? If Mary dies first, then Nate owns the house. Even if Mary tells Nate that the house is eventually to go to her children, Nate is under no legal obligation to give anything to Mary's children, Sam and Sarah. This is true even if Mary's will expressly states that all her assets are to be equally divided among her two children. Because legal title controls, not the will, it doesn't make any difference what her will says. If it is Mary's intent to leave her property to her children, she should not add Nate as a joint tenant because she has no way of ensuring the property will pass to whom she wants.

It is easy to see how joint tenancy can have the unintended consequence of disinheriting children if a surviving spouse remarries after the death of the first spouse and puts her new spouse on as a joint tenant on the family home. If she then predeceases her new spouse, her children from her first marriage will not receive anything.

TAX ISSUES

But this scenario isn't the only problem we see with joint ownership. There are also tax consequences! Let's look at the tax consequences of what happens if Mary dies with son Sam on title to the property as the other joint tenant.

Tax Issues: Gift Tax Consequences

Avoiding probate is generally the most significant benefit of holding property in joint tenancy. However, gift tax consequences are often overlooked. When a parent places a child on title to property as a joint tenant, the parent is typically unaware that he or she has made a gift of one-half of the value of the property to the child. If the value of that gift exceeds the annual gift-tax exclusion amount, $12,000 in 2008 ($13,000 in 2009), it is a taxable gift requiring the filing of a gift tax return. In some cases, a gift tax may have to be paid.

Tax Issues: Income Tax Consequences

Another problem with joint tenancy is that the surviving joint tenant will not receive the full step-up in cost basis he or she would receive if he or she inherited the property instead (or held title to the property as community property in a community property state). Here is an example: Mary and her son, Sam, jointly buy a house as joint tenants for $50,000 and today it's worth $650,000. Upon Mary's death, only her half of the property receives a step up in cost basis. So if Sam sells the house for $650,000, Sam has a $300,000 gain on the sale which is subject to capital gains tax.

What happens if Mary "gives" the property during her lifetime to son Sam, who then sells it for $650,000? Because Mary transferred title to Sam while she was living, the house retains Mary's old cost basis of $50,000. That means Sam now has a $600,000 capital gain on the sale which is subject to capital gains tax.

Let's look at what happens if, instead, Mary leaves her home to Sam as an inheritance — either through a will or a living trust. Sam sells the house for the same $650,000. But, because he received the house as an inheritance after Mary died instead of as a gift while Mary was living, the property receives a new stepped-up cost basis. The basis is now the fair market value on the date of Mary's death — $650,000. So now when Sam sells the house, there is no gain on the sale and no capital gains tax to pay.

Tax Issues: Property Tax Consequences

Let's assume that Mary had a will dividing her property equally among her two children, Sarah and Sam, and that is the way she wanted it. But, what Mary didn't realize is that because the family home was titled in joint tenancy with Sam, her daughter Sarah is not legally entitled to any of the property. It is all Sam's and he is under no legal obligation to share any of it with his sister.

Even if Sam decides that he will honor his mother's wishes and agrees to give his sister one-half of the property, this could trigger some unpleasant tax consequences. There could be gift tax consequences if Sam ends up giving Sarah more than the annual exclusion amount ($12,000 in 2008, and $13,000 in 2009). Moreover, at least in California, there will be property tax consequences. A transfer between siblings will trigger a property tax reassessment for one-half of the property, which could be problem if the children had intended to keep the property.

Federal Estate Tax Consequences

Although title to the property passes by operation of law to the surviving joint owner, the value of the owner's interest in the property is still included in his or her estate for federal estate tax purposes. Because individuals using joint tenancy often have not consulted with an attorney, they may be completely unaware of their federal estate tax liability and may not have made adequate provision for payment. It's also possible that an owner's beneficiaries may pay federal estate taxes on property they do not receive.

ADVANTAGES OF JOINT TENANCY

So why would anyone ever hold property in joint tenancy? First, joint tenancies are easily understood, so there is a perceived advantage due to its simplicity. Also, joint tenancy can be used to avoid probate, because the property does pass by operation of law without a court proceeding at the first joint tenant's death. Finally, joint tenancies often represent a relationship commitment and people who care about each other may want to hold property jointly and don't know of a better alternative.

IN SUMMARY

1. Joint tenancy ownership does not really avoid probate, it only postpones it.

2. The original joint tenant could end up in a lawsuit if the other joint tenant is sued over an accident that involves the jointly owned asset. The asset is exposed to the other owner's debts and the property could be seized as settlement. Your joint tenant's divorcing spouse may also make a claim to the property.

3. If a co-owner becomes incapacitated, a court may get involved. This would limit the control the other owner has over the joint tenancy property.

4. It's always easy to add a joint tenant onto a deed. However, getting the joint tenant off the deed if there is a change of mind is not always as easy. If the co-owner doesn't agree, the joint tenants could end up in court.

5. If the original owner dies first, there is no way of controlling what ultimately happens to the asset and there could be an unintentional disinheritance of the original owner's family.

6. Tax consequences! Lots of them. The consequences will vary widely depending on a number of factors. Suffice it to say, putting a family member on title as a joint tenant is not as easy as it sounds and it can have many consequences reaching far beyond what the parties intended.

7. The disadvantages of joint tenancy usually far outweigh any advantages, so careful consideration should be taken before holding title to property in joint tenancy.

Attorney Darlynn Morgan has been practicing law in Orange County, California, since 1996. Her practice is focused in the Trusts and Estates area. Contact her at www.morganlawgroup.com or 949.260.1400.

2008 Unified Federal Estate and Gift Tax Rate Schedule

	FEE SIMPLE	TENANCY IN COMMON	JOINT TENANCY WROS	COMMUNITY PROPERTY (BETWEEN SPOUSES)
Included in Gross Estate	100%	Percentage of ownership	Spouses — 50% Nonspouses — based on portion of purchase price paid	50%
Included in Probate	Yes	Yes	No	Yes
Rights of Survivorship	No	No	Yes	No
Property Disposed Via Will or State Intestacy Law	Yes	Yes	No	Yes
Consent of Others Needed for a Sale or Gift	No	No	Yes — interest is converted to tenancy in common	Yes
Receives Stepped-Up Basis at Decedent's Death	Yes	Yes — owner/decedent's portion only	Yes — owner/decedent's portion only	Yes — both owner/decedent's portion and spouse's portion

Classification of Property Interests as Present Interests, Contingent Future Interests, or Vested Future Interests

BRIAN ALBEE (Madison, Wisconsin)

Because an understanding of vocabulary is important to any communication, let's start by defining our terms:

Property refers to the thing to which certain rights (or interests) are attached. Property is classified as either real or personal. Real property is land and things attached to the land (houses, for example). Personal property is everything else.[1]

Interests are the rights in the thing (the property). Sometimes referred to as a "bundle of rights," interests include the right to possess, use, encumber[2], transfer[3], and exclude others.

Property interests are classified as either present interests or future interests, as follows:

> A **present interest** is an interest that can be presently exercised (that is, the interest holder can presently possess, use, encumber, transfer, or exclude others).

> A **future interest** is an interest that can only be exercised upon the happening of a future event, at which time it becomes a present interest.

Future interests are further classified as either contingent future interests or vested future interests, as follows:

> A **contingent future interest** is a future interest where the future event IS NOT certain to occur.

> A **vested future interest** is a future interest where the future event IS certain to occur.

There is no such thing as a contingent present interest. A present interest, by its very definition, is an interest that can be presently exercised. It is not contingent on anything, and if it were, it would be a future interest.

TYPES OF INTERESTS

Common types of interests include a fee simple, leasehold, life estate, remainder, and reversion:

A **fee simple** is sometimes referred to as absolute ownership. You have a fee simple if you have all of the bundle of rights.

A **leasehold** is an interest bound by time. It terminates at some point in the future.

A **life estate** is an interest that exists only so long as a person lives. A life estate can be based on the interest-holder's life or the life of another.

A **remainder** is a future interest that another holds (either contingent or vested) after the termination of a prior interest (for example, after a life estate).

A **reversion** is a future interest the grantor holds (either contingent or vested) after the termination of a prior interest (for example, after a life estate where no remainder interest is specified).

Consider the following conveyances (assume the grantor had a fee simple):

"To Adam." That's about as simple as it gets. Adam has a fee simple. The grantor has nothing.

"To Adam for 10 years." Adam has a present interest called a leasehold. The grantor has a vested future interest called a reversion.

"To Adam for life, then to Baker." Adam has a present interest called a life estate. Baker's interest is clearly a future interest because Baker can only exercise his rights in the property upon the happening of a future event (Adam's death). But is it contingent or vested? It is contingent because if Baker is dead when Adam dies, the property reverts to the grantor.

"To Adam for life, then to Baker or Baker's heirs." Adam still has a present interest but now Baker has a vested future interest because Adam is sure to die. Once Adam dies, Baker or Baker's heirs will have a fee simple. Before Adam dies, Baker can convey his future interest during life or at death. After Adam dies, it is no longer a future interest. It is a present interest.

"To Adam for life, then to Baker if he has reached age 25." Again, Baker's interest is clearly a future interest because Baker can only exercise his rights in the property upon the happening of a future event (Adam's death). Actually, there are two future events that must occur before Baker can exercise his rights — reaching age 25 and Adam's death. Until Baker reaches age 25, he has a contingent future interest, because the future event of reaching age 25 is not certain to occur. After

he reaches age 25, it is a vested future interest because the contingency of reaching age 25 has been satisfied, and the remaining future event (Adam's death) is certain to occur. But what if Adam dies before Baker reaches age 25? The property reverts back to the grantor. The grantor is said to hold a reversionary interest called a possibility of reverter.

"To Baker, <u>so long as</u> the property is not subdivided." Baker has a present interest in fee simple, but because it is subject to a condition subsequent (that it not be subdivided), it is said to be a defeasible fee simple. Further, because "so long as" are words determining when the fee simple will terminate, it is said to be a fee simple determinable. And if it terminates, the property will revert to the grantor. The grantor has a contingent future interest (a reversion) called a possibility of reverter.

"To Baker, <u>if</u> the property is not subdivided." Notice the difference from the last example. Using "if" instead of "so long as" makes a world of difference. The law looks at "if" as a word allowing the grantor to defeat Baker's interest, but the grantor must take some action. It is not automatic as it is with "so long as." If the grantor does not take action within a reasonable time, the grantor's interest is terminated. Here, Baker still has a defeasible fee simple, but we call it a fee simple subject to condition subsequent, rather than a fee simple determinable. The grantor has a contingent future interest (a reversion) called a power of termination (or right of entry).

Well, that's all fine and good, but how is classifying property important to estate planning? It is important for understanding the value of a person's estate. Since estate valuation is based on a willing buyer, willing seller standard, there is a significant difference in what a willing buyer will pay for a contingent future interest versus a vested future interest, depending on the contingency and the extent of the future interest.

Property interests can be very complex, and valuing a property interest that has not met the light of the free market often requires the expertise of an appraiser who specializes in estate valuation appraisals.

Brian F. Albee specializes in developing document automation systems in the estate planning field. In addition, he has taught real property law at the junior college level.

---

1. As an historical note, the term "property" did not refer to the thing itself, but to the rights (or "interests") a person has in the thing. Therefore, historically, one would refer to "property" rather than its modern equivalent "property interest." So, in modern usage, "property" refers to the thing, and "property interests" refers to the rights in the thing.

2. "Encumber" means to allow another person to attach a legal right to the property. There are two types of encumbrances, those affecting title, and those affecting physical condition. A lien on property to secure a loan is an example of an encumbrance affecting title. An easement allowing someone else to cross the property is an example of an encumbrance affecting physical condition.

---

3. "Transfer" means to convey one's interest to another. This can be confusing when we consider present and future interests. You could have the present right to transfer a future interest, but such does not give you a present interest in the property. In order to have a present interest in the property, you must have the power to presently exercise at least one of the other property interests.

ESTATE PLANNING DOCUMENTS AND DRAFTING ISSUES

CHAPTER 8

Intestate Law Overview

ELLEN GAY MOSER (Naperville, Illinois)

When you don't have a will, the state will make one for you. Your property will go to your heirs under the laws of the state in which you reside by intestate succession.

MOST AMERICANS DON'T HAVE A WILL

When you die without a will you have little control over what happens to your assets and how or when your minor children take their shares. The purpose of intestate statutes is to distribute the decedent's property in the way the average person would have designed his or her estate plan, if he or she had a will. However, who knows what you really want unless you write it down? Even if you have expressed what you would like to see happen; such as, "If both my husband and I are killed, you would raise our children," unless your wishes are written in a valid will, your wishes may be ignored.

WHO GETS YOUR STUFF?

If you are married and want your surviving spouse to have your entire estate, you must write a will because your state's laws may only give your spouse a portion of your assets. Do you want your spouse to report annually how he or she is managing the money of the minor children? Do you want your spouse to have to borrow money from your kids, or ask them if he or she can sell some stock to buy a new car? Do you want your children to receive all of their inheritance at such a young age that they are not ready for the responsibility? If you want to protect your loved ones, you must plan to sign a will and (often) a revocable living trust before it is too late. You must decide who gets what and when they get it. You can only control who gets your stuff if you create an estate plan.

1990 Uniform Probate Code

The 1990 Uniform Probate Code (the Code) is the starting point for many states' intestacy laws. State laws vary, but generally you can assume your close relatives will take your property before distant relatives. The people who get your property first would be your surviving spouse, then your descendants (kids and grandkids).

If they are not living, or if you have none, your parents would take, then your siblings, and then your nieces and nephews. If none of them are living, your grandparents would take and next, your aunts and uncles and cousins. Adopted descendants are the same as if naturally born. If you have no living relatives, your property goes to the state.

Probate

With or without a will, your estate will go through probate unless you have created an estate plan with a revocable living trust. Some states do allow smaller estates to be administered outside of the probate process if they are under a certain amount (e.g., under $100,000 and contain no real estate). If the costs of probate and attorney fees plus the time delays become a burden, a surviving spouse may ask the court for an advance against the estate.

Costs and fees of probate may reduce an estate by three to five percent. Your "net estate" is the amount left for distribution to heirs after all debts, taxes, and administrative expenses have been paid. Settlement of an estate through the probate process may take a year or more. Probate is public and denies you the privilege of keeping your most personal affairs private. When an estate goes through probate, your friends and neighbors may attend court hearings deciding who gets the kids and who gets the house.

WHO GETS YOUR KIDS?

If you die without a will, under which you would normally name guardians of your minor children, the court will decide who qualifies to raise your kids and who will manage their money. Under state law, a minor or incompetent person may have a guardian of their person and a guardian of their property appointed. If you do not want your children in the hands of strangers — the court, lawyers and bankers, you must take the time to decide who gets your children.

After the Marshall University plane crash in which some families suffered the loss of both parents, minor children were in court for a couple of years while relatives fought for the right to raise the children. Grandparents were pitted against their other surviving children, and both petitioned the court to be considered favorable as guardians. Inherited funds were delivered to bank trust officers who were to keep the funds safe until the children were of legal age to take their money.

If you want to prevent family disharmony and protect your loved ones from themselves, predators, and well-meaning friends and relatives, prepare your estate plan with a Revocable Living Trust naming trustees to manage the money and a Pour Over Will designating guardians to raise your children.

Ellen Gay Moser counsels individuals and families to: Protect their assets; exit their business; provide for loved ones and obtain peace of mind. Her mission is to "Protect Family Values for Generations."

CHAPTER 9

Wills – Testamentary Capacity and Undue Influence

CHRISTOPHER BERRY (Farmington Hills, Michigan)

Many of the wills challenged in court are challenged on either the basis of a lack of testamentary capacity or on the basis of undue influence.

Not just anyone is able to execute a will. To execute a will, you must have "testamentary capacity." Check your state law for your state's definition. Typically, however, there will be an age requirement — generally 18 years old, along with a mental requirement of a "sound mind."

Satisfying the age requirement is cut and dry. To make a will, you must be the required age. The portion of testamentary capacity that is often more problematic is the mental requirement.

Typically, to have testamentary capacity, the testator — the one creating the will — must be able to comprehend the nature and extent of his or her property, the ability to know the natural objects of his or her bounty, and to determine and understand the disposition of property which he or she desires to make.

If a testator executes a will and it is subsequently challenged, the testator does not have the burden to prove testamentary capacity. That burden falls on whoever is challenging the will. They have to prove the lack of testamentary capacity at the time the will was drawn. More often than not, they challenge the will on the grounds that the testator did not have a "sound mind."

You often see wills challenged for lack of testamentary capacity when dealing with the elderly or disabled. For example, a senior individual suffering from Alzheimer's disease, a middle-aged man who has suffered a head injury, or a woman who suffers from Schizophrenia all could have their wills challenged due to lacking a "sound mind."

While the burden is not on the testator to prove testamentary capacity, there are keys to make it more difficult for a will to be challenged on this basis. First, illiteracy or lack of education has little to no bearing on the "sound mind" requirement. Nor does the lack of wisdom or fairness in the disposition of the property provisions of the will. Weakness of mind and forgetfulness, are likewise, insufficient of themselves to invalidate a will due to lack of testamentary capacity. Furthermore, just because a person may suffer from a mental disease or disability does not automatically mean he or she lacks a "sound mind" in terms of testamentary capacity. If the testator has lucid moments, and witnesses can attest to those lucid moments, that is enough testamentary capacity for the person to create a valid will.

For example, a testator suffering from dementia may have many bad days in a row. Then one day, he or she is very lucid, aware of his or her surroundings, property, what he or she wants to do with the property, and the effect of his or her decisions. The testator signs and executes a will that day. Then he or she falls back into dementia and passes away a week later. The will the testator executed is valid because at the time the will was drawn, he or she had a "sound mind" and testamentary capacity. If the testator had created a will on another day, it may not have been valid.

One strategy you can use to aid your argument that a testator has testamentary capacity is quiz the testator on current events while reviewing and signing the documents while witnesses are around. For example, if you are having the testator sign the will and are able to carry on a conversation about yesterday's baseball game or any other current events, that can be used as evidence of a lucid, "sound mind." If someone subsequently decides to challenge the will on testamentary capacity and "sound mind" grounds, you have established, with the aid of witnesses, evidence of the "sound mind" requirement during the signing and execution of the document.

Along with testamentary capacity, undue influence is a second common reason wills are challenged. Undue influence occurs when the testator has testamentary capacity, but that capacity is subjected to and controlled by another individual who has manipulative, selfish intentions.

For example, a testator in a nursing home creates a will benefiting his children. However, a nurse discovers that the testator is very wealthy and begins to take steps to keep the children away from the testator, while at the same time becoming the testator's confidant. Over a period of time, the nurse continues an entire course of conduct designed to overpower the testator's mind and manipulate the testator to hate the children. Eventually, the testator executes a new will naming the nurse as beneficiary. This new will may be challenged because of undue influence.

However, just because there is influence, does not mean there is "undue influence," and that a will can be successfully challenged. For example, a testator has two sons and creates a will to benefit both equally. Over the next five years, one son spends more time taking care of the testator. Along with this, the caregiving son pleads for more of the testator's estate. The testator then creates a new will benefiting the son who helped out more and, shortly thereafter, passes away. This scenario most likely would not rise to the level necessary to challenge on the basis of undue influence because there is not the level of manipulation and domination required by most state laws.

Undue influence must amount to force and coercion that overcomes and destroys the free agency of the testator. In our examples, the nurse was forcing the testator's children away, while in the second example, the son who was helping out was not forcing or manipulating. He was making his wishes known, but there was not the level of deceit present as there was with the nurse.

As you are creating a will, you need to keep in mind the two concepts of testamentary capacity and undue influence and take steps to ensure your documents do not erroneously get challenged on these grounds.

Witzke Berry, PLLC, help our clients create, implement, and maintain their estate plans designed to capture the past and secure the future for both our clients and their beneficiaries.

CHAPTER 10

Types of Wills

ALEXANDRA GADZO (Palo Alto, California)

A will is used to designate how, when, and to whom your assets will pass at your death. In addition to naming an Executor or Executrix (sometimes called a Personal Representative) to collect and distribute your assets, your will is the document in which you name guardians for your minor children.

If you have a living trust, a pour over will is generally used so that at your death, the will "pours" any assets not in your living trust into the trust so the assets can be distributed according to the trust's terms. There may or may not need to be a probate first depending on the amount of the assets.

REQUIREMENTS OF A WILL

You can draft a typewritten will or have an attorney draft a will for you. In California, the requirements for a will to be legally effective are as follows:

- the testator must be 18 years or older;
- the testator must be of sound mind;
- the document must state that it is a will;
- it must be type-written or created and printed using a computer;
- you need to appoint at least one executor;
- the will must provide for the disposition of your assets;
- the will must be signed and have a date of execution; and
- two witnesses who are at least 18 years of age must be present when the testator signs the will.

These witnesses must also be of sound mind and understand they are witnesses for your will. The witnesses may not be beneficiaries of the will, and the witnesses must see the testator and the other witness sign your will.

WHAT IS A HOLOGRAPHIC WILL?

A holographic will is a will that is handwritten by the testator (the person who would like to leave property after his or her death). This type of will can range from simple to complex, and drafted with or without the assistance of an attorney. In California, the only requirements for a holographic will are that the will is handwritten by the testator, the testator signs the will (anywhere on the handwritten document), and the signature authenticates the will (i.e., it cannot be instructions for an attorney to later draft a will). Although a date is not necessary for a holographic will, the Testator should date the document.

WHY WOULD YOU WANT TO WRITE A HOLOGRAPHIC WILL?

You may have wanted to visit an attorney for advice on drafting a will, but due to time or financial constraints, have not been able to do so. If you must go to the hospital unexpectedly, an attorney can dictate over the phone what to include in your holographic will. You can also draft your holographic will without the assistance of an attorney, and your wishes will be respected by a court of law.

WHY WOULD YOU NOT WANT TO WRITE A HOLOGRAPHIC WILL?

Not all states recognize holographic wills as valid. Even states that do recognize holographic wills may restrict property that can be transferred by holographic will to personal property or to a small dollar value, such as $500. Additionally, by only leaving a holographic will, your estate will have to be probated. The court ultimately decides whether the will is valid. If the will is not dated, it can easily be argued that it was written before another will was drafted, causing it to be invalidated. Even if the holographic will has a later date, some states do not allow holographic wills to revoke properly executed, typewritten wills. Before you decide to write a holographic will as your final draft, consult with an estate planning attorney to ensure your choices will be carried out in the way you intend.

WHAT IS A STATUTORY WILL?

Statutory wills are form wills you fill out to designate who will receive your assets. These forms are written by the state and forms can be purchased through the State Bar. While this may seem like a great idea, only four states recognize them as valid, namely California, Maine, Michigan, and Wisconsin. While the concept sounds very simple and user-friendly, your choice of recipients for your property can be very limited, making these statutory forms useless in many situations. Additionally, if you have a trust, statutory wills cannot pour over your assets to your trust. However, if you are leaving all your assets to your spouse or children, a statutory will may be a good choice. Check with your state to see if this form of document may be the right choice for you.

The requirements of a statutory will are similar to those of a will drafted by an attorney. Besides having to meet all the other requirements of a typewritten will, an additional requirement is that you should not edit, change, add, or delete words to the statutory will form.

Alexandra Gadzo of the Gadzo Law Firm specializes in estate, gift, income tax, and business succession planning in the San Francisco Bay Area.

CHAPTER 11

Who Are Your Descendants?

RICHARD F. NEVINS (Riverside, California)

Descendants are the people authorized by your state's laws who will inherit and receive your possessions when you die.

Your state has a set of rules called the laws of intestate succession. These rules act as a substitute will and include a list of your descendants, also known as heirs. The state law ranks them in order of how they will divide your possessions among them. Lineal descendants are the direct line of relationships starting with your children and continuing down through your grandchildren and great-grandchildren. Collateral descendants include your siblings, nieces, and nephews.

Each state has its own variety of intestate succession laws. Each state's law provides that the property is to be distributed to the closest surviving relatives. In most states, priority goes to your surviving spouse, followed by your children, your parents, your siblings, your nieces and nephews, and your next of kin. Many states require that your surviving spouse and children each receive a fractional share of your estate.

If you use a do-it-yourself will kit and your will is incomplete or incorrect, most state laws will consider your document to be invalid, which means your desires will not be followed and the intestate succession rules will apply.

One of the dangers of relying upon your state's intestate succession laws to define your descendants is that the rules may not match your true distribution wishes. Suppose you want to make sure that your grandchildren receive most of your estate so they can attend college or simply have a better life than their parents. Most intestate succession statutes give your children priority over your grandchildren. If you want someone who is not a relative to inherit your assets you will need to specifically name them in your will, because without a will, your life partner, significant other, lifelong friend, or favorite charity, for example, will be out of luck because they are typically not included on a state's list of intestate descendants. To make matters worse, if you do not have any surviving relatives, all your property that you spent a lifetime acquiring will be legally assigned (i.e., escheated) to the state.

However, you can use your state's intestate succession statutes as a backup planning tool to cover situations when your beneficiaries have died before you. For example, your will leaves your entire estate to your wife and child, but they die before you. Your will could provide that if your beneficiaries predecease you, then one-half of your estate is to be distributed to your heirs at law and one-half of your estate goes to your wife's heirs at law, as defined in your state's rules of intestate succession.

Intestacy laws will also apply in situations where your will has improperly excluded someone from receiving a share of your estate, such as when a spouse or minor child is completely excluded from a will contrary to state law. A pretermitted heir is someone who is included on your state's list of intestate descendants but who was not mentioned in your will. The most common type of pretermitted heir is a child born out of wedlock or a child who is estranged from the family. If you fail to mention the existence of all of your children, or you fail to mention your wife, your will can be considered void and the person you failed to mention can claim a share of your estate through application of the intestate succession rules.

If you attempt to exclude an heir and your will does not provide for the disposition of all of your property, then you will have died partially intestate. The portion of your estate that is not included in your will is then subject to the rules of intestate succession. Accordingly, that person whom you wanted excluded from taking an inheritance under your will could receive property by operation of the laws of intestate succession. When preparing your will, be sure you have accounted for all of your property and all of your family members so that the final document will not be ruled invalid and void.

The Law Office of Richard F. Nevins provides legal services in the areas of wills, trusts, probate, and business formation in Riverside, California.

CHAPTER 12

Designating Fiduciaries

SHERI PETERS (Munroe Falls, Ohio)

WHO IS YOUR PERSONAL REPRESENTATIVE?

When you die, your estate (the assets you own at death) will transfer to your loved ones one of three ways: 1) by contract; 2) by will; or 3) by the laws of intestacy of the state of your residence at death. Only the first two ways of transferring assets permit you to choose who receives your assets. Under the third method, the laws of intestacy, the state of your residence chooses who receives your assets.

However, if you die with assets in your name alone, generally they can only be transferred through the probate process. This is true whether you have a will or whether you die intestate (without a will). Your affairs will be handled by the Personal Representative of your estate. If you have a will, you are able to choose someone to handle your affairs. That person is called an Executor or Executrix. If you do not have a will, the court will select someone to handle your affairs and that person is called an Administrator or Administratrix. The generic term for these positions is the "Personal Representative."

Obviously, it is more beneficial for you to choose the person who will handle your affairs by making a will. That person has many duties and responsibilities, and you want to ensure your wishes are carried out properly. They must first gather and marshal all of the assets that are in your name alone. They must also obtain information about any of your assets transferring by a contract, because this may be relevant for death tax purposes. In this process, all of your assets are valued at their fair market value as of your date of death. Included in marshalling your assets is the duty to inventory all of your household furnishings and personal possessions.

The Personal Representative must also diligently search your records to find your creditors. The second function of the Personal Representative is to ensure all your outstanding bills are paid, including those caused by your death.

Another responsibility is sending a notice of death to the post office, utility companies, banks, and credit card companies. Notification of death to the Social Security Administration is required, as well as the civil service or military when applicable, and the Department of Health Services if the decedent was receiving Medicaid.

The third aspect of the Personal Representative's duties deals with the determination and payment of any death taxes that may be due by reason of your death. There are two types of taxes, the Federal Estate Tax and potentially, depending on your state, State Estate/Transfer Tax. All assets must be valued at the date of death value, including those being transferred by contract. Death taxes are generally computed on these values. All payments made to creditors after death are allowed as deductions in computing the amount of death taxes to be paid.

Once these taxes are paid and the clearances are received from the taxing authority, the Personal Representative can take the final steps to fulfill his or her duties. These steps involve distributing the assets of your estate, under the terms of your will or according to your State's laws of intestacy, to those entitled to receive them. Usually, all of these duties are performed with the help and guidance of an attorney who is experienced in the probate process. In addition, the court must approve the Personal Representative's actions before closing the estate.

In distributing estate assets, the Personal Representative should be sure to collect receipts for the estate records, which will be used to file an accounting with the court. When all is complete, the court will issue an order closing the estate. The Personal Representative should be sure to notify the IRS that the estate is closed.

If a testamentary trust needs to be established after the decedent's death or the decedent created a trust before death, a trustee is named to manage those assets. Being a trustee is an honor and a responsibility for the person you have entrusted to carry out your wishes. Serving as an executor or a trustee requires thoroughness and organization. It is an honorable task to be carried out soberly and responsibly.

CHOOSING A FIDUCIARY

In selecting a fiduciary, whether it is an executor named in a will, or a trustee for a testamentary or inter vivos trust, several factors should be considered.

The executor is in charge of the assets in a probate estate, whereas the trustee is the person who is in charge of the assets in a trust. Both are considered fiduciaries. He or she acts as the captain of a ship or the president of a corporation. The fiduciary must manage the assets, invest them, and distribute them in accordance with the will or trust document.

However, who should serve as a fiduciary upon death or incapacity? Here are some factors to consider:

Management

The fiduciary has the responsibility of managing the assets. Ideally, the fiduciary should be someone who can keep records and follow the instructions of the will or trust document. While the fiduciary need not be a financial genius, the fiduciary should know his or her own limits and be able to select appropriate advisors.

Distributions

The executor will be responsible for following the instructions for distribution in the will while the trustee often has broad discretion in when and how to distribute assets. The trustee should be someone who will exercise discretion fairly, without favoritism or vindictiveness.

Congeniality

The administration of an estate or trust is a delicate matter. Emotions can run high. The fiduciary should be someone who follows your instructions in the document without unnecessary friction. Can this person get along with the beneficiaries?

Trust

While bound by a fiduciary duty, the trustee typically has broad discretion in use of the assets. The best way to sum up the qualifications of a trustee is that you trust his or her abilities and discretion to make decisions as you would make them if you were able to do so yourself.

Many people name their son or daughter as successor trustee. This can be an excellent selection if the son or daughter has the aforementioned abilities. However, people often feel obligated to name a child even if he or she lacks some or all of these abilities. There are other options — family members or close friends often make effective trustees. If there are no appropriate family members or friends, a bank trust department or other corporate trustee can be an excellent choice.

If there are complex family dynamics with a history of friction, a corporate trustee can help diffuse family resentments and tensions. A corporate trustee can be unbiased and decide objectively between competing positions of conflicting beneficiaries. A corporate trustee has experience in administering trusts and managing assets.

You can choose one person to serve as a successor trustee or several people to serve as co-trustees. Of course, a single successor trustee will be more efficient. However, co-trustees will be less likely to act impulsively. Appointing more than two or three co-trustees can turn into a logistical nightmare. When appointing multiple trustees, consider the personal dynamics among those trustees. The trustees must work together to accomplish your goals.

Choosing a trustee to succeed you upon your incapacity or death is crucial to achieving your goals and providing a smooth transition. A qualified estate planning attorney can help counsel you in this important decision.

Attorney Sheri A. Peters has spent the last seventeen years focusing her practice in estate planning, elder law, and probate law.

CHAPTER 13

Make Sure Your Property Is Distributed the Way You Want if One of Your Children Dies Before You

RANDY GARDNER (Leawood, Kansas) and LEWIS W. DYMOND (Frisco, Colorado)

If you do not have a will, your state's intestate laws will determine who receives your property. If you have a will or trust, you determine who will receive your property. Among the legal phrases that appear in state intestate laws and wills and trusts are the terms "per stirpes" and "per capita." These terms significantly affect the way your property is distributed, particularly if one of your children dies before you and leaves children.

Per stirpes, which from the Latin means "by the roots," allows lineal descendants to inherit property their parents would have received. Per stirpes is sometimes referred to as "by right of representation." Per capita, which from the Latin means "by the head," requires surviving heirs to receive an equal share of the property. The distinction between per stirpes and per capita is best understood with an example.

> **EXAMPLE:** Assume you are unmarried and have two children. Child One (C1) has two children (C1A and C1B). Child Two (C2) has one child (C2A).

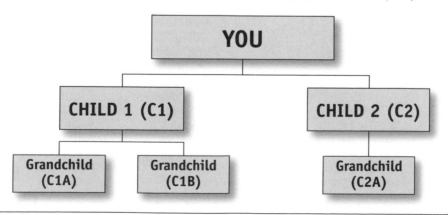

SCENARIO 1: If you die survived by your children, C1 and C2 will share equally in your property under either per stirpes or per capita language, unless you include a different distribution arrangement in your will or trust.

SCENARIO 2: If C1 dies before you, who inherits your property if you die without a will? If you live in a state following traditional "per stirpes" rules of descent, C2 receives ½ of your property and C1A and C1B split C1's ½ interest. C1A and C1B each receive ¼. If both C1 and C2 die before you, then C1A and C1B take the property their parent, C1, would have received. C2A takes C2's share. In other words, C1A and C1B each receive ¼, and C2A receives ½.

Many think this unequal distribution at the grandchild level is not desirable. Consequently, many states have adopted a hybrid of per stirpes called "per capita at each generation per stirpes."

SCENARIO 3: Continuing the facts of Example 1, if C1 dies before you, C2 receives ½ of your property and C1A and C1B split C1's ½ interest. C1A and C1B each receive ¼ (the per stirpes outcome from Scenario 2 above). If both C1 and C2 die before you, then C1A, C1B, and C2A share the property equally (⅓ each) (the per capita outcome from Scenario 1 above).

None of these approaches is intrinsically good or bad or right or wrong. What matters is whether the distribution pattern produces the result you want.

Distribution Approach Followed in Each State's Intestate Statute

STATES FOLLOWING THE TRADITIONAL PER STIRPES APPROACH (SCENARIO 2)	STATES FOLLOWING THE PER CAPITA AT EACH GENERATION PER STIRPES APPROACH (SCENARIO 3)	
CONNECTICUT	ALABAMA	NEW MEXICO
DELAWARE	ALASKA	NEW YORK
FLORIDA	ARIZONA	NORTH CAROLINA
GEORGIA	ARKANSAS	OHIO
ILLINOIS	CALIFORNIA	OKLAHOMA
IOWA	COLORADO	OREGON
KANSAS	HAWAII	PENNSYLVANIA
KENTUCKY	IDAHO	RHODE ISLAND
LOUISIANA	INDIANA	SOUTH CAROLINA
MARYLAND	MAINE	TENNESSEE
MINNESOTA	MASSACHUSETTS	TEXAS
MISSISSIPPI	MICHIGAN	UTAH
NEVADA	MISSOURI	VIRGINIA
NORTH DAKOTA	MONTANA	WASHINGTON
SOUTH DAKOTA	NEBRASKA	WASHINGTON, D.C.
VERMONT	NEW HAMPSHIRE	WEST VIRGINIA
WISCONSIN	NEW JERSEY	
WYOMING		

OVERRIDING YOUR STATE'S DISTRIBUTION APPROACH WITH A WILL OR TRUST

If the distribution pattern applicable in your state does not reflect your wishes, you can override it in your will or trust. For example, if you want a per capita distribution similar to Scenario 1, you would include language similar to the following in your will or trust.

If my spouse does not survive me, I give the residue of my estate to my descendants, per capita.

If you want a traditional per stirpes distribution similar to Scenario 2, you would include language similar to the following in your will or trust.

If my spouse does not survive me, I give the residue of my estate to my descendants, per stirpes.

If you want a per capita at each generation per stirpes distribution similar to Scenario 3, you would include language similar to the following in your will or trust.

If my spouse does not survive me, I give the residue of my estate to my descendants, per capita at each generation per stirpes.

What you should do: Check your state's intestate statute to see which distribution approach your state has adopted. If you have a will or trust, check the language contained in the document to see which approach was used. Think about the approach you feel is fair, and perhaps discuss it with your family. Be sure your estate planning documents reflect your wishes.

Randy Gardner, JD, LL.M, MBA, CPA, CFP® is the Director of Education for WealthCounsel, LLC and also a Professor of Tax and Financial Planning and Director of the Certificate in Financial Planning Program at the University of Missouri – Kansas City.

Lewis W. Dymond is president and founder of Dymond Consulting, Inc. located in Frisco, Colorado, a WealthDocs™ consulting, auditing, and customized drafting solution for wealth planning professionals.

CHAPTER 14

No-Contest Clauses in Wills and Trusts

ROLAND ACHTEL and OLGA ÁLVAREZ (San Diego, California)

WHAT IS A NO-CONTEST CLAUSE?

A no-contest clause is a provision in a will or trust instructing the executor or trustee to disinherit a beneficiary completely if that beneficiary objects to or contests what he or she is to inherit.

Policy Behind No-Contest Clauses

The rationale for a no-contest clause is to dissuade beneficiaries from competing over your estate after you are gone. The clauses are essentially designed to motivate beneficiaries to accept whatever you have left for their benefit without argument.

Example of a No-Contest Clause

One example of a well-drafted and broad sweeping no-contest clause is as follows:

> *"If any person shall, in any manner, directly or indirectly, attempt to contest or oppose the validity of this agreement, (including any amendment to this agreement) or commences, continues, or prosecutes any legal proceedings to set this agreement aside, then such person shall forfeit his or her share, cease to have any right or interest in the trust property, and shall, for purposes of this agreement, be deemed to have predeceased both of us."*

No-Contest Clauses and State Law

Each state has its own set of rules regarding the application and interpretation of no-contest clauses. A well drafted no-contest clause considers your particular circumstances and goals as applied to your home state's laws. Often no-contest clauses apply not only to legal proceedings, but also to negotiations or other similar efforts to alter a will or a trust.

Good Reasons to Have a No-Contest Clause

The following is an example of a good application of a no-contest clause:

EXAMPLE: Harold and Wanda are married with two children. They have a joint revocable trust with a no-contest provision as stated above. Harold and Wanda have left half of their assets to their children (one-quarter to each child, one-quarter to their church, and one-quarter to Wanda's sister). Harold's and Wanda's children are currently in the middle of a long-standing argument going back years, and it is always a little strained when everyone is together around the holidays. Harold and Wanda want to ensure their wishes are respected and their estate is divided equally among the four beneficiaries without argument. They are uncertain how their children and Wanda's sister will react to one another after Harold and Wanda are no longer around to keep the peace.

The no-contest clause protects Harold's and Wanda's estate against fighting among the beneficiaries, because the beneficiaries are unlikely to risk disinheritance to challenge the trust. This clause also prevents further strife between the siblings or, in a more extreme scenario, it prevents a long and expensive court battle. Even in the most congenial family, issues can arise after the death of a loved one leading to squabbling over last wishes and estate assets.

NARROWING OR OMITTING A NO-CONTEST CLAUSE

Often, it will be in your best interest to omit or narrowly draft a no-contest clause in your will or trust. The following example shows a typical problem that could arise when a no-contest clause has been included in your trust or will:

EXAMPLE: Henry and Wendy are both over 75 years old and live on a 50 acre farm. They have three adult children, Andy, Bella, and Cara. They have a joint trust with a no-contest provision as stated above. They love their children dearly and all of them seem to get along well. Andy is successful and lives out-of-state in a large city. He visits twice a year. Bella lives an hour away with her son in an apartment. She has never been very responsible. Cara lives next door to her parents with her family. For the past ten years, Cara has maintained her farm, her parents' farm, and has helped care for her parents.

In their trust, Henry and Wendy leave 50% of their assets to Cara, including the farm, 25% of their assets to Andy outright, and 25% of their assets to Bella in trust.

Henry dies and Wendy goes into a deep depression. She is not her cheerful self, but is managing to pay her bills and keep her house relatively clean. Cara checks on her daily. A few months pass and Cara leaves on a three-week vacation. Cara asks Bella to stay with Wendy while she's gone. When Cara returns, Wendy is much worse than she had been. Cara takes Wendy to the doctor. The doctor determines that Wendy lacks capacity and needs 24-hour care. A few months later

Wendy dies. Unbeknownst to Andy and Cara, an amendment to the trust surfaces with Wendy's signature dated two weeks before Wendy was deemed to lack capacity. The amendment left the farm and the 50 acres to Bella, and the remaining assets are divided equally among Andy, Bella, and Cara.

The no-contest clause makes it difficult for Cara or Andy to challenge the trust amendment without being disinherited. If Cara decides to contest the amendment and loses, she is completely disinherited. Even if Cara is justified in challenging the amendment, it may be difficult to prove undue influence and manipulation by Bella before a court. Therefore, Cara is likely to forego the contest rather than risk losing her inheritance entirely.

Narrowing the No-Contest Clause

You may consider a narrowly drafted no-contest clause as an option. In the above example, if Henry and Wendy had narrowly drafted the no-contest clause so that it did not apply to amendments, then Cara would not have had to risk her inheritance to challenge the suspicious amendment.

CONSIDERATION OF A NO-CONTEST CLAUSE IN YOUR ESTATE PLAN

You may want to include a no-contest clause in your estate plan depending on your particular circumstances. A competent attorney will help you evaluate your circumstances and determine if a broad clause, a narrow clause, or no clause at all is best for you and your family. You should carefully consider your family dynamics in reaching your decision on this issue, in conjunction with the overall goals of your estate plan.

The Achtel Law Firm is dedicated to integrated estate planning and estate dispute resolution. This specifically includes preparing estate documents, Medi-Cal planning, handling conservatorships, and resolving will or trust contests.

AVOIDING PROBATE
(What Happens After You Die?)

The Pros and Cons of Probate

DIEDRE DENNIS WACHBRIT (Westlake Village, California)

Probate is your state's method of transferring the property of someone who has died to its new rightful owners. If you have no estate plan, your assets will go through the probate process. If you have a will, your assets will go through the probate process. If you have a revocable living trust and you have placed your assets into that trust, they will not go through probate.

PROBATE IS A PUBLIC PROCESS

Probate gives relatives and friends a forum to bring suits against those who claim your property.

PRO: This can be advantageous if there has been elder abuse or if your will was changed when you were subject to undue influence, fraud, or dementia.

CON: Probate increases the likelihood of conflict after your death. Your estate could be consumed by legal fees as relatives battle each other over a wide variety of issues. They can argue about the validity of your will. They can argue about whether they are entitled to a monthly allowance from your estate. They can argue about your debts and whether they are valid.

Everything about your estate — from the value of your jewelry to the age of your beneficiaries — is made public. This is particularly unfortunate for young beneficiaries who may not have the maturity to handle incoming solicitations.

PROBATE IS COURT-SUPERVISED

PRO: You don't have to select your Executor as carefully as you select a Trustee of a Revocable Living Trust because everything an Executor does is supervised by the court. If you don't select an Executor, the court will select one for you. Because that person may not be a good choice for the job, court supervision can give your beneficiaries some safety and protection.

CON: Your Executor has much less flexibility to administer your estate in probate. Probate is controlled by your state's probate code, a thick book of laws, and by the probate cases that have been tried in your state, many more thick volumes. Your Executor is bound by these laws, which are designed to restrict the Executor and avoid mistakes, not to maximize the ease of administering your estate. Your

Executor will have to seek court permission for most transactions on behalf of your estate and will not be able to invest your funds in a well-diversified stock portfolio. In fact, in most probates, assets are managed as little as possible and stock losses are not uncommon.

Most people find the courtroom stressful. Probate forces your loved ones to go through a court process, an unpleasant experience even with the best attorney.

PROBATE IS INSURED

The Executor in a probate typically must get a bond. A bond is an insurance policy that will pay your beneficiaries if your Executor commits wrongdoing. Many wills waive bond.

PRO: Your beneficiaries are protected with a bond.

CON: Bond is another cost your estate will have to pay. Typically, bond is about ¼ of 1% of your estate each year.

PROBATE DOES NOT REQUIRE ADVANCE PLANNING

Probate is available to anyone and requires no will or trust.

PRO: Probate requires no effort on your behalf.

CON: Because no advance planning is required, you never have the opportunity to think about and care for your loved ones in a way that expresses your values and your love.

WITHOUT A WILL, PROBATE RELIES UPON THE LAWS OF INTESTACY

PRO: The laws of intestacy are designed to mimic what most people would put into their wills if they had done planning. In most cases, the spouse inherits one-half to all of the estate and the children inherit the rest. Where there is no spouse or children, assets typically go to parents and siblings, then to nieces and nephews, then to cousins.

CONS:

Your next of kin may not be your chosen heirs. The law makes assumptions about whom you would wish to inherit your estate. Those assumptions may not be correct. Perhaps you don't want to leave assets equally to children from different marriages. Or perhaps you do not want your brother or sister to inherit. Without a will, your wishes will not be followed.

Your divorcing spouse gets everything. If you die in the midst of a divorce and you have not created a will disinheriting your spouse, your spouse will typically inherit one-half to all of your estate.

Your loved ones inherit because of the law, not because you made provisions for them. When provisions have not been made for people, that is, when they inherit because of the law and not because you chose them, the inheritance is not a gift. It is a right under law. This changes the feeling the heirs have about you and changes how they treat the inheritance (more like "found money" than an inheritance that must be stewarded).

Young people get full control of their entire inheritance at age 18. When you fail to create a trust for young people, their inheritance is controlled by guardians, who must invest it very conservatively. Then, at age 18, they receive whatever is left — no strings attached. I say whatever is left, because spending the inheritance is up to the guardian until the children turn 18. Because you did not choose the guardian, you have no way of assuring the money will be spent wisely.

PROBATE CAN BE EXPENSIVE

PRO: Your estate's attorney and Executor are nicely rewarded for their hard work.

CON: In some states, probate can consume as much as 8% of your estate, leaving less for heirs. And that 8% is based on the gross value of your estate, not the net value. In other words, if you have a $500,000 home with a $450,000 mortgage, your heirs pay for probate based on its $500,000 value, and after fees and costs, may inherit nothing. Even if your state's fees are more reasonable, a revocable living trust will almost always cost less to administer than a probate. In some states, the filing fee to open a probate (paid to the court) is a percentage of the estate.

PROBATE CAN BE TIME-CONSUMING

Most probates take six to eighteen months to complete.

PRO: The probate process provides plenty of time for heirs to adjust to the idea of their inheritance. It also provides plenty of time for challenges to be brought.

CON: Your beneficiaries must wait to receive their inheritance. Your Executor must work on your estate throughout the process, completing form upon form.

While probate has been reformed in a few states, it remains an unpleasant and expensive process for most. If you find yourself in the midst of a probate, be sure to retain an experienced attorney and to follow the probate court's rules closely.

*Diedre Dennis Wachbrit, a board-certified specialist in estate planning, trust, and probate law, has been quoted in the **Wall Street Journal, Time Magazine, and The New York Times**.*

CHAPTER 16

Types of Probate Administration – Formal and Informal

RICHARD DAYTON (San Jose, California)

This chapter will describe the different types of probate, what it is, how to avoid it, and how some states deal with it.

Probate happens after someone dies. It is the process of proving a will is valid and thereafter administering the estate of the deceased person according to the will, or via the state's intestacy statutes if someone dies without a will. In the simplest terms, probate is nothing more than the process of getting an asset from the person who died to the person who is alive. The person who died is called the decedent and for our purposes, the person who is alive is the beneficiary. An asset can be a home, a car, money, books, furniture, or any other type of property. It includes retirement plans, IRAs, 401(k)s, etc.

Probate is frequently thought of as a bad thing. It is a time-consuming, expensive, court-supervised, and public process. However, avoiding probate is not always the best answer. Having the court oversee the process provides protections to the people who are supposed to receive the property of the decedent; it can ward off family arguments; it can ensure creditors are paid; and it generally assures everything is handled correctly.

In general, there are two types of probate — formal and informal. Formal probate is what most people think about when they hear the word probate. This is the "long, drawn-out, expensive court process" in states such as California. In states other than California, probate can be handled relatively quickly and inexpensively. Livingston County Michigan Probate Court, for example, has defined informal probate as a method of administering an estate of the deceased individual without the intervention of the Probate Judge.

The person handling the probate can have many different names, such as executor, executrix, administrator, special administrator, and others. We will use the general term administrator.

Formal probate generally consists of a very formal process with specific steps. These steps are taken by the administrator and must be followed exactly and in a timely manner. Each step is supervised by the probate court and normally by a judge.

Formal probate steps usually consist of establishing that the decedent really died by producing a death certificate, determining who should be appointed as administrator, determining how formal the court supervision will be, notifying creditors, determining what the decedent owned upon death, and determining which assets will have to go through probate. The administrator is also responsible for paying bills, terminating credit cards, notifying state agencies, and paying taxes. Finally, the administrator must obtain the court's permission to distribute property to the decedent's beneficiaries and then closing the probate. Closing the probate is very important to the administrator as this is when he or she is no longer responsible for handling the estate's issues.

In California, a formal probate cannot realistically be done in less than six months for the simplest estate, and usually takes longer. As mentioned, probate can be expensive. In California, the formal probate of an estate consisting of one home with a value of $1,000,000 and a mortgage of $990,000 is $23,000 for legal fees, $23,000 for administrator fees, and approximately $700 in costs. So as you can see in California and other states with similar formal probate proceedings, it is very important to avoid probate if you can.

Informal probate, on the other hand, can be very simple and not even involve the court. The informal probate process varies considerably between states. California's informal process, although simple, can only be used when the value of real estate is less than $20,000 and the total value of all property going through the informal process is less than $100,000. Usually, judges are not involved and the longest waiting time is the initial 40 day waiting period required before an informal process can be used. In Alaska and Maine, informal probate is simpler than formal probate but still involves the courts. In Michigan, Minnesota, and Wisconsin, informal probate involves the courts and many of the same steps as a formal probate. Please keep in mind that we are only touching on the highlights of probate. There are many different ways of completing the probate process. It is very important to check with your local court for the process to follow.

Probate can be avoided by several methods. However, the selection of one or more of the following mechanisms must be considered in context with your overall planning goals. Each idea is correct for a specific situation but might not be appropriate in the next situation or for you.

- Have pay-on-death or transfer-on-death beneficiaries named for bank accounts and other accounts with this feature.

- Have detailed beneficiary designations and name back-up beneficiaries on life insurance and retirement accounts such as 401(k)s, IRAs, and 457 plans.

- Hold joint ownership property title in such a way that property will pass to other joint owners upon your death (subject to the cautions detailed in other chapters).

- Create a revocable living trust (discussed in other chapters).

The foregoing are just a few ways probate can be avoided. Later chapters provide more detail about how to keep your property out of the probate process.

In summary, formal probate is a court-supervised process that is normally time-consuming, expensive, and detail-oriented. Informal probate can be simple, quick, inexpensive, and much less complex. Probate can be avoided using a number of techniques, but avoiding probate is not always the best choice for your situation. Be sure to consult with an attorney before making a final decision.

Richard Dayton is a Certified Specialist in Estate Planning, Trust, and Probate Law by the State Bar of California Board of Legal Specialization. His practice is located in San Jose, California.

Non-Probate vs. Probate Assets – Why You Should Care

SUSAN MCMAKIN (Richmond, Virginia)

When you die, like most other people, you will probably leave assets that need to be transferred to the person, persons, or organizations (charitable or other) that you have named in your will or living trust. If you die without a will, your property will go to whomever your state's law says it will go.

An asset will be a probate asset if your state law requires the property to be administered under your state's probate process before it can be transferred to your beneficiaries after your death.

Assets fall into three categories: 1) property you own as an individual, 2) property you own with another, and 3) property for which you have named a beneficiary, such as a life insurance policy or a retirement plan.

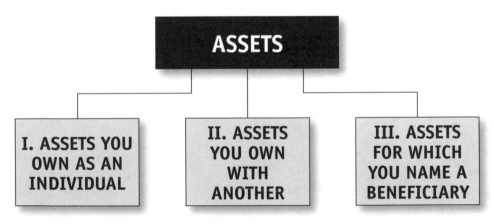

I. ASSETS YOU OWN AS AN INDIVIDUAL

An asset you own as an individual at the time of your death (that does not otherwise avoid probate as described in Section III below) is a probate asset because the probate process in your state will require certain steps to be taken for individually held assets to be transferred to your heirs or beneficiaries.

II. ASSETS YOU OWN WITH ANOTHER

Usually, an asset you hold jointly with another individual or individuals will not be a probate asset. For example, assets such as a residence, bank account, or brokerage account you own as joint tenant with right of survivorship with your spouse are not probate assets because at your death the surviving joint owner — in this example, your spouse — gets title to the asset because of the survivorship feature of this type of ownership. However, an asset you hold with another person or persons could still be considered a probate asset. Let's say you and two friends invest in a piece of real property. In this case you own a one-third share of the property along with your two friends, each of whom also owns a one-third interest. In this case, the property is owned as tenants-in-common instead of jointly with right of survivorship as in the first example. At your death your one-third share is a probate asset because you are the sole owner of that one-third interest at the time of your death.

III. ASSETS FOR WHICH YOU NAME A BENEFICIARY

Generally, assets for which you name a beneficiary are not probate assets. Accordingly, the underlying assets of most life insurance policies, annuities, qualified retirement plans, individual retirement accounts, and accounts that provide for transfers on death pass directly to the named beneficiary by contract and need not pass through the probate process. But, what if the beneficiary named on your life insurance policy or retirement account is your estate? What if there is no named beneficiary, or the named beneficiary has predeceased you and you have failed to name a contingent beneficiary? When this occurs — and it often does — the asset is subject to the probate process, either because you purposely named your estate as the beneficiary, or your beneficiary designation lapsed, causing the assets by default to vest in your estate.

The probate system varies from state to state. While there are certainly situations where it is advisable to utilize the statutory probate process (for example, where the protections of the court system are necessary to guarantee the interest of beneficiaries and/or fiduciaries), in the overwhelming majority of circumstances probate is an unnecessary hassle. For years, advice has been rendered about how to avoid it. Even the simplest formal probate requires probate fees, inventories, and accountings. A complex scenario could drag on for years. In between these two extremes, the process entails numerous statutory requirements, meticulous record-keeping, precise attention to detail, and strict timetables, all resulting in unnecessary expense and time-consuming inconvenience. Witness a paraphrase of a letter recently sent by a probate official to an attorney acquaintance of this writer:

> *Dear Counsellor:*
>
> *Thank you for the final account for the referenced estate.*
>
> *Your total on the summary sheet for line 5 is $203,199.50, but the total for line 11 is $203,199.51 which is off by one cent.*
>
> *The will bequeaths numerous items to named individuals. You will need*

to show each of these items as distributions in the account; the signed receipts are insufficient.

The receipt you sent for Section 3 says it was for a horse, but you had previously informed this office that the horse was dead. Should this receipt be for the dog instead of the horse?

You also show $25,000.00 to each of five heirs in your disbursements, but these should be shown as distributions to beneficiaries.

You show the distribution of the 1995 Toyota Corolla and the 1989 Dodge truck to the beneficiaries but state below this that the 1995 Toyota Corolla went to Donna Drake and the 1989 Dodge truck went to John Drake. If the two individuals mentioned received these vehicles then you do not show it also distributed to the beneficiaries.

We will need the canceled check written to Somerset County on April 5, 2006 for $40.25; the receipt is not sufficient.

Please redo the account and resubmit it to this office as soon as possible. Please consult our published fee schedule for the appropriate fee for resubmission.

Sincerely,
The Probate Department

Not the letter your executor or your attorney wants to receive after everyone thinks the matter has been finalized.

What you should do: Consider using a revocable living trust as the controlling document distributing your assets at your death. Transfer individually held assets for which joint ownership or beneficiary designations are not options or not advisable (residence, interests in real estate, bank accounts, brokerage accounts, and your stuff — golf clubs, jewelry, pianos, cars, boats, household items, and maybe even horses — to you as Trustee of your trust by deed, re-registration, or affidavit of transfer. That way when you die, your successor trustee will have title to the assets and can distribute them according to the instructions contained in your revocable living trust and avoid probate of these assets. Remember if your joint co-owner of property predeceases you, you as the surviving joint owner, will be the sole owner and the property will be a probate asset. At the death of a co-owner, transfer the asset to your trust. Be sure to keep beneficiary designations on life insurance policies, annuities, and retirement plans up-to-date to avoid distribution by default to your estate. With advice of your tax advisor, accountant, and/or attorney you may wish to consider naming your revocable living trust as the beneficiary of these types of assets.

Parker & McMakin Law Group is a personal practice limited to estate and business planning, trusts, and trust and estate settlement. Additional firm services include corporate and business planning and litigation dealing with estates and businesses.

Probate and Non-Probate Assets

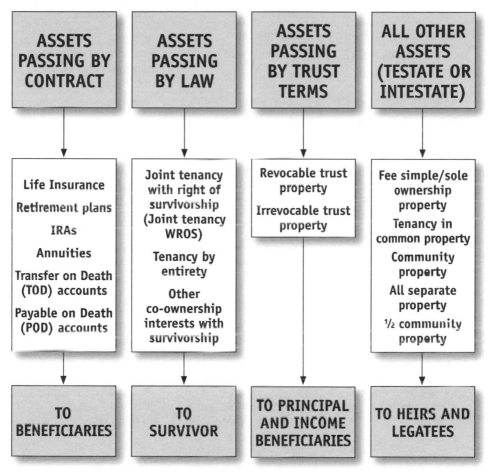

ASSETS PASSING BY CONTRACT	ASSETS PASSING BY LAW	ASSETS PASSING BY TRUST TERMS	ALL OTHER ASSETS (TESTATE OR INTESTATE)
Life Insurance Retirement plans IRAs Annuities Transfer on Death (TOD) accounts Payable on Death (POD) accounts	Joint tenancy with right of survivorship (Joint tenancy WROS) Tenancy by entirety Other co-ownership interests with survivorship	Revocable trust property Irrevocable trust property	Fee simple/sole ownership property Tenancy in common property Community property All separate property ½ community property
TO BENEFICIARIES	TO SURVIVOR	TO PRINCIPAL AND INCOME BENEFICIARIES	TO HEIRS AND LEGATEES

Will Substitutes Compared

	JOINT TENANCY WROS	REVOCABLE TRUST
What property is used?	Real or personal.	Real or personal.
How do you set it up?	Sign a document.	Attorney creates a trust document and owner re-titles assets to the trust.
How much does it cost?	Minimal cost.	Moderate cost.
What are the gift tax consequences?	Spouse — none. Nonspouse — may be a taxable gift.	None since no completed gift has been made.
What are the income tax consequences?	Income splitting between joint tenants.	Income is taxed to the grantor.
What are the estate tax consequences?	Spouses — 50% is included in the decedent's gross estate. Nonspouses — Entire value is included unless the survivor made contributions.	Entire value of trust assets is included in grantor's estate.
How much control does the owner retain?	Owner gives up control of property.	Owner/grantor can change trust at any time, thus retains control until incapacity or death.
Do assets avoid probate?	Yes, pass to survivor.	Yes, pass to income and principal beneficiaries.
Do the assets receive a step up in basis at death?	Spouses — Yes, ½ of property receives a step up in basis. (Note: Full step up in basis is for property held as community property in community property states.) Nonspouses — Yes, to the extent of inclusion in the decedent's estate.	Yes, 100% of property receives a step up in basis.
Will the assets qualify for the marital deduction?	Spouses — Yes, ½ of property qualifies. Nonspouses — No, none of the property qualifies.	Depends on the trust document.
Will the assets qualify for the unified credit?	Spouses — No, none of the property qualifies. Nonspouses — Yes, value included in decedent's gross estate qualifies.	Depends on the trust document.

CHAPTER 18

Trust Terminology and Types of Trusts

ARLYN J. BOSSENBROOK (East Lansing, Michigan)

People create trusts to implement their plans for themselves, their family, and their property. There are many different types of trusts. Trusts can be customized to fit a person's or family's particular circumstances.

Revocable Living Trusts. A Revocable Living Trust is a written document containing the Grantor's plans for his or her property and his or her family. The Trust comes into existence when it is signed by the Grantor. (Grantor, Settlor, Creator, Trustmaker, and Trustor are names for the person who establishes a Revocable Living Trust.) The Trust may be revoked or amended by the Grantor.

Trustee. The Trustee is in charge of managing the trust property. The Grantor usually appoints himself or herself as the initial Trustee. Upon the Grantor's incapacity or death, a Successor Trustee takes over the management of the trust property and is responsible for carrying out the Grantor's instructions. Trustees may be individuals or institutions. Trusts can be managed by more than one Trustee, called Co-Trustees.

Trust Beneficiary. The Trust Beneficiary is the person or entity entitled to receive distributions of Trust property. During the Grantor's lifetime, the Grantor is also the Trust Beneficiary. Upon the Grantor's death, the Trust's subsequent beneficiaries are changed to the Primary Beneficiaries and if any of them have predeceased the Grantor, to the Contingent Beneficiaries. Charities or non-family members may be named as beneficiaries.

Trust Funding. Trusts control property held in the name of the Trust. The Grantor funds the trust by transferring title to his or her property to the Trust. The property then becomes "trust property." Trust Funding is accomplished by sending a letter to banks and other financial institutions asking them to change title on the accounts from the Grantor's individual name to the Trust. Real estate is transferred to the Trust by deed. Trusts may also be the beneficiary of the Grantor's life insurance policies or retirement accounts, but this should be done on a case-by-case basis with the advice of an attorney.

Avoiding Probate. Property that is "trust property" will avoid Probate Court proceedings at the incapacity or death of the Grantor.

Sub-Trusts. A Revocable Living Trust may contain Sub-Trusts which come into being upon the happening of an event. For example the Trust may state, "Upon my death, if my spouse survives me, my estate will be divided into a Marital Trust and a Bypass Trust." The Trust may go on to state, "If my spouse has predeceased me, my Trust property shall be divided into equal trust shares to my children." The Marital Trust, the Bypass Trust and the trusts for the children are Sub-Trusts contained in the Grantor's Revocable Living Trust.

Bypass Trust (Family Trust, Credit Shelter Trust) & Marital Trust. If a husband and wife have a combined estate valued at more than the Federal Estate Tax exemption amount ($2 million in 2008, and $3.5 million in 2009), the Trust document will divide the Trust property into a Bypass Trust and a Marital Trust in order to minimize Federal estate taxes. The surviving spouse may be the Trustee and Beneficiary of the Bypass Trust and the Marital Trust.

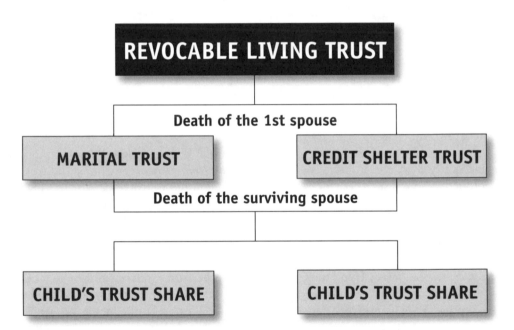

A Qualified Terminal Interest Property Trust (QTIP Trust). A Qualified Terminal Interest Property Trust, commonly referred to as a QTIP Trust, is a special type of Marital Trust which may be used in a second marriage when a Grantor wants to provide trust distributions to his or her spouse during the spouse's lifetime and upon the spouse's death, distribute the remaining trust property to the Grantor's children from his or her first marriage.

Separate Trusts and Joint Trusts. If husband and wife have a combined estate valued at more than the Federal Estate Tax exemption amount, they may have separate trusts which provide for Federal Estate Tax planning or they may have one joint trust which provides for Federal Estate Tax planning.

Protective Trust. An inheritance left to a child outright could subject the inheritance to the child's creditors, marital problems, addiction problems, inability to manage money, and Federal Estate Taxes on the child's estate. Leaving the child's inheritance to the child in a Protective Trust, rather than outright, will address these concerns. Dynasty Trusts are special types of Protective Trusts which continue to hold property in trust for the benefit of succeeding generations.

Trust Amendment. After the Grantor has established a Revocable Living Trust, he or she may change all or any part of the Trust by signing a Trust Amendment. A Trust Amendment must be signed and dated by the Grantor.

Testamentary Trust. A Testamentary Trust is a trust contained in someone's will. It comes into existence upon death and is subject to Probate Court proceedings.

Irrevocable Trust. An Irrevocable Trust is created during the Grantor's lifetime and cannot be amended by the Grantor. Irrevocable Trusts may be used for gifting and for reducing Federal Estate Taxes.

Life Insurance Trust. A Life Insurance Trust, or ILIT, is an Irrevocable Trust established to be the beneficiary of a life insurance policy. If the premiums are gifted to the Trust, the life insurance proceeds will not be included in the Grantor's estate for Federal Estate Tax purposes.

Special Needs Trust. A Special Needs Trust is a trust established for the benefit of a child who has disabilities and is entitled to government assistance. An inheritance for a disabled child held in a Special Needs Trust will not disqualify the child from receiving government assistance. Distributions from the Trust are made at the discretion of the Trustee for the child's special needs. A Special Needs Trust may be established as a stand-alone trust or it may be a Sub-Trust contained in a Revocable Living Trust.

Asset Protection Trusts. A Grantor's property held in a Revocable Living Trust is not protected from the claims of the Grantor's creditors. Property held in a Bypass Trust or a Protective Trust is protected from creditor claims against the Trust's Beneficiary. Several states now permit Domestic Asset Protection Trusts, which allow a Grantor to transfer his or her property to an irrevocable trust of which he or she is the beneficiary. If the statutory requirements are met, the property is protected from the Grantor's creditors.

Arlyn J. Bossenbrook, P.C. designs estate plans which gives clients control during their lifetimes and passes their estate to their loved ones as they desire, while minimizing taxes and costs.

Comparison of Revocable and Irrevocable Trusts

	REVOCABLE TRUSTS	IRREVOCABLE TRUSTS
Avoids probate	Yes	Yes
Gift tax applies	No, not a completed gift	Yes, is a completed gift
Estate tax avoidance	No	Yes, unless an exception applies
Income taxed to grantor	Yes	No, unless grantor trust rules
Owner retains control over assets in trust	Yes	No

CHAPTER 19

Overview of the Taxation of Trusts

DAVID ALLEN HIERSEKORN (Santa Ana, California)

The general rule is that all trusts are separate taxpayers, each with its own tax year and accounting method. The exception to this rule is trusts that are ignored for income tax purposes under the "grantor trust" rules discussed in more detail below.

Just like their human counterparts, trusts are taxed on income and receive deductions for certain authorized expenses.

Unlike human taxpayers, however, trusts are taxed under a compressed rate schedule which results in a significantly higher tax at any given level of income. As shown in the trust tax rate schedule below, the highest bracket is reached at just $10,050 in taxable income, whereas an individual would need an income of $357,700 in 2008 to reach that same tax bracket.

Trust Tax Rates 2008

IF TAXABLE INCOME IS...		THEN ESTIMATED TAXES ARE...		
Between	But Not Over	Base Tax	+ Rate	Of the Amount Over
$0	$2,050	$0	15%	$0
$2,050	$4,850	$307.50	25%	$2,050
$4,850	$7,400	$1,007.50	28%	$4,850
$7,400	$10,050	$1,721.50	33%	$7,400
$10,050	—	$2,596.00	35%	$10,050

Bear in mind that these compressed rates only apply to ordinary income. Capital gains and dividend income are taxed the same for individuals and trusts.

Because of the substantial disparity between individual tax rates and those for trusts, it is important to understand exactly how trusts are taxed. For our purposes, trusts will be divided into three categories: grantor trusts, simple trusts, and complex trusts. Each will be discussed in more detail below.

GRANTOR TRUSTS

A grantor trust is the exception to the general rule that all trusts are taxpayers. Therefore, grantor trusts are ignored for income tax purposes. Under the Internal Revenue Code, a trust is a "grantor trust" if the grantor retains one or more of the powers listed in Internal Revenue Code Sections 673 through 677. It is also possible for a third party who is not the grantor to be deemed the owner of a trust if that person has control over the principal or income of the trust as described in Internal Revenue Code Section 678.

In essence, this means that if the grantor (or a third party) has the kind of control over the trust property that would ordinarily be consistent with ownership of the property, the trust will be ignored for income tax purposes and the deemed owner will be taxed on all income to the trust as if it were his or her own income.

By far, the most common type of "grantor trust" is the revocable living trust. Because it is virtually impossible to create a revocable living trust without retaining one of the grantor trust powers (e.g., power to designate beneficiaries), anyone creating a revocable living trust does not need to worry about filing a separate income tax return for the trust. Even though grantor trust status is virtually guaranteed for a revocable living trust, it is still a good idea to state in the trust that the grantor is specifically retaining one or more of the grantor trust powers.

EXAMPLE: GRANTOR TRUST STATUS LANGUAGE

By reserving the broad rights and powers set forth in this Article, I intend to qualify my trust as a "Grantor Trust" under Sections 671 to 677 of the Internal Revenue Code so that, for federal income tax purposes, I will be treated as the owner during my lifetime of all the assets held in my trust as though I held them in my individual capacity.

During any period that my trust is a Grantor Trust, the taxpayer identification number of my trust shall be my Social Security number, in accordance with Treasury Regulation Section 301.6109-1(a)(2).

INTENTIONALLY "DEFECTIVE" GRANTOR TRUSTS

Perhaps one of the most unfortunate vocabulary choices in the estate planning field lies with the "Intentionally Defective Grantor Trust," or IDGT. Many clients have blanched at the idea that their trust would be "defective." But, the term only means the trust was intentionally created so that the grantor retained one of the powers listed in the Internal Revenue Code's grantor trust rules.

This powerful technique takes advantage of a quirk in the tax code classifying the owner of the trust differently for estate tax purposes than for income tax purposes. Therefore, a gift in trust may be complete for estate tax purposes but not for income tax purposes. A gift is only complete for income tax purposes if you give away all of the powers in the grantor trust rules. If you retain any of the listed powers, then the gift is "defective," which means the trust will be considered a grantor trust, and you will pay income tax on all of the trust's income.

This schism creates two planning opportunities. First, you cannot sell something to yourself for tax purposes. That is, a sale transaction where you are both the seller and the buyer is not considered a "transfer" for income tax purposes. That means you can create and fund an intentionally defective grantor trust, which is outside your estate for estate tax purposes, and then sell an asset to that trust without incurring any capital gains tax on the sale. This technique also avoids other penalties and consequences that may apply to certain transfers, such as transfers of life insurance.

The second key benefit is that, when the grantor pays income tax on the trust's income, it is effectively the same as making a tax-free gift to the beneficiaries equal to the amount of the income tax he or she would pay if the trust were a non-grantor trust.

NON-GRANTOR TRUSTS: SIMPLE OR COMPLEX?

Non-grantor trusts (i.e., trusts that are not considered grantor trusts) are divided into two categories. A non-grantor trust will either be a simple trust or a complex trust, depending on how it handles distributions to beneficiaries.

A simple trust must pass three tests. It must distribute all income to the beneficiaries; it cannot distribute principal; and it cannot make distributions to charities. A complex trust, by comparison, is one that does one or more of the things that a simple trust cannot do. That is, it can accumulate income, distribute principal, or make distributions to charity.

In other words, a trust must qualify as a simple trust, or else it will be considered a complex trust. The difference between the two lies in the way that the trust deducts distributions to beneficiaries.

In a simple trust, all income is treated as distributed to the beneficiaries. In such a case, the trust reports all income annually, but is entitled to a deduction for the entire amount distributed to beneficiaries. The result is that the trust only pays tax on capital gains. (Note that it is possible in some states to treat capital gains as income if permitted by the trust. In those instances, a simple trust would distribute all income and capital gains.)

With a complex trust, distributions can include ordinary income, dividends, capital gains and, perhaps, principal. It is also possible that the trust earns income that is not distributed, and there may be a deduction for distributions to charities. The result is that the allocation of the tax and any deductions between the trust and its beneficiaries — and among beneficiaries — can be quite complex. Hence, the name.

A complex trust may not distribute principal unless all income has first been distributed. However, it is actually more complex than this. The rules require that all ordinary income be distributed before dividends; all dividends be distributed before capital gains; and all capital gains be distributed before principal. The result is what tax lawyers call "worst in, first out" — that is, the worst character of income must be exhausted before moving to the next tier.

When these distributions are made, the trust is entitled to a deduction for any income distributed to beneficiaries. However, because the income (and certain deductions) must be allocated equitably among the trust and the beneficiaries, it is necessary to calculate what the tax code refers to as the Distributable Net Income, or "DNI."

How DNI is determined is beyond the scope of this chapter. However, it should suffice to know the DNI represents the amount that must either be distributed to beneficiaries or be taxed to the trust. It represents the upper limit on the trust's deduction for distributions and the upper limit on the amount of income taxable to the beneficiaries.

Because of the nature of the tax rules for complex trusts, careful planning and coordination between your investment, legal, and tax professionals is critical.

David Hiersekorn helps affluent families and business owners protect their assets and create a lasting legacy.

CHAPTER 20

Generation-Skipping Transfer Tax and the Rule Against Perpetuities

JIMMIE L. JOE (City of Industry, California)

THE GENERATION-SKIPPING TRANSFER TAX

The generation-skipping transfer (GST) tax is imposed on any transfer you make to a skip-person (i.e., a relative two or more generations below you, such as a grandchild or great-grandchild, or an unrelated person 37½ years younger than you). The reason for the tax is that the federal tax system seeks to tax transfers at each generational level. Otherwise, if you transferred property directly to your grandchild, you would have "skipped" a generation so that there would be no estate tax triggered on the property when your child dies because your child would not have owned the transferred property at the time of his or her death.

Congress enacted the GST tax to capture this lost tax revenue. The GST tax is a second additional tax to the estate and gift tax that applies to any transfers to any skip-person. The GST tax is more punitive than the estate and gift tax in that property is taxed as a flat tax at the highest estate and gift tax rate in effect at the time of a transfer. It taxes every dollar at this highest rate, whereas the estate and gift tax rate schedule taxes property at increasing rates. Because of this, it is almost always better to pay an estate tax rather than a GST tax on all but the largest estates. Table 1 shows the GST tax rates and exemption amounts between 2008 and 2011.

Table 1: GST Tax Rates

YEAR	GST RATE	GST EXEMPTION
2008	45%	$2 million
2009	45%	$3.5 million
2010	Highest Individual Income Tax Rate (Applies Only for Gift Transfers)	Repealed (Except for Gifts)
2011	55%	$1 million (Indexed for Inflation)

THE GST EXEMPTION

Like the estate and gift tax, you have a GST tax exemption you can use to exempt property from the GST tax. The exemption is a dollar-for-dollar reduction. In 2008, the GST tax exemption is $2 million, which means you can transfer up to $2 million of your property to your grandchild and have it avoid the GST tax. The GST exemption is available for lifetime gifts you make to your grandchildren. Any unused GST exemption remaining at your death is available to exempt your estate, wholly or partially, on transfers you make to your grandchildren.

The GST tax exemption increases to $3.5 million in 2009. Unless new legislation is passed, the exemption will decrease to $1 million (indexed for inflation) in 2011 and thereafter.

USING THE GST TAX EXEMPTION WITH DYNASTY TRUSTS

One highly effective way to preserve, grow, and protect wealth for several generations is through use of a dynasty trust. Since wealth that is never taxed grows far greater than wealth that is taxed at each generation, a dynasty trust is a great wealth builder. To illustrate the effectiveness of a dynasty trust, you need to understand the effect of estate taxes when wealth passes to several generations:

> **EXAMPLE:** Assume John Knight inherits $2 million in 2008 directly from his parents. Since the government taxes everything owned at death, at John's death, his $2 million inheritance is subject to estate taxes. Each time wealth passes down a generation, the government will again tax it. So, assuming no investment growth, if everyone in the Knight family is already in the 50% estate tax bracket and everything they inherit is added to their taxable estates and subject to estate taxes, not only will John's inheritance be subject to estate tax, shrinking it to $1 million when it passes to John II, but at John II's death, the amount will again be subject to estate taxes and will shrink further to $500,000 before it passes to John III. At John III's death, the amount will once again shrink further after estate taxes to $250,000. After three generations, 87% of the family's wealth will have been paid to the government, leaving less than 13% for the Knight family.[1]

> If John Knight had received his inheritance in a dynasty trust, however, and his parents had allocated their unused $2 million GST exemption to it, there would be no estate taxes at each generational level. This outcome occurs because the entire trust is exempt from GST tax. Once exempted, the assets of the trust, including all future growth and appreciation of the trust assets, remain exempt from estate and GST taxes as long as the assets stay in the trust. Thus, John Knight would be able to pass the entire $2 million at his death to John II. If John II were named as the Trustee of the trust, he could control and invest the trust's assets. Assuming he were able to double the trust assets over his lifetime, John II would be able to pass $4 million to John III free of estate and GST

taxes. If John III were also able to double his $4 million received in trust over his lifetime, he would be able to pass $8 million to John IV. This is because the assets of the dynasty trust avoid paying GST and estate taxes. Moreover, the example does not account for the power of compounding. Assuming a 7% annual growth rate, a dynasty trust funded with $1 million could grow to $867.7 million after 100 years according to an analysis done by Wilmington Trust.[2]

It is because this type of planning is so effective in transferring significant wealth without being taxed that Congress enacted the GST tax. However, with proper planning, you and your spouse can leave up to $4 million to your children and grandchildren free of estate and GST taxes in 2008. In doing so, you will have used your GST tax exemption to its fullest extent instead of wasting it.

Besides the enormous tax savings to your family over time, there are other important reasons to plan with a dynasty trust. Proper long-term planning can protect your family's wealth from lawsuits, divorces, and your beneficiaries' poor money management skills. Furthermore, you can pass your values to your children and grandchildren. Proper long-term planning can provide for future education, influence behavior, promote entrepreneurship, promote family harmony, and encourage philanthropy. For many families, it only seems logical to extend these planning benefits to children, grandchildren, and beyond.

LEVERAGING GST TAX PLANNING WITH YOUR INSURANCE TRUST

One of the most powerful techniques for building wealth for generations is to create an irrevocable life insurance dynasty trust that utilizes your GST tax exemption to its fullest extent. In 2008, you can make annual exclusion tax-free gifts of up to $12,000 per beneficiary ($13,000 in 2009) to the life insurance trust. These tax-free gifts can be made without reducing your gift tax exemption. If your spouse is not a beneficiary of the trust, he or she can also transfer $12,000 annually to it for each beneficiary. So, if you and your spouse have three children and two grandchildren, you can both transfer up to $120,000 ($12,000 x 2 [of you] x 5 [children and grandchildren]) tax-free to the irrevocable life insurance dynasty trust each year. In doing so, you and your spouse can also allocate part of your GST tax exemptions to the gifts, so that the entire $120,000 gift is exempt from GST tax.

Your trustee can use the trust money to purchase a second-to-die life insurance policy on you and your spouse. When the life insurance pays the death benefit to the trust, the entire amount will be exempt from estate and GST tax for generations. If you and your spouse make these gifts to the trust for ten years, you will have both used $1.2 million of your combined $4 million lifetime GST tax exemption (as of 2008). However, when the death benefits are paid to the trust, the entire amount, which could be several million dollars, will be exempt from estate and GST tax. As the trust grows exponentially, you will have leveraged your GST tax exemption and created significant wealth for many generations.

THE RULE AGAINST PERPETUITIES

As discussed above, the use of a dynasty trust can provide many generations with tax-efficient transfers and protection from lawsuits, divorces, irresponsible behavior, and money mismanagement. State law determines how long a dynasty trust can last, however. Many states have limited the duration of dynasty trusts through an old law known as the Rule against Perpetuities. This law is complex and in most states limits a trust's existence to around 90 years.

Many states have modified or abolished the Rule against Perpetuities. In these states, no limits exist on the duration of a trust, or the limits have been greatly extended. Table 2 sets forth those states that have modified or abolished the Rule against Perpetuities.

Table 2: States That Have Abolished or Extended the Rule Against Perpetuities

STATE	LIMIT
North Carolina, South Dakota, Washington	150 yrs
Florida	360 yrs
Alaska, Delaware, Idaho, Maryland, Nevada	365 yrs
Colorado, Maine, Nebraska, New Jersey, Rhode Island, Utah, Virginia, Wisconsin, Wyoming	1,000 yrs
Arizona, District of Columbia, Illinois, Missouri, New Hampshire, Ohio	opt out

The good news is that you do not have to live in a state that has abolished the Rule against Perpetuities to receive all of the trust and tax benefits of a perpetual dynasty trust. The trust only needs to be located in one of these states to receive the benefits. A dynasty trust may contain a provision to allow the trust to change its location to a state that has abolished the Rule against Perpetuities. Below is an example of language that may be used to add flexibility to a dynasty trust and allow it to be moved to a state that has abolished the Rule against Perpetuities:

> ### Changing the Governing Law and Situs of Administration
> *Our Trustee may, at any time, change the governing law of the trust, remove all or any part of the property or the situs of administration of the trust from one jurisdiction to another, or both. Our Trustee may elect, by filing an instrument with the trust records, that the trust will thereafter be construed, regulated, and governed as to administration by the laws of the new jurisdiction. Our Trustee may take action under this Section for any purpose our Trustee deems appropriate, including the minimization of any taxes in respect of the trust or any beneficiary of such trust, and may do so with or without providing notice to any beneficiary.*

Jimmie Joe's practice specializes in assisting clients with their estate and business planning needs by helping clients understand the opportunities available through planning to attain specified goals and objectives.

1. W. Edward Dean, "Multi-Generational Trusts: Planning, Drafting, and Implementing Multi-Generational Tax-Exempt Trusts," *WealthCounsel, LLC* (2005) II-2.

2. Rachel Emma Silverman, "Building Your Own Dynasty," *The Wall Street Journal*, September 14, 2004: D2.

Three Types of Generation-Skipping Transfers

TYPE	DESCRIPTION	GST TAX PAID BY
Taxable distribution	Trust makes payment to skip-person	Trust or skip-person
Taxable termination	All interest in trust passes to skip-person	Trust
Direct skip	Assets pass to skip-person: • If related, two or more generations below donor • If unrelated, 37.5 years younger than donor	Donor

Strategies to Reduce Generation-Skipping Taxes

STRATEGY USED	EFFECT
Gift-splitting	Value of gift is split with consenting spouse.
Annual exclusion	In 2008, donor can give $12,000 ($13,000 in 2009) annually to each individual without GST tax consequences. Gift-splitting allows a married couple to give $24,000 ($26,000 in 2009) per donee without GST tax consequences. Trusts must meet special rules.
GSTT exemption	In 2008, allows taxpayer to gift $2 million ($3.5 million in 2009) during lifetime without GST tax consequences.
Qualified transfers	Allows taxpayer to directly pay educational institutions and providers of medical care on behalf of others without GST tax consequences.
Reverse QTIP election	Postmortem planning in which deceased spouse is treated as transferor of QTIP trust, so GST exemption can be allocated to the trust.

CHAPTER 21

Planning for Estates Worth Less Than the Generation-Skipping Tax Exemption

W. EDWARD DEAN (San Francisco, California)

The Generation-Skipping Tax (GST) exemption makes the Generation-Skipping Transfer Tax (GSTT) irrelevant to unmarried clients with a net worth of less than the exemption amount. These clients can transfer all their wealth to grandchildren and other skip beneficiaries, including multi-generational bypass trusts, with the assurance that all their transfers will be exempt from the GSTT. No matter how large a multi-generational trust grows over many generations after the death of a client whose taxable estate is less than the GST exemption, no GSTT liability will result from any direct skips, taxable terminations, or taxable distributions with respect to trust assets.

PLANNING FOR UNMARRIED CLIENTS WITH ESTATE LESS THAN THE GST EXEMPTION

Assuming a $3.5 million GST exemption, an unmarried client can establish a testamentary, multi-generational bypass trust for his or her descendants.

EXAMPLE: Grandmother's living trust leaves Daughter $3.5 million in an asset-protected, beneficiary-controlled bypass trust. Upon Daughter's death, the trust passes to Granddaughter under the same terms after it has grown to $14 million in value, then to Great-Granddaughter upon Granddaughter's death when the trust has grown to $56 million.

Result: Although there are two taxable terminations during the trust term, the first one equal to $14 million when Daughter dies, and the second one equal to $56 million when Granddaughter dies, the entire value of the trust will pass free of estate taxes under the bypass trust provisions because everything Grandmother transferred to the trust was covered by her GST exemption (and is automatically allocated to the trust to shelter its assets). Thus, the trust will be fully exempt from the GSTT, regardless of its increasing value.

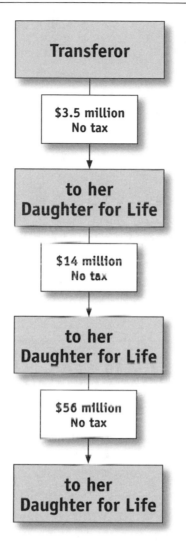

PLANNING FOR COUPLES WITH COMBINED ESTATES LESS THAN $7 MILLION

A husband and wife (or any unmarried couple for whom the estate tax marital deduction is not available) can leave $7 million to their heirs (assuming each member of the couple has $3.5 million) by establishing a bypass trust upon the death of the first spouse. A living trust plan for such a couple would look like this:

EXAMPLE: Grandfather and Grandmother each leave $3.5 million to a bypass trust for the benefit of the survivor of them, then leave Daughter $7 million in an asset-protected, beneficiary-controlled bypass trust. Upon Daughter's death, the trust passes to Granddaughter under the same terms after it has grown to $28 million in value, then to Great-Granddaughter upon Granddaughter's death when the trust has grown to $112 million.

Result: Although there are two taxable terminations during the trust term, the first one equal to $28 million when Daughter dies, and the second one equal to $112 million when Granddaughter dies, the entire value of the trust will pass free of estate taxes under the bypass trust provisions because everything Grandfather and Grandmother transferred to the trust was covered by their GST exemptions (?· ' is automatically allocated to the trust to shelter its assets). Thus, the trust will be fully exempt from GSTT, regardless of its increasing value.

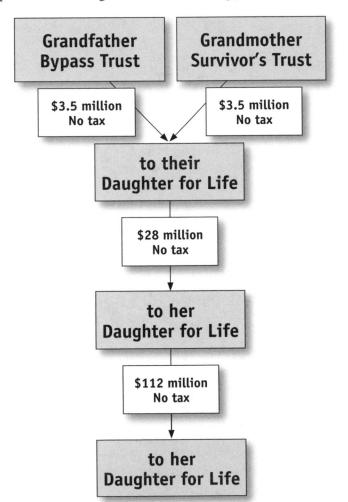

As these two plans illustrate, even the heirs of small estates can benefit from GSTT planning because 1) even if the estate of a client is small, adding it to the estate of an otherwise nontaxable beneficiary can raise that beneficiary's estate above the $3.5 million (as of 2009) taxable threshold, 2) compound growth can turn a nontaxable estate into a taxable one over time, and 3) the flexibility and freedom to pass wealth from generation to generation of beneficiaries free of estate tax and GSTT allows you to plan for several generations of beneficiaries without having to worry about subjecting them to future transfer taxes.

These examples also illustrate that, if the GSTT exemption remains the $3.5 million level it will be in 2009, under current law, GSTT planning will save all but fantastically large estates from being taxed when they pass to second, third, and fourth generations of beneficiaries, no matter how much the estates grow over the generations.

W. Edward Dean is the principal of W. Edward Dean, P.C., located in San Francisco, California. He is a tax attorney who protects wealth through estate, income, and charitable tax planning.

CHAPTER 22

Health Care Durable Powers of Attorney and Durable General Powers of Attorney for Property Management

RICHARD PETERSON (Greenwood Village, Colorado)

Good estate planning not only addresses lifetime and after-death issues but gives you the opportunity to address issues that are raised if you become disabled. It is a fact of life that you will at some point in your life, become physically or mentally unable to give prompt and intelligent consideration to business matters. You simply do not know when that stroke, automobile accident, or other event may render you incapable of taking care of yourself and your affairs. Who is going to handle those matters on your behalf? The answer is: your "agent." That agent is appointed by you in your Durable General Power of Attorney for Property Management and Durable Health Care Power of Attorney.

WHAT IS AN AGENT?

In this context, an agent is a person authorized by another to act for him or her. Both the principal (person giving the power) and the agent must be adults who are both mentally competent when the power of attorney is signed.

WHAT DOES "DURABLE" MEAN?

Under the body of law we inherited from England, known as the common law, a power of attorney was only as good as the principal who created it. If the principal became disabled, so did his power of attorney.

Then along came a proposed uniform law, which most state legislatures have now adopted in one form or another. The Uniform Statutory Power of Attorney Act allowed a power of attorney to contain the words "this power of attorney shall not be affected by disability of the principal." Such language allowed the power of attorney to endure even though the principal became disabled. The power endured and therefore became "durable."

The beauty of the reverse in common law is its simplicity in contrast to the former need to have conservators appointed by a court to manage and account for financial matters of the disabled person and the need to have guardians appointed by a court to make decisions regarding medical care of the disabled person. Often, the disabled person had little choice as to who was appointed. Under the "durable" provision, the principal has the opportunity to select in advance who serves as his or her agent after disability.

WHEN SHOULD YOUR AGENT'S POWER BECOME EFFECTIVE?

You can literally turn on or turn off the power under your Power of Attorney any time you wish. Also, the choice of when powers are to become effective may depend upon the type of power of attorney you want to use.

Health Care Power of Attorney

Most people do not want to delegate decisions regarding their health care until such time as they are not mentally or physically competent to make medical decisions themselves. However, they also realize there can come a time when it is simply not in their own best interests to be making health care decisions.

The point at which a health care power of attorney becomes effective for the agent is in your hands as the principal. It could be as precise as setting a specific date or age. However, more often than not, the principal has the power "spring" into existence when disability occurs. A well-drafted power of attorney defines "disability" in terms with which you as the principal are most comfortable. For example, disability can be defined as a time when two licensed physicians concur you are no longer capable of responsibly conducting your own business affairs or making your own medical decisions. Keeping in mind that an agent must act in the best interests of the principal in all matters, this so-called "springing power" can contain very simple criteria to spring it into effect or more arduous criteria may be used, such as requiring spousal or family member to concur with the opinion of a physician or two physicians. For these reasons, it is best that you make these determinations now while you are not disabled.

The "springing" event need not be as broad as any and all disability. It can be limited to other criteria such as a confirmed diagnosis of a particular disease like Alzheimer's disease, or factors such as marital status, your financial condition, or literally anything else that is important to you in deciding when to turn over your right of self-determination.

General Power of Attorney for Property Management

Just when a Durable General Power of Attorney for Property Management is to become effective merits separate evaluation from the effective date of the Health Care Power of Attorney. For example, perhaps you have reached a stage in life when you would like to be relieved of the daily responsibility of managing your own financial affairs. Doing the banking, paying the bills, keeping track of certificate of deposit maturities, maintaining records for income tax returns, and so forth are simply burdens you simply no longer wish to bear. You can simply turn all of that over to a trusted child or friend immediately while still being able to monitor the checking account, investment account statements, and all other records as you wish from time to time.

A "springing" effective date can also be selected for a general power of attorney for property management. The springing event could be disability (as you define it), the sale of your business, or any other milestone or trigger you select.

WHO SHOULD SERVE AS MY AGENT?

Once again, there is often a distinction between those you choose to make your health care decisions and those you choose to make your financial decisions in the event of your disability.

Parents with adult children sometimes approach the selection process based on what can be called the "committee approach." Not wanting to hurt anyone's feelings, the parents have all the children jointly serve as the health care agents and the property management agents. What is overlooked is the administrative difficulty of having, in some cases, three signing off on an informed consent form for surgery or to make other medical decisions on the spot. Imagine the frustration when all three of them need to sign all the papers at a real estate closing when the title insurance company typically prepares the documents the day before closing. Picture the frustration when the physician-assistant daughter must leave the bedside of her mother to attend a board of director meeting for the family business, which her brother with the MBA says is crucial for the survival of the family business.

All these scenarios are avoided by a more considered approach, the selection of single agents in succession. That is, naming one adult child at a time to serve as agent with an accompanying explanation. The oldest adult child will understand that selecting the youngest child, who lives in closest proximity to his or her parents, will make practical sense. That perception is particularly true when direction is given to the first agent to consult with the other adult children in making decisions.

Sometimes it is best to look outside the family to persons with particular skills in managing financial affairs or medical care. Once again, a simple explanation regarding such appointment will salve most wounded feelings.

Of course, it is a good idea to have successors in place should a designated agent cease or fail to act. The "cease or fail" language in a document covers all circumstances such as the agent's refusal to serve, his resignation, death, or disability.

HOW DO YOUR POWERS OF ATTORNEY AFFECT YOUR LIVING WILL?

Over the last several decades, many people have heard about the so-called "Living Will." Most states have adopted statutes which limit the use of life-sustaining procedures. Usually this limitation applies only in very dire medical circumstances, such as being in a terminal condition, in a coma, and being kept alive on a respirator and feeding tube. If you have signed a Living Will, you should reference it in your

Powers of Attorney. Then you can state that in the event your Living Will applies to the particular circumstances confronting your agent, the terms of the Living Will govern if it is in conflict with your Power of Attorney.

DO I ALSO WANT AN AFFIDAVIT OF POWER OF ATTORNEY?

A well-drafted Power of Attorney may contain up to 25 pages because it must contain authority to handle all the things you routinely do for yourself. You give little thought to the number of times you are asked to give authorizations to third persons in order to conduct your affairs. The simple act of signing on your behalf involves banks, insurance companies, car dealers, repair estimates, credit companies, taxing authorities, and so on. Because your disability does not allow your Agent to add things to your Power of Attorney after the fact, your "suitcase" of powers must be packed in advance.

The question then becomes whether your Agent needs to provide the entire document every time a transaction is needed. The answer for most transactions is "No," if an Affidavit of Power of Attorney is available to your Agent. The Affidavit contains language which includes the following points:

- Any person may rely upon the Affidavit of Power of Attorney as evidence that the Power of Attorney is currently in full force and effect and that such third person is relieved of any obligation to verify that any transaction entered into by the Agent is consistent with the terms and conditions of the Power of Attorney

- If the third person deems it absolutely necessary, copies of the signature page and specific power allowing the transaction will be provided.

- The signers of the Affidavit are currently the acting Agent of the Power of Attorney and that the foregoing statements and any attached portions of the Power of Attorney are true and correct under penalty of perjury.

Such an Affidavit including a notary verification should take only one page. It will save trees, data storage, and the size of a transaction file.

CONCLUSION

Durable Health Care Powers of Attorney and Durable General Powers of Attorney for Property Management are powerful tools for dealing with your own disability. Your thoughtful approach to each of their components will serve you well in the event of your disability.

Richard G. Peterson has provided estate planning services for 40 years, during which time his abilities were rated by judges and his peers as "A" (very high to pre-eminent) and "V" (very high ethical standards).

CHAPTER 23

Advance Health Care Directives

PETER S. MYERS (San Francisco, California)

Some states, such as California, have combined the various legal documents concerning medical or health care into a single document known as an "Advance Health Care Directive" (also known as an AHCD). The purpose of an AHCD is to make it easier and more practical for you to state your medical care wishes in a legally binding format.

FOR WHOM IS AN ADVANCE HEALTH CARE DIRECTIVE APPROPRIATE?

AHCDs are appropriate for people who are residents of those states which recognize them, or for people who travel frequently to those states. For example, if you suffer an injury or accident in California, you will likely be treated at a California-based medical facility, at least on an emergency basis. In that instance, you would want the hospital to have access to a form the medical staff would find familiar.

Anyone who is an adult may sign an AHCD. The age of majority varies from state to state, but is usually 18. For minor children or others under the age of majority, the child's legal guardian would have the right to determine medical treatment. If that legal guardian has also been injured or has died, their wishes for the child would likely be honored by the medical staff and, if a dispute arises, the courts.

WHAT MATTERS DOES THE AHCD ADDRESS?

An AHCD combines four of your health care documents into one document: 1) your nomination of a health care agent, 2) your nomination of a conservator, 3) your wishes with regard to the continuation of medical treatment in the event you are in a persistent vegetative state (PVS) with no likelihood of recovery, and 4) your wishes regarding organ donation.

Why Would I Want To Set Forth All Of These Matters in an AHCD?

The consequences of failing to have health care documents in place can be expensive and even disastrous. In 2004, the life of Terry Schiavo of Florida took the national stage. Schiavo, who had suffered a severe brain injury, was receiving artificial nutrition and hydration for more than ten years while her relatives battled about whether to withdraw such treatment. Ultimately, the courts decided that her husband's desire to withdraw her artificial feeding tubes should be honored, and shortly after those treatments were withdrawn, Ms. Schiavo died.

The Schiavo matter could have been avoided completely had Ms. Schiavo signed an AHCD nominating her agent (e.g., her husband or her parents) to make decisions for her, or stating whether or not she wanted to be kept alive with artificial nutrition or hydration if doctors determined she was unable to recover from her illness or injury.

Lawyers throughout the country could discuss similar matters or situations they've encountered where their clients were forced to go to court to decide the fate of a loved one. Medical staff is very reticent about making life and death decisions that relatives with different opinions can second guess and force into the courts.

Moreover, if you are injured or gravely ill, wouldn't you want your medical caregivers to know exactly from whom they needed to obtain permission in order to treat you? Similarly, you want those agents to have some idea of what your wishes are in the event there is an important medical decision to be made (for example, whether to undertake the risk of surgery to alleviate a condition where the risks and benefits can be explained to your agent and he or she can determine what you would want under the circumstances).

WHAT ARE MY OPTIONS FOR NOMINATING A CONSERVATOR IN THE AHCD?

In most instances, you will want your personal conservator (also called a guardian in some states) to be the same person as your health care agent. Occasionally, your health care agent will not be the appropriate choice. Perhaps he or she lives far away, or he or she has some medical knowledge, but no knowledge of your desires about your personal living situation. In those instances, the nomination of the conservator over your person might be someone more familiar with the local facilities and options for local long-term treatment and care, or perhaps someone more intimately familiar with your personal care needs, as opposed to merely your medical treatment desires.

Are There Different Kinds of Conservators?

Yes. In many states, there is a distinction between the conservator over your person and the conservator over your estate. The conservator over your person makes decisions about your personal care; while the conservator over your estate makes decisions regarding your property and financial affairs. In some cases, these may well be two different people.

Suppose, for example, that your sister is very loving and caring, and you respect her judgment when it comes to your day-to-day living wishes. She may know all about the local facilities for assisted living, or perhaps she has a medical background. But you may have concerns about her ability to manage your portfolio of stocks and your real estate. Suppose further that you have another sister who has an MBA and who manages assets and properties of her own. She may not be as familiar with your personal care wishes as your loving sister, but she is good with money. In that instance, you may wish to nominate your loving, caring, familiar sister as the conservator over your person and your sharp, frugal, money-mogul sister as the conservator over your estate.

What if There Is No One in My Family Who Fits These Descriptions?

Sometimes there is no one among your family or loved ones who is an appropriate choice for conservator. In that instance, you might check with a "private professional fiduciary" — someone who provides these services for a living. If you are alive and well, you are in a position to interview possible nominees and determine whether he or she might be an appropriate person to serve in this role on your behalf.

WHAT ARE MY OPTIONS FOR ANATOMICAL GIVING?

Most states permit you to specify whether you wish to make anatomical gifts and, if so, for what purpose(s) you would like those gifts to be used. You can, for example, limit your gifting to organs to be used specifically for transplant. Other options are for therapy (e.g., tissues for therapeutic uses), research (e.g., to investigate possible cures for your condition), or education (e.g., to train medical students about the human body).

Peter S. Myers, The Myers Law Firm, P.C. Estate, Tax, and Business Succession Planning

Techniques to Use for Incapacity Planning

	DURABLE POWER OF ATTORNEY	HEALTH CARE DURABLE POWER OF ATTORNEY OR ADVANCE HEALTH CARE DIRECTIVE	LIVING WILL	REVOCABLE TRUST
When is it effective?	• Immediately or • Springing – Continues after incompetency – Ends at death	• Immediately or • Springing – Continues after incompetency – Ends at death	• Used only for a terminal condition • Only effective after incompetency	• Immediately if funded or • After incompetency if it is a standby trust – Can continue after death
Can it be used for estate planning after incompetency?	Yes, if attorney is given broad powers.	No.	No.	Yes, if a successor trustee is provided in the event of incapacity.
Is it useful for health care decisions?	No.	Yes, it can authorize health care decisions.	Yes, but only for terminal conditions.	No, the trustee makes decisions on property only.
What potential drawbacks exist?	• Third parties are not required to accept it. • Attorney-in-fact is not required to act.	• Third parties are not required to accept it. • Attorney-in-fact is not required to act.	Requires a terminal condition.	Attorney fees and title transfer costs will be incurred.

CHAPTER 24

Long-Term Care and Disability Insurance

PETER J. PARENTI (San Antonio, Texas)

What is the difference between long-term care insurance and disability insurance and what are their purposes?

Long-term care insurance is insurance that will cover the cost of long-term care from a disability due to age, illness, or injury. Long-term care can include care at home, or care in a skilled care facility such as a nursing home or convalescent care facility. Long-term care insurance will pay for room, board, and skilled care by doctors, nurses, and other skilled health care persons. Long-term care insurance policies, premiums, and coverage can be designed with any number of variables that can include:

1. A waiting period of various lengths of time before benefits will begin;

2. A variable coverage period from any number of years to life; and

3. A variable monthly dollar maximum amount of benefits to be paid.

Just like any other kind of insurance, long-term care insurance can only be purchased when the benefits are not needed and the proposed insured is healthy. However, most people do not usually consider acquiring such coverage until they are at least in their fifties. When estate planning for disability, you and your estate planning attorney should work closely with a long-term care insurance advisor who can design coverage plans.

Disability insurance coverage is intended to be income replacement insurance. This kind of insurance is usually acquired during your working years prior to age 65 and will usually provide benefits of up to 60% of your current income if you become disabled due to illness or injury. Similar to a long-term care insurance policy, premiums and coverage under a disability policy can be designed with any number of variables that can include:

1. A waiting period of various lengths of time before benefits will begin;

2. A variable coverage period from any number of years up to age 65; and

3. A variable monthly dollar maximum amount of benefits to be paid, usually up to 60% of your current income.

Another kind of disability insurance that can be acquired is known as business or professional overhead expense insurance. This type of insurance will cover the normal overhead expenses of a business or professional practice should a business owner or professional become disabled. It will help to keep the business or professional practice continuing during the period of disability of the business owner or professional person by paying the salaries of employees, the rent or mortgage for the business building or office, and the utilities and other expenses that would normally be paid for by the revenue that would have been generated by the business owner or professional had he or she not become disabled.

When estate planning for disability for a business owner or a professional, you and your estate planner should not only bring up the discussion of disability insurance and business or professional overhead expense coverage, but you should also work closely with a disability insurance advisor who can design a plan for them.

Peter J. Parenti is a wealth strategies, estate planning, and tax attorney in San Antonio, Texas. In addition to advanced wealth strategies planning, estate planning, and probate and tax law, his practice specializes in real estate transactions, business entity planning, business buy-outs and sell-outs, charitable estate planning, living trusts, family limited partnership creation, and design and asset protection estate planning.

CHAPTER 25

Special Needs Trusts

DIEDRE DENNIS WACHBRIT (Westlake Village, California)

When a loved one has a disability, providing for that person can become the central goal of estate planning. The tool estate planners use is the Special Needs Trust, or "SNT." The purpose of an SNT is to ensure the loved one receives needed public benefits (such as Supplemental Security Income and Medicaid) while also enjoying the little extras that provide for a good quality of life.

Two sources of funds for the SNT require two different sorts of trusts. One, called a "Third Party" SNT, is funded as part of an estate plan. By that, we mean the source of funds going into the SNT is from a friend or family member. The second type is called a "First Party" SNT, where the source of funds going into the SNT is from the disabled person himself or herself. This SNT has many complicated requirements that do not apply to the "Third Party" SNT. Nevertheless, it can be useful to preserve the inheritance of a beneficiary for whom a Third Party SNT was not created, or to preserve the proceeds of a judgment or settlement. There are two types of First Party SNTs. One is set up by a parent, grandparent or the court and can be drafted to allow the beneficiary to choose his or her trustee. Another, called a Pooled Trust is already set up and the beneficiary simply joins the existing trust with his or her own sub-account pooled together for investment purposes with other sub-accounts. However, because this is a book about estate planning, we will focus on the first type, the Third Party SNT funded as part of an estate plan.

Estate planning SNTs have few rules. They must contain very particular standards about how distributions for the benefit of the beneficiary are to be made but otherwise are flexible tools. In practice, the way an SNT works is the beneficiary (or his or her guardian or conservator) asks the Trustee to make a distribution. The Trustee considers whether he or she is permitted to make the distribution and whether making the distribution is in the best interests of the beneficiary. If all is well, the Trustee makes the distribution by paying for the good or service directly from the trust account to the vendor. The money never passes through the beneficiary's hands. This is important because any money the beneficiary receives may reduce his or her Supplemental Security Income or may even cause a total loss of Medicaid benefits.

When creating an SNT, a grantor (the person setting it up) should consider a variety of tools. While an SNT can be a very short, very simple document, the best working SNTs often have more detailed provisions in them to ensure the beneficiary's well-being. Some provisions to consider include the following.

TRUSTEE

The SNT must have a Trustee. This person will have tremendous power and responsibility. In addition to deciding which distributions will be made and which will not be made, the SNT Trustee must invest the funds prudently so they last for the lifetime of the beneficiary. While it is tempting to name family and friends as Trustee, consider the fact that the beneficiary may outlive them. Consider also whether those potential Trustees have the time and inclination to keep thorough records, invest the trust assets wisely, file tax returns, and ensure their distributions comply with government benefits laws. Being a Trustee is hard work!

Many corporations, including banks and brokerage houses, have trust departments that will manage SNTs as Trustee. Ask your attorney which corporations in your area have the best reputation for handling SNTs. Not all trust departments handle SNTs, and of those that do, there is a wide variety in the way they handle SNTs. Do they assign a single trust officer to the account? Will that person ever meet the beneficiary? Do they hire Care Managers or Advocates to ensure the best possible care? What is their investing philosophy and track record?

Corporations charge a percentage of the trust assets each year as their fee. Individual Trustees either charge a percentage or are compensated on an hourly basis for the work they do.

ADVISORY COMMITTEE

Once you have chosen a Trustee, consider who else might want to be involved in ensuring your beneficiary has a good quality of life. Those people can be named to an Advisory Committee to advise the Trustee. The Advisory Committee is a formal body that can arrange itself in any convenient manner. Some meet by phone. Some meet in person. Some are composed of just two or three people. Others have twelve members. Committees of between three and twelve people seem to work best.

ADVOCATE OR CARE MANAGER

If your Trustee is a corporation or a person who cannot personally ensure the beneficiary is receiving the best possible care, it may make sense to authorize or even require the Trustee to hire an Advocate or Care Manager. This person's job is to visit the beneficiary and make recommendations about living arrangements and distributions. Advocates and Care Managers usually charge for their time by the hour.

TRUST PROTECTOR OR ADVISOR

Because benefits laws are constantly changing, it is possible your trust could become invalid in time, which would cause your beneficiary to lose benefits. You can nominate a person or firm to make administrative changes to your trust to enable it to keep pace with legal changes. If you don't nominate anyone, there is always the opportunity to go to court to ask the court to change the trust but that may be expensive and uncertain. There is no guarantee the court will say "yes."

Many families name their attorney or CPA as the Trust Protector but you can choose anyone who is legally savvy enough to hire an experienced attorney and follow his or her advice.

MEMORANDUM OF INTENT

While your trust can contain many of your wishes for how your money is spent, it is best limited to those things that will not change. For example, if your beneficiary loves to fly in airplanes, perhaps your trust will recommend (it cannot require without breaking the SNT rules) that the Trustee purchase a couple of round-trip plane tickets for the beneficiary each year. If, however, your beneficiary's current passion is electricity and how it works, it may be best to leave that out of the trust as it might change. For all those things that are important to your beneficiary but may change, the Memorandum of Intent fills the gap. It is a place to list your beneficiary's doctors and therapists, to write about your beneficiary's preferences, to decode your beneficiary's non-verbal communications, or just to make your caring voice heard throughout your beneficiary's lifetime.

The Memorandum of Intent should be referenced in the trust but is not a part of the Trust. This is because you might accidentally say something that could invalidate the Trust if the Memorandum of Intent were actually incorporated into the Trust. Think of the Memorandum of Intent as a letter to your Trustee explaining how things should really work.

YOUR ATTORNEY

Choosing an attorney to draft an SNT is not always an easy task. Drafting an SNT is highly specialized and you want someone who is experienced in this area. Be sure the attorney you are working with devotes a substantial portion of his or her practice to special needs planning. Choose someone whom you can trust because an SNT lasts for the lifetime of your beneficiary and the attorney you choose is a crucial member of the SNT team.

Special needs planning can seem daunting. With the right attorney, however, it is an exploratory process leading to great peace of mind. It can also lead to new discoveries. You might discover you want more people to surround your beneficiary and set about to make new friends. You might discover your beneficiary is surrounded by caring family and now the financial piece is in place to ensure they can follow your wishes. No matter what, you will find that having a Special Needs Trust in place provides you with a sense of peace because you will know your beneficiary will be well taken care of.

---

*Diedre Dennis Wachbrit, a board-certified specialist in estate planning, trust, and probate law, has been quoted in the **Wall Street Journal, Time Magazine, and The New York Times.***

ESTATE TAX
PRINCIPLES

CHAPTER 26

What Is Included in Your Estate?

KRISTINE KYLLANDER (San Diego, California)

Comprehensive estate planning includes an analysis of the estate tax liability you may be facing. Whether one of your personal estate planning goals is to minimize estate taxes or not, it is important to understand what taxes may become due as a result of your death so you can define how those taxes will be paid and who will bear the burden of payment. The first step towards determining if you have an estate tax issue is defining what property and assets the IRS will include in your gross estate. This chapter will answer the question: What assets are included in your estate for federal estate tax purposes?[1]

There are generally two broad categories of assets that will be included in your gross estate: 1) property owned by you at the time of your death; and 2) certain property transfers made during your life. The statutory authority for these categories can be found in Internal Revenue Code (IRC) Sections 2033-2044. If an interest in property is not described in IRC Sections 2033-2044, then it will not be included in your gross estate.

PROPERTY OWNED AT DEATH

The general rule under IRC Section 2033 is that your gross estate includes all property in which you have an interest at death. This language is meant to capture *any* interest you have in any property at your death, even if you do not own title or have complete rights to the property.

EXAMPLE: JOINT INTERESTS

a) Assume you are married and you and your spouse own an asset as joint tenants with right of survivorship. If you predecease your spouse, at your death one-half of the value of the asset will be included in your gross estate under IRC Section 2040(b). This principle applies regardless of how the asset was acquired or who paid for the asset in the first place. This is also how any vested community property assets will be treated.

b) Assume instead that you own the asset with your brother (or anyone other than your spouse) as joint tenants with right of survivorship. If you predecease your brother, the full value of the asset will be included in your gross estate subject to two exceptions: 1) if you and your brother received the asset by gift or bequest, or 2) your brother furnished a portion of the funds used to acquire the property in the first place.

EXAMPLE: LIFE INSURANCE & ANNUITIES

a) Assume you own a life insurance policy payable at your death. The proceeds will generally be included in your gross estate. However, if you do not retain any incidents of ownership in the policy *and* the policy proceeds are not payable to your estate, then the proceeds will not be included in your gross estate.

b) If you own a straight life annuity (an annuity which terminates on your death), the annuity will not be included in your gross estate.

c) If you own an annuity with a term certain or a joint life/survivor annuity, the asset may have value after your death. If so, that value will be included in your gross estate to the extent you contributed to the value remaining to be distributed.

EXAMPLE: INCOME BENEFICIARY OF TRUST

a) Assume you are the beneficiary of an irrevocable trust (not established by you) which entitles you to income from the trust for life and leaves you no power of appointment at your death. The underlying assets of this irrevocable trust would typically not be included in your estate at death.

b) Exception: Let's now assume the irrevocable trust is actually a QTIP trust and you became the income beneficiary of the trust upon your spouse's death. If you make an election to take a marital deduction with respect to this trust, then the underlying assets of this trust are included in your gross estate. The trust is designed to allow a couple's assets to avoid estate taxes at the death of the first spouse but not after the death of both.

PROPERTY TRANSFERRED DURING LIFE

Gifts Made Within Three Years. Under current law, certain gifts of life insurance or transfers in trust made within three years of your death may be pulled back into your estate at death. In addition, the amount of any gift tax payable on *any* gift made within three years of your death will also be included in your gross estate.

> **EXAMPLE:** Today you make an outright gift to your daughter and pay $200,000 in gift taxes on that gift. If you die within three years, your gross estate will include the value of the taxes paid ($200,000).

Gifts Made With Continued Possession/Enjoyment. If you transfer property during your lifetime but you (or your legal dependents) retain the right to income from that asset during your lifetime, the asset will likely be included in your gross estate.

Gifts Made With Retained Power to Change the Transfer. If you transfer property but retain the right to change the terms of the gift (e.g., to substitute beneficiaries or to revoke the gift in full), it is likely that the value of the property gifted will be included in your gross estate at your death.

VALUATION OF INCLUDED ASSETS

In determining the value of assets included in your estate, the fair market value of the assets as determined on the date of your death is typically used. In some cases, your personal representative may make an election to value the property six months after the date of your death.

By focusing on three core components of Incapacity Planning, Wealth Transfer Planning, and Beneficiary Protection, we deliver high-quality drafting with the superior customer service expected from a boutique firm.

1. Not all States that impose an estate tax at death follow the federal definition of the Gross Estate under IRC Section 2031. A state by state analysis of what is included in a gross estate is beyond the scope of this chapter.

CHAPTER 27

Estate Tax Deductions

STEVEN B. SPEWAK (St. Louis, Missouri)

When you die, it is likely that those charged with administering your final affairs will have responsibility for paying, from your estate or revocable trust, a variety of costs, expenses, and other financial obligations on your behalf. These may include your funeral expenses, debts you owe at your death, and expenses required to administer your estate. The good news is that these expenses are deductible on your estate tax return, which in turn, can produce estate tax savings for your family. The even better news is that if you do not owe an estate tax at your death, many of these expenses can instead be taken as income tax deductions, thereby translating into income tax savings for your family. However, it is important that those who administer your estate understand these rules in order to obtain the tax savings available.

There are four types of expenses that qualify as estate tax deductions. They are:

Funeral Expenses. Examples include funeral and cemetery charges and payments to officiating clergy.

Administration Expenses. Costs incurred to administer your final affairs are also deductible for estate tax purposes. These deductible expenses include accounting fees to prepare your final income tax return, income tax returns for your estate or trust, and your estate tax return, if necessary. They also include attorney fees, executor fees, trustee fees, and probate costs necessary to administer your property and affairs. Finally, administration expenses include other miscellaneous expenses, such as appraisal fees, and expenditures to maintain property in good condition prior to distribution to beneficiaries.

Claims. Claims are amounts you owe at your death that your estate is legally obligated to pay. They include items such as final utility bills for the month in which you die, credit card balances owed at your death, and any other financial obligations you have incurred but which are still unpaid at your death. They also include any income taxes due for income you earned in the year of your death.

Mortgages. Any indebtedness secured by a mortgage on real estate you own at your death also qualifies for an estate tax deduction. For example, if you die with a

$100,000 mortgage on your home and an additional home equity loan of $25,000, a deduction of $125,000 can be taken on your estate tax return.

In addition to deducting the foregoing expenses, any casualty losses, such as theft losses or losses resulting from a fire or flood occurring during the administration of your estate not otherwise compensated by insurance are deductible for estate tax purposes.

The biggest impediment in making use of estate tax deductions is that for the majority of people who die, no estate tax is due regardless of whether estate tax deductions are claimed. This occurs for two reasons. First, if you are married when you die and leave your estate to a surviving spouse, there is no estate tax due regardless of the size of your estate because of the unlimited marital deduction. Second, if the value of your estate is less than the amount of the estate tax exemption in the year of your death, no estate tax will be due. For example, for persons dying in 2009, the amount of the estate tax exemption is $3.5 million. Therefore, if you die that year with an estate less than that amount, there is no estate tax.

The fact that no estate tax is due does not mean your family cannot benefit from estate tax deductions, because the portion of your estate tax deductions that qualify as administration expenses, if not deducted on an estate tax return, may be deducted on the income tax return for your estate or revocable trust during the administration of your estate or revocable trust. In addition, medical expenses incurred by you prior to your death paid within one year of your death may be deducted on your personal income tax return for the year in which you incurred those expenses if they are not deducted on your estate tax return.

The examples that follow will help clarify how your family can best benefit from your available estate tax deductions.

SCENARIO 1: At the time of your death, you are not married, and your estate has a value of $4.5 million. The estate tax exemption at that time is $3.5 million and the estate tax rate is 45%. Your estate is entitled to the following estate tax deductions:

Funeral bill	$ 5,000
Credit card balances	2,000
Other debts	5,000
Appraisal fees	2,000
Executor and Trustee fees	10,000
Accounting fees for income and estate tax return preparation	10,000
Attorney fees	10,000
TOTAL DEDUCTIONS	**$44,000**

Since the estate tax rate in this example is 45%, taking $44,000 in deductions on your estate tax return saves your family $19,800 in estate taxes ($44,000 x 45%).

SCENARIO 2: The facts are the same as in Scenario 1 except that you are married at the time of your death. If your estate plan took advantage of the unlimited marital deduction, there is no estate tax due even though the gross value of your estate exceeds the exemption amount. Therefore, no tax benefit would result by claiming your estate tax deductions on an estate tax return. However, those estate tax deductions that qualify as administration expenses can be deducted on your estate's income tax return. In our example, all expenses other than the funeral bill, credit card balances, and other debts qualify as administration expenses. These administration expenses total $32,000. If your estate is in a 33% income tax bracket and these are taken as deductions on the estate's income tax return, your family will save $10,560 in income taxes ($32,000 x 33%).

SCENARIO 3: At the time of your death, your estate has a value of $1 million, and the estate tax exemption is $3.5 million. Whether or not you are married, there will be no estate tax due because the exemption is greater than the value of your estate. As in our prior example, there would be no tax benefit by claiming your estate tax deductions to reduce your estate tax. However, as in Scenario 2, those estate tax deductions qualifying as administration expenses can be deducted on your estate's income tax return. If those expenses and the tax rate are the same as in the previous scenario, the same $10,560 in income taxes is saved for your family.

SCENARIO 4: There is no estate tax due upon your death. However, $50,000 in medical expenses are incurred in the year of your death in connection with your final illness. If those medical expenses are paid within one year of your death and are not claimed as estate tax deductions, then you are entitled to claim the medical expenses as an itemized deduction on your personal income tax return for the year of your death.

What you should do: Carefully choose the parties who will act as executors of your will and/or trustees of your revocable trust to be sure that they have the experience and know how to take advantage of the tax saving opportunities available after your death. Include language in your estate planning documents to grant them the flexibility they need to take advantage of those opportunities. Such language would be similar to:

> *"My Trustee's authority to make tax elections shall include, but shall not be limited to, the right to elect whether to take administration expenses as estate tax deductions or income tax deductions."*

Steven B. Spewak works with his clients to preserve wealth and protect assets while achieving personal and family objectives, minimizing taxes, and providing comfort and peace of mind.

CHAPTER 28

Marital Deduction

JOSEPH O'BRIEN (Brighton, Michigan)

Understanding the marital deduction is very important to successfully prepare your estate plan. The marital deduction can help you save or even eliminate estate taxes if implemented properly. It is very important that you understand how the marital deduction operates so you can plan accordingly and avoid any negative consequences by utilizing the deduction improperly.

WHAT IS THE MARITAL DEDUCTION?

In the latest revision of the Internal Revenue Code, you have been provided with one of the most powerful federal tax deductions for estate planning purposes, known as the marital deduction. The marital deduction allows an unlimited amount of lifetime and testamentary tax-free transfers from one spouse to another. Simplified, the marital deduction is a type of tax deduction which allows you to give your assets to your spouse while effectively reducing or eliminating taxes.

WHO QUALIFIES FOR THE MARITAL DEDUCTION AND WHAT ARE THE REQUIREMENTS?

The marital deduction encompasses the entire value of the property given to your spouse to the extent that property is includable in your gross estate. It does not matter whether the property passes by will, intestacy, beneficiary designation, titling, or any other manner. What is required, however, is the following:

1. The decedent must be survived by a spouse;

2. The property must pass from the decedent to the surviving spouse;

3. The property is included in the decedent's gross estate;

4. The property is transferred outright and not as a life estate or other terminable interest (unless specific requirements are met and the property is passed by way of utilizing a qualified terminable interest property (QTIP) election).

Of the four requirements, the first requires that the parties be married. Also it is imperative that some form of a "simultaneous death" clause be placed in your will and other estate planning documents to protect the marital deduction if both you and your spouse die and the survivor cannot be determined. If there is no presumption of survivorship in the will or your other estate planning documents, many states follow the Uniform Simultaneous Death Act which presumes that each spouse survived the other, reducing the benefit of the marital deduction for you or your spouse.

The QTIP election provides an exception to the requirement that the property transferred does not include property of a life estate or terminable interest. The election allows property to qualify for the marital deduction that would otherwise not qualify, as long as additional requirements are met including the following:

1. The property would qualify for the marital deduction for all other reasons other than it being considered a terminable interest; and

2. The election is made on the federal estate tax return to qualify the property for the marital deduction.

THE MARITAL DEDUCTION AND GIFT TAXES

The marital deduction can apply to either estate taxes or gift taxes. Most of what we discussed above is applicable to estate taxes. However, the marital deduction is also available for the full value of any property transferred to your spouse as a gift. Typically, the gift is given outright to your spouse; conversely, it may be held in trust subject to two further requirements:

1. If the gift is held in trust, your spouse must have the absolute right to income for life; and

2. Your spouse must have a general power of appointment over such property.

Once again, the QTIP election allows you to remove the general power of appointment requirement and still qualify for the marital deduction by requiring an irrevocable election claimed when filing a gift tax return.

HOW THE MARITAL DEDUCTION WORKS

Marital Deduction on First to Die Spouse

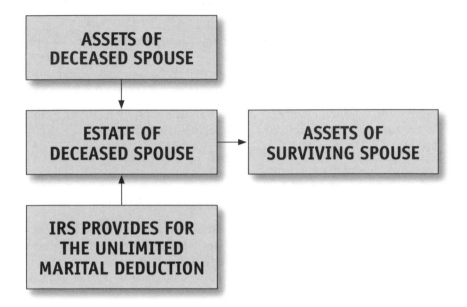

Marital Deduction on Surviving Spouse's Death

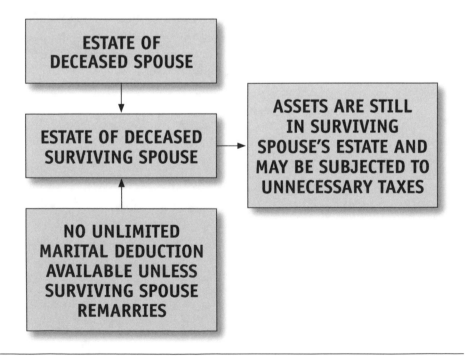

WHAT OTHER CREDITS AND DEDUCTIONS SHOULD I KNOW ABOUT TO PLAN PROPERLY?

For many, the unlimited marital deduction may be the simplest solution to estate tax problems. However, the marital deduction may not solve all of your estate tax problems. To properly plan and utilize the marital deduction, it is imperative that you also understand the unified credit.

The unified credit allows an individual to dispose of assets without tax liability up to a specified amount — currently $2 million. By utilizing the unified credit and the marital deduction, assets will be preserved from estate taxation upon the death of the first spouse, and with proper planning will preserve some or all of the assets from taxation in the second estate.

The unified credit allows you to pass a certain amount of assets estate tax-free to your heirs. Congress has provided the following unified credit exemption amounts per individual per year.

YEAR	EXCLUSION AMOUNT	MAX AND TOP TAX RATE	YEAR	EXCLUSION AMOUNT	MAX AND TOP TAX RATE
2002	1,000,000	50%	2007	2,000,000	45%
2003	1,000,000	49%	2008	2,000,000	45%
2004	1,500,000	48%	2009	3,500,000	45%
2005	1,500,000	47%	2010	Unlimited	0%
2006	2,000,000	46%	2011	1,000,000	55%

COMMON PLANNING EXAMPLES:

TOTAL ESTATE VALUE FOR HUSBAND AND WIFE IS BELOW THE UNIFIED CREDIT AMOUNT: If your and your spouse's combined estimated estate value is below the unified credit exemption amount, currently $2 million, the marital deduction is enough to prevent any estate taxes at the federal level. For example, if your estate is worth $1 million and your spouse's estate is worth $500,000, the total estate value after the assets are transferred after the first death is $1.5 million. This amount is under the unified credit amount and is thus exempt from federal estate taxes.

TOTAL ESTATE VALUE FOR HUSBAND AND WIFE IS ABOVE THE UNIFIED CREDIT AMOUNT: If your and your spouse's combined estimated estate value is above the unified credit exemption amount, currently $2 million, the marital deduction is not enough to prevent all estate taxes and more planning is needed to ensure tax savings are maximized. For example, in 2008, federal estate tax is not owed on a combined $3 million estate when the estate passes from one spouse to another because the marital deduction allows for the transfer. However, upon the death of the surviving spouse, an estate tax of $450,000 (not including any possible state tax) is owed. With proper planning, this $450,000 tax can be saved.

Joseph O'Brien (www.josephdobrien.com) provides estate planning, business, and tax services. His knowledge of estate planning and tax law allows him to solve even the most complex estate planning problems.

Marital Deduction Planning

PROPERTY INTEREST	AMOUNT THAT QUALIFIES FOR MARITAL DEDUCTION
Outright bequest to spouse	Full amount
Joint tenancy WROS with spouse	One-half
Tenancy in common	To the extent of decedent's interest
Community property	Full amount (one-half)
Life insurance death benefit	Full amount if payable as a lump sum (installment option and life income) None if interest only
Life estate	None
QTIP	Full amount
Terminable interest	None
Power-of-appointment trust	Full amount
General power of appointment	Full amount
Special power of appointment	None
Qualified domestic trust (QDOT)	Full amount

CHAPTER 29

Using Credit Shelter and Marital Trusts to Reduce Estate Taxes

JULIE GARBER (Key West, Florida)

If you are married and your combined estate with your spouse exceeds the amount exempt from estate taxes, you will need to incorporate estate tax reduction strategies into your estate plan. The most common technique used by married couples to reduce their estate tax bill and pass more on to their beneficiaries is the use of a Credit Shelter Trust, also referred to as a Bypass or Family Trust, coupled with a Marital Trust, also referred to as a Marital Deduction Trust or QTIP Trust.

The amount exempt from federal estate taxes is $2 million in 2008, $3.5 million in 2009, unlimited in 2010, and unless the law is changed, $1 million in 2011 and thereafter (indexed for inflation).

Aside from the federal estate tax, many states impose their own separate estate tax, so even if your estate is not taxable at the federal level, it may very well be taxable at the state level. Thus, proper estate tax planning is crucial to insure your beneficiaries receive the maximum amount possible. (Because many states that collect their own estate tax have an exemption that is "decoupled" from the federal exemption, this chapter will focus on the federal estate tax and how to minimize it. For those who live in a state with its own estate tax, you will need to consult with an attorney in your state to insure the effective use of both your state and federal exemptions.)

If you do not incorporate the Credit Shelter/Marital Trust strategy into your estate plan, you and your spouse will end up wasting the estate tax exemption of one spouse. Here is why: while spouses can leave any amount to each other at death free from estate taxes (as long as the surviving spouse is a U.S. citizen — the rules are very different for non-citizen spouses), if it all goes outright and free from estate taxes at the first death, there will be no need to use the deceased spouse's exemption. However, later, when the surviving spouse dies, he or she will only have his or her own estate tax exemption left.

However, by using the Credit Shelter/Marital Trust strategy in your estate plan, you and your spouse can leave two times the amount of the estate tax exemption to your heirs before any estate taxes will be imposed. Here is how:

1. **Incorporate Credit Shelter and Marital Trusts into Your Estate Plan.**
This can be done in your Last Will and Testament or Revocable Living Trust. (See illustrated examples below.)

2. **Divide Your Assets.** In non-community property states, you will need to divide your assets so you and your spouse have approximately an equal amount in your individual names (or in the names of your trusts). This is an important step that is often overlooked. If your assets remain jointly titled, then the Credit Shelter and Marital Trusts cannot be funded because the joint assets will pass by right of survivorship instead of under the terms of the deceased spouse's will or trust.

3. **Upon the First Spouse's Death, Fund the Credit Shelter and Marital Trusts.** The amount funded into each trust will depend upon the year of death. For example, if the death occurs in 2009, then the first $3.5 million of the deceased spouse's assets will be placed in the Credit Shelter Trust, and the excess (if any) will be placed in the Marital Trust. The Credit Shelter Trust can provide for the needs of the surviving spouse as well as your children or other beneficiaries, but it must include certain restrictions so that the balance of the trust will not be included in the surviving spouse's estate when he or she later dies. The Marital Trust can only be used for the benefit of the surviving spouse and all the trust income must be distributed to the surviving spouse.

4. **Upon the Surviving Spouse's Death, Use His/Her Estate Tax Exemption.** When the surviving spouse later dies, he or she will still have his or her own estate tax exemption, so his or her assets, valued up to the exemption amount, will pass to available heirs free from estate taxes. Anything over the exemption amount is taxed, as well as anything remaining in the Marital Trust.

5. **Pass Assets Remaining in the Credit Shelter Trust Estate Tax-Free.** Whatever remains in the Credit Shelter Trust when the surviving spouse dies will pass estate tax-free to your heirs.

EXAMPLE (Credit Shelter/Marital Trust Planning): Assume you are married and have two children, your combined estate with your spouse is valued at $8 million, and your estate plan includes two Revocable Living Trusts that incorporate Credit Shelter/Marital Trust planning. Assume your husband dies in 2009 when the federal estate tax exemption is $3.5 million, and then you later die in a year when the federal estate tax exemption is also $3.5 million and the estate tax rate is 45%.

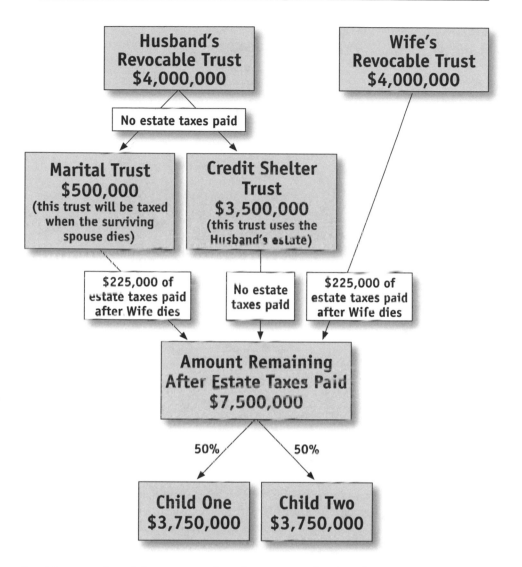

In this example, while your combined estate is valued at $8 million, both your federal exemptions are effectively used so that only $1 million of your estate is subject to estate tax. After paying $450,000 in estate taxes, $7.5 million passes to your children. Compare this with an estate plan without any Credit Shelter/Marital Trust planning.

EXAMPLE (No Credit Shelter/Marital Trust Planning): Assume you are married and have two children. Your combined estate with your spouse is valued at $8 million and all assets are jointly titled. Assume your husband dies in 2009 when the federal estate tax exemption is $3.5 million, and then you later die in a year when the federal estate tax exemption is also $3.5 million and the estate tax rate is 45%.

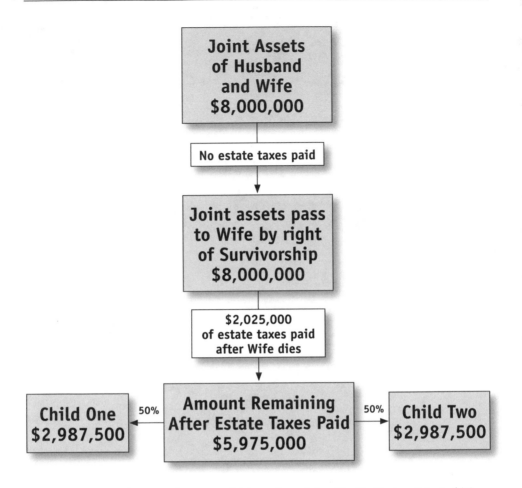

These examples illustrate the powerful benefits of the Credit Shelter/Marital Trust estate tax planning strategy: Without Credit Shelter/Marital Trust planning, your children will pay $2,025,000 in estate taxes before receiving their inheritance. The choice of the difference of $1,525,000 going to your children or to the IRS is yours to make.

What you should do: Consult with a qualified estate planning attorney in your area to learn if your state has its own estate tax and how you can effectively use both your federal, and, if applicable, state estate tax exemptions to leave more to your heirs after you die.

Julie Ann Garber, J.D., The Andersen Firm, A Professional Corporation, located in Key West, Florida, practices in the areas of estate planning, probate, and estate and trust litigation.

CHAPTER 30

A QTIP Trust Can Protect Your Children's Inheritance if You Remarry

TROY WILSON (Salt Lake City, Utah)

If you have children with someone other than your current spouse, you risk disinheriting them unless you plan properly. Consider the following example.

You are in your second marriage and you and your spouse each have adult children from prior marriages. If you die without a will or trust, most states' intestate laws provide for a nominal amount of your estate to first pass to your current spouse (in Utah, it is the first $50,000). After that initial amount is paid, your remaining estate will be split between your current spouse and your children from your prior marriage. Again, this ratio varies from state to state (in Utah, one-half of the remaining assets would pass to your spouse and the other one-half would pass to your children).

If you and your spouse have executed wills which name each other as sole beneficiaries, your children will receive nothing at your death unless your spouse chooses to make a gift to them.

Now suppose following your death, your spouse remarries. If your surviving spouse were then to die without a will, his or her assets transfer under the same rules as above (remember, this now includes the assets you left your spouse at your death). The assets will transfer either to the new spouse and his or her children (not your children) under the state intestate law, or if a new will was executed in favor of the new spouse, entirely to the new spouse. Either way, your children are disinherited from either a substantial portion or all of the inheritance you may have intended for them to receive. This same result occurs if you and your spouse own property in joint tenancy with right of survivorship. Ownership of the property vests entirely in the surviving joint owner, possibly disinheriting your children altogether.

For most people, this paints a picture much different from what they would desire. On the one hand, you may want to preserve your spouse's standard of living by making all of your assets available for his or her lifetime. A transfer of nearly half your assets to your children at your death could have a substantial impact on your spouse's lifestyle. This is especially true if your main asset is the family home. In some circumstances, a forced sale of the home may be ordered. Additionally, your children may be too young or immature to properly manage a significant inheritance upon your untimely death. However, you may ultimately want to leave all of your assets not consumed during your spouse's lifetime to your children upon your spouse's death.

One option is to rely on your spouse to honor your wishes and leave your assets to your children. The reality is that no matter how well-intentioned your spouse may be today with regard to passing your estate on to your children, people change their minds, change behaviors, and circumstances change. In addition, your spouse has his or her own children to consider. Through commingling, remarriage, and other life events, the separate identity of your assets may be lost and your children may be disinherited, either intentionally or unintentionally.

Fortunately, you do not have to choose between your spouse and your children. With proper estate planning, you will be able to provide for your spouse, yet ensure your children receive the inheritance you intend for them to receive.

QTIP TRUST TO THE RESCUE

The solution to this dilemma is making use of a properly drafted Qualified Terminable Interest Property Trust, commonly referred to as a QTIP Trust. This special type of trust is authorized under Internal Revenue Code Sections 2056(b)(7) and 2523(f).

Generally, to qualify for the marital deduction and avoid estate tax at your death, your property must pass to your spouse outright or in a trust where he or she has full access to the principal. A QTIP Trust is an exception to this general rule. A QTIP Trust allows you to separate your property into two portions: one portion is the interest or income the property can generate; the other portion is the property itself, called the corpus or principal. An example is an apartment building (corpus) that generates rental income (income). Another example is a portfolio of stocks and bonds (corpus) generating dividends and interest (income).

By separating your property into two portions, you can direct that each portion benefits a different person or group of people. So long as the QTIP Trust directs that all of the income will benefit your spouse during his or her lifetime, it will qualify for the marital deduction. That means the corpus can be preserved and distributed to the remainder beneficiaries, usually your children, following your spouse's death with no adverse estate tax consequences.

Properly drafted and executed, a QTIP Trust provides you with the following benefits:

1. The trust grants to your surviving spouse, during his or her lifetime, a "terminable interest" in the income portion of your assets. This interest in the income portion terminates at your spouse's death.

2. At your spouse's death, the corpus of the trust property passes to remainder beneficiaries you designate in the trust, typically your children from a prior marriage.

3. The trust "qualifies" for the unlimited marital deduction, rendering the assets in the QTIP trust exempt from estate taxes at your death.

The following flowchart illustrates how the QTIP works.

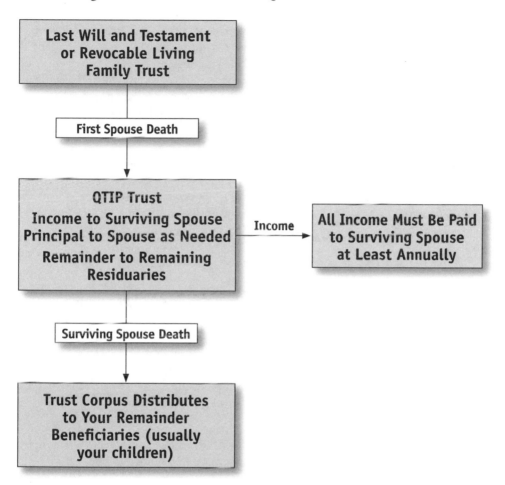

This type of trust is very powerful and commonly used in blended family situations. When either you or your spouse have children from a prior marriage, it is not uncommon for each spouse to have a bias in favor of his or her natural children over his or her step-children. Without a technique such as a QTIP Trust, your natural children may not receive the inheritance you intend.

While blended families are perhaps the most common scenario where a QTIP is put in place, any situation where you wish to protect principal, but allow interest to be accessed by your surviving spouse is a viable use for a QTIP. For example, if your spouse is a spendthrift or has creditor issues, you may want to protect the assets from his or her creditors or from frivolous spending habits. The same holds true if your spouse is an unsophisticated money manager or particularly vulnerable.

SIMPLE, YET TECHNICAL

QTIP Trusts have been used for years, if not decades. This strategy is by no means a cutting-edge strategy, nor overly complicated. The strategy is well known by qualified estate planning attorneys, but the technical requirements are strict. Also, the drafting attorney as well as the grantor (you) putting this strategy in place should have a very thorough understanding of the marital deduction and the potential estate tax liability of the particular estate being planned. The first step is to draft language in your current estate planning documents such as a last will and testament or a revocable living trust that directs a QTIP Trust be created at your death. To do this, your document may contain language similar to the following:

Qualified Terminable Interest Property

I intend that the Marital Trust property shall constitute qualified terminable interest property for federal and state death tax purposes if and to the extent my Trustee or Personal Representative makes the necessary elections. This agreement shall be interpreted to accomplish such intent.

Termination of the Marital Trust at the Death of My Spouse

The Marital Trust shall terminate upon the death of my spouse.

Following your death, your estate plan will likely become irrevocable. Therefore, it is important that the provisions of the QTIP Trust be carefully considered. You will also want to carefully select the personal representative or trustee who will carry out the instructions, and appoint them in your trust. You must specify who the beneficiaries are, both the income beneficiary (remember, this must be your spouse for his or her lifetime) and the remainder beneficiaries. Finally, you should identify what property you would like to transfer into the QTIP Trust, or the formula your personal representative or trustee will follow when transferring property to your QTIP.

While putting in place language to allow for a QTIP election is relatively simple, deciding whether or not to elect QTIP treatment can be quite complicated.

POSTMORTEM QTIP ELECTION, ADMINISTRATION, AND PLANNING

Following your death, there is a limited time period for the personal representative of your estate or trustee of your trust to make an election for property to receive QTIP treatment. This election is made on IRS Form 706, the U.S. Estate and (Generation-Skipping Transfer) Tax Return, which must be filed no later than nine months following your date of death. Whether or not to make a QTIP election, thereby qualifying property for the marital deduction, is a fact-specific determination. The maximum estate tax rate is currently 45%; so depending on the size of your estate, the year of your death, and current law, this decision can have significant tax consequences.

Since an affirmative election must be made, this presents yet another opportunity for your heirs to examine the estate and take appropriate action. Your spouse and children may be at odds about making a QTIP election. Therefore, it is important that your personal representative or trustee know what goals are most important to you and that he or she consult with qualified tax counsel well before the nine month deadline to allow time for counsel to analyze the alternatives and make recommendations.

QTIP WRAPPED UP

What you should take away from this discussion is that if you are in a blended family situation where either you or your spouse has children from a prior marriage or relationship, your planning may not be as simple as the wills your neighbors have. Fortunately, the QTIP Trust is a simple solution which provides a customized estate plan for your unique family's goals and objectives.

Wilson Law Office PC practices in the areas of Estate and Business Planning, Elder Law and Medicaid Planning, and Trust Administration and Probate.

CHAPTER 31

Use of Disclaimers

DAVID HAROWITZ (Tempe, Arizona)

Your wealthy Uncle Louie dies leaving a trust. It says, "Nephew, I leave you my $500,000 diamond." What response might you have? You most likely will grab the diamond and run. Do you know that you can politely decline to accept the diamond?

Believe it or not, in administering the estate of a deceased person, declining to accept the diamond may be the best choice! In estate planning, this refusal to accept the property is called a "disclaimer." By disclaiming you are legally saying, "I know you have left me the diamond, but I do not want to accept it. Treat me as though I died before you, and let the diamond pass to the next person in line."

Disclaimer planning can be used when there is no will or when there is a will or a trust. If there is no will, every state has intestate laws which list the order a person's assets pass upon death. If you are the person who will receive the assets under the law and you disclaim, the assets go to the next listed person. If the person who dies has a will or a trust, that document, if properly drafted, will specify who receives the assets if you disclaim.

Disclaimers may be used in any situation where a person is left an inheritance. This includes being named in pay-upon-death accounts or as the survivor in property titled "with right of survivorship." You may also use a disclaimer when you are named as a beneficiary under a life insurance policy or a retirement asset, such as a 401(k) plan or an IRA. You may disclaim all or only a part of what is left to you.

An effective disclaimer is "qualified" under the Internal Revenue Code and satisfies the requirements of state law. Generally, you must deliver a disclaimer in writing to the donor or personal representative of the estate within nine months of the gift or the decedent's death, respectively, and before you receive benefits from owning the property (e.g., rental or dividend income). You should contact a knowledgeable attorney immediately after the death of an individual to determine if a disclaimer will be helpful, which will prevent you from taking actions that may make it impossible for you to disclaim, and to make sure the disclaimer will be qualified under state and federal law.

Disclaiming may make sense in situations where a husband and wife have provisions in their will or trust that create a Bypass Trust, passing property to the children at the first death and taking advantage of the federal estate tax exemption, and a Marital Trust, passing property to the surviving spouse and taking advantage of the marital deduction. This approach is used primarily to legally avoid or minimize estate taxes for the children upon the second spouse's death. The Bypass Trust is an irrevocable trust that locks in its terms and beneficiaries such that the surviving spouse can not change them. The Marital Trust usually allows the surviving spouse to change its terms and do whatever he or she wants to do with the assets.

EXAMPLE 1. Assume that on the first death a will or trust provides that the property of the spouse who died will go to the Bypass Trust and the surviving spouse's property will go to the Marital Trust. The will or trust also provides that any assets disclaimed by the beneficiaries of the Bypass Trust will go to the Survivor's Trust and any assets disclaimed by the beneficiaries of the Marital Trust will go to the Bypass Trust. Assume further that each spouse has $2 million in assets and that the amount each spouse can pass to their children free of estate tax is $3.5 million. In this example, no disclaimer is necessary as this structure allows the $2 million on the death of the first spouse and $2 million on the death of the second spouse to pass to the children free of estate tax.

EXAMPLE 2. Continuing the above example, if the family did not think the surviving spouse had sufficient assets for his or her lifetime or maintaining the Bypass Trust would be problematic, the beneficiaries of the Bypass Trust might disclaim all or part of their interest.

EXAMPLE 3. Again continuing the above example, if the surviving spouse is concerned that the maximum amount allowed ($3.5 million exemption in 2009) was not passed to the children at the first spouse's death, then the surviving spouse, as Trustee of the Marital Trust, might disclaim some of the property passing to the Marital Trust.

There may be problems associated with disclaiming from a Bypass Trust due to the fiduciary duties owed to the children by the Trustee. In such a situation, a will or trust may be written to provide that both spouses' property will go to the Marital Trust. If the combined estate of both spouses is $2 million and the amount that can pass free of estate tax on the second death is $3.5 million, no disclaimer will be filed. If the combined estate is $5 million and the amount that can pass free of estate tax is $3.5 million, the surviving spouse, as trustee of the Marital Trust, will disclaim $1.5 million of the inheritance from the deceased spouse. The amount may be larger or smaller depending on the expected growth in the value of the assets and the spending needs of the surviving spouse, but the property now goes to the Bypass Trust and estate taxes are avoided when the surviving spouse dies. The same result is accomplished without violating any duties owed to the children by the Trustee of the Bypass Trust. The risk is that more estate tax may be owed if the surviving spouse does not want to give up control of the property.

Disclaimer planning between the Bypass Trust and the Marital Trust allows estate tax planning to occur upon the death of the first spouse when the total estate value and the Congressionally determined estate tax exemption are known. In most cases, this flexibility is lost if the planning documents are not drafted anticipating possible disclaimer planning and an attorney knowledgeable in disclaimer planning is not consulted immediately after the death of the first spouse.

David J. Harowitz, P.C. limits their practice to helping clients plan ownership and distribution of their assets to maximize the clients' goals while minimizing taxes, costs, and risks.

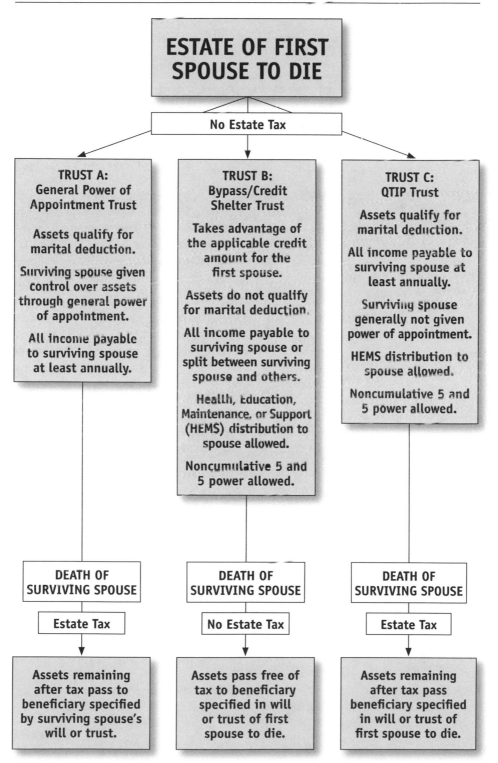

ESTATE OF FIRST SPOUSE TO DIE

No Estate Tax

TRUST A:
General Power of
Appointment Trust

Assets qualify for
marital deduction.

Surviving spouse given
control over assets
through general power
of appointment.

All income payable
to surviving spouse
at least annually.

TRUST B:
Bypass/Credit
Shelter Trust

Takes advantage of
the applicable credit
amount for the
first spouse.

Assets do not qualify
for marital deduction.

All income payable to
surviving spouse or
split between surviving
spouse and others.

Health, Education,
Maintenance, or Support
(HEMS) distribution to
spouse allowed.

Noncumulative 5 and
5 power allowed.

TRUST C:
QTIP Trust

Assets qualify for
marital deduction.

All income payable to
surviving spouse at
least annually.

Surviving spouse
generally not given
power of appointment.

HEMS distribution to
spouse allowed.

Noncumulative 5 and
5 power allowed.

**DEATH OF
SURVIVING SPOUSE**

Estate Tax

Assets remaining
after tax pass to
beneficiary specified
by surviving spouse's
will or trust.

**DEATH OF
SURVIVING SPOUSE**

No Estate Tax

Assets pass free of
tax to beneficiary
specified in will
or trust of first
spouse to die.

**DEATH OF
SURVIVING SPOUSE**

Estate Tax

Assets remaining
after tax pass
beneficiary specified
in will or trust of
first spouse to die.

CHAPTER 32

Non-Citizen Spouses and the Qualified Domestic Trust (QDOT)

MATTHEW T. MCCLINTOCK (Oklahoma City, Oklahoma)

The unlimited marital deduction does not generally apply to property passing to a surviving spouse who is not a citizen of the United States.[1] Marital transfers to a special "qualified domestic trust" or QDOT,[2] however, enable a decedent spouse to set aside property for the surviving non-citizen spouse without incurring immediate estate tax liability.[3]

The reason for not allowing the marital deduction for transfers to non-citizen spouses is to prevent the surviving spouse from receiving assets free of the federal estate tax regime and then expatriating those inherited assets to a jurisdiction that does not have an estate tax treaty with the United States. Rather than allow for a distribution to or for the surviving spouse free of estate tax, the QDOT provides a structure that merely defers the estate tax otherwise due at the decedent spouse's date of death (and at the decedent spouse's applicable estate tax rate) until the property is actually distributed free of the trust.[4]

In order to qualify as a QDOT, the trust must meet several strict requirements. Failure of any of these will cause the trust to fail and will make the entire balance of the QDOT immediately subject to estate taxation in the decedent spouse's estate if the Trustee and beneficiaries do not reform the trust to comply with these requirements before the filing deadline for the deceased spouse's federal estate tax return.

- First, the QDOT must require that at least one of the Trustees of the QDOT be a citizen of the United States or a domestic corporation as the "U.S. Trustee";[5]

- The Trustee may not distribute any cash or property from the QDOT unless the U.S. Trustee is empowered to withhold the estate tax attributable to the principal distribution;[6]

- The deceased spouse's fiduciary must irrevocably elect to treat the property as marital deduction property on the deceased spouse's federal estate tax return;[7] and

- If the fair market value of the assets distributed to the QDOT exceed

$2 million (a fixed value, not adjusted for inflation), the trust must meet additional requirements designed to provide adequate security to ensure payment of the estate tax liability imposed on the transferred property.[8]

In addition to these special requirements, the structure of the QDOT must otherwise meet the requirements of a trust that will qualify for the marital deduction.[9]

STRUCTURING THE MARITAL SHARE TRUST

The options for designing the Marital Share trust have some common elements. To qualify for the marital deduction, the trust must state that the spouse is entitled to receive all of the income from the trust at least annually. In addition, the spouse must be able to compel the Trustee to convert any non income-producing property to income-producing property. Whether the spouse has the ability to appoint the Marital Trust property in favor of other beneficiaries is a function of the particular design of the trust. Recall that a "general appointment trust" requires that the surviving spouse hold either a lifetime or testamentary power of appointment; the QTIP trust or QDOT trust may or may not grant a power of appointment. (Remember that the spouse cannot hold any lifetime power of appointment over a QTIP trust.[10]) Aside from these requirements, the Marital Trust may have other features that limit or expand the surviving spouse's access to the Marital property.

The trust need not give the surviving spouse access to trust principal to qualify for the marital deduction. Depending on the client's objectives, however, it may be desirable to allow for distributions of principal to the surviving spouse to augment the spouse's income interest. Because the value of the Marital Trust is already included in the surviving spouse's gross estate, allowing distributions of principal from the Marital Trust to the surviving spouse is estate tax neutral. Nevertheless, granting access to principal can have other significant consequences you must explore with an estate planning attorney during your counseling and plan design process.

Matthew T. McClintock is Co-Executive Director of WealthCounsel, LLC, an attorney membership organization dedicated to providing the best knowledge and tools to estate planning attorneys.

---

1. I.R.C. § 2056(d).

2. I.R.C. §§ 2056(d)(2), 2056A.

3. For a general discussion on QDOT requirements and administration, see Stephens, Maxfield, Lind, Calfee & Smith, *WG&L Estate Planning Treatises Federal Estate and Gift Taxation – Part II The Estate Tax,* Chapter 5: "The Taxable Estate" ¶5.07. Section 2056A. Qualified Domestic Trusts.

4. I.R.C. § 2056A(b).

5. I.R.C. § 2056A(a)(1)(A), Treas. Reg.§20.2056A-2(c).

6. I.R.C. § 2056A(a)(1)(B). See I.R.C. § 2056A(b)(1)(A). Note that not all distributions of principal trigger estate tax liability. See Stephens, et al., *WG&L Estate Planning Treatises Federal Estate and Gift Taxation – Part II The Estate Tax* Chapter 5: "The Taxable Estate" ¶5.07[4][a][i].

7. I.R.C. § 2056A(a)(3).

8. Treas. Reg. § 20.2056A-2(d)(1).

9. Treas. Reg. § 20.2056A-2(b)(1). Although this requirement is not apparent in the text of I.R.C. § 2056A, it is contained in the legislative history. HR Rep. No. 101-247, 101st Cong., 1st Sess. 1431 (1989). It is also a logical extension in the context of I.R.C.§§2056(d)(2)(A) and 2056(a).

10. Remember that no one can be permitted to distribute property to anyone other than the surviving spouse in a QTIP trust. See the discussion in Chapter 30.

CHAPTER 33

Planning for Nontraditional Relationships and the Evolving Definition of Marriage

JERRY CHASEN (Miami, Florida)

A growing number of Americans consider themselves family even though marriage is not part of the equation. If you cannot marry – as is true for most gay and lesbian couples in the United States, or choose not to marry — as is increasingly common, particularly among elderly couples, the absence of a marriage certificate has wide ranging consequences. Some of these we can "plan around"; others we just keep in mind.

Over 1,100 federal and 500 state determined rights, benefits, and privileges are conditioned on marriage. Many state laws deal with the issues raised in this book. For example, the laws of intestacy - who inherits property when there is no will, and the laws of guardianship — who will take care of your financial matters if you're incapacitated and haven't signed a pre-need appointment of a guardian or a power of attorney, will be determined by state law. Many of us watched the battle between Terri Schiavo's husband and parents (numbers one and two on the default state list of health care surrogates) over decisions about her care. Other consequences of no marriage license include denial of employer benefits for a surviving partner, less advantageous access to retirement plans, and lack of shared Social Security benefits.

Bottom line: without being pro-active, if the two of you are unmarried but consider yourselves family, you're not likely to be able to care for each other in the event of disability and make emergency health care and financial decisions for each other, nor will you inherit from each other, nor settle your partner's affairs after death.

Let's suppose Pat and Chris live together, consider themselves family, and yet haven't legally "tied the knot." They want to buy a home together and are considering how to title their property. An easy way to pass property at death is through legal title. Like many unmarried couples, Pat and Chris may find it emotionally satisfying to own property as "Joint Tenants with Right of Survivorship." They also like the fact that property owned this way passes from one to the other in the event of death without probate.

But owning property this way has its own drawbacks. First, both people will be needed to transfer title, so if one becomes disabled, there must be a "durable power of attorney" or similar document allowing the non-disabled partner to handle the affairs for both of them. If Pat has a taxable estate and predeceases Chris, Chris will have to prove Chris' contribution to the property, or the entire value of the property will be included in Pat's estate — not just half, but all of it, due to a presumption in the federal tax law.

Suppose Chris is in an accident, and can't make medical decisions. Unless Pat is named as Chris' health care surrogate or proxy, the law will likely provide that Chris' parents, or if they're not around, Chris' siblings, have the right to make those decisions. If Chris' condition is terminal, unless Pat is named in a living will, Pat won't be able to make decisions about discontinuing Chris' care, even though Pat probably knows more about Chris' feelings about end-of-life care than anyone else. Moreover, Pat won't be able to take care of Chris' financial affairs, even if their finances have been intertwined for years. Heck, without the proper documents, Pat may not even be allowed to visit Chris in the hospital or obtain Chris' medical file!

Suppose they are living in a house owned by Chris. If this accident proves fatal, then without planning, Pat is out of the house. Chris' family — again, at the top of the state's default list — will be the ones who manage Chris' estate and Pat will be left with nothing but memories.

Now suppose Pat and Chris did some planning before the accident occurred. First, you would expect to see a Health Care Proxy which would assure Pat could make decisions for Chris if Chris were incapacitated. There would also be a living will, authorizing Pat to make decisions about "pulling the plug." (Note that in some states these documents are combined into a single document called an Advance Health Care Directive.) Chris would also give Pat a durable power of attorney for property management so Pat could make decisions regarding Chris' financial affairs. Another document would ensure Pat would be appointed legal guardian if Chris were incapacitated.

Chris' will would appoint Pat as the executor to handle Chris' estate, and also ensure Pat has the right to continue to live in their house (assuming, of course, it is Chris' intent). All in all, a lot of the worst consequences could readily be avoided.

A particularly useful document in this area is a revocable living trust. Think of a folder. A trust, like a folder, holds what's put into it. The difference is that on the cover of the folder, the person setting up the trust — the "grantor" or "trustor" — lists instructions about what to do with what's in the folder, both in the event of disability and death — so this becomes the primary estate planning document. And like the "joint tenancy" title we discussed before, trust property — the property in our hypothetical folder — also passes outside of probate, without the tax presumption problem of joint tenancy.

Critically, the lack of a marriage license impacts planning because there is no federal or state gift and estate tax "marital deduction." A legally married couple can transfer assets between them during life and at the death of the first, and no gift or estate tax will be due the government until both partners have passed away. Pat and Chris have to plan with the expectation that tax will be due when each one dies.

Everything we've talked about so far applies to the couple regardless of Pat's or Chris' sex. But if Pat and Chris are of the same sex, they may wonder about tying the knot, now that it is an option available in some states in some form or other.

The answer: the lawyer's standby — "It depends." First, it depends on where they live. If they live in a state that has some sort of legalized same-sex union, they will at least get the benefits and have the obligations of a married couple under their state law. But presently, that marriage will have no effect on the federal level, because federal law provides that marriage is only between a man and a woman. When it comes time to pay taxes, they may be faced with filing as a married couple for state tax purposes, and as single individuals for federal tax purposes.

It gets more challenging if the couple moves to another state, or gets married elsewhere and returns home. If the home state, like the federal government, only recognizes opposite sex marriages, then the union is likely to have no legal effect whatsoever — unless the couple wants to dissolve it. If that happens, their home state may well look at a divorce petition and say, "Because we don't recognize this marriage, we can't even dissolve it." This becomes even more tricky with "marriage equivalents" like civil unions, which have been created in many states, but are unknown in others.

Given the uncertainty, what should Pat and Chris do? By all means, they should get married if that's the degree of commitment they have towards one another. But until the law becomes a good deal more settled, marriage is no substitute for good estate planning!

Jerry Simon Chasen, Chasen & Associates, P.A. Estate & Charitable gift planning for traditional and nontraditional families.

AVOIDING ESTATE TAX WITH LIFETIME TRANSFERS

CHAPTER 34

Annual Exclusion Planning

BRIAN C. LAYMAN (Canton, Ohio)

U tilizing the annual gift tax exclusion is a simple planning technique that reduces potential exposure to federal estate taxes. You may have heard that you can give away $10,000 tax-free a year to as many people as you want. The amount was indexed to $12,000 in 2008 ($13,000 in 2009). If you are married, you and your spouse can each make annual exclusion gifts, essentially doubling the amount you can gift. A spouse can also agree to apply his or her annual exclusion amount to a gift made by his or her spouse by "gift-splitting." The annual exclusion gifts will not reduce your lifetime gift exemption amount (currently $1 million).

As with many other tax planning techniques, the benefits of annual exclusion gifting are compounded over time. The following example illustrates the power of a lifetime gifting program:

EXAMPLE

Assumptions

- **Donor's age** – 60
- **Number of annual exclusions** – 1
- **Donee's annual after-tax return on gifts** – 4% (assuming the person who receives the gift invests all of the gifted money)
- **Annual exclusion inflation adjustment** – 3% (this is the amount used to determine how quickly the annual exclusion will be increased by $1,000 increments)
- **Donor's estate tax bracket** – 50%

Calculations

- **Donor's life expectancy** – 24.2 years
- **Total gifts** $426,000
- **Estate tax savings** $213,000

- **Projected value at life expectancy** $667,905

- **Estate tax savings if donee invested** $333,952

In this example, if you are 60 years of age, the tax savings for a single annual exclusion gift over your life expectancy is significant. In addition to removing $426,000 from your estate, all future growth and income generated from the gifted assets is also removed from your estate. In this example, the projected growth of the gifted assets is $241,905 ($667,905 - $426,000). This example assumes you only make annual exclusion gifts to one person. If you make lifetime gifts to more than one person, the tax benefits are even more powerful.

For various reasons, you may hesitate to make outright gifts to your beneficiaries. Once you make an outright gift, the beneficiary has complete control over the gifted asset and you no longer have any control over it. You may be concerned that the beneficiary is too young to receive the gift. The beneficiary may have substance abuse, bankruptcy, or creditor problems, or you also may not want to establish an expectation of future gifts. However, there are additional planning techniques you can utilize to overcome these obstacles. If the gift recipient is too young, it may be best to make a custodial gift or a gift to a minor's trust, both of which are discussed in subsequent chapters. Another alternative is to make a gift to a Crummey Trust, named after a taxpayer who won a case against the IRS.

Trusts provide a great deal of flexibility. A trust can dictate who will receive benefits from the trust, at what time, and under what circumstances. This flexibility comes at a cost, however. Gifts to most trusts will not qualify for the annual exclusion. In order to qualify for the annual exclusion, the tax rules require that the gift be of a "present interest." In other words, the gift recipient must be able to access the gifted property. Most trusts do not give the beneficiary access to the gifted property because the person making the gift is not comfortable making an outright gift for the reasons discussed above. As a result, gifts to these trusts do not qualify for the annual exclusion.

To maintain the desired flexibility of the trust and at the same time, qualify it for the annual exclusion, the trust can include a Crummey withdrawal right, also commonly called a "Crummey power." The Crummey power gives a beneficiary the right to withdraw assets you gift to the trust. The courts have ruled that the Crummey power gives the beneficiary the required access to the gifted property in order to qualify it for the annual exclusion. The beneficiary must have notice of his or her Crummey power and have a reasonable amount of time to exercise the power before it lapses. It is common to give the beneficiary at least 30 days to exercise the power. Once the time period expires, the beneficiary no longer has the ability to withdraw the assets you gift to the trust.

Can the beneficiary really withdraw the assets you just gifted to the trust? Yes. Otherwise, the IRS would say that the beneficiary's right was illusory and deny your use of the annual exclusion. You cannot have an implied or express agreement that the beneficiary will not exercise the Crummey power. However, if the beneficiary did withdraw the gifted assets, you probably would not make another gift for the benefit of that beneficiary, so it would not be in the beneficiary's best interests to do so.

In addition to the annual exclusion, there is also an unlimited gift tax exclusion for direct payments of qualifying medical and educational expenses. This unlimited exclusion applies regardless of your relationship to the recipient of the medical or educational services. To qualify, the payments must be made directly to the medical provider or educational institution. Gifts to a trust will not qualify even if the trustee is only permitted to make distributions for the beneficiaries' medical and educational needs.

The IRS Regulations clearly define which payments qualify for the unlimited exclusion. Qualifying educational expenses include tuition, but not books, supplies, dormitory fees, board, or other similar expenses. The exclusion applies to any educational institution that maintains a regular faculty and curriculum, and includes grade school, high school, and higher educational institutions. Qualifying medical expenses include expenses incurred for the diagnosis, cure, mitigation, treatment, or prevention of disease, or for the purpose of affecting any structure or function of the body, or for transportation primarily for and essential to medical care. In addition, qualifying medical expenses include payments for medical insurance on behalf of any individual. However, amounts paid for medical care reimbursed by the donee's insurance are not qualifying medical expenses.

The unlimited health and education exclusion provides an extremely valuable deathbed planning opportunity. For instance, the IRS has privately ruled that negotiating and prepaying non-refundable tuition qualifies for the exclusion. While private rulings cannot be relied upon by other taxpayers, the rulings provide insight regarding the IRS's interpretation of the tax rules. Following the IRS's logic in those rulings it will be interesting to see if a donor could negotiate with a health insurance provider to prepay health insurance for a wide number of "donees." The health and education exclusions are truly unlimited. If you have a number of beneficiaries who have tuition or medical expenses, you can greatly reduce your taxable estate by utilizing these techniques.

The annual exclusion and unlimited health and education exclusion provide simple yet effective tax savings techniques. The earlier a gifting program is implemented, the more the benefits can accrue.

Layman, D'Atri & Associates protects everything you love – family, friends, and favorite charities by developing unique and innovative wealth preservation strategies for the firm's individual clients, families, and businesses.

CHAPTER 35

Advantages and Disadvantages of Gifting

JEFFREY ROTH and DAVID BACON (Port Clinton, Ohio)

DEFINITIONS

It is always best to start the discussion of any topic by first defining the terms to be discussed.

What is a gift?

A gift is the transfer of any asset from one person to another for less than adequate compensation. A gift contemplates the surrender of the original owner's control of the asset to another person or entity.

TAXES

Who pays the tax caused by a gift?

The person making the gift is referred to as the Donor of the gift. The person receiving the gift is referred to as the Donee of the gift. Gifts are never taxed as income to the Donee. If there is a gift tax generated by the making of a gift, generally it is paid by the person making the gift, the Donor.

Are all gifts taxable?

No, there are several exceptions.

ANNUAL GIFT EXCLUSION

The first exception is often referred to as the annual gift exclusion amount. The federal gift tax rules currently provide that you may give an amount not exceeding $12,000 in 2008 ($13,000 in 2009) to any other person once each year. Gifts of this amount or less are excluded from the payment of any federal gift tax. There is no limit as to the number of persons to whom you make annual exclusion gifts in any one year.

If you are married, you may give twice the annual exclusion amount ($24,000 in 2008, and $26,000 in 2009) to a donee using your and your spouse's annual gift exclusion amount even though all the assets comprising the gift may be made from one spouse. However, in no event can you and your spouse give an amount in excess of $24,000 (in 2008) to any one individual in any one year and use their annual gift exclusion amount as an exception to shield the gift from gift tax.

In order to qualify for the annual exclusion, your gift must be made with absolutely no restrictions. If there is a restriction made on the gift, such as, "Here is $12,000, son. You can do whatever you want with the money, but you can't buy a car with it," then your gift does not qualify for the annual exclusion. The transfer is still a gift, but unless the transfer is covered by another exception, the transfer may be taxable to the Donor.

Gifts to minors (persons under legal age or the age as set by state statute for this particular exception) under the Uniform Gifts to Minors Act may be subject to restrictions yet still qualify for the annual gift exclusion. When the minor reaches the age of majority, these restrictions are removed and the Donee of the gift is thereafter free to do whatever he or she desires with the gift.

If a gift is made of $12,000 or less to any one person in 2008 is the Donor required to file a gift tax return?

No. There is no requirement that a gift tax return be filed by the Donor for gifts of $12,000 or less to any one person in 2008 ($13,000 in 2009).

LIFETIME GIFT EXEMPTION

Are there other exceptions to the gift tax in addition to the annual exclusion amount just discussed?

In addition to your ability to make any number of annual gift exclusion gifts to Donees each year, a Donor may, over the course of his or her lifetime, make up to $1 million in gifts.

Gifts utilizing the Donor's $1 million lifetime exemption must be reported on a federal gift tax return (Federal Gift Tax Form 709) on or before April 15th of the year succeeding the year in which the gift was made.

ESTATE TAX INCLUSION

In 2008, you can die leaving an estate of not more than $2 million before you are required to pay federal estate tax. Is this $1 million lifetime gift tax exemption in addition to your $2 million federal estate tax exemption, or a part of it?

The $1 million gift tax exemption for lifetime gifts is part of the $2 million estate tax exemption available at death. Accordingly if you have used your $1 million lifetime exemption for gifts during your lifetime, your estate tax exemption is reduced accordingly, so you only have $1 million of your federal estate tax exemption remaining. The estate tax exemption increases to $3.5 million in 2009. However, the lifetime gift tax exemption will remain at $1 million.

The federal government changes the rules regarding gift and estate tax exemptions and exclusion amounts. Prior to undertaking any estate or gift tax planning strategies, you should consult an attorney to review the current rules and regulations and the probable tax effects of gifting.

INCOME TAX CONSEQUENCES

Are there income tax consequences of gifting in addition to the potential gift tax consequences?

Generally the Donee of a gift takes over the basis and holding period of the Donor. Consequently, when the Donee sells the property, the Donee may recognize gain that occurred while the Donor held the property.

> **EXAMPLE.** You own ten acres of land you purchased for $1,000 per acre. In 2008, each of these acres is now worth $12,000. You wish to use your $12,000 annual exclusion to gift one acre to your son. Your gift tax consequences are determined by the current value of the asset on the date of the gift. Accordingly, you can give your son one acre and avoid the payment of any gift tax.
>
> The receipt of the acre as a gift is not income taxable to your son, as gifts are not income taxed to Donees.
>
> However, if your son thereafter elects to sell this acre for $13,000, he will not use the value of the asset on the day he received it ($12,000) as his basis in calculating his taxable gain realized by the sale. Because your son received the acre as a gift, he will instead use your basis in the property as his basis for purposes of calculating his taxable gain on the sale. If the sale price is $13,000, the basis of the son in the acre is your original basis of $1,000 and the taxable gain is $12,000.

For this reason, when a gift of an appreciated asset is made to a Donee, the Donor and the Donee should pay close attention to the Donor's basis and holding period in the gifted asset. In contrast, assets passing by reason of death under current estate tax laws are stepped up (or down) to fair market value on the date of death and automatically receive long-term capital gain or loss treatment. You should contemplate in advance the income tax consequences to the donee or heir upon a subsequent sale.

Jeffrey P. Roth graduated from the University of Miami (1969) and obtained his J.D. from Capital University, Columbus, Ohio. Mr. Roth is admitted to practice in both Ohio and Florida.

David F. Bacon is an Ohio State Bar Association Board Certified Specialist in the areas of Estate, Trust, and Probate Planning. He has authored treatises on estate and business planning.

CHAPTER 36

Avoiding Estate Tax Through Lifetime Transfers: Gift Splitting

RICHARD REDGRAVE (Boca Raton, Florida)

A BRIEF OVERVIEW OF THE ESTATE AND GIFT TAX

When you die, the government will impose a tax on your estate if its value exceeds the applicable exclusion amount for the year of your death. For example, in 2008 the applicable exclusion amount is $2 million. In 2009, the applicable exclusion amount is $3.5 million. If you die in 2009, the first $3.5 million of your estate will be sheltered from taxation, but the portion of your estate in excess of this amount will be subject to estate tax.

Therefore, if you anticipate that upon your death the value of your estate will exceed the applicable estate tax exclusion amount, there are a number of planning techniques you should consider that could allow you to avoid this potential tax liability.

A simple method to reduce the value of your estate is by making gifts to another party during your lifetime. However, the government limits the amount you may gift during any given year (the annual exclusion is $12,000 per year per recipient in 2008, and $13,000 in 2009) as well as the total amount you may gift during your lifetime ($1 million). If you exceed the lifetime exemption, you will be forced to pay a gift tax.

For example, suppose you have two children. In 2008, you can gift $12,000 to each child ($12,000 x 2 = $24,000 total) and not be subject to any gift tax liability. However, if later that same year, you gift an additional $5,000 to each child, the additional amount ($5,000 x 2 = $10,000 total) must be reported on a federal gift tax return. However, you would not incur any gift tax liability since the excess can be deducted against your $1 million lifetime gift exemption ($1 million - $10,000 = $990,000 remaining).

Also, it should be noted that the estate and gift tax is "unified" such that any amounts deducted from your lifetime gift exemption are also, in effect, deducted from your estate tax exclusion amount. Thus in the above example, if you were to die in 2009 and had used $10,000 of your lifetime gift exemption, you would have $3,490,000 remaining as your estate tax exclusion amount.

Despite these limitations, gifting remains a common and valuable estate planning strategy and the concept of gift splitting makes the strategy even more effective.

GIFT SPLITTING

Gift splitting is a technique available to married individuals that allows spouses to agree to classify gifts made to a third party as made one-half by the donor and one-half by the donor's spouse. The primary benefit of gift splitting is that it allows a married couple to take full advantage of both spouses' exemptions despite any economic disparity between the two spouses. The wealthy spouse does not have to transfer assets to the other spouse (which may be an undesirable option, particularly in a second marriage) in order to accomplish the couple's gifting intentions.

Moreover, the actual process of gift splitting is relatively straightforward. After you make a gift, your spouse consents (on your timely filed gift tax return) to treat your transfer as having been made one-half by each party. Once filed, this election is irrevocable for the year in question and will apply to all gifts made during that year (i.e. you cannot elect on a gift by gift basis). The only requirements are that the spouses must be married at the time the gift is made, and both must be either U.S. citizens or resident aliens.

Consider the following example: You are married and have two children from a prior marriage. Using the principles of gift splitting (and with your spouse's consent), in 2008 you are now able to gift $24,000 to each child ($26,000 in 2009) without triggering any tax consequences. Note that in this example, despite the fact that the gifts did not exceed the annual exclusion amount, a gift tax return indicating the election to gift split is still required. Thus, one minor disadvantage of gift splitting is that it requires a gift tax return to be filed regardless of the amount in question.

Nevertheless, the advantages of gift splitting become even more apparent in the following scenario: you wish to make a gift of $1.5 million to your child. Without the use of gift splitting, the $500,000 above the lifetime exemption ($1 million in 2008) would be subject to gift tax (payable by you, the donor). Instead, your spouse agrees to gift split, and accordingly, $750,000 is allocated against the exemption of each spouse. Each spouse has a sufficient lifetime exemption to cover this amount; consequently you avoid potential tax liability.

While the preceding examples present relatively basic applications of gift splitting, the fundamental principles can be extended to more advanced scenarios. Gift splitting is often employed to pay premiums on life insurance policies owned by Irrevocable Life Insurance Trusts. In another context, if you can obtain a discounted valuation on an asset (such as a closely held business interest), then you can use gifting splitting to maximize the interests being transferred.

Ultimately, gift splitting allows you to leverage the annual exclusion and the lifetime exemption to transfer significant amounts of wealth.

A. Richard Redgrave provides clients with comprehensive legal solutions to matters involving estate planning, asset protection, taxation, and business planning.

Strategies to Minimize Gift Taxes

STRATEGY USED	EFFECT
Gift-splitting	Value of gift is split with consenting spouse.
Annual exclusion	Donor can give $12,000 in 2008 ($13,000 in 2009) to each individual without gift tax consequences. Gift splitting allows a married couple to give $24,000 in 2008 ($26,000 in 2009) per donee without gift tax consequences.
Unified credit	Allows taxpayer to gift $1 million during lifetime without gift tax consequences.
Qualified transfers	Allows taxpayer to directly pay educational institutions and providers of medical care on behalf of others without gift tax consequences.
Gifts to a spouse	Marital deduction eliminates gift tax for U.S. citizen spouses.
Gifts to charity	Charitable deduction eliminates gift tax.
Bargain sales	Gift is bargain element (FMV less sales price).
Net gifts	Donee is required to pay gift taxes, which reduces amount of the gift.
Partial-interest gifts (GRATs, GRUTs, QPRTs, etc.)	Grantor retains an interest so assets are transferred at reduced gift tax values.
Valuation discounts	Discounts for lack of marketability and minority interests can be used for family limited partnership interests and stock in closely held corporations.
Gifts of life insurance	Small premiums can be leveraged into large death benefits.
Trusts	Gifts to Crummey trusts and 2503(b) and (c) trusts for minors are eligible for the gift tax annual exclusion.

What to Do with Various Types of Properties

Highly Appreciated Property	Gift to a person in a lower tax bracket.
Property Likely to Appreciate	Gift to remove future appreciation from donor's estate, especially if there is a concern about higher estate taxes in the future.
Loss Property	Do not gift. Sell the property, take the loss, and gift the proceeds.
Income-Producing Property	Gift to a person in a lower tax bracket.
Depreciable Property	Keep in order to take advantage of depreciation.
Depreciated or Cost-Recovery Property	May be good for using the gift-leaseback technique.
Life Insurance	Gift that will have a high value at the date of death and a low value (replacement value) for gift tax purposes.
Out-of-State Real Property	Gift to avoid ancillary probate.
Closely Held Stock	Use caution in gifting. Estate may be disqualified from using Section 303 or 6166.

CHAPTER 37

Custodial Accounts for Minors

NANCY KAUPP EWIN (La Mesa, California)

By definition, custodial accounts are established by adults as custodians for minor children. Both the custodian and the minor must be residents or resident aliens of the United States or its territories. The accounts are established under the Uniform Gifts to Minors Act (UGMA) or Uniform Transfers to Minors Act (UTMA) on a state-by-state basis. While custodial accounts are available in the vast majority of states, they differ slightly regarding the age for distribution. Therefore, each separate state's law must be consulted.

WHAT IS A CUSTODIAL ACCOUNT?

A custodial account is simply an account established with property gifted by an adult. It is a gift under Internal Revenue Code Section 2503(c) and can be used for annual gift tax exclusion gifts.

You establish the account in the name of the custodian for the minor child as, for example, "[Custodian Name], as custodian for [Minor Child Name] under the [Name of State UGMA/UTMA Act])." Income generated by the account is reported to the Internal Revenue Service under the social security number of the child.

The custodian manages the account for the benefit of the minor to whom the gift has been made. Management includes keeping records of all transactions for the account/property. Generally, the custodian has broad management powers, both as to the type of investments which comprise the account and as to the uses, if any, by the minor prior to reaching the stated age for distribution (usually 18 years of age). The custodian has a duty to act as a prudent person responsible for the property of another and not invest in risky or speculative investments.

The account, once established, is irrevocable. "Irrevocable" means the account cannot be terminated by the adult once established, and it cannot be taken back. It is a completed gift.

WHAT TYPES OF PROPERTY CAN BE TRANSFERRED TO CUSTODIAL ACCOUNTS?

The UTMA/UGMA Act permits transfer of any kind of property to title ownership in custodial format. For example, money, securities, U.S. savings bonds, life insurance, annuities, partnership interests, real property, and tangible personal property can be transferred under the Act. You must refer to your own state's version of the act to verify the foregoing, however.

CAN THE ACCOUNT BE USED BY THE MINOR, IF NEEDED, PRIOR TO THE MINOR ATTAINING THE AGE OF MAJORITY?

If you establish a custodial account, the account can be used for the benefit of the minor prior to the minor reaching the age of majority. The adult custodian is the only one who can access the account and must determine that the minor's access to the account satisfies the purpose for which you established the account, for example, to pay for music lessons, to buy a car, or to participate in an after-school program.

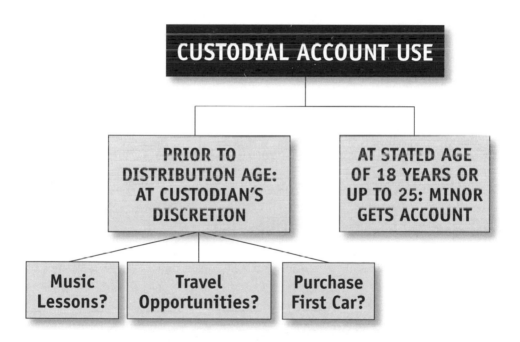

AT WHAT AGE CAN A CHILD ACCESS THE ACCOUNT?

Normally a child can access the account upon attaining the age of majority, usually age 18. In some states, a custodian can state a slightly higher age before allowing access, age 21, for example, or, in some states, even up to 25 years of age. You will have to check the requirements in your state before establishing the account.

WHAT ARE THE BENEFITS OF A CUSTODIAL ACCOUNT?

Custodial accounts are easy and inexpensive to set up. You can establish a custodial account for any minor. There is no minimal amount required to establish a custodial account. There is no requirement that additional contributions be made, nor is there any requirement that the account be used for a specific purpose (e.g. education).

WHAT ARE THE DISADVANTAGES OF CUSTODIAL ACCOUNTS?

As previously stated, the custodial accounts are irrevocable, meaning that once you establish one, the account belongs to the minor, with only the requirement being that he or she attain a stated or statutory age. While the accounts can be accessed by the custodian prior to the minor attaining the age of majority, you may be nervous about giving an 18 year old, or even a 21 year old, a substantial amount of money or a valuable asset. The accounts are statutory so they are inflexible. If you change your mind about the age for distribution, it is too late. The account, as established, stands.

For larger value assets, a custodial account may not be the best option for dealing with minor beneficiaries due to the inflexibility of the account.

WHAT IF THE CUSTODIAN DIES BEFORE THE MINOR REACHES THE AGE OF MAJORITY?

What happens when the custodian dies prior to distribution to the minor is extremely problematic. In this case no one has access the account and the minor must wait until the stated age to claim the property. It may require a court order to install a new custodian. Most state statutes, however, allow a personal representative or trustee to name a successor custodian.

WHAT HAPPENS IF THE MINOR DIES?

If the minor dies prior to the stated age for distribution, the account passes according to state law, not necessarily back to you as donor. The beneficiaries of the account are likely to be the parents of the minor child according to state laws of intestate succession.

WHO PAYS THE TAXES ON INTEREST OR DIVIDENDS EARNED ON THE ACCOUNT?

The tax identification number on a custodial account is the minor's social security number. Any income earned will be reported to the IRS under the minor's social security number and taxed to the minor. One exception arises if the custodian uses the account to discharge a parent's obligation of support to the minor child, in which case the income is taxed to the parent.

TO WHOSE ESTATE DOES THE CUSTODIAL ACCOUNT BELONG?

Custodial accounts are part of the minor's estate in the event of the minor's or custodian's death prior to the minor attaining distribution age unless you, as the donor who established the custodial account, are also the custodian. If estate taxes are an issue for you, name someone other than yourself as custodian on the account.

WHAT ALTERNATIVES TO A CUSTODIAL ACCOUNT EXIST?

There are alternatives to a custodial account, which you should examine before making a final decision. Some alternatives are Coverdell accounts, 529 plans for education, and traditional or Roth IRAs. You can also explore establishing a trust for the minor child. Considerations in making your decision include: 1) the amount of money or value of property involved; 2) the purpose for which you want to set aside the assets for the minor child; 3) the terms for management and distribution of the assets to the minor child; and 4) the cost to effectuate the plan.

Nancy Kaupp Ewin has practiced for over 26 years exclusively in the areas of estate planning, trusts, wills, powers of attorney, elder law issues, conservatorship, probate, trust administration, elder law, and Medi-Cal planning.

CHAPTER 38

Providing Education and/or Nest Egg Funding for Young Beneficiaries

TIMOTHY M. HALLIGAN (Atlanta, Georgia)

You may be a parent or a grandparent planning to fund a child's or grandchild's college education. You may be an aunt, uncle, or adult mentor with a similar desire to help fund the education of your favorite young niece, nephew, or friend. What better financial investment, you are thinking, can you make in a child's future?

If that is your wish, you are in luck because there are many effective ways to accomplish your objectives and there are numerous tax benefits available that will enable you to do so in a tax-efficient way. There are so many alternatives, in fact, that your main challenge will be to determine which education-funding mechanism is most suitable to your circumstances. In a nutshell, your range of options includes direct gifts to or for the benefit of a minor, gifts to custodial accounts, gifts in trust, and gifts to Section 529 accounts. So how do you determine which strategy will work best for you?

First, it helps to understand the pros and cons of each form of education funding. Direct gifting to minors is very simple: you make out a check in the name of the child and deliver it to the child's parents and they deposit the check in an account in the name of the child. The downside of the strategy is that the child will gain control of the account upon attaining the age of majority in the state of his or her residence. There is a risk that the child will not use the gifted monies for education or other worthwhile purpose. If direct gifting is nonetheless desired, a better alternative might be to make a direct tuition payment to an educational institution for the benefit of a child enrolled there, and this technique could be used for pre-college private schools as well as for college funding. Such a direct tuition gift qualifies for the unlimited gift tax exclusion for tuition payments.

Custodial accounts, similarly, have advantages and disadvantages. Under most Uniform Gifts to Minors or Uniform Transfers to Minors Acts, the child will not gain unfettered access to the account until he or she attains age 21. Thus, in the many states that have an age of majority of 18, the custodial account will allow the account to stay out of the child's control a little longer than a non-custodial account, perhaps until the completion of the child's college education. But what if the account appreciates in value during the child's pre-college years and there is much more than is needed for the child's education? Or what if the child has qualified for significant grant or scholarship money or has elected not to go to college? Then the custodial account doesn't look as favorable because the child, who may not be financially responsible yet, may have access to a lot of capital at age 21. The child might waste the money on depreciating assets or frivolous pursuits. The child might decide not to seek employment and live off the capital.

If it is foreseeable that gifted monies will grow substantially over the child's pre-college years and exceed the amount required to fund the child's education, such that the monies will also create a future nest egg for the child, then trusts are usually the preferred funding vehicle. Specialized trusts designed to qualify contributions for the gift tax annual exclusion are typically used for this purpose. One such trust is usually dubbed a "Minor's Trust." It is a special form of trust described in Section 2503(c) of the Internal Revenue Code that qualifies for the annual exclusion. The problem with this form of trust is that the child for whom it is established must be given the right to withdraw all of the trust assets when he or she attains age 21. If the trust still holds a lot of assets at that time, then the same potential problems arise that exist with custodial accounts. Maybe the child will agree to allow the assets to continue to be held in a trust for his or her benefit, but there is always a risk that the child will opt to pull the assets out. Another possible disadvantage with this form of trust is that the trust instrument must require the Trustee to make distributions for the "best interests" of the child. The trust cannot be tailored for educational or more finely tuned purposes.

Because of the inherent drawbacks with Minor's Trusts, tax practitioners developed an alternative form of trust which enables contributions to qualify for the gift tax annual exclusion while allowing the creator of the trust to postpone the date at which the child can take possession of the trust assets. This form of trust is usually referred to as a "Crummey Trust," its name having been borrowed from the brave soul who litigated and succeeded in one of the early cases testing this type of trust's qualification for the gift tax annual exclusion. With such trusts, the beneficiary is given the power to withdraw contributions for a limited time (30 days for example) after a contribution is made to the trust. There is little risk that the withdrawal powers will be exercised while a child is a minor because only the child's parents (or guardians) can exercise the withdrawal rights. Once the withdrawal period passes, the property can be held in trust for the child's benefit for the time period the trust creator chooses, even for the child's lifetime or beyond (for a child's children or siblings, for example). Thus, this form of trust is especially useful if there is a chance that residual value above and beyond a child's education costs will build up over years. The trust instrument can be tailored to provide funding to the child for education and other desired purposes. Trusts such as the Crummey and Minor's Trusts are also very good creditor protection vehicles because they can be designed as discretionary trusts that do not give the child rights to income or principal that can be garnished or attached by a creditor or made part of a property settlement in a divorce.

The newest option in the planning arsenal is the Section 529 account, another device created in the Internal Revenue Code. This special kind of account is similar to an IRA account, but it is geared toward funding college costs. There are several unique characteristics which make a Section 529 account a special planning vehicle. First, if the account assets are used to pay for education costs, then the account's earnings (i.e., its income and gains) are not subject to federal income tax. Second, the initial account contributor can take back property by withdrawing it from the account. This makes it unlike any other kind of "gifting" strategy. Third, the account can be front-loaded with up to five times the amount of the gift tax annual exclusion ($60,000 in 2008, and $65,000 in 2009), or twice this amount for a married couple, if a special five-year election is made to treat the gift as though it were made over a five-year period. Fourth, the beneficiary can be changed after the account is established.

There are some drawbacks to Section 529 accounts, which should also be considered. First, the accounts can only be funded with cash. Thus, they are not suitable for contributors who wish to contribute closely held or publicly traded securities, land interests, or other non-cash assets. Second, if amounts are distributed from the account for anything other than education costs, such non-qualifying amounts are taxable to the recipient at ordinary income rates and a 10% penalty is imposed. Consequently, if a large portion of the assets would, upon sale, be otherwise taxed at capital gain rates, this would be disadvantageous. Third, your investment options are limited with Section 529 plans. Each state operates at least one of these plans and each of these plans typically uses one mutual fund family and offers no more than a half dozen investment choices within those mutual fund families. Typically, you can only make changes in your investment allocation once per year. Therefore, these accounts might not be suitable for you if you do not want to have your investment choices limited or believe that you can invest with greater success than the investment managers used by your state's Section 529 plans. A fourth drawback with these accounts is that a number of issues exist with these accounts that have not yet been settled by the Internal Revenue Service. Results are not as predictable as you might like them to be on issues such as what happens to an account upon the death of the account owner or upon the death of a beneficiary.

Given the myriads of education funding choices and their advantages and disadvantages, there are several conclusions that can be drawn about their relative suitability.

- First, if it is possible you will accumulate capital that significantly exceeds what will be required for a child's education, consider using a trust. This approach is especially beneficial if you have a sizeable estate and wish to shift wealth out of your estate to your children and grandchildren and if you intend to invest in assets with explosive growth potential such as stock in a company planning to go public. If, on the other hand, you anticipate that all of the funds will be used for a child's education, a Section 529 account may be the best option because of the tax-free growth such accounts afford. Trusts can adapt well to changed circumstances (such as the death of a beneficiary); Section 529 plans may not adapt as well. However, it is possible under some states' 529 plans to open a Section 529 account in the name of a trust, and that option may make such accounts in those states much more adaptable to change.

- Second, if you wish to get some of the funded money back, you will want to use a Section 529 account.

- Third, if you intend to contribute non-cash assets, trusts and custodial accounts are the only available choices.

- Fourth, if you want to invest the gifted monies yourself or hire your own investment manager, you will want to use a custodial account or a trust.

- Fifth, if creditor protection is of paramount concern, consider using a trust. However, some states have enacted spendthrift laws and other creditor protection measures for Section 529 plans (and some federal bankruptcy protection is available for 529 accounts). In those states, Section 529 plans may offer strong creditor protection as well.

Timothy M. Halligan has an estate planning practice that caters to families desiring to coordinate their personal tax and investment planning with their retirement and wealth transmission planning.

Comparison of Various Types of Transfers to Minors

	UGMA/ UTMA	SECTION 2503(B) TRUST	SECTION 2503(C) TRUST	CRUMMEY TRUST
What are the transfer requirements?	Property vests in the minor at date of transfer.	Income must be distributed to beneficiary. Principal can be retained by the trust.	Trustee must have power to use property and/or income for the benefit of donee until age 21. The donee must receive all accumulated income and principal at age 21. If donee dies before age 21, all accumulated income and principal must pass to the donee's estate as the donee appoints.	Beneficiaries must have power to remove trust assets for a specified period of time. Notice must be given to beneficiaries of any additions to the trust subject to the power. Beneficiary must be given a reasonable time to exercise the power. Donee's lapse of power may create a gift if assets subject to withdrawal exceed the 5 and 5 limitation.
Is the annual exclusion available for gifts to the trust?	Yes, for the entire FMV.	Yes, for the FMV of the income interest.	Yes, generally the FMV.	Yes, for the FMV of property subject to the withdrawal power.
What are the consequences if the donor is also the custodian/ fiduciary?	Included in donor's estate if custodian at time of death.	Included in donor's estate if donor has discretionary power to distribute principal.	Included in donor's estate if donor has discretionary power to distribute income and principal.	Included in donor's estate if donor has discretionary power to distribute income and principal.
What are the income distribution rules?	May accumulate in account or be distributed to or for the benefit of the minor/donee.	Must be distributed to beneficiary.	Trustee must follow trust instrument. May accumulate income in trust or distribute to the beneficiary. If donor is trustee, trust may be treated as grantor trust.	Trustee must follow trust instructions. May accumulate income in trust or distribute to beneficiary.
What are the income tax consequences?	Income is taxed to minor/donee. If under age 24, income is taxed at parents' marginal rates. If income is used to satisfy the donor/grantor's legal obligation to support, that portion of income is taxed to the donor/grantor.	Donee/ beneficiary is taxed on income since it is required to be distributed. If income is used to satisfy the donor/grantor's legal obligation to support, that portion of income is taxed to the donor/grantor.	Taxed at trust level unless distributed. Distributions are taxed to beneficiary. If any portion of the income is used to satisfy the donor/grantor's legal obligation to support, that portion of income is taxed to the donor/ grantor.	Generally, taxed at trust level unless distributed. IRS may consider donee to be the owner of any portion subject to withdrawal power. Distributions are taxed to the beneficiary. If income is used to satisfy the donor/grantor's legal obligation to support, that portion of income is taxed to the donor/grantor.

CHAPTER **39**

Intra-Family Loans

SEAN KENNEY (San Francisco, California)

Bank borrowing is a common method for obtaining a loan. However, banks may not always be practical sources for funds for children and other heirs. The following example illustrates this principle. Assume Laura and Lenny, a married couple, have accumulated wealth of $50 million. Their son Bruce, 23, recently found a wonderful place in the Hamptons costing $2 million that he feels he must own. Laura and Lenny love Bruce so much they have offered him any type of assistance in buying a home. In fact, Laura and Lenny have told little Bruce they would purchase the home for him outright if only they had not already exhausted their available gift tax exemption buying him gold-plated GI Joe action figures last year.

Bruce acquired his parents' business acumen and recently launched a successful chain of Bolly Burgers, netting approximately $250,000 annually. However, Bruce's credit is poor, due to failed business ventures in the past, and banks refuse to lend him any money. Laura and Lenny love little Bruce dearly, but do not want to pay any transfer taxes this year so they refuse to buy a home for Bruce outright. What is Bruce to do?

Bruce has a couple of options: 1) go to the neighborhood loan shark and obtain a loan at a 30% annual interest rate; or 2) borrow money from Laura and Lenny. Wisely, Bruce has opted to choose the latter. Laura and Lenny want to ensure no tax exposure results from this transaction, but also want to give Bruce the best possible loan terms. Thus, Laura and Lenny decide to seek counsel from their attorney.

To their dismay, their attorney advises Laura and Lenny that they cannot make a $2 million loan interest-free. The United States Supreme Court has held that any type of transfer of property or property rights — such as an interest-free loan — with substantial value is deemed a gift and the interest not charged is still treated as income. Thus, if Lenny and Laura make a loan to Bruce interest-free, when in fact the applicable rate should be 5% annually, they could be taxed on a $100,000 gift at the federal gift tax rate of 45% ($45,000) for every year the loan exists. Lenny and Laura would also have to treat the interest they would have received ($100,000) as income taxed at their income tax marginal rate of 35% ($35,000). Reluctantly, Laura and Lenny agree to loan little Bruce $2 million at an annual interest rate of 5%, thereby avoiding the gift tax but not the income tax.

Having diligent business minds, and recognizing that the IRS may still attempt to impute a gift based upon the nature of the relationship between themselves and

Bruce, Laura and Lenny inquire how they may make the consequences of this transaction more certain. Their attorney advises them that a promissory note, security agreement, and guarantee agreement will document the transaction. These steps will avoid problems with the IRS. However, Laura and Lenny have no idea what these types of documents are, or what they mean.

A promissory note recites the terms, amount, and the interest rate of the loan in question. A promissory note also discusses what will happen if the borrower, here Bruce, decides to default on the loan. The promissory note may be interest only with a balloon payment at the end, which greatly interests Bruce, as he can only afford to make small payments at the current time.

The promissory note needs to be "secured" in the case of default by Bruce. Put simply, if Bruce fails to meet the obligations spelled out in the promissory note, Laura and Lenny can take (foreclose upon) the Hampton house and sell it to pay off any type of obligation owed to them by Bruce. Thus, if Bruce made interest and principal payments throughout the term of the loan, and owed $1 million on the principal balance, then upon Bruce's "default" (failure to pay when due), Laura and Lenny could foreclose and sell the house for $2 million. In that instance, Laura and Lenny would only be entitled to receive $1 million. The remaining amount would go back to Bruce, who could buy a more modest house loan free.

Finally, a guarantee agreement allows for a third party to act as guarantor for little Bruce's loan. Laura and Lenny could proceed against the third party without proceeding against Bruce on the loan if he defaults. A guarantee agreement is especially useful if, for example, the Hampton house burned down due to Bruce's playboy lifestyle, and Bruce owed Laura and Lenny close to all of the principal on the loan. Under these circumstances, Laura and Lenny could proceed against a third party to collect any debt owed to them. Of course, Laura and Lenny would not want to proceed against Bruce at all in such circumstance (or his guarantor). However, if they did not proceed against Bruce or the third-party guarantor in such a situation, any amounts uncollected would be viewed as a gift and taxed accordingly.

Laura and Lenny are glad they spoke with their attorney and they enter into an agreement to loan little Bruce $2 million for a term of 30 years at a rate of 5% annually. Bruce will make interest-only payments for the first 29 years of the loan, with the remainder to be paid on the 30th anniversary of the promissory note. The note is secured by Laura and Lenny taking an interest in the home, and the loan is guaranteed by Bruce's childhood friend, Bob, who has also done quite well for himself. Bruce is extremely happy he did not have to get a loan for his home at a 30% rate from the loan shark. Laura and Lenny are doubly glad they did not have to pay any gift tax. Everybody comes out ahead, except the IRS of course.

For smaller loans, the benefits are even greater. Loans of $10,000 or less are not subject to the gift tax and income tax treatment of interest-free loans. The imputed gift and income from loans between $10,000 and $100,000 is limited to the lesser of the investment income of the borrower (Bruce) or the applicable federal rate.

If Bruce used the loan proceeds to buy the house or attend graduate school, earning no investment return, no income is imputed to the parents.

Sean R. Kenney, Myers Law Firm, P.C., provides estate, tax, and business succession planning.

CHAPTER 40

Sales, Installment Sales, and Self-Canceling Installment Notes

HENRY WEATHERBY (Bloomfield, Connecticut)

SALES

Asale is an asset transfer from you to a third party (someone other than your spouse) for consideration. Consideration is, alone or in any combination, cash, a promissory note, or relief from existing debt. The problem with a sale is if you receive more than your adjusted tax basis in return for the assets you are selling, you will be subject to tax. If you have held the asset for less than one year, the gain will be classified as a short-term capital gain. If instead, you have held the asset for one year or more, the gain will then be classified as long-term capital and will be taxed at a somewhat lower rate. If the sale involves a depreciable asset, the sale may be subject to depreciation recapture, which like a short-term capital gain, will be taxed at ordinary income tax rates. A taxpayer's original basis in a depreciable asset will diminish over time as the taxpayer depreciates the asset. A classic example of a sale that may generate depreciation recapture is the sale of rental property.

In a sale, all the gain is recognized at once, and accordingly, all tax on the recognized gain will be due by April 15th of the year following the year of the sale. If the gain is large enough you may find the Alternative Minimum Tax (AMT) will be owed instead of long-term capital gains. If the debt owed on the asset sold is large enough, and the tax burden created by the sale is large enough, you can possibly find yourself in the unwelcome position of owing more than you actually received from the sale.

INSTALLMENT SALES

An installment sale is a sale by which some or all of the payments are made over more than one calendar (tax) year. As the seller, you will have received a promissory note in addition to any other consideration. The benefit of spreading the payments out over time is that the tax on the gain is likewise spread out over time.

In an installment sale, the total gain for the sale will be the sales price minus your adjusted tax basis. Dividing the gain by the sales price yields the gross profit percentage. The gain you will recognize for each payment will be the principal payment multiplied by the gross profit percentage. The IRS has established rules as to the minimum rate of interest that must be charged. These rates are updated monthly and are known as the applicable federal rate (AFR). Loans at rates below the appropriate AFR will create imputed interest, on which you must pay tax, even though none, or only a part, was actually paid.

For sales to relatives, it is important that the assets be sold for "full and adequate consideration" in order to avoid adverse gift tax consequences. Sales for less than full and adequate consideration will result in the sale being categorized as a gift. To avoid a taxable gift, the transaction must be properly documented, and the principal amount of the note must be equivalent to the fair market value of the assets being sold.

The primary risk in an installment sale is that the note may never be paid off in full. Any unpaid principal remaining upon the transferor's death will remain in the transferor's taxable estate. If the purpose of the sale was to convert otherwise illiquid assets into a steady income stream, that purpose will be thwarted if the payments cease. Therefore, the transferor will always need to consider the credit risk of the transferee.

Self-Canceling Installment Note

A self-canceling installment note (SCIN) is used in an installment sale where the seller agrees that any balance remaining on the note is automatically canceled upon his or her death. This means the unpaid balance on the note is not includable in the transferor's estate. Accordingly, an appropriate risk premium is added to the promissory note in a SCIN to account for the possibility that the full value of the note may never be paid. This may be done by increasing the amount of the principal to be paid, or by increasing the interest rate above the AFR rate. You should consult a professional to calculate the appropriate premium for either principal or income because the rules concerning this transaction are complex.

Estate Planning Uses of Installment Sales and SCINs

An installment sale can be a good way for parents to remove assets from their estates and transfer them to their children or other beneficiaries. Payments on the note can be used to satisfy the parents' income requirements during the term of the note. If interest rates are low and income requirements are likewise low, the note could call for interest-only payments with a balloon payment at the end of the term, which makes the purchase very affordable in most cases. Installment sales can also be a good way for parents to transfer illiquid closely held business interests to their children, in which case, the utility of the installment sale may be heightened by leveraging discounts on the assets transferred due to transfer restrictions and illiquidity.

Another good use for an installment sale in the estate planning context is a sale to an intentionally defective grantor trust (IDGT) for the benefit of the seller's children. During the seller's lifetime, there is no income tax due on the sale. However, for income tax purposes, the seller will continue to be taxed on income generated by the asset. The payment of income tax on earnings is effectively a tax-free gift to the children, which substantially increases the total wealth transferred. There is a difference of opinion among tax practitioners about whether or not the accrued gain on the assets sold will need to be recognized if the principal amount due is cancelled due to the seller's death.

Henry C. Weatherby, JD, ChFC, CLU, CEBS, focuses on Business, Estate Planning, Elder Law, Estate and Trust Settlement. Value to clients comes from being a concerned, informed, thoughtful advisor.

CHAPTER 41

Private Annuities – a Simple Strategy for Estate Planning, Business Succession Planning, and Asset Protection

RYLAND F. MAHATHEY (Boca Raton, Florida)

A sale for a private annuity describes a sale of property in exchange for a privately issued unsecured annuity contract under which a series of payments is made to the seller or annuitant (hereinafter Annuitant) usually for the Annuitant's lifetime. A private annuity is issued by a private individual or obligor, typically a family member; whereas a commercial annuity is issued by an organization in the business of issuing annuities, such as an insurance company. Such a transaction may be useful for estate planning, business succession planning, and asset protection purposes. Most often, appreciated property is sold by a family member in the senior generation to children, or to a trust for their benefit, in exchange for the privately annuity.

ESTATE PLANNING CONSIDERATIONS

For estate tax purposes, the value of property sold for a private annuity is removed from the Annuitant's gross estate. Further, and perhaps more importantly, after the transfer is complete, any appreciation or earnings from such property is now outside of the Annuitant's estate. At the Annuitant's death, the annuity obligation terminates and similar to a Self-Canceling Installment Note (SCIN) nothing is included in the Annuitant's gross estate. In effect, appreciating property that would otherwise be included in the Annuitant's gross estate and subject to estate tax has been converted into a life estate, which will not be included in the Annuitant's gross estate.

A private annuity is a means of transferring wealth between generations without gift tax consequences or immediate income tax consequences (but see discussion of the IRS Proposed Regulations below). Also, because the annuity calculation is based on the Internal Revenue Code (IRC) Section 7520 rate in effect at the time of the annuity and the Annuitant's life expectancy, this strategy may be particularly attractive if the Annuitant has less than a normal life expectancy; in effect creating a bargain purchase for the buyer or obligor. However, IRS actuarial tables cannot be used to value the annuity if the Annuitant is known to have an incurable illness or other deteriorating physical condition, such that there is at least a 50% probability that the Annuitant will die within one year.

Another advantage of a private annuity is that the Annuitant receives a stream of payments or cash flow for life. A private annuity may, in effect, provide a means of generating cash flow from otherwise non-income producing property.

Business Succession Planning

In certain circumstances, the private annuity strategy may also serve as an effective means of succession planning or exit planning for a closely held business. The private annuity can be used to transfer business ownership interests, either in increments or all at the same time, from the owner to junior family members without gift tax consequences, while providing the owner with a cash flow for life generated from the cash flow of the business. Given possible immediate income tax recognition as discussed below, it is advisable to obtain a valuation of the business interests from a qualified business appraiser. Such an appraisal should take into consideration various valuation discounts so that the resulting valuation will be the lowest possible supportable value. To this end it may be possible to structure the transaction to achieve significant valuation discounts either through the sale of minority ownership interests, or possibly by contributing the business ownership interests to a Family Limited Partnership or Limited Liability Company prior to the sale.

Asset Protection Possibilities

In some states, such as Florida, an annuity is protected from creditors. Florida Statute 222.14 provides that proceeds from an annuity contract issued to a Florida resident are not subject to attachment, garnishment, or legal process in favor of any creditor of the beneficiary of the contract. The Florida courts have broadly construed this statutory exemption to include both commercial annuities and privately issued annuities between family members. Further, under Florida law there is no limitation on the amount of the annuity that may be protected. Therefore, converting individually owned property, which may be subject to the claims of future creditors, to a private annuity, is a means of asset protection.

Income Tax Consequences

In the past, if appreciated property were exchanged for a private annuity, any capital gain would be postponed and recognized by the Annuitant over his or her lifetime as a portion of each annuity payment received. The IRS approved of this result in Revenue Ruling 69-74. As a result, a private annuity was a particularly useful strategy to transfer highly appreciated property with a large built-in capital gain and defer recognition of that gain.

However, on October 18, 2006, the IRS issued Proposed Regulation Sections 1.72-6(e) and 1.1001-1(j) that generally would require gain (or loss) to be recognized immediately when the property is exchanged for the annuity contract (unless the property exchanged is cash). When finalized, the Proposed Regulations would be applicable to private annuity transactions after October 18, 2006, or after April 18, 2007 where an unsecured annuity contract is issued by an individual. Although there may be changes to the Proposed Regulations which carve out exceptions for private annuities before the Regulations become final, these new rules could make other estate freeze strategies such as installment sales or SCINs more attractive, although each of these strategies also produce income tax consequences to the Annuitant's estate or beneficiaries. Also of concern is whether the capital gain tax rate, currently at a historically low 15%, will increase in the near future.

EXAMPLE

To illustrate the workings of a private annuity, assume an Annuitant, age 60, sells appreciated property with a fair market value of $5 million and a tax basis of $1 million to a junior family member for a lifetime annuity, payable at the end of each year. Based on the Annuitant's life expectancy and a 4.2% Section 7520 rate in effect for August 2008, the Annuitant will be entitled to annual annuity payments of $389,363 for almost 24 years. Each annual annuity payment will consist of a nontaxable return of capital and taxable ordinary income of $210,971 and $178,392, respectively.

Following the Regulations, the Annuitant would be required to pay capital gains tax of approximately $600,000, calculated at 15% on the $4 million capital gain. However, the potential federal estate tax savings, assuming the Annuitant is in the 45% marginal estate tax bracket, is $2,250,000, less the increase in estate tax due to the receipt and retention of incoming annuity payments. Upon the Annuitant's death, the annuity obligation terminates and nothing is included in the Annuitant's gross estate. Finally, any appreciation, growth, and earnings from the property after it is sold for the annuity is outside of the Annuitant's gross estate.

Advantages

1. The value of property sold for a private annuity is removed from the Annuitant's gross estate.

2. All appreciation and/or earnings from the annuity property after the sale are outside of the Annuitant's estate and not subject to estate tax.

3. Upon the Annuitant's death, the annuity obligation terminates and nothing is included in the Annuitant's gross estate.

4. A private annuity may result in a bargain sale when the Annuitant's actual life expectancy is less than his or her actuarially calculated life expectancy.

Disadvantages

1. Uncertainty concerning IRS Regulations which require immediate recognition of income upon sale of property for the private annuity.

2. The Annuity is generally unsecured.

Other Considerations

The private annuity may be a particularly useful technique to ensure certain property remains inside the family, which may be vital if the property consists of ownership interests in a family-owned or closely held business. However, the Annuitant should be comfortable transferring the property to the obligor, given that the annuity is unsecured. In most cases, the Annuitant should have other assets available to live on in case the annuity is not paid.

Ryland F. Mahathey practices primarily in the areas of sophisticated estate, asset protection, and business succession planning. He is a CPA and holds an LL.M in Taxation from the University of Florida.

Sale to an Intentionally Defective Grantor Trust vs. a Grantor Retained Annuity Trust

CHARACTERISTIC	IDGT	GRAT
Income stream	To grantor for term of the note	To grantor for term of the trust
Interest rate used to value property transferred	Section 1274 AFR	Section 7520 rate (120% of Section 1274 AFR)
Effect of death of grantor during term	Value of note included in grantor's estate; Post-transfer appreciation in value of underlying property is removed from grantor's estate	Entire value of property held in trust included in grantor's estate, including post-transfer appreciation in value
Allowance of balloon note payments	May be allowed; If note not fully repaid at death of seller, there may be income tax consequences	Not allowed as annuity payments in one year may not exceed 120% of the payments made in the immediately preceding year
Amount of taxable gift	None if note equals FMV of property transferred	If properly structured, zeroed out GRATs with no taxable gifts are possible
Subsequent increase in the value of the property transferred by an IRS audit	Results in dollar-for-dollar increase in amount of taxable gifts	Will not result in a dollar-for-dollar increase in amount of taxable gifts because value of retained annuity interest also increases
Assumption of risk if value of assets decreases	Beneficiaries	Grantor
Disclosure of sale	Required on federal estate tax return (Form 706)	None required if grantor dies after term of trust

CHARITABLE TRUSTS

CHAPTER 42

Outright Gifts

JACKSON DOGGETTE (Tampa, Florida)

Y ou are an adult. You may be young. You may be old. You may be single. You may be married. You may be in a relationship considered to be nontraditional. You may have children. You may not have children. You may own real estate. You may not own any real estate but you do own some type of property. You may not have much. You may be rich. You may be healthy. You may be sick. Whatever your situation, you have decided you want some professional to make decisions about the things you own or over which you have stewardship.

Many people believe that consulting with an estate planning attorney is only important when you have decided to take steps to plan for your death. However, the word is getting out that estate planning is also about making plans that affect you while you are alive. So, you select an estate planning lawyer, and make an appointment to get some advice. At your appointment, your lawyer leads you through a discussion of, among other things, what might happen if you do not establish a plan for the things you own. Perhaps the government takes too much in taxes, or the property is distributed to heirs in ways that do not reflect your wishes. Because you do not like the results of that decision, you begin to decide what you want to do with your material possessions. Who should get them? How should they get them? When should they get them?

You may already know whom you want to receive your property. One of your options is to give your possessions away as outright gifts. You even have options regarding when and how you give outright gifts.

A gift of property, whether real or personal, is a voluntary and complete transfer from the one who owns the property to someone else without any requirements or strings attached. That means there is no payment or other consideration or expectation of anything in return for the gift.

Who can legally give a gift? The owner, who can be a person, a corporation, or another legal entity the law recognizes as eligible to give a gift.

Who can legally receive a gift? Like an owner, the recipient can be a person, a corporation, or another legal entity the law recognizes as eligible to receive a gift. There are four requirements to meet to legally give a gift. The owner of the property must have the capacity to give the property as a gift and the intent to give the gift. The gift must be delivered to or for the recipient, and it must be accepted by the recipient. Therefore, capacity, intent, delivery, and acceptance are the four requirements for a gift to be considered a legal gift.

You have options regarding when to give an outright gift. You can give the gift while you are living. This is called an inter vivos gift. You can give the gift after you are dead through a written instrument. This is called a testamentary gift.

There are some advantages in giving outright gifts while you are living. First, you can experience the joy and good feelings that come with seeing someone receive and benefit from your gift. Second, you remove the gifted property from your estate. This might have positive tax consequences for you. This chapter is not designed to detail those advantages. However, those advantages may exist depending upon your circumstances.

Imagine giving a gift to your favorite charity which is advancing a mission about which you are passionate. That gift may be in the form of money, stocks, bonds, real estate, or anything else you own. Doesn't the very thought of giving it while you can see the good it will generate inspire joyful feelings even as you are thinking about it now?

Think about the happiness you promote by giving a gift to your spouse or significant other, your children, or a dear friend. Can you feel the warmth and gladness right now? That is probably the greatest advantage of giving an outright gift inter vivos. You are alive to enjoy the results of it.

However, there are some disadvantages in giving outright gifts while you are alive. First, you no longer have control of the property. Second, the property may be of a type that appreciates over time and you may wish for the recipient to benefit from the appreciated value of the gift at a later time. Third, there may be some negative tax consequences for you or the recipient in giving the property away during your life.

You can give the outright gift as a testamentary gift, meaning, through a testament or will after you are dead. How do you accomplish this? You might simply state what the gift is and who receives it in the language of your will. The will might say something like: *"I give my stamp collection to Joe Jones, my son."* Another way to give an outright gift by will is to use what is called a Memorandum for Distribution of Personal Property. An outright gift using a Memorandum for Distribution of Personal Property requires two steps. First, the language in your will might say something like:

I give all of my remaining tangible personal property, together with any insurance policies covering such property and claims under such policies in accordance with a "Memorandum for Distribution of Personal Property" or other similar writing directing the disposition of such property, which shall be dated and signed by me.

Second, you write down what you want to give and to whom you want to give the personal property on a separate piece of paper stating what the gift is, who gets the gift, and sign and date the paper. Talk with your lawyer, however, before you attempt to give an outright gift in this manner.

There are some advantages in giving testamentary gifts. First, you get to enjoy the property all the time you are alive. Second, you can direct who gets your property after you have no use for it any longer. Third, there may be some tax advantages for you and/or the recipient (such as a step up in basis) by waiting to give the outright gift through your will.

There are also some disadvantages in making testamentary gifts. First, you will not experience the joy and good feelings that come from seeing someone receive and use the outright gift from you. Second, you do not effectively remove the property from your estate before the outright gift is completed. This could have negative tax consequences. Third, the recipient could predecease you and never receive the gift.

We have briefly explored the outright gift. Whether you give an outright gift during life or after death to a person, charity, government, or other legal entity, giving is ultimately necessary because "you can't take it with you."

Doggette Law Firm, P.L. is an estate planning and nonprofit corporate counsel law firm designed to meet the non-litigation, transactional legal needs of families and nonprofit organizations.

CHAPTER 43

Charitable Remainder Trusts
(How to Benefit Yourself and Others)

STEPHEN J. BAILEY (Anniston, Alabama)

WHAT IS A CHARITABLE REMAINDER TRUST?

A Charitable Remainder Trust (CRT) is a way you can donate to your favorite cause while benefiting yourself and your family. It is a powerful income tax and estate tax planning tool that can:

- Defer capital gains taxes on the sale of appreciated assets;

- Provide you with a new source of income;

- Provide you a substantial current income tax charitable deduction; and

- Provide you future estate tax deductions.

A CRT delivers best results when you have a highly appreciated asset — such as real estate or stocks — that provide little or no income. Owning such assets is a double-edged sword. You cannot sell the assets without experiencing the costly bite of state and federal capital gains taxes. On the other hand, if the asset is still in your estate when you die, it will increase your estate taxes. Of course, you could donate the asset directly to charity and gain an immediate income tax charitable deduction. This would reduce the value of your estate — and thus future estate taxes — as well as avoid capital gains taxes, but you miss out on any income the asset could generate. The CRT neatly overcomes these problems.

HOW DOES A CRT WORK?

Step 1

You and your estate planning attorney create a CRT. You, or whomever you designate, is designated as trustee of the CRT so you can remain in control of the CRT's investment decisions. The terms of the CRT provide that it will pay you an income stream (more about this later!) based on either a certain term of years (not to exceed 20) or over one or more lifetimes (whichever you choose to meet your needs). The CRT also provides that whenever the term or lifetimes are over, the remaining trust assets, if any, will go to a charity or charities of your choosing.

Step 2

You transfer a highly appreciated asset that you cannot afford to sell because of potential income taxes to the CRT in return for the trust's obligation to provide you with an income stream over the term or lifetimes you choose, in an amount that is actuarially computed using the expected length of the income stream and the expected earnings rate. The annual income stream cannot be less than 5% of the asset's value and may range upward to as high as 50% depending on the term over which you have chosen to be paid and the prevailing interest rate.

Step 3

The CRT sells the appreciated asset but pays no tax because of its favorable tax status.

Step 4

The CRT, from its liquid resources provided by the sale, pays you an income stream for the term or lifetimes you have designated.

Step 5

After the term for which the CRT is obligated to pay you is over, it distributes any remaining assets to the charities you have designated and the CRT terminates.

SO, HOW MUCH IS MY INCOME STREAM?

Your income stream from the CRT depends on how you choose to be paid. You may choose to have the CRT pay you a fixed annuity that equals a percentage of the fair market value of the assets transferred to the CRT, or you may choose to have the CRT pay you a percentage of the fair market value of the CRT's assets as they are revalued annually.

Conservative investors who want a predictable income year after year may prefer the Charitable Remainder Annuity Trust — or CRAT for short. A CRAT will provide you a fixed annual income regardless of the investment performance of its assets. Because your tax deductions and income are based on the value of the asset as of the day it is transferred to the Trust, the CRAT is probably better suited if you suspect the CRAT's assets may lose value in the years ahead.

Regardless of the economic winds, your income is fixed. So, if the CRAT's assets do not earn enough to pay your annual income, more principal will be used to make up the difference. On the other hand, if the markets turn bullish and the CRAT's assets outperform your expectations, the surplus will be added to the principal and ultimately benefit your charities.

The chief drawback of the CRAT is also its strength; it protects you against swings in the financial markets. Thus, in a stagnant or declining market, you come out ahead. However, in a strong market experiencing investment growth, the charity will ultimately benefit the most. That's why you may prefer the Charitable Remainder Unitrust if you hold more bullish views on investing.

A CRUT offers a couple of advantages over the CRAT. First, unlike the CRAT, you may make as many contributions as you like. And for the sake of determining annual income, it is the asset's current fair market value (revalued annually), not its value on the date it was transferred to the CRUT, which is used in the calculations.

As for its income opportunities, the CRUT allows you to ride the financial markets and enjoy the investment performance of the CRUT's assets. That means, of course, that in some years you may receive less, in other years more. When lean years keep you from receiving your full due, a "make-up provision" can allow for additional income in future years to make up for the shortfall.

A CRUT requires you to receive a minimum income of 5% of the asset's current fair market value, and not more than 50%. You can also opt to receive your chosen percentage or the trust's net income, whichever is less.

An example may help you understand the confluence of your income tax charitable deduction, estate tax charitable deduction, and income stream.

ASSUMF:

- You and your spouse are both 70 years old.

- You own a non-income-producing farm with a $10,000 tax basis that is worth $1 million today.

- You would like to generate some retirement cash flow from the farm for both you and your spouse.

- You have a taxable estate.

- You can earn 5% income on invested assets.

- You have identified the farm as an underperforming asset that you want to re-deploy.

The chart below compares alternative courses of action you may take regarding the farm.

	DO NOTHING	YOU SELL FARM AND REINVEST NET PROCEEDS @ 5%	ESTABLISH CRAT AND THEN CRAT SELLS FARM	ESTABLISH CRUT AND THEN CRUT SELLS FARM
Your income stream after sale	$0	$40,100[1]	$60,280[2]	$143,710[3]
Your income tax charitable deduction	$0	$0	$263,565	$100,010
Net value inherited by your heirs	$550,000[4]	$441,100[5]	$0[6]	$0

The chart demonstrates that you can significantly increase your cash flow and also receive a significant income tax charitable deduction. However, your family receives no part of the farm, so they have, in fact, lost $550,000 of their expected inheritance. How can we remedy this for them? By taking a portion of the excess cash flow from the CRAT or CRUT and buying $550,000 of life insurance in an Irrevocable Life Insurance Trust that will not be subject to estate tax at your death.

DID YOU KNOW YOU CAN ALSO USE A CRUT AS AN ANCILLARY RETIREMENT PLAN?

Imagine, instead of the example above, that you are a 50 year old couple who have maxed out their retirement contributions and would to like to put more aside for retirement. How can we do this using a CRUT?

Bear with me — to understand how this works, you need to know about some options that can be built into a CRUT.

As we have seen, the standard CRUT pays you (or whomever you wish to designate) an amount determined by multiplying a fixed percentage of the net fair market value (FMV) of the trust assets, valued each year. On the death of the last beneficiary (or at the end of the trust term if the income term is measured by a term of years), the charity gets the remainder.

You may, however, construct a CRUT that pays only the trust's income if the actual income is less than the stated percentage multiplied by the trust's FMV. Deficiencies in distributions (i.e., when the CRUT income is less than the stated percentage) are made up in later years, when and if the trust income exceeds the stated percentage. This type of trust is called a Net Income Makeup Charitable Remainder Unitrust (NIMCRUT).

So assume you placed the above farm into a NIMCRUT at age 50. The NIMCRUT just holds the farm until you retire at age 65, and then it sells the farm. If the farm appreciates at 8% per year, it will be worth about $2,937,194 in 15 years.

During the intervening years, before the farm is sold, the NIMCRUT will not make any distributions to you because its net income is zero, and therefore less than the 6.864% computed for the standard CRUT. In the fifteenth year, when you retire (or really any time you choose), the farm is sold, creating a capital gain of 2,927,194 ($2,937,194-10,000)[7]. Now the trust can start making up payments to you that were skipped in earlier years when the NIMCRUT had no income. So in year 15 you receive $1,863,721 to "make up" for prior distributions not made and then you start receiving a unitrust amount that starts at $53,674.

What if you don't need the large make-up distribution? What if, instead, we had the NIMCRUT convert into a standard CRUT upon the sale of the farm? This is known as a FLIP-CRUT. In this case, the percentage is recalculated on the increased amount in the CRUT ($2,937,194) and results in an initial payment of $201,609.

SUMMARY

As you can see from our few examples, the CRT is a very flexible and powerful income tax and estate tax planning tool. Using it in your arsenal of tax planning techniques can truly benefit you while doing good for others.

Our mission is to honor and serve God by loving and protecting families. We do this by managing client risk through asset protection, estate, and VA and Medicaid benefit planning.

1. Net proceeds after 20% capital gains tax (1,000,000 -($1,000,000-10,000) x 20%)) invested at 5%.

2. This same payment is made for every year of you and your spouse's joint lifetime (21.8 years under current life expectancy tables).

3. This is the first year's payment — each subsequent payment will equal 14.371% of the balance at the end of the previous year.

4. $1,000,000 asset value less $450,000 estate tax.

5. $802,000 after income tax value less $360,900 estate tax.

6. The assets of the CRAT or CRUT are excluded from your estate and revert to the charitable beneficiary.

7. $3,172,159 sales price less $10,000 basis in the farm.

CHAPTER 44

The Charitable Lead Trust

SCOTT GUNDERSON (Reno, Nevada)

Would you like to support one or more charities at your death without reducing your children's or grandchildren's inheritance? Would you like to reduce the estate or gift tax on the transfer to your children to zero? Would you like to create a fund that can be available to benefit your family for generations to come — without ever being subject to the estate or gift tax?

The Charitable Lead Trust (CLT) might be right for you.

HOW DOES IT WORK?

The CLT is a split-interest trust. That is, the value of the trust is split into two components, income and remainder. During the term of the CLT the income is paid to a qualified charity and at the end of the term the remainder is paid to individual (non-charity) beneficiaries, generally your children or grandchildren. The gift of the remainder interest is a taxable gift by the donor to the individual (non-charity) beneficiaries. The value of the gift is determined by subtracting the net present value of the stream of cash flow payments made to the charity during the term of the trust from the amount initially contributed to the trust. The variables in the calculation are the amount paid to the charity each year, the number of years those payments are made, the Applicable Federal Rate (AFR) in effect at the time of the initial contribution to the CLT, and the structure of the CLT.

The CLT can be structured in one of two ways either as an "annuity" trust or as a "unitrust." An annuity trust pays a fixed amount each year to the charity beneficiary based upon a percentage of the initial value of the contribution. A unitrust pays a fixed percentage each year of the then current value of the trust to the charity beneficiary. The structure selected greatly impacts the value of the remainder interest paid to the non-charity.

EXAMPLE:

Charitable Lead Annuity Trust (CLAT)

If you contribute $1 million to a CLAT which by its terms will pay out 7% of the contribution each year to a charity for 20 years, the remainder amount (the taxable gift amount) is $65,304. If the assets in the trust grow at 10%, the actual remainder balance paid to your children is $2,718,250. Your generosity also results in $1,400,000 being paid to your favorite charity. If you extended the CLAT term to 23 years, the remainder value (taxable gift amount) is $0 and the actual remainder value to your children is $3,386,291, with $1,610,000 going to charity. The zero remainder value would hold for any size gift (e.g., a $10 million gift to a CLAT with a 7% payment to charity for 23 years will result in a zero remainder value).

Charitable Lead Unitrust (CLUT)

If you contribute $1 million to a CLUT which by its terms will pay out 7% of the value of the CLUT each year to a charity for 20 years, the remainder amount (the taxable gift amount) is $248,914. If the assets in the trust grow at 10%, the actual remainder balance paid to your children is $1,806,111, with $1,880,926 being paid to charity. If you extended the CLUT term to 30 years, the remainder value (taxable gift amount) is still $124,207 and the actual remainder value to your children is $2,427,262, with a whopping $3,330,279 going to charity.

Thus, it is possible with a CLAT to transfer any amount of assets to your children at a zero gift or estate tax cost with the right combination of annuity rate, term, and applicable federal rate.

It is not possible to reduce the transfer tax to zero using a CLUT because of the theoretical impossibility of reducing the remainder to zero. This outcome occurs because the most the trust can pay to a charity is a percentage of its holdings at the time of the payment. Since there will always be something left in the trust after every payment, the trust cannot be exhausted so there will always be a gift or estate tax associated with the gift to a CLUT.

CLAT OR CLUT?

Even though it is not possible to reduce the remainder value of a CLUT to zero, as is possible with the CLAT, the CLUT has a significant advantage over the CLAT if the intended beneficiaries are your grandchildren. Transfers to grandchildren are subject to a tax in addition to the gift or estate tax, called the Generation-Skipping Transfer Tax (GSTT). This tax is imposed at the highest marginal gift or estate tax rate (currently 45%). You have a lifetime credit ($2 million in 2008, and $3.5 million in 2009) that you can apply against the GSTT. You can apply your GSTT credit to a CLUT but not to a CLAT.

So in the above examples, you could apply $248,914 of your GSTT credit to the CLUT at the time it is created and the trust would then be GSTT exempt. That is, it would not be subject to GSTT at the time it distributes its assets to your grandchildren, or even to subsequent generations. However, you cannot apply any amount of GSTT credit to the CLAT at the time it is created. In fact, you must apply the GSTT credit at the time it terminates and is distributed to your grandchildren. In the above example, application of even your full $2 million of GSTT credit to the CLAT in year 20 would not be enough to exempt the entire balance of $2,718,250, so a portion of every distribution from the CLAT to your grandchildren is subject to an additional GSTT.

WHAT CHARITIES CAN YOU CHOOSE?

You can choose any qualified 501(c)(3) charitable organization you like. You can choose more than one charity. Most commonly though, the charity is a family foundation run and managed by the family to support a variety of the family's charitable goals.

PLANNING OPTIONS

Commonly, CLTs are put in place at your death. These are called Testamentary CLTs. They operate in the same way as CLTs you set up during your life, but defer the gifts to your children and grandchildren for many years after your death. Often, a grantor will obtain life insurance and hold it in a life insurance trust for the benefit of children or grandchildren, so that the children or grandchildren receive an inheritance at the death of the grantor with no need to wait an extended time to receive the benefits of the CLT.

Many times a grantor will contribute interests in Limited Partnerships or Limited Liability Companies to a CLT because these interests may be subject to valuation discounts. The discounts have the effect of increasing the potential annuity or unitrust payout rate, resulting in a shorter term for the CLT and earlier distribution to children or grandchildren.

If you prefer a CLUT, it often makes sense to establish the CLUT in a state which has abolished the Rule against Perpetuities so that the CLUT can benefit not just your children and grandchildren, but subsequent generations as well.

SUMMARY

The Charitable Lead Trust (CLT) is one of the most powerful tools in the estate planner's arsenal for estate or gift tax planning and for providing large contributions to one or more charities. Properly drafted and implemented, this strategy can reduce estate or gift taxes to zero for any size gift. A CLT can also provide the means to create and preserve multi-generational family wealth.

Scott Gunderson is a Certified Estate Planning, Trust & Probate Specialist by the State Bar of California Board of Legal Specialization. Admitted in California and Nevada, he focuses on estate, charitable, business, and asset protection planning.

Charitable Trusts Compared

	CHARITABLE LEAD TRUST	CHARITABLE REMAINDER TRUST	POOLED-INCOME FUND
Purpose	Property is transferred to a trust that distributes income to a charitable beneficiary for a period of time or for the life or lives of designated individuals. Remainder interest reverts back to donor or some other noncharitable beneficiary.	Split interest gift in which donor receives either a fixed or variable annuity for a period of time not to exceed 20 years or for the life or lives of designated individuals and remainder goes to charity.	Investment fund created and maintained by target charity. Pools property from all contributors and pays a pro rata share of income earned by commingled trust assets.
Income Tax Consequences	**Grantor trust:** If created during life, grantor claims income and receives charitable deduction for the present value of the total anticipated income during the lead period. **Nongrantor trust with remainder beneficiaries other than grantor:** Grantor does not claim income and cannot receive charitable deduction.	If created during life, donor receives immediate charitable contribution deduction for FMV less present value of retained interest. Annual income is taxable to the income beneficiary.	If created during life, donor receives immediate charitable contribution deduction for FMV less present value of retained interest. Annual income is taxable to the income beneficiary.
Estate Tax Consequences	**Grantor trust:** If created during life, the value of the asset is generally out of the estate. **Nongrantor:** The value of the asset is out of the estate.	Value of property is included in gross estate, but an equivalent charitable deduction reduces the taxable estate amount to zero.	Value of property is included in gross estate, but an equivalent charitable deduction reduces the taxable estate amount to zero.
Planning Opportunities	Noncharitable beneficiary can be grantor, spouse, child, or other person. Good for clients who have a large amount of highly appreciating assets and can forgo the income from these assets. When interest rates are low, this increases the valuation of the deductible interest donation.	Contributions allowed only at setup for CRAT. CRUT allows contributions after initial setup. While CRAT provides a fixed annuity, CRUT can provide a hedge against inflation. When interest rates go up, the deductible charitable remainder interest goes up.	No tax-free securities can be contributed. A good choice for those who do not want to set up and maintain a trust. Many colleges and universities maintain these.

Retirement Savings Vehicles:
Charitable Remainder Trusts vs. Qualified Plans

	CHARITABLE REMAINDER TRUST	QUALIFIED PLAN
Subject to ERISA.		X
Subject to Internal Revenue Code rules on coverage and contribution requirements.		X
Contributions are fully deductible within prescribed limits.		X
Full amount of assets is available at retirement.		X
All or a portion of the distributions may consist of tax-free income.	X	
Borrowing funds from the account is not subject to an excise tax on self-dealing.		X
Distributions prior to age 59 ½ are not subject to the 10% excise tax.	X	
Upon death, remaining balances passes to the beneficiaries of the participant.		X

CHAPTER 45

Charitable Deductions and Contributions of Partial Interests in Property

DAVID STRAUS (Las Vegas, Nevada)

The transfer of a "partial interest" in property refers to one of two types of transfers: transfers of an undivided interest in the transferor's entire interest in the property; and transfers of term, annuity, life estate, or remainder interests, so-called split interests, in property contributed in trust or not in trust.

INCOME AND TRANSFER TAX DEDUCTION FOR TRANSFERS NOT IN TRUST[1]

General Rule

Internal Revenue Code (IRC) Section 170(f)(3)(A) provides the general rule that contributions of partial interests in property, not in a trust, are not deductible.[2] Note that there is no deduction allowed for contributing use of an item of property, which is considered a partial interest.[3] Congress disallows a deduction for the use of property to prevent a double tax benefit to the donor: a lack of taxation on the income from the property used by the charity; and a charitable deduction for full rental value of the property.[4] Likewise, an interest-free loan of money to a charity is not deductible because it is a partial interest in property.[5] However, there are exceptions provided in IRC Section 170(f)(3)(B) for remainder interests in a residence or a farm, or an undivided portion of the donor's entire interest in the property, or a conservation contribution.[6]

Undivided Fraction or All of the Donor's Interest

An undivided portion of the donor's entire interest in the item of property refers to a fraction or percentage of each and every substantial interest or right the donor owns in the property.[7] Assume a donor owns a life estate in a building and donates a fraction of the life estate to a charity. The contribution of the fractional interest, not in trust, is deductible by the donor because it is a fraction of each substantial interest or right the donor has in the property.[8] Likewise, if the donor contributed the entire life estate, not in trust, it would be deductible.[9]

If the owner of an annuity interest in a charitable remainder annuity trust, presumably a unitrust, contributes that annuity interest to the remainder charitable beneficiary, not in trust, it is treated as a deductible contribution by the donor.[10]

If a donor gives a life estate to one charity and the remainder interest in the property to another charity, the contribution qualifies as a deduction of the donor's entire interest in the property at its fair market value.[11] However, if property is intentionally divided into separate interests to circumvent the partial interest rules, any such contribution is denied a deduction.[12]

Remainder Interest in a Residence or Farm

While a deduction is allowed for the contribution of a remainder interest in a residence or a farm, not in trust, a deduction is not allowed for the proceeds of the sale of the remainder interest if the remainder interest is required to be sold.[13] The residence may be any residence of the donor and does not need to be the principal residence of the donor.[14]

> A farm is defined as: any land used by the taxpayer or his tenant for the production of crops, fruits, or other agricultural products or for the sustenance of livestock. The term 'livestock' includes cattle, hogs, horses, mules, donkeys, sheep, goats, captive fur-bearing animals, chickens, turkeys, pigeons, and other poultry. A farm includes the improvements thereon.[15]

If property is subject to a mortgage, it is treated as a bargain sale. If the donor continues to make mortgage payments, they constitute additional contributions deductible to the extent attributable to the remainder interest.[16] Depreciation must be taken into account on the contribution of a remainder interest in real property.[17] The specific rules for depreciation are beyond the scope of this section.

Qualified Conservation Contribution

> A qualified conservation contribution is defined in IRC Section 170(h) as a contribution:
>
> a) of a qualified real property interest;
>
> b) to a qualified organization;
>
> c) exclusively for conservation purposes.

A qualified real property interest is one of: 1) the entire interest of a donor other than a qualified mineral interest; 2) a remainder interest; and 3) a restriction (granted in perpetuity) on the use which may be made of the real property.[18] A qualified organization is any of: 1) a governmental unit or a publicly supported charity described in clause (v) or (vi) of subsection (b)(1)(A) of IRC Section 170; 2) a publicly supported organization described in section 501(c)(3) which meets the requirements of section 509(a)(2); or 3) a support organization that meets the requirements of section 509(a)(3) and is controlled by a governmental unit or publicly supported charity,[19] that uses the property for a conservation purpose as defined in IRC Section 170(h)(4).

Limitation on Charitable Contributions of Tangible Personal Property

For contributions made after August 17, 2006, IRC Section 170(o) limits the deduction for contributions of partial interests in tangible personal property, limiting the ability of donors to make fractional donations, or term interests, of art and other valuable tangible personal property to charities unless the charities ultimately own or have exclusive use of the entire property, as part of its exempt purpose, within the earlier of the death of the donor or ten years.

INCOME AND TRANSFER TAX DEDUCTIONS FOR PARTIAL INTERESTS CONTRIBUTED TO A TRUST[20]

Qualified Annuity, Unitrust Interests, or Pooled Income Funds

No deduction is allowed for a partial interest, split interest, contribution to a trust, or typically a life estate, term, or remainder interest, unless the transfer is to a charitable remainder annuity trust or unitrust as described in IRC Section 664,[21] a charitable income trust (charitable lead annuity or unitrust) pursuant to IRC Section 170(f)(2)(B), or a pooled income fund under IRC Section 642(c)(5).

The rules for deducting partial interests for income, estate, and gift tax purposes are quite complex and require additional research beyond simply reading this chapter.

David A. Straus, JD, LLM, CPA, is AV rated by the Martindale Hubble Law Directory and works out of Las Vegas, Nevada. He focuses on Estate, Charitable, and Asset Protection Planning.

---

1. References to the Internal Revenue Code (Code) are to the Code of 1986 as amended to the date of publication.

2. The same general rules also apply for the gift tax deduction under Code Section 2522(c)(2) and Treasury Regulation (Reg.) 25.2522(c)-3(c)(2) (See RR 86-60 infra.) For estate taxes, see Code Section 2055(e)(2) and Reg. 20.2055-2(e)(2)(i),(ii),(iii), and (iv).

3. Code Section 170(f)(3)(b).

4. Id.

5. See H.R. Report No. 9-413 pt 1 (1969), 1969-3, C.B. 200 237

6. Reg. 1.170A-7(d)(Ex. 3)

7. Code Section 170(f)(3)(B)(i)(ii).

8. Treasury Regulation (Reg.) 1.170A-7(b)(1).

9. Id.

10. Id.

11. Revenue Ruling 86-60 1986-1 C.B. 302

12. Reg. 1.170A-7(a)(2)(ii)

13. Reg. 1.170A-7(a)(2)(i)

14. Rev. Rul. 77-305, 1977-2 C.B. 72, but see Blackford Est. v. Comm., 77 TC 1246 (1981), acq., 1983-2 C.B. 1, where the remainders under state law could have insisted on the remainder interest rather than the proceeds of sale.

15. Rev. Rul. 75-420, 1975-2 C.B. 78 (Vacation residence qualified)

16. Reg. 1.170A-7(b)(4)

17. PLR 9329017

18. Code Section 170(f)(4)

19. Code Section 170(h)(2)

20. Code Section 170(h)(3)

21. The same general rules also apply for the gift tax deduction under Code Section 2522(c)(2)((A)(B) and Reg. 25.2522(c)-3(c)(2)(v)(vi). For estate taxes, see Reg.20.2055-2(e)(2)(v)(vi).

22. Code Section 170(f)(2)(A).

CHAPTER 46

Conservation Easements – How to Give Your Land Away but Still Use It

MATTHEW BROWN (Irvine, California)

WHAT IS A CONSERVATION EASEMENT?

Do you own a ranch in Montana or forest land in Colorado? Do you overlook that perfect canyon view, that serene spot at the beach, or that to-die-for piece of lakefront property? Whatever piece of splendor you own, you probably want to see it preserved and transferred to future generations. A conservation easement may be just the right planning tool.

You can create a conservation easement by giving your land (or just a piece of your land) to charity while retaining extensive rights to use the land. You will also receive a charitable income tax deduction and can pass the land to your descendants at a substantially reduced estate tax cost.

WHAT RIGHTS DO I RETAIN?

Envision your land ownership as a bundle of sticks. Each stick represents a right to do something with your property. Gifting a conservation easement simply relinquishes one or more development rights. But you, and ultimately your descendants, retain the right to enjoy many other benefits of land ownership.

You may want to retain hunting rights, the right to build a home, extract minerals, lease the property, or pass the property to your children. The more rights you retain, the less the value of any charitable income tax deduction.

And remember, this is not an all-or-nothing deal. You do not have to give an entire piece of land. You can retain a portion of the land with full development rights and then grant a conservation easement limiting development on your remaining land.

WHAT ARE THE TAX ADVANTAGES?

You may be eligible for both income tax and estate tax benefits. The income tax deduction will be the amount by which the development restrictions reduce the value of your land. The deduction is limited to 50% of your Adjusted Gross Income the year of the gift. If you cannot use the entire deduction the first year, you can carry the deduction forward for an additional 15 years, with the same 50% limitation applying in those years as well.

For estate tax purposes, the value of the land is reduced up to $500,000 by the drop in value created by the development restrictions. Therefore, the estate tax, which is calculated based upon the value of the land, may be reduced by up to $225,000 (assuming a 45% estate tax rate). Of course, conservation easements on larger properties may reduce the value of the land by more than $500,000. But this value reduction would not translate into estate tax savings.

The bottom line is that you can obtain a double tax benefit – you can take an income tax deduction to pass land to your descendants at a drastically reduced estate tax cost.

WHAT KIND OF LAND CAN I GIVE?

You can give any piece of land with significant conservation value. This includes, for example, beach property, ranch property, scenic property, forests, wetlands, and endangered species habitats. Stated more broadly, you must satisfy one of the following conservation purposes:

1. Protection of a relatively natural habitat of fish, wildlife, or plants of a similar ecosystem;

2. Preservation of open space, including farmland and forestland, if the preservation provides a significant public benefit;

3. Preservation of an historically important land area or certified historic structure; or

4. Preservation of land for outdoor recreation for, or education of, the general public.

Some of the preservation-based land grants that have satisfied these tests include:

1. Grants made to preserve land as a public garden;

2. Grants made to preserve farmland to assist a state flood control program;

3. Grants made to preserve forests along a highway to maintain a scenic view from the highway;

4. Grants made to preserve a stretch of undeveloped oceanfront property to maintain a scenic view from the highway; and

5. Grants made to preserve a thin strip of riverfront property, immediately behind which was the landowner's home.

WHO OWNS AND MANAGES THE LAND?

You will continue to own the land. You will bear all of the ownership costs and liabilities, and you will have the right to keep people off of your land. Unless you create a conservation easement allowing the public onto your land, you have no obligation to allow anyone onto your land.

WHERE DO I GIFT THE CONSERVATION EASEMENT?

Private foundations are generally not a fit for conservation easements — not even a friend's private foundation. You should give your conservation easement to a public charity. However, because most public charities are not capable of properly monitoring a conservation easement, it is best if you give your conservation easement to a public charity routinely engaged in conservation efforts with extensive experience in conservation easements. The Nature Conservancy is perhaps the best known organization routinely accepting these types of gifts.

If you gift the conservation easement to a private foundation, you will not receive an income tax deduction. Additionally, you may run into estate tax challenges and/or may violate certain private foundation prohibitions against self-dealing.

HOW LONG DOES IT LAST?

A conservation easement is perpetual, which means it lasts forever. The charity will monitor the property over time and will, if necessary, take legal action to enforce the conservation easement.

SAMPLE LANGUAGE

Conservation easements are long, complex documents. We have reproduced below a statement of purpose from a conservation easement. You will likely see similar language in your own document.

1. *This Conservation Easement assures that the Property will be perpetually preserved in its predominately natural, scenic, historic, agricultural, forested, and open space condition. The Purposes of this Conservation Easement are to protect the Property's natural resource and watershed values; to maintain and enhance biodiversity; to retain quality habitat for native plants and animals, and to maintain and enhance the natural features of the Property. Any uses of the Property that impair or interfere with the Conservation Values are expressly prohibited.*

2. *The Donor is the Owner of the Property and is committed to preserving the Conservation Values of the Property. The Owner agrees to confine use of the Property to activities consistent with the Purposes of this Easement and the preservation of the Conservation Values.*

3. *The Conservancy is a qualified Recipient of this Conservation Easement, is committed to preserving the Conservation Values of the Property, and is committed to upholding the terms of this Conservation Easement. The Conservancy protects natural habitats of fish, wildlife, plants, and the ecosystems that support them. The Conservancy also preserves open spaces, including farms and forests, where such preservation is for the scenic*

enjoyment of the general public or pursuant to clearly delineated governmental conservation policies and where it will yield a significant public benefit.

Matthew Brown is a Partner with the Orange County, California, law firm of Brown & Streza LLP, which provides integrated estate, business, and charitable planning.

CHAPTER 47

Modest Philanthropy – Encouraging Modest Gifts Using "The Expression of Charitable Intentions"

TIMOTHY BORCHERS (Medway, Massachusetts)

In 25 years of advising clients, I have found that given a choice, most clients would like charity to receive some part of their assets when they die. Given the record for generosity among Americans, this finding is not surprising.[1] Nonetheless, without prompting and assistance, most plan to give nothing to charity, even to causes they care deeply about. By removing obstacles to modest giving, however, you can bridge the gap between what you want to give and what you feel you can give.

YOUR LEGACY OF GIVING LOST

Most clients want to leave a legacy besides money.[2] A large inheritance is great, but most clients want their heirs to live responsibly with the resources they receive, large or small. Yet when estate plans are written, the focus is on probate and taxes, with some attention on how to make discretionary spending decisions, with far less attention on motivating heirs to pursue purposes beyond preserving wealth for themselves and their heirs.

Assuming that giving is a value you care about, would you like to be able to transfer that legacy to your heirs? According to the survey cited above, you would. Yet, unless you are truly exemplary, the ideal of giving will not be conveyed merely by example. Your children may associate you with generosity. But, without direction, you can fairly predict that your children will let the ball drop on your causes. Likely they will not catch the spirit and use their windfall to start or boost giving of their own; heirs rarely volunteer to help any cause beyond their own pocketbook.

FRUSTRATED IN GIVING

As important as charitable giving is to ordinary Americans, clients are not knocking down the door to give to charity in their plans. There are many reasons for this phenomenon.

"Charity begins at home." This saying is an excuse to "give it all to the little darlings." Come to think of it, they're not always little and not always darling. Giving is demonstrated at home, but it naturally extends outward as the fervor for helping overflows the domestic confines. Why not encourage that passion?

Fear of short-changing the heirs. It seems that people have guilt around not leaving every last dime to their descendants. But, will they really miss that $1,000, $5,000, or $10,000 out of the $100,000, $500,000, or millions that they likely will inherit? It is not their entitlement, unless you let it be.

Advisors ask the wrong questions. The question (if it gets asked at all), "Do you wish to leave anything to charity?" is usually an afterthought or is saved for those who have no children or who have great wealth. Why should they get all the fun?[3]

Lack of information. You know how to give to your faith, your alma mater, and your community group. But what if your heart goes out to the animals you've seen rescued on TV? You have the urge to help, but you don't know how.[4]

Conflict and competition. You'd like to give to the rescue league, but you already help starving children. It strikes you that you could leave something in your will, but your spouse feels differently.

"Circumstances may change." While living, you base your giving on circumstances, such as the strength of your conviction, your bank balance, tax advantages, and so forth. How can you plan ahead to give to causes and institutions that may change or fold? How can you set the amount, years In advance?

"My gift won't matter." We get the impression that "Platinum" donors — the ones pictured in charity publications — are the ones who matter, at least to tax advisors and institutions who promote fancy techniques for giving.[5] Advisors often ignore small donors, but the small gifts add up.

MODEST PHILANTHROPY[6] AND THE EXPRESSION OF CHARITABLE INTENTIONS

Thinking creatively about this problem led to a technique called the "Expression of Charitable Intentions" for clients who, though charitably inclined, need an alternative to the formal charitable bequest. Using this form, clients simply ask heirs to make donations in their memory, based on the same factors that determined giving during life. Some features of the Expression:

- The Expression can guide the descendants to give for specific purposes, in specific amounts, or as a percentage of the estate, and can be amended at any time.

- The Expression can also be generic, as in: "It is my request that you make a gift in my memory [anonymously, in honor or memory of another] to charities and causes that were important to me during my lifetime."

- The Expression can encourage giving invented by the beneficiaries themselves. After all, the idea is to promote the ideal of giving.

- To add credence, the Expression of Charitable Intentions is referred to in the trust instrument as something that may be completed. An amount may also be supplied in the trust.

- Recipients need not be "qualified" charities. Gifts to grandchildren or other persons can even be mentioned (i.e., let some charity begin at home!). If there is to be an income tax benefit, the children (or other beneficiaries) will get the deduction.[7]

- The Expression may be done individually instead of as a couple to maximize the individuality of the giving.

- Remind your heirs to give cheerfully. Those who give are happier than those who don't.[8]

The Expression of Charitable Intentions provides a flexible method to express good will and to share the spirit of giving with the next generation. The amounts clients give using this method are typically modest — hundreds or low thousands of dollars, but the important thing is not the amount. The satisfaction that this form of giving provides to all concerned is substantial. In the end, the cumulative effect of this giving is great.

Since 1985, providing legal solutions for the care of loved ones, organizations, and assets in estate and tax planning, asset protection, philanthropy, business succession, and estate administration.

1. Source: The Center on Philanthropy, Indiana University: The average American donates 2.6% of his or her income. Households earning less than $50,000 give an average of $971 annually; $50,000-$100,000 households give $1,918; above $100,000, $3,975.

2. When individuals across generations and continents were asked, "What would you like most to leave your family," 60% worldwide and 81% of US respondents said they want their heirs to inherit their personal values and only 19% wanted their heirs to inherit assets. "Investing in Later Life" conducted by the insurance company HSBC, the largest study of its kind in the world. Source: Business Wire 2008, May 13, 2008.

3. When asked the right way, clients not only reveal that they wish to leave behind a modest charitable gift (if not a substantial bequest), but they are relieved and grateful, and loved ones appear to be delighted at the prospect of fulfilling this mission as well. For ideas, feel free to e-mail the author.

4. You'll find charities listed by subject at charitynavigator.org. To vet a charity, visit guidestar.org or give.org.

5. The Giving U.S.A. Foundation says that 65% of the contributions that help fund soup kitchens, for example, are small gifts from families earning less than $100,000, many of them, a lot less.

6. The term MODEST philanthropy, standing for Model Ordinary Donor Estate Solution and Therapy — is so called for its therapeutic effects on our clients! For more information on how you can participate in the Expression and for model forms, feel free to e-mail the author.

7. In the case of large gifts, specific gift amounts or percentages of the estate can be provided for in the trust itself without displacing the Expression for other, modest gifts. After comparing the estate and individual tax rates applicable to the gift, it may be best to place the gift in the trust to be sure that the estate gets the write-off instead of the beneficiary.

8. In case proof is needed of this point, a 2008 study shows spending money on others boosts our own happiness. University of British Columbia, Source: ScienceNOW 20 March 2008

CHAPTER 48

Setting Up a Private Foundation in Your Will or Trust

THOMAS J. RAY, JR. (Arnold, Missouri)

Recently, the Internal Revenue Service released sample trust forms for private foundations on its Web site at http://www.irs.gov/charities/foundations/article/0,,id=141239,00.html. Among the provisions that should be included in your will or trust to establish a private foundation are the following.

REQUIREMENTS FOR PRIVATE FOUNDATIONS

Purpose Clause. Federal law requires that a donor organize and operate his or her charitable foundation "exclusively for religious, charitable, scientific, testing for public safety, literary, or educational purposes..." To show compliance with this requirement, the trust document should include a purpose clause. The grantor can define the charitable purposes of his or her foundation broadly or narrowly.

Chapter 42 Language. Code Section 508(e)(1) requires that all private foundations, whenever and however organized, include language requiring compliance with Chapter 42 of the Internal Revenue Code: "The Foundation shall distribute its income for each tax year at such time and in such manner as not to become subject to tax on undistributed income imposed by Section 4942 of the Internal Revenue Code. Further, the Foundation shall not engage in any act of self-dealing as defined in Section 4941(d) of the Internal Revenue Code, nor retain any excess business holdings as defined in Section 4943(c) of the Internal Revenue Code, nor make any investments in such manner as to incur tax liability under Section 4944 of the Internal Revenue Code, nor make any taxable expenditures as defined in Section 4945(d) of the Internal Revenue Code." Section 1.508-3(d) of the Treasury Regulations deems a foundation's governing instrument to conform with the requirements of Section 508(e) if valid provisions of state law have been enacted that: 1) require it to act or refrain from acting so as not to subject the Foundation to the taxes imposed by Sections 4941 (relating to taxes on self-dealing), 4942 (relating to taxes on failure to distribute income), 4943 (relating to taxes on excess business holdings), 4944 (relating to taxes on investments which jeopardize charitable purpose), and 4945 (relating to taxable expenditures); or 2) treat the required provisions as contained in the Foundation's governing instrument. The Internal Revenue Service has listed those states that have enacted provisions complying with this Regulation in Revenue Ruling 75-38.[1]

Private Inurement. The governing instrument should state that "No part of the assets, income or profit of the Foundation shall be distributed to or inure to the benefit of private persons except that the Foundation shall be empowered to pay reasonable compensation for services rendered and to make payment and distributions in furtherance of the purposes of the Foundation." The law — through a doctrine imbedded in the Internal Revenue Code called the "private inurement doctrine" — prohibits a charity from using any part of its net earnings for a private use.[2] "The inurement prohibition serves to prevent anyone in a position to do so from siphoning off any of a charity's income or assets for personal use."[3] The Internal Revenue Service requires that the governing instrument include a prohibition against violating this foundational doctrine of charitable jurisprudence.

Prohibition Against Political Activities. The governing instrument of all Foundations should contain a statement similar to the following: "No substantial part of the activities of the Foundation shall involve carrying on of propaganda, or otherwise attempting to influence legislation and the Foundation shall not participate in or intervene in any political campaign on behalf of any candidate for office." Like the prohibition against private inurement, the prohibition against lobbying and campaigning activities is a fundamental part of our charitable jurisprudence.[4] So, again, the Internal Revenue Service requires that the governing instrument include prohibition against lobbying and campaigning.

Dissolution Clause. The law does not treat an organization as organized exclusively for charitable purposes unless the organization dedicates its assets to exempt purposes, even when the organization terminates.[5] So, as a rule,[6] federal law requires the governing instrument to state how the Foundation will disburse its assets if the organization goes out of existence. A typical dissolution clause will read, "Upon the dissolution of this organization, assets shall be distributed for one or more exempt purposes within the meaning of Section 501(c)(3) of the Internal Revenue Code, or corresponding section of any future federal tax code, or shall be distributed to the federal government, or to a state or local government, for public purposes."[7]

Thomas J. Ray, Jr. is an estate and tax attorney with offices in the Greater St. Louis metropolitan area, and the primary drafter of WealthDocs™ charitable components. He has lectured and written extensively in the charitable tax planning area, and he has conducted seminars and workshops for attorneys, accountants, financial advisors, development officers, and donors throughout the United States.

---

1. 1975-1 C.B. 161.

2. Treas. Reg. § 1.501(c)(3)-1(c)(2).

3. Gen. Coun. Mem. 39862.

4. Treas. Reg. § 1.501(c)(3)-1(b)(3). The prohibition for private foundations is even more restrictive.

5. Treas. Reg. § 1.501(c)(3)-1(b)(4).

6. Rev. Proc. 82-2, 1982-1 C.B. 367 says an express clause is not necessary if governing state law's cy pres doctrine protects the ultimate charitable purposes of the charity, even upon dissolution.

7. Id.

REVOCABLE LIVING TRUSTS

Revocable Living Trusts, Pour Over Wills, and Probate Avoidance

DONNA L. WILSON (Williamsburg, Virginia)

Should I have a Revocable Living Trust? Why? These are the first of many questions new clients ask their estate planning attorney. In order to properly answer these questions, the clients' goals, dreams, hopes, fears, concerns, needs, and plans for themselves, their families, and their loved ones need to be analyzed. Each family has unique planning concerns, and each plan should be customized to accurately reflect those goals and dreams in order to satisfy the three basic principles of estate planning: maintaining control during incapacity; expedient and cost-effective wealth transfer at death; and legacy planning to protect beneficiaries.

So, what is a Revocable Living Trust? A revocable or "living" trust (RLT) is a legal document utilized as a will-substitute. Like a will, the trust names beneficiaries who inherit your property upon your death. The trust document sets the criteria and conditions by which the property is to be held and distributed. Many clients use a RLT to maintain control of assets in the event of incapacity or death, distribute assets in a timely and cost effective transfer at death, and to avoid probate.

To the layperson, trusts can appear complicated. However, they entail use of fairly simple concepts, which include a set of instructions about how you want your "stuff" managed when you are not able to do so yourself, whom you want to manage it, and for whom you want it managed.

The RLT is initiated upon the signing of the trust by the grantor and trustee and funding the trust, which puts the trust legally into place. The trust is designed to continue during the grantor's lifetime and may be designed to continue after his or her death. A RLT is a legal entity established by you, the grantor (the person creating the trust, either individually or jointly, e.g., husband and wife), with a trustee (the person or entity managing the trust property, again, either individually or jointly), and a beneficiary (the person or entity for whose benefit the trust is managed and administered, which is typically the grantor until death).

A grantor may, should, and usually does, name himself or herself as trustee of a living trust during his or her lifetime, and should name a series of successor trustees to act upon the grantor's incapacity or death. At the grantor's death, the successor trustee distributes the assets of the trust in accordance with the trust directions.

The grantor of a revocable living trust can change (amend), or revoke (terminate) the terms of the trust any time after the trust is initiated. This means you can revise, cancel, and/or change trustees and beneficiaries during your lifetime. Using a "revocable" trust, you reserve the right to assert complete control of the assets and change the terms of the trust whenever you like, as long as you have the capacity to do so.

Funding or re-titling property into the name of the trust is a critical step to trust implementation. Unlike a will, assets held in trust do not have to go through probate. Thus, the assets are distributed to beneficiaries without the costs and delays typically associated with probate proceedings. A funded RLT is designed to avoid the procedural requirements of probate, as well as the possible costs and inefficiencies related thereto. Assets funded to the living trust do not have to go through the probate process because, although the trustmaker of the trust has died, the trust, as the owner of the assets, remains. It is important to note, however, that probate is avoided only for the assets titled to the name of the trust while the trustmaker was living.

> **RLT SCENARIO 1:** Mr. X creates a RLT. The terms of the trust state that on his death his assets will go equally to his children. He has a fully funded trust and upon his death, his son, as his successor trustee, divides the trust assets among his siblings and transfers title of those assets to them.

> **RLT SCENARIO 2:** Mr. & Mrs. X create a joint RLT. The terms of the trust state that upon the death of the first of them, the spouse will continue to be the trustee and continue to use the trust assets, and upon the death of the second of them, the assets will be divided equally among their three children and put into legacy trusts for asset protection.

Many methods and strategies used to reduce estate tax liability involve RLT-based estate plans. A RLT with tax provisions is designed to maximize the use of both spouses' unified credit exemption amount — the "credit" against federal estate taxes. An A-B Trust, referred by some as a "Credit Shelter Trust," "A-B Bypass Trust," "Bypass Trust," or "Federal Credit Trust" can be used to reduce, and, in some cases, eliminate, federal estate taxes, also known as the "death tax," by taking full advantage of the combined value of the marital deduction and the unified credit. Usually, RLT-utilized tax planning is created by married couples whose estate currently exceeds, or will grow during their lifetime to exceed, the federal estate tax exemption.

With a RLT, you maintain complete control of your assets as long as you have capacity, and then the successor trustee of your choosing takes over for you, temporarily upon your incapacity, and then permanently at your death, based on your specifications. Upon incapacity, you can avoid expensive court proceedings for a conservatorship. Upon death, you can transfer "protected" assets to your beneficiaries according to your wishes, with a minimum of cost and delay, and avoid costly lawsuits due to will contests. Note that the RLT does not create adverse income tax or property tax consequences during the lifetime of the grantor. The trust is classified as a grantor trust by the IRS, and all income the trust assets generate is reported on the grantor's individual income tax return.

Some advantages of using a revocable living trust-based estate plan:

- RLTs may eliminate issues that can arise when certain financial entities apply 'expiration dates' to Durable Powers of Attorney.

- RLTs may reduce estate and gift taxes.

- RLTs are private and confidential. Survivors do not have to reveal the extent of the trust's assets through a public filing that would occur through the probate process. (A will mandates probate.)

- RLT assets avoid probate. Titling your local and out-of-state real property to your trust avoids probate in every state where the property is located.

- RLTs provide for your incapacity/disability. Your successor trustee steps in without court action or intervention to manage the trust property according to your directions in the event you, the grantor, become mentally or physically incapacitated, until such time that you are physically capable of managing your own affairs again.

- RLTs typically reduce the time required to settle the estate affairs after death, because unlike the probate process, there are no set administration time periods that tie up assets.

- RLTs avoid court intervention. Your estate is handled by the trustee you name in your trust, in accordance with your instructions.

- RLTs protect assets for your spouse, through the family trust (tax planning trust).

- RLTs can utilize special needs planning to protect a dependent's needs-based government assistance, such as SSI benefits. An inheritance given outright (not in trust) to such an individual could be more harmful than helpful as it could disqualify them from receiving their benefits for the statutory penalty period.

- RLTs protect assets for your beneficiaries through legacy planning. Legacy planning provides for children who are not good with money, and protects their inheritance from future divorces, judgments, bankruptcy, creditors, and predators. As long as funds are available, subject to your state's Rule Against Perpetuities, your RLT can continue to operate indefinitely, passing from your children, to their children, and so on, for generations.

- RLTs may include remarriage protection. This type of clause, when included in a RLT, protects trust assets for remainder beneficiaries in the event the surviving spouse remarries, ensuring the inheritance eventually goes to the beneficiaries whom both spouses, as co-grantors, originally intended.

- RLTs may include business management planning, such as directions for management of your business, in order to facilitate a smooth transition of business management.

- RLTs may include court contest planning, utilizing no-contest provisions to make your estate less susceptible to attack by disgruntled heirs. Only beneficiaries of the trust have standing to sue, but a no-contest clause acts as a deterrent, putting them at risk of being disinherited if they do so.

A pour over will works as a safety net for the RLT, protecting assets left outside of the trust, either because they were not titled to the trust, or because they were made payable to the name of the estate. Upon the death of the last grantor, assets left outside of the trust will go through probate if necessary, and then be "poured over" into the trust, to be distributed according to the terms of the trust. Property passing this way is subject to probate requirements. In many states, if there are no assets outside of the trust, the will does not need to be admitted. If you have minor children, the pour over will also serves to name their guardians and conservators.

> **SCENARIO:** Ms. Y creates a RLT. The terms of the trust state that upon her death, her assets will be divided equally among named charities and her nieces and nephews. She transfers her primary residence into her RLT, but does not transfer some rental real estate, or any other assets, to the trust. At her death, the trust can distribute the primary residence through the trust, avoiding the probate process. However, the rental property and any other asset subject to probate will have to go through the probate process according to the laws of that state. After the probate process has concluded, based on the directions of the pour over will, the assets will be transferred to the trustee, who will then distribute the assets according to the terms of the trust.

Many clients implement a RLT to avoid probate, thereby avoiding delay and expense. Probate is a mandated legal process supervised by Court, in which an executor is nominated; the will is validated; heirs and beneficiaries are identified; all assets are identified; an appraisal is prepared if required by the court; a Judge enforces the will instructions; the Court orders payment of debts and taxes; any will disputes are settled; and, finally, the assets are transferred to the beneficiaries. The probate process was carefully designed to fairly transfer assets to the beneficiaries and creditors of an estate. However, many factors, such as the character of the specific assets, valuation problems, creditor claims, and will contests, can cause difficulties and obscure the true intent of the testator. Understanding the process and the significant distinctions that exist between States can help you determine if probate avoidance is truly your goal. If complications surface, the process can be more time-consuming and expensive. However, it is important to note that many estates are not complicated and the probate process may not be as onerous as initially perceived.

When asking yourself if a RLT is appropriate for your situation, consider the array of estate planning tools available to meet your specific needs, and work with a knowledgeable estate planning attorney who will apply the three basic principles of estate planning to assist you — planning for life, dealing with death, and providing legacy planning for your loved ones.

Wilson Law, PLC specializes in Estate, Legacy Preservation, Asset Protection, and Special Needs Planning. Our goal is to help families plan for life, deal with death, and allocate a legacy.

CHAPTER **50**

Revocable Living Trusts – Separate or Joint

KAREN REAGLER (Hot Springs, Arkansas)

You have decided on a revocable living trust because you like the speed, convenience, and privacy a trust offers. Now, should you and your spouse put all of your assets into one trust or should each of you have your own? Picking the right type of trust can make life easier for you and for those who have to manage your trust when you cannot do so yourself.

If your estate is larger than the federal estate tax credit ($2 million in 2008 and $3.5 million in 2009), part of your revocable trust will include tax planning. Tax planning can mean the creation of a new trust after your death for your spouse's benefit (or after your spouse's death for your benefit). The new trust takes advantage of the estate tax credit and various planning options. A typical joint revocable trust for an estate worth more than the estate tax credit works like this.

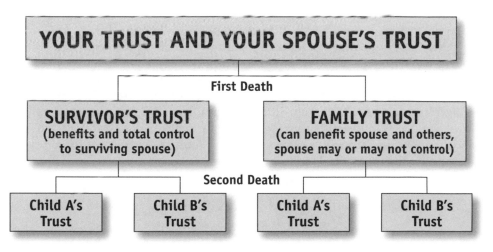

Trusts for the benefit of the same person can usually be consolidated, but your trust is still rather complicated with lots of sub-trusts. The more complicated a trust, the more difficult it will be for your successor trustee to take over. The more trusts you put in one document, the bigger the document and the more cumbersome it is.

If you chose a trust for its privacy, having more trusts inside your trust could jeopardize that privacy. Often copies are required of various trusts — a special needs trust will need to be sent to the state for approval and some banks require a copy of the entire trust before accepting an account. If you have everything in one trust and a copy is required of a particular part, you may need to provide the entire document and your privacy will be lost.

If you are in a second (or subsequent) marriage, you may want separate trusts. A separate trust contains only your assets. Your spouse can have a separate trust with only his or her assets. You can choose to support your surviving spouse, and even allow your spouse to be trustee, while still insuring your family benefits. Stepchildren worry that the stepparent will disinherit them, which can be a viable concern. A separate trust insures your children know that although you are providing for your surviving spouse, they will still get their great-grandmother's piano and their grandfather's Exxon stock. Having stepchildren act as trustees for a surviving spouse is generally not a good idea. Every dollar spent on your surviving spouse is a dollar your children do not get, which is a classic conflict of interest. To reduce potential sources of conflict, using a corporate trustee or an impartial friend may be your best option.

If you brought assets to your marriage, a separate trust is a good option. Perhaps you inherited the money, or it came from a prior marriage, or you married after you had already created wealth. A separate trust requires that the assets be kept separate. If you do not keep an asset separate, by putting the asset into a joint bank account, for example, and barring a written agreement to the contrary, you have given half of it to your spouse (laws differ by state, however, and you should consult with an attorney in your state). Although you can argue later that it was not a gift — a difficult argument to prove — separating the assets later is no easy task.

Even with an estate totaling less than the amount of the federal estate tax credit, revocable trusts are wonderful for the simplicity, beneficiary protection, and control they provide. If your estate is less than the federal estate tax credit, you do not expect much asset growth, you and your spouse own everything jointly, and — most importantly — you want the same people to get all of your assets, then you have a perfect situation for a joint trust. In a joint trust, both you and your spouse place all of your assets in the same trust. You and your spouse may be the initial trustees and both of you can make changes. A typical joint trust structure for an estate totaling less than the federal estate tax credit looks like this:

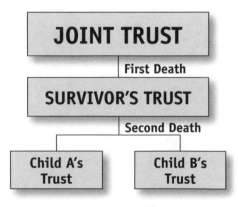

A joint trust is also a great idea in Community Property states: Arizona, California, Idaho, Louisiana, Nevada, New Mexico, Texas, Washington, and Wisconsin. Community Property law (in general) provides that all assets acquired during marriage from the work of either spouse are owned half by each spouse. A joint trust preserves the status of the Community Property and its considerable estate tax advantages.

The estate tax advantages include a double-step up in basis of the Community Property at the death of the first spouse. Basis is your investment in an asset. If you buy stock for $1, your basis is $1. If you later sell it for $10, you have a gain of $9 (Sale price minus basis). You pay capital gains tax on gains. The greater the basis, the less your gain and the less capital gains tax you pay.

In Common Law jurisdictions (non-Community Property States), any property that you own jointly with your spouse is considered half yours. Only half is included in your estate and only half receives a step up in basis. If you own that same $1 stock jointly with your spouse and it is worth $10 when you die, the basis in the stock increases from $1 to $6. The basis in your half ($1) stepped-up to the date of death value ($5) plus your spouse's basis ($1). In Community Property jurisdictions, both your half and your spouse's half receive a step up in basis. So at your death, you and your spouse have a total basis in the stock of $10. If you sell the stock in a Common Law jurisdiction, you will pay tax on $4 ($10 - $6). If you sell the stock in a Community Property jurisdiction, you own no capital gains tax ($10 - $10).

Karen Baim Reagler, Hot Springs office of Baim, Gunti, Mouser, Havner & Worsham, PLC, has been an attorney for over ten years and focuses her practice on elder law.

CHAPTER **51**

What Happens After the First Death

BRAD WIEWEL (Austin, Texas)

The loss of a spouse is often one of the most devastating experiences a person will encounter. Avoiding a costly and uncertain future from that point forward involves proactively planning for that eventuality with a competent and concerned estate planning attorney. Getting from the graveside to a fulfilling life for the surviving spouse requires careful advance preparation.

REMARRIAGE

Perhaps the most overlooked aspect of "first death planning" is what happens if the survivor remarries. Nothing can bring more joy or more devastation than remarriage. The loss of a life-long spouse can be accompanied by depression, loneliness, and isolation. Men particularly seem vulnerable. No estate planning, a simple Will, accounts held in joint tenancy, or naming a new spouse as a beneficiary on life insurance and retirement assets can lead to a "Bimbo-Gigolo" problem. Because the surviving spouse has full control of this property if no prior planning is in place, he or she is perfectly capable of redirecting it to someone outside of your "family." Experienced estate planning attorneys have heard numerous stories of wealth and heirlooms lost to a new husband or wife who seems to have little connection with the original family.

One real life example involved an older couple who had accumulated a substantial estate. Mom died first, and the adult children arranged for a housekeeper to take care of dad. The housekeeper did an excellent job of taking care of dad, and soon enough dad and the housekeeper were getting married. A few weeks following their wedding they visited a lawyer to re-draft their Wills. No long after that, dad died. Then a few weeks later, the housekeeper died. According to the new Wills, the housekeeper's children inherited ALL of Mom's and Dad's property, including the large and valuable family home and all of their heirlooms. Mom's and Dad's kids received nothing!

How could this have been prevented? First, Mom and Dad could have included a Bypass trust and/or a QTIP trust in their Will or their revocable living trust. These trusts have certain tax savings features that will be discussed below, but in addition to the tax savings, such trusts can give the surviving spouse control over the entire estate, while prohibiting him or her from transferring the deceased spouse's share of the couple's assets to a new spouse either during the survivor's lifetime or at the second death.

Another option, growing in popularity, is to include a requirement in the Will or revocable living trust that the surviving spouse must have any subsequent fiancé sign a prenuptial agreement prior to getting married. A prenuptial agreement is an agreement in which prospective marriage partners outline their respective rights in the assets each brings into the marriage and the status of money earned during the marriage. The real advantage of including this type of provision in the Will or revocable living trust is two-fold. It gives the surviving spouse an excuse to obtain a prenuptial agreement because their "hands are tied" by the estate plan. This takes the emotional "heat" off of a potentially explosive conversation. Furthermore, when there is a remarriage, the adult children often see the new spouse as a threat to their inheritance. Having a valid, binding prenuptial agreement in place can go a long way toward making the second wedding a joyful, rather than a painful event.

PROPERTY ISSUES

The surviving spouse's emotions following the funeral are complex and confusing. Having access to money is often the highest priority because of the feeling of vulnerability that almost always seems to occur. With up-to-date documents in place, the pain and frustration can be minimized, although probably not completely eliminated. The first order of business is ascertaining what property the couple owned, and how it was titled at the date of death. Property titled in the sole name of the deceased or in the name of the deceased and another person as tenants-in-common will almost always involve probate proceedings. This happens because the name of the deceased must be removed so that the heir — the surviving spouse in most instances, can have title to that property put in his or her own name so that he or she can control it.

Assets held in joint tenancy with rights of survivorship, or assets with beneficiary designations, automatically become the property of the beneficiary or joint tenant, but transferring these types of assets can present estate tax problems, as well as the type of remarriage problems outlined above. Many people, in their quest to avoid probate, inadvertently create large tax bills and other vulnerabilities that could otherwise be easily avoided with proper advice from a competent estate planning attorney. Revocable living trusts are designed to make the transition of assets from one spouse to the other as smooth as possible while avoiding probate, saving on taxes, and protecting the estate from a predator. Most people have never been to court, or at least do not relish the thought of doing so under the cloud of death. A properly funded revocable living trust can achieve most, if not all of a couple's goals in this regard.

TAX PLANNING

The best opportunity married couples have to save significantly on federal estate taxes is at the first death. Through the use of a properly implemented Bypass trust (sometimes called a Credit Shelter or "B" Trust) a married couple can legitimately shelter millions of dollars in wealth from onerous estate taxes. However, unless a couple's Will or revocable living trust is designed to create a Bypass trust on the date of the first death, the ability to save significant taxes and keep the surviving spouse in control of the entire estate cannot be achieved.

Most estate plans containing Bypass trusts also have a QTIP trust. A QTIP trust is a special trust that allows the deceased spouse to provide for the future needs of the survivor, but be assured that the money passes according to his or her wishes on the second death. The property in the QTIP trust remains in the estate of the survivor for the imposition of estate taxes on the second death unless the couple has engaged in other estate tax reducing techniques.

Bypass trusts and QTIP trusts are highly technical, both in terms of their creation and in terms of their implementation. After the first death, the role of the estate planning attorney, in concert with the family CPA and financial advisor is to first value the property of the deceased, and to decide which property is to be placed in the Bypass trust, which property is to be placed in the QTIP trust, and which assets are to remain under the complete and absolute control of the survivor.

Brad Wiewel is a Board Certified Estate Planner in Texas, the host of a legal call-in radio show, and an instructor at the University of Texas CFP Training Program.

CHAPTER 52

Revocable Living Trusts – Trustee Distribution Powers

WILLIAM CARMINES (Yorktown, Virginia)

Imagine someone gave you $500,000 and said you could invest the money and use the income, but only the income it produced, for any purpose you chose. Assuming you could invest the $500,000 in a manner that would produce an 8% return each year, you would have $40,000 a year to enjoy. That is a pretty nice gift. However, now imagine the next day, you were in a car accident and needed medical care that cost roughly $6,000 a month. Suddenly, that $40,000 a year would not be sufficient to take care of your needs. Wouldn't it have been better if the person who gave you the $500,000 had given you a little more flexibility about how you could use the money?

It is important that people weigh the benefits of flexibility given to the Trustee, against the possibility of misuse by the Trustee, when creating their Revocable Living Trust ("Trust"). Many people are uncomfortable with the idea of allowing someone else to decide to simply give their hard-earned money away for any reason. However, if you become incapacitated and are unable to make your own decisions, it is important you have someone you trust who is able to manage your assets and effectively care for you and your beneficiaries.

There are several options to consider that can make your Trust flexible enough to ensure that you and your beneficiaries will be taken care of no matter what happens while still allowing you to feel comfortable that your Trustee is not able to make ill-advised decisions.

OPTION 1: SPECIFICALLY AUTHORIZE CERTAIN TYPES OF DISTRIBUTIONS

Many Trusts include language authorizing a Trustee to distribute assets from the principal of the trust to beneficiaries for specific reasons. Three common reasons are to continue a pattern of gifting you may have established during your lifetime to charities, organizations or people, to pay medical expenses for your beneficiaries, and to prepay tuition costs for your beneficiaries. These are all sound reasons for allowing your Trustee to distribute assets from your Trust, but they may not offer your Trustee enough flexibility to manage your Trust.

OPTION 2: DISTRIBUTIONS LIMITED TO THE FEDERAL ANNUAL GIFT TAX EXCLUSION AMOUNT

Often, Trusts contain the following language authorizing the Trustee to make gifts from the Trust to your beneficiaries:

> *My Trustee may make gifts on my behalf, limited in amount to the federal annual gift tax exclusion amount, to or for the benefit of any remainder or contingent beneficiary named in this agreement for purposes my Trustee considers to be in my best interest or in the best interest of the beneficiary, including, without limitation, the minimization of income, estate, inheritance or gift taxes.*

While it is wise to include such language, this will only authorize your Trustee to distribute a limited amount ($12,000 in 2008, $13,000 in 2009) to a beneficiary once a year. That $12,000 may not be enough to sufficiently take care of one of your beneficiaries or to lower your tax burden.

OPTION 3: DISTRIBUTIONS IN EXCESS OF THE ANNUAL EXCLUSION AMOUNT

Alternatively, you could insert language into your Trust that allows your Trustee to make gifts in excess of the annual federal gift tax exclusion. The authority to make larger gifts provides your Trustee with a significant power and you may be concerned about this idea. However, if you use the following language, you can give your Trustee this power while minimizing the risks involved:

> *If our Trustee determines that gifts in amounts in excess of the annual federal gift tax exclusion are in the best interests of both the incapacitated Grantor and our beneficiaries, our Trustee, by unanimous vote if more than one Trustee is serving, shall appoint an Independent Special Trustee unrelated by blood or marriage to any Trustee to review the facts and circumstances and to decide whether the gifts should be made.*

By requiring your Trustee to appoint an independent special trustee to authorize gifts in excess of the federal gift tax exclusion amount, you can be assured that these gifts will not be made unless it is in the best interests of both you and your beneficiaries.

While the thought of someone else making such significant gifts of your assets may be troubling, you should remember that it may be necessary. A common scenario more and more people face is the possibility of having to live in a nursing home for significant periods of times. If your Trustee cannot make larger gifts from your Trust, he or she may not be able to get you qualified for governmental or veterans assistance. If your Trustee cannot get you qualified for these programs then you risk a significant amount, if not all, of your assets going to pay for your nursing home care instead of being preserved for the well-being of your beneficiaries. Similarly, given the present uncertainty regarding estate and income taxes, there may be a good financial reason why significant amount of your assets should be gifted in a particular year. This type of power provides your Trustee with flexibility to adapt to changing circumstances.

OPTION 4: GIVE YOUR TRUSTEE DISTRIBUTION GUIDELINES

If you are concerned that if you became incapacitated, your Trustee may give away your assets to other people with little regard for your well-being, then you should consider putting distribution guidelines during your incapacity into your Trust.

You can instruct your Trustee to distribute assets out of your Trust for your benefit first and only if you are provided for, then for the benefit of others, or for your benefit and your spouse's benefit, and then for the benefit of others (including your children, beneficiaries, etc.), or you can instruct your Trustee to distribute assets from your Trust for the benefit of you and others equally. Instructing your Trustee to distribute your assets for your benefit first and only then for the needs of others may be the selection that gives you the most peace of mind that your assets will not be given away. But if you have minor children or beneficiaries who are dependent on you, you may want to consider the more flexible option.

OPTION 5: DISTRIBUTIONS ONLY FOR ASCERTAINABLE STANDARDS

If you are leery of authorizing your Trustee to distribute assets from your Trust for any reason while you are incapacitated, then you can limit distributions to your beneficiaries to an ascertainable standard. You can instruct your Trustee only to make distributions to your beneficiaries for their health, education, maintenance, or support. You can further restrict the standard by authorizing your Trustee to only make distributions for health and education. This offers flexibility while also providing your Trustee with important guidelines.

OPTION 6: BALANCE FLEXIBILITY WITH RESTRICTIONS

If you are concerned about giving your Trustee so much authority, you do have some alternatives.

- You can appoint joint Co-Trustees and require all of them to agree before making any distributions.

- You can authorize your Trustee to make distributions to your Agent under your Durable Power of Attorney, who will make distributions according to the terms of that document.

- You can appoint an independent person or professional fiduciary to serve as a Distribution Trustee. That person reviews any distributions and determines whether they are in your and your beneficiaries' best interests before the distributions are made.

What you should do: When deciding how much flexibility to provide your Trustee to make distributions from your Trust, you should balance your concerns of giving your Trustee too much power with the understanding that you want to enable your Trustee to take care of you and your beneficiaries no matter what happens in the future. You and your attorney should discuss your concerns and consider the options outlined above to ensure your Trust will protect your assets as much as possible for you and your beneficiaries for the rest of your lives.

For the past 15 years, this firm has helped clients in the Hampton Roads region of Virginia with elder law, estate planning, estate administration, and special needs planning.

CHAPTER 53

Choosing a Trustee for Your Living Trust

GLENN PRICE (Bellevue, Washington)

One of the most important aspects of executing a successful estate plan for yourself and your family is the selection of a trustee. Because a trustee's responsibilities are serious and sometimes time-consuming, it is prudent to evaluate your options carefully before making a selection.

What are your trustee's duties? A trustee is the legal owner of the trust assets and has a fiduciary duty to manage, invest, and distribute those assets in the best interests of the trust's beneficiaries. The trustee's authority comes, first and foremost, from the duties, powers, and instructions described in the trust instrument. In faithfully following that authority, as well as your state's laws, the Internal Revenue Code, and Treasury Regulations, your trustee should always be willing to seek out the advice and guidance of an experienced estate planning attorney, tax advisor, or other advisors. Your trustee is duty-bound to deal with the trust property as a "prudent person" would deal with the property of another. The trustee has a duty of loyalty to carry out the trust's provisions in the best interests of the beneficiaries, without personal conflict or even the appearance of self-interest.

Whom should you choose as trustee? If you are creating a revocable living trust, you will probably serve, at least initially, as the sole trustee if you are single, or as a co-trustee with your spouse if you are married. You are essentially wearing three hats as the: 1) grantor — setting up the trust and putting assets into it; 2) trustee — owning, managing, and distributing the trust assets; and 3) trust beneficiary. A critical decision you must make is who to name to serve as your successor trustee if you should resign, if you become disabled or incapacitated, and when you die.

Considerations in choosing your successor trustee. In selecting a successor trustee, you want the best assurance that your wishes and desires will be carried out, that the trustee will be a responsible person whose judgment, common sense, good organizational skills and willingness to seek professional guidance you can trust and rely upon, and that the successor trustee is available and willing to serve. Your successor trustee could be your spouse, family member, relative, friend, business associate, professional advisor, or a corporate fiduciary such as a bank or trust company. Considerations in making your selection could depend upon the nature and value of the trust assets, the expected length of the trust term, the complexity of the trust's provisions, the age, nature, and circumstances of your beneficiaries, or other factors.

Selecting a family member as trustee. Many people choose family members to serve as trustee. They may not charge a fee (but, as with any trustee, they are entitled to "reasonable compensation" for services performed), and they generally have a personal stake in the trust's success.

If your family member is competent to handle the trust's finances, has the time and interest to do so, exercises reasonable judgment, has administrative capabilities, will follow the trust's (your) instructions, can avoid family conflicts, will be unbiased and unemotional, is familiar with your beneficiaries' circumstances, personalities and abilities, and can be sensitive and unbiased in making decisions, this can be an appropriate choice for a small to medium-sized trust.

The potential downsides of such a choice are lack of expertise and diligence, emotional decision-making, inadequate financial resources to cover mistakes, financial mismanagement, existence of family rivalries and conflicts, and, of course, your trustee's disability or death.

Selecting a corporate trustee. Banks and trust companies are permanent institutions that can manage your trust for decades. If friends or family members are unavailable or unreliable, institutional trustees can have the following advantages: 1) managing trusts is their everyday business; 2) they act objectively and follow trust instructions unemotionally; 3) they have estate administration, tax, and investment expertise; 4) they don't die or become incapacitated; 5) they are highly regulated by government agencies; 6) they have the resources to cover errors and mistakes; and 7) the law holds them to a higher standard of care as professional fiduciaries.

Potential disadvantages of corporate trustees are: 1) their fees; 2) their objective and unemotional decision-making can be perceived as cold and impersonal; 3) they lack specific knowledge and insights about your goals and wishes, your beneficiaries particular needs and personalities, and family dynamics; 4) they can be extremely conservative in interpreting trust terms and making distributions to beneficiaries; and 5) they aren't always the best choice for administering real estate and/or a family business.

How about your advisor? A trusted professional advisor such as your attorney, tax advisor, or investment advisor can be an appropriate selection as trustee if he or she is willing to serve and can do so without conflict of interest.

Co-trustees: The best of both worlds? Naming a family member and an institution as co-trustees can be an effective way to combine familiarity with the beneficiaries with the experience, stability, and expertise of a corporate trustee. Each party complements the other's strengths, better serving the beneficiaries' interests. The family member can mentor the children in financial responsibility while the institutional co-trustee manages the trust. An increasingly popular middle course between naming an institutional trustee and an immediate family member is choosing a relative as sole trustee and hiring a bank or investment company as an independent advisor. This can maximize advantages while reducing fees.

Your attorney can help you choose. As your estate planning attorney carefully shepherds you through the crucial estate planning design process, he or she acquires invaluable insights into your circumstances, goals, fears, concerns, and family dynamics. This insight and knowledge about you and what you wish to accomplish allows both of you to collaborate in evaluating and arriving at the best choices for the critically important roles of trustee, successor trustee, and alternate trustees of your living trust. Take advantage of your attorney's professional ability to help you create the very best estate plan you can. You and your family deserve it.

Glenn D. Price, working closely with his clients' other professional advisors, dedicates his practice exclusively to client-centered estate, tax, retirement, business, and family wealth preservation planning.

Factors to Consider in Selecting a Trustee

X	GOALS
	Willingness and ability to devote the time required during the trust term
	Good judgment and decision-making ability
	Integrity
	Independence from the grantor and beneficiaries (if needed for decision-making)
	Adequate financial, business, tax, and legal knowledge
	Financially secure
	Fair and impartial (no conflicts of interest)
	Accurate understanding of grantor's goals
	Knowledge of individuals involved with the trust, including their personalities
	Knowledge of any family assets to be placed in trust
	Adequate administrative ability, attention to detail, and flexibility
	Capable of working with third parties the trust may hire
	Discretion with respect to confidential matters
	Adequate proximity to trust assets and beneficiaries for the trust term
	Previous experience as a trustee
	Reasonableness of fee structure
	Inclusion of tax preparation and asset management services as trustee and associated fees

CHAPTER 54

Revocable Living Trusts – Timing Distributions After the Second Death

KEVIN FORBUSH (Colorado Springs, Colorado)

How you choose to distribute trust assets after your death and the death of your spouse is one of the pillars of your revocable living trust, the effects of which reach far into the future. For this reason, there are many factors to consider when determining the timing of distributions from your trust. The methods and techniques are almost limitless and depend on your specific objectives and the needs of your beneficiaries. Your decisions regarding the timing of such distributions should be made only after you have discussed your objectives with your counseling attorney and after you fully understand the possible outcomes.

As a preliminary matter, you need to decide whether your assets will be distributed to your beneficiaries outright or in trust. An outright distribution is the simplest way to distribute property. It immediately gives the beneficiary full access to the money or assets at the time of distribution with "no strings attached." Outright distributions are simple, immediate, and easy to understand. One disadvantage is that you lose control over the way your beneficiaries use the assets they receive. Further, you will have missed the opportunity to provide protection for the assets you intend to distribute — or ensuring they go to your beneficiaries, and not to their "creditors or predators."

If, on the other hand, you decide to control your assets by leaving them in trust, you have two main options for handling distributions, each of which can be broken down to further meet the needs of your beneficiaries. The first option is to allow distributions of income and principal only, at the Trustee's discretion. The second option is to require the Trustee to make distributions of income and principal pursuant to a set plan or schedule.

If you decide to have your Trustee exercise discretion in making distributions, you will want to define the criteria your Trustee will use when exercising this discretion. You may require that your trustee use the same criteria for distributions to all beneficiaries, or you may choose to implement different distribution instructions for different beneficiaries.

However, most people choose that their trust assets — specifically the income of the trust — be distributed according to a fixed schedule. One reason for this is that undistributed income triggers relatively unfavorable income tax consequences for your trust; the income tax consequences are generally worse at the trust level than at the level of an individual beneficiary. It is important to note, however, that there are circumstances where, after considering all factors, your beneficiaries are better off with the Trustee exercising discretion to retain income in your trust and paying relatively higher taxes on your trust's income.

After choosing a method of distribution for your trust's income, you have many options for distributing trust principal. First, you can choose to set an age when your beneficiaries have a "demand right," which is simply the ability of a beneficiary to demand principal at any time and for any reason.

It is important to realize that once a beneficiary has the right to demand principal from the trust, the beneficiary loses valuable protection over those assets. For this reason, the best demand right age often varies from beneficiary to beneficiary, and depends on all the facts and circumstances. For some, a younger age, such as 30, may be appropriate. Other beneficiaries may have a greater long-term need for asset protection, and age 50 will be more appropriate. Other beneficiaries may never be ready for a demand right, and a trust that does not allow for any demand right during the beneficiaries' lifetime may be best. Common risk factors you might consider when making your demand right decision include the risk of divorce, fear of lawsuits, and fear of business failure.

Certain beneficiaries may be best served by having a series of demand rights that are triggered by the occurrence of various events. Many people use the attainment of specific ages as triggers for demand rights. For example, you might decide your beneficiary should have a demand right over one-third of his or her trust principal at age 30, one-half of the remaining trust principal at age 40, and the balance at age 50. Such a tiered distribution could consist of equal or unequal distributions. Other examples include creating demand rights at specific time intervals (i.e., at five years after your death, ten years after your death, etc.) or upon the occurrence of one or more specific events such as upon a beneficiary's marriage, the birth of a grandchild, or when a child or grandchild begins college.

Another option is to distribute trust principal when the beneficiary successfully completes certain tasks. You may specify that "Kimberly shall receive $10,000 upon completion of a four-year degree from an accredited college or university." This type of distribution plan might be referred to as a "motivational" distribution plan.

The timing of principal distributions can also be affected by the character of the assets. For example, $250,000 in cash and the family cabin that Grandfather built may have equal monetary value, but their relative "emotional" values are very different, and therefore, necessitate a different distribution plan. You might distribute the cash right away or in one of the ways described above; Grandfather's cabin, however, might never be distributed.

The unique characteristics of your beneficiaries will also affect the timing of distributions from your trust. The age of the beneficiary could be a major factor in your decision. Any beneficiary who is a minor should receive income and principal distributions only when the Trustee exercises discretion to do so. The same is true for any incapacitated beneficiary. Careful drafting in cases of minor or incapacitated beneficiaries will minimize or eliminate Court involvement in the beneficiaries' affairs. Court involvement can add unnecessary time, expense, and frustration for all parties involved. A well-qualified counseling attorney should advise you of your options.

Finally, if you have several children and one or more of them are minors, you might choose to establish a "common pot" trust. A "common pot" trust is used to hold all your assets together to ensure each of your children can use family assets to support them through their minority. If your estate is divided into shares for your children before the younger ones reach adulthood, your younger children may end up paying their medical and educational expenses from their own "shares" of the trust estate while your older children will have received their shares "net" of the expenses you already spent to raise them to adulthood.

There are many options for the distribution of your trust assets after both you and your spouse have passed away. What we have shared here gives you a good idea of the timing and distribution options available to you. Remember to consult your estate planning attorney to design trust distribution and timing provisions best suited to your specific needs and the needs of your beneficiaries.

At Forbush Legal we specialize in Business and Estate Planning in a collaborative environment. We focus not on transactions, but on counseling, fostering enduring relationships with clients and their advisors.

CHAPTER 55

Revocable Living Trusts – Independent Trustees and Trust Protectors

DENNIS SULLIVAN (Wellesley, Massachusetts)

If you have a Revocable Living Trust in place to avoid probate and control your family legacy, have you considered how that Trust will be administered after you are gone? We find that many families have a plan in place to minimize taxes and maximize children's and grandchildren's inheritances, but have little idea of the next steps they should take to make those inheritances last for the long term. Independent Trustees and Trust Protectors can join with your family team to guide them to create a lasting family legacy.

WHY AN INDEPENDENT TRUSTEE?

If you have a Revocable Living Trust, you very likely have chosen a family member as a successor Trustee to manage and distribute assets for you if you are incapacitated, or for your family when you pass away. A family member is an excellent choice for responsive management and for understanding family dynamics and circumstances, but most people know very little about the asset protection, investment, tax, accounting, and the fiduciary duties of a Trustee.

A family member Trustee who is inexperienced with legal, tax, and financial matters may inadvertently make mistakes or omissions that can create personal liability for himself or herself, or for the beneficiaries of the trust. Family conflicts and lower investment returns can destroy a hard-earned family legacy.

ASSET PROTECTION

A Trust that continues to operate after you are gone can provide significant advantages to your children and grandchildren. As the trust was created by you with your money, the assets in the trust are significantly less vulnerable to your children's or grandchildren's creditors (including lawsuit creditors and divorcing spouses). However, to utilize the benefits of an ongoing Trust for children or grandchildren, all but a few jurisdictions require that an Independent Trustee serve as Trustee of the Trust.

If there is no Independent Trustee, one of the primary benefits of an ongoing Trust — the opportunity to retain enormous flexibility, along with protection from divorce, lawsuits, and other creditors, will be lost.

INVESTMENT MANAGEMENT

One of the least understood duties of a Trustee is that the Trustee acts as a fiduciary, overseeing all the Trust assets and investments to ensure they remain productive and available for the beneficiaries as required by the terms of the Trust. Few Trusts have specific instructions about how a Trustee should manage assets.

While a fiduciary does not have to personally oversee each aspect of the investment process, the fiduciary is the overall manager of the process. It is the fiduciary who may be personally liable if the Trust's investments are too risky and funds are lost or if the Trust's investments are too conservative and the income stream provided by the Trust does not keep up with inflation.

An Independent Trustee with a solid understanding of the process is a resource to guide the family member Trustee in the investment process, as well as a way to ensure the Trustee's fiduciary duties are fulfilled.

TAXES AND ACCOUNTING

Trust accounting is another area that even most bright, educated family member Trustees may know little about. Once you pass away, your Revocable Living Trust will become irrevocable and will be required to file its own annual income tax returns. An Independent Trustee should have the knowledge and experience to make the appropriate distributions to income and principal beneficiaries and then be able to file the Federal Form 1041 income tax return correctly.

AUTHORIZING DISTRIBUTIONS
Beyond the usual health, education, maintenance, and support standard

In order for your trust to provide effective asset protection for your beneficiaries, the role of Interested Trustees, that is Trustees who are also beneficiaries, must be limited. The most common way to limit them is to restrict distributions of income and principal that Interested Trustees can make to an ascertainable standard, most commonly for the health, education, maintenance, and support of the beneficiary.

However, an Independent Trustee is not similarly limited to these standards. If you wish, you can allow an independent Trustee complete discretion in distributing assets to the beneficiaries, allowing safe access to the Trust funds for the beneficiary under nearly any circumstances.

TRUST PROTECTORS:
Facilitating a productive trust for a lasting legacy

What is a Trust Protector?

A Trust Protector may be an individual, a group of individuals, or a corporation, and can include your attorney, accountant, or a Trust company. Trust Protectors are appointed in advance as a part of your Revocable Living Trust and they do their work after the Trust becomes irrevocable due to your death or disability. The Trust Protector is usually authorized to monitor and then fire or replace non-family member Trustees if they become ineffective, and to amend a Trust that is otherwise irrevocable if legal changes, IRS opinions, or scriveners' error have made it impossible for the Trustees' to fulfill your original wishes and intent.

Why a Trust Protector?

When you pass away, your Trust becomes irrevocable and the provisions cannot be changed. However that does not mean there will be no changes in tax law or family circumstances. By naming a Trust Protector in your Revocable Living Trust you take steps to preserve your original intent, minimize the impact of taxes, particularly the generation-skipping transfer tax as assets pass from your children to your grandchildren, and allow your family the flexibility it needs.

> **EXAMPLE 1:** If you drafted your original Trust while your children were childless or unmarried, but when you pass away they would like to use the Trust funds to pay for their own children's college or other education, there may be significant tax and asset protection implications by using funds from the Trust if there has not been prior planning for this contingency.

This is where a Trust Protector can step in to amend your Trust to provide for the proper generation-skipping transfer tax allocations.

> **EXAMPLE 2:** If you have young children, you probably do not want them to have direct access to or responsibility for funds until they have reached the age where they understand and are comfortable with tax and legal decisions. In this situation, many people will choose both a family member and a professional Trustee, together, to help their children until they are of age. However, in the current age of rapidly merging banks and Trust Companies, it is critical to have a third party available to monitor the Trust and Trustees. A Trust Protector can ensure the Trustees comply with their responsibilities, provide your children with the funds they need without allowing them to waste their inheritance, and step in to find a new Trustee if your previous Trustees cannot or will not be viable choices.

SO WHAT SHOULD YOU THINK ABOUT AS YOU DRAFT OR REVIEW YOUR REVOCABLE LIVING TRUST?

Consider your family's personal and financial circumstances and experience when determining who will serve as Trustee upon the death or disability of you and your spouse. You want to provide for your family, not leave them with a potential lawsuit or a tax and accounting nightmare. A good Independent Trustee, working with a solid, well-informed Trust Protector, can take most of the burden off your family's shoulders and allow them to concentrate on the things that are most important to you and to them.

Dennis Sullivan & Associates is a team dedicated to helping people concerned with losing their assets to increasing medical and nursing home costs, taxes, and the costs and delays of probate.

CHAPTER 56

"Funding" Your Trust

CHRIS CASWELL (Sarasota, Florida)

The process of "funding" a trust involves transferring title and ownership of your property into the name of the trustee of your trust. It also involves changing designated beneficiaries on insurance policies, annuities, and retirement plans to the trustee of your trust, when appropriate. See below, however, for some reasons why you may need to get professional advice before you transfer title or change any beneficiary designations.

Why should you go through the process of funding your trust? There are numerous benefits from ensuring title to your property is in the name of your trustee, and some of the benefits may depend upon state law, as well as your specific circumstances. Therefore, the rest of this chapter will provide general guidance, but you should confirm the effect of any funding action with qualified counsel before you undertake it. Also, trusts can be funded while you are alive and after your death, but for the purposes of this chapter, we will only address the funding of your trust while you are alive. The mechanics, however, are the same.

Fundamental to the concept of using trusts is that all rules and issues for the management and transfer of your property are included within the terms of the trust document. No court action is normally required to implement your wishes for handling your property when you are not able to do so.

So some of the advantages of a properly funded trust are:

- Avoidance of living probate (guardianship or conservatorship) and death probate.

- Minimizing the delays and hassles of managing and transferring property in a living or death probate action.

- The costs of administering your trust assets are far less then the costs of going through living or death probate.

- If you have property located in several states, you will not need to open up separate probate actions to handle the transfer of your property upon your death.

- Compared to property held in joint title, you can control how ownership of your property will pass even after your death through your trust.

- In many states, it is not clear what property rights domestic partners have and property in a trust can provide certainty rather than uncertainty.

You should remember that even if you fail to completely fund your trust, a good estate plan will include a pour over will which will serve to get any unfunded property into your trust after your death. However, normally a probate action will be required, so you would not be able to benefit from many of the valuable advantages you would otherwise have if you had funded your trust while you were alive. Also, if you leave your property in joint ownership, have a payable-on-death or transfer-on-death designation, or have a beneficiary designation, it keeps the property out of your trust, and the property does not pass title through your probate estate so the pour over will is not effective as to that property.

How do you fund your trust? The method of funding your trust varies depending on the type of property.

- Real estate is transferred by a deed (or other appropriate method of transferring real estate in your state).

- Stocks and bonds held in your name are transferred by reissuing the certificates in the name of your trustee.

- Investment accounts and bank accounts are transferred by having your stockbroker or banker change ownership on the accounts to your trustee. (Sometimes this might require opening a new account and sometimes it only requires new signature cards.)

- Ownership and interests in private companies, partnerships, and limited liability companies may require an assignment or stock power and reissuing ownership certificates in the name of the trustee.

- Personal property is transferred by a bill of sale or other assignment document to your trustee.

- Notes, mortgages, and other receivables due you will generally be transferred by assignment.

- IRAs, retirement plans, annuities, and life insurance generally will not have ownership transferred to your trust due to potential tax implications, and must be evaluated on a case-by-case basis with the advice of qualified counsel.

- Inheritances, gifts, or lawsuit judgments not yet received can generally be transferred by assignment to your trustee.

An example of the proper titling language to use is (you should change this to match your particular trust description) is as follows. The bracketed language is desirable to create a more complete description.

John Smith as trustee [, or his successor in trust,] of the John Smith
Revocable Living Trust dated 1/1/2001 [and any and all
amendments and restatements thereof]

If there are co-trustees, you would add the name of the additional co-trustee
as well.

**Why do they talk about "balancing" your estate and what does that have
to do with funding your trusts?** The technical reasons behind "balancing" your
estate are beyond the scope of this chapter. However, the basic concept is that
generally the value of a married couple's total estate should be split equally, or
balanced, between each person's living trust. If you are advised to prepare and use
a joint trust, the question of balancing may not come up initially, and instead may
become an issue for the survivor after the death of the first spouse.

The goal behind balancing is to ensure there are enough assets allocable to the estate
of each of the spouses to take advantage of the available federal estate tax exemption
on the death of the first spouse. You should review other chapters of this book to
understand the concept of the available federal estate tax exemption.

Sometimes it can be difficult to balance an estate because of certain ownership
restrictions on an asset. For example, professional practices may not be able to be
owned by a non-licensed professional. Also certain stock options and other contract
rights governed by plans and documents may prohibit the transfer of an asset even
among spouses.

What records do you have to keep for the funding of your trust? For several
reasons, it may be necessary to document and prove that your assets are funded into
your trust. Therefore, you need to keep all written documentation of your requests
to fund your assets into your trust, as well as all confirmations that that funding
has been completed. This may consist of bank and investment account statements,
written beneficiary designation forms, copies of deeds and assignments, copies of
title certificates, and copies of correspondence.

**Why you may or may not be able to handle your own funding and what
might go wrong?** Changing titles on accounts and changing beneficiaries may
sound like activities that do not require professional assistance. But there are several
issues that may affect how title can be transferred or even if it should be transferred.
Some of these issues may be tax-related and some may depend on your particular
state law, and some may even depend on the preferred strategies recommended by
your professional advisors.

Some of these issues include:

- **Your residence.** Although generally you should deed your residence to
  the trustee of your trust, legal professionals may differ in their advice to
  you. Some of this may depend on state law issues, some may depend on
  asset protection availability, and some may depend on local, state, federal,
  property, and capital gain tax issues.

- **Business interests.** Any business entities you have elected to have taxed under Subchapter S of the Internal Revenue Code (S Corporations and certain limited liability companies) have certain limitations on owners. You may need to determine whether ownership by your trustee complies with those limitations. Also, shareholder, operating, or partnership agreements which govern the ownership of business interests may have limitations on transfers with which you will need to comply.

- **IRAs and retirement plans.** Changing ownership of IRAs and retirement plans could trigger negative tax effects and early distribution penalties. That is why you typically only want to change the beneficiaries rather than ownership.

- **Community property.** The rules applicable to community property may require property agreements or other documentation to appropriately establish the proper funding of your trust.

- **Using the correct forms.** Sometimes an institution will not recognize a transfer or beneficiary change request unless it is on an approved form. Therefore, it is important to not only use the correct form, but to also obtain confirmation that the change has been accepted.

- **Real property.** It is important that the transfer of title to your trustee does not trigger any due on sale clause on any mortgage on your property, or avoid or reduce any insurance coverage. Therefore, it may be appropriate to obtain the consent of your lender before initiating the transfer. Also, you may need to determine whether your insurance company might re-rate your policy due to ownership by the trustee. Finally, you may need to obtain an endorsement to your title insurance to make sure adequate coverage is continued after the transfer.

- **Certificates of deposit.** You should make sure that retitling a certificate of deposit does not trigger an early withdrawal penalty.

- **Stock options and other assets governed by a plan.** These types of assets are governed by a written third-party plan and may also have tax and legal issues associated with the transfer. You will need to consult with your CPA and the plan administrator to determine the process and ramifications of transferring title to a trustee. Also, some stock is governed by transfer rules that may prohibit any transfer or may subject it to requirements such as obtaining an attorney opinion letter.

- **Annuities and life insurance.** You should consult with your financial and insurance advisors to determine the effect of any transfer of ownership of annuities and life insurance policies, which may include income tax and capital gain issues, as well as an alteration of payout options due to title being held by a trustee. As previously stated, funding this type of asset is usually implemented by changing beneficiary forms rather than by changing ownership.

- **Contract rights, leases, obligations.** Contract rights may have terms and conditions which restrict or prohibit any transfer and you may need to obtain consents before you can assign those rights.

- **Direct deposits.** If an account into which direct deposits, withdrawals, or other transfers are made, is closed out or the ownership is transferred, you may need to reestablish the transferor relationship with the new or retitled account.

- **Insured bank and investment accounts.** In order to maintain the maximum FDIC or other insurance available on your bank and investment accounts, you should review the structure of the accounts set up in the name of the trustee with your banker or financial advisor.

TIMING OF FUNDING AND FINAL THOUGHTS

You should expect the complications and communications involved in funding your trust will result in a *process* of funding rather than an *event*. Depending on the complexity of the asset transfers and the various companies and bureaucracies that may be involved in the transfers, several attempts and letters of direction may be necessary in order to complete the transfer of an asset to your trustee. Many times the delays result in you putting the completion of funding on the back-burner. As you can see from the advantages listed at the beginning of this chapter, incomplete funding can result in extensive additional costs and delays in the management and transfer of your property during any disability and after death.

Treating funding as a process means you and/or your professional advisors will review your asset holdings and titling on a monthly, quarterly, or annual basis. Every time an asset is acquired, you need to revisit the funding process, and of course, you should always obtain competent professional advice to make sure you are completing the process properly.

Christopher Caswell, JD, MBA, CFP® provides Business and Personal Planning and Counseling in the areas of Business, Real Estate, and Wealth and Estate Planning.

CHAPTER 57

Trust Administration
to Reduce Estate Taxes

CRAIG R. HERSCH (Fort Myers, Florida)

Before revocable living trusts became popular, when someone died, the will was probated to take care of assets titled in the decedent's name. Probate is simply a court-supervised process under which the decedent's last will is admitted to probate, and the personal representative (executor) is appointed by the court to marshal the decedent's assets, pay off the decedent's creditors, file the decedent's tax returns, and ultimately distribute the assets to the beneficiaries named in the will.

Some attorneys proclaim that one of the beneficial attributes of a revocable living trust is the fact that assets transferred into the trust avoid the probate process. So does this mean that the trustee of the trust can simply make immediate distribution to the trust beneficiaries following the grantor's death without regard to creditors, taxes, or legal claims against the estate? The answer to this question is a resounding "no."

State laws have evolved over the years to impose on the trustee of a decedent's trust many of the same responsibilities assumed by the personal representative of an estate. These responsibilities include ensuring: the proper trust is being administered, including all amendments properly executed by the grantor; the decedent's creditors get paid; interested parties have the opportunity to object to the validity and/or terms of the trust; taxing authorities are cleared; and ultimately proper distribution is made to beneficiaries.

This chapter will review the various duties most states impose on the trustee of the trust when the grantor dies. While many states have implemented some version of the Uniform Restatement of Trusts Third, it is incumbent upon anyone serving as a trustee of a trust to obtain competent legal counsel to ensure all legal requirements are satisfied. Failure to comply with most state statutes results in the trustee having personal liability to a harmed party.

ADMINISTERING THE MOST RECENT VERSION OF THE TRUST

In many revocable living trust scenarios, the grantor of the trust initially serves as his or her own trustee. Usually the person named as successor trustee only begins serving upon the incapacity or death of the grantor. Therefore it is important for the successor trustee to ensure he or she is administering the most recent version of the grantor's trust. Since most revocable trusts are, by definition, amendable and revocable, it is not uncommon for a trust to have one, two, or even multiple amendments altering its terms.

Hopefully, the successor trustee is familiar with the grantor's advisors, including the trust attorney who drafted the instrument. Most of the time, the grantor's attorney can verify the proper trust to be administered and has knowledge about its amendments.

Because the trust administration process is not governed by any court, there is no judge to determine whether the version of the trust being administered is the proper version. Most state trust administration laws therefore impose the primary duty on the trustee to provide a copy of the trust and any relevant amendments to any interested party who so requests.

It is usually good form, even if not expressly required by state statute, to provide the surviving spouse, beneficiaries, and other interested parties a copy of the current trust instrument following the grantor's death. This, along with the statutory notice provisions discussed below, starts the clock ticking for anyone who may have knowledge of another version of the trust, who believes that the trust being administered is legally invalid, or who wishes to make a statutory claim — such as a spousal elective share. If a party fails to file a challenge to the trust instrument within the legally prescribed time period, he or she generally loses the ability to do so.

It is important to explore these issues before distribution is made under the terms of the trust. If the trustee were to make distribution before giving all parties due process to present a claim or a challenge, the trustee could be held personally liable to a party. The trustee should avoid the unfortunate position of having potential liability to a party who did not get due process without having the assets at the trustee's command to satisfy the liability.

LEGAL NOTICES AT THE INCEPTION OF THE ADMINISTRATION

Most state statutes require the trustee to issue certain notices to interested parties when administering the trust following the death of its grantor. In Florida, the first notice is a "Notice of Trust." This Notice of Trust may be filed with the probate court and identifies the fact that a person died, that he or she had a revocable living trust at the time of his or her death, the name and contact information for the acting trustee of the trust, and the attorney acting for the trustee. This Notice serves as a "bridge" for potential creditors who may wish to file claims against the estate. Creditor claims aspects of a trust administration are discussed below.

The second notice is usually an "Acceptance of Trusteeship." This Acceptance indicates that the person named as successor trustee following the death of the grantor has accepted the office and responsibilities as trustee. The Acceptance is usually forwarded to all institutions (banks and brokerage firms) holding trust assets in order to transfer the ownership on the trust's existing accounts from the decedent's name as trustee to the name of the successor trustee in his or her capacity as trustee of the trust. The Acceptance is also mailed to the beneficiaries of the trust, so they know who is responsible for the trust administration and how to contact that person.

TAXPAYER IDENTIFICATION NUMBER

While the grantor of the revocable living trust is acting as a trustee, the grantor's Social Security number usually serves as the trust's taxpayer identification number. Once another party takes the office of trustee for the trust, a new taxpayer identification number is required.

CREDITOR'S RIGHTS

If there are no assets in the decedent's name individually, which would require opening a probate administration, the trust will be required to stand behind any claims made against the estate during the applicable time period prescribed by statute. In Florida, for example, without the due process afforded to creditors under the probate statutes, a creditor has a two-year statute of limitations in which to file a valid claim against the estate.

Depending upon applicable state law, the trustee may wish to open an empty probate to clear creditors. Looking at Florida again, the statutory claims period is shortened to three months by opening a probate administration and publishing a notice to creditors as directed under Florida law.

In most situations there are few creditors, and if there are, their claims probably arise from expenses related to the last illness or funeral expenses, which are usually paid in due course. A trustee should, however, assemble a list of any claims or potential claims that may be known or otherwise "reasonably ascertainable." Recent case law has held that a recurring payee in the decedent's checkbook is deemed a reasonably ascertainable creditor.

Copies of the decedent's credit card statements, bank statements, check registers, and computer logs should be reviewed to determine which creditors may have claims against the estate assets. The trustee should work carefully with the trust attorney to ensure any and all creditors who may have claims against the trust estate are provided proper notice and are duly satisfied, where necessary, prior to the final distribution of trust assets.

ACCOUNTINGS

Each "qualified beneficiary" (a legal term defined under the Uniform Restatement of Trusts Third) is entitled to an accounting of the trust assets at least annually, and again upon the termination of the trust. This provision may be, and frequently is, waived by the beneficiaries, but in this instance it will be important for the trust attorney to prepare a proper waiver from the qualified beneficiaries to protect the trustee.

Frequently, family members will waive the accounting requirement, but the more beneficiaries there are, the less likely it will be that everyone will be willing to waive. It is therefore very important that the trustee keep accurate records of all receipts and disbursements for the trust, and that these records are kept consistently throughout the course of the trust administration.

When there are ongoing "testamentary" trusts benefiting one or a group of individuals with income, while other beneficiaries are entitled to the "remainder" interest after the primary beneficiaries' interests terminate, it will be important for the trustee to account separately for the receipt and disbursement of income items, and the receipt, gain or loss, and disbursement of principal items.

Here you will need a qualified attorney or CPA to properly account for trust income and principal. Income generally refers to items such as dividends and interest, while principal typically refers to items such as capital gains and corpus.

While this might seem like a simple concept, in practice, accounting for income and principal can be quite difficult without the assistance of a qualified professional. Consider the complications arising from depreciable real estate or annuities, for example. Most state laws devote whole chapters to the rules surrounding what is considered income and what is considered principal when performing trust accountings and when making trust distributions. It is therefore important for the trustee to engage the services of a qualified professional to properly account for these items.

TAX RETURNS AND VALUING THE TRUST ASSETS

It is generally the trustee's duty to ensure that all necessary trust tax returns have been filed and that any taxes due have been paid. These returns typically include the decedent's last 1040, the trust income tax return 1041, the federal estate tax return Form 706, state income tax returns, as applicable, and if taxable gifts were made prior to the decedent's death, a federal gift tax return Form 709.

In most cases, the trustee will be responsible for determining the date of death values of the assets held by the trust. The trustee must usually hire a real estate appraiser to determine property values. A good faith estimate by a realtor or real estate broker is typically not acceptable to the IRS, so the trustee should ensure he or she is using a licensed appraiser familiar with the neighborhood or county in which the property is located.

Date of death values for stocks, bonds, and mutual funds is easier to obtain, commonly with the assistance of the trust's stock broker or financial professional. When the date of death falls on a weekend, the financial advisor should average the Friday and Monday high and lows for the stocks, bonds, and mutual funds to determine the date of death values.

When the trust owns closely held business interests, partnerships, or interests in land trusts, often the trustee must hire a qualified valuation specialist to value these types of assets.

In some taxable estates, the trustee may also be required to obtain "alternate valuation date" values for the trust assets. If the trust assets fall in value, the "alternate valuation date" (six months past the decedent's date of death) may be used for valuation purposes on the federal estate tax return.

The date of death values are important to obtain even if the estate will not be required to file a federal estate tax return Form 706. The beneficiaries to the trust assets will generally receive a step up in basis equal to the date of death values. Consequently, for the beneficiaries to verify the gain or loss on the sale of an inherited asset on their own personal tax returns, they must know its date-of-death value.

PRUDENT INVESTOR RULE

Generally, the duty of the trustee is to administer the trust diligently for the benefit of the beneficiaries. In carrying out these duties, the trustee is required by law to invest and manage the trust assets during the course of the administration as a "prudent investor." The trustee is advised to retain the services of a qualified investment advisor to assist with this duty if the trustee does not personally have sufficient credentials or skills as a money manager.

If the trust owns a concentration of assets in one or a few securities, it is usually prudent to diversify the holdings. Similarly, because most trust administrations are short-term in duration, a prudent investor would be expected to liquidate more volatile assets in favor of more conservative holdings, unless the beneficiaries sign a direction, such as a "letter of retention" directing the trustee not to sell certain holdings.

The trustee is charged with the responsibility of ensuring the assets do not fall in value following the valuation date used for the federal estate tax return. The trustee, in other words, does not want to be in the situation where the trust estate is paying tax on asset values that have since declined. Consequently, the prudent investor rule leans toward a conservative, asset preservation mode as opposed to a more aggressive growth mode during the course of the trust administration.

Because many assets receive a step up in basis equal to the date-of-death value, the trustee usually does not have to risk incurring capital gains on the sale of volatile assets. These issues should be discussed with the trust attorney, CPA, and financial professional prior to the trustee taking action.

SALE OF REAL PROPERTY

The sale or disposition of real property, particularly homestead real property presents unique issues. Some of these issues involve whether the trustee has proper and clear vested title, or whether certain court orders must be obtained before clear title can be transferred.

Therefore the trustee should not list to sell, contract to sell, or transfer real property without consulting trust counsel. The trustee does not want to be in the situation where he or she has a contractual obligation to pay a commission to a broker or to close a transaction when the trust has a legal impediment, such as a tax release, homestead order, or other contingency which must occur before the trustee has authority to close the transaction.

In other words, the trustee needs to avoid the situation where he has contractually obligated the trust to act when in fact there are circumstances beyond the trustee's control (court orders might take longer to obtain than originally anticipated, for example) that prevent him from acting and therefore renders the trust in breach of the obligation. Competent real estate and trust counsel can assist the trustee in avoiding these situations.

DUTY TO ACT IMPARTIALLY

Often the trustee charged with the duties and responsibilities of administering the trust is also a beneficiary of the trust. Here, the trustee must be very careful to administer the trust impartially, without regard to his or her own or any particular beneficiary's interest.

Suppose a child of the grantor is named as the trustee of the trust following the grantor's death. Assume further that the trust continues for the benefit of the child's stepmother for the rest of her life, paying her income, while principal may be invaded for the stepmother's health, maintenance, and support.

The child/trustee understands that if the trust is balanced more for income than for growth, this will adversely affect his own interest and benefit his stepmother's interest. Further, if the child were to distribute principal for the stepmother's benefit during her lifetime, these dollars will not end up with the child/trustee's remainder interest.

Nevertheless, when accepting the office of trustee, the child assumes the role of an independent, impartial, and disinterested fiduciary and must carry out his or her duties without regard to personal gain or loss. Instead, the trustee should always consider what the intent of the grantor would have been had the grantor been alive to provide further instruction.

TRUSTEE AND PROFESSIONAL FEES

Generally speaking, most trusts and state statutes provide that the trustee may take a reasonable trustee's fee and may also employ legal, accounting, tax, appraisal, and other advisors. The trust assets are used to pay these fees, and the fees are normally tax-deductible.

In cases where the trustee is also a family member or beneficiary, trustee fees may be waived. As one can determine by reading this chapter, however, acting in the capacity of trustee takes a substantial amount of time and effort and is fraught with liability. For other beneficiaries to expect the person acting as trustee to take on these obligations without compensation is not a reasonable position.

Costs, such as filing fees, newspaper publication costs, and the like, should also be paid by the trust assets. Where the trustee or another person has forwarded these costs on behalf of the decedent, the trustee can use trust funds to reimburse the party.

Certain expenses, such as those associated with family members attending funeral services, are not deductible by the trust or the estate and are generally considered not to be expenses that should be reimbursed by trust assets. The trustee should consult with the trust attorney prior to making any such reimbursements.

IS A TRUST ADMINISTRATION AS BURDENSOME AS A PROBATE?

After reviewing this chapter, you may inquire whether having a revocable living trust is worth it, given the fact that the trustee has so many obligations to satisfy. If one considers that the trust administration process is private and rarely do issues appear in a public forum such as the probate court, then one can come to the conclusion that a trust administration is preferred to a probate administration.

Couple this with the fact that one does not have to wait for a court to respond to pleadings, something that can often delay a probate administration for weeks or months given most probate court's crowded dockets, and one can easily surmise that having a revocable living trust is preferable to not having one.

Many of the rules surrounding the obligations of trustees have been around for quite some time. It is only in recent history that these common law rules have been codified into state statutes to provide clear guidance to trustees and their advisors, ensuring everyone affected by the grantor's death is treated fairly and responsibly.

Craig R. Hersch is a Florida Bar Board Certified Wills, Trusts & Estates Attorney and CPA. He practices in Fort Myers, Florida, and is a shareholder in Sheppard, Brett, Stewart, Hersch, Kinsey & Hill P.A.

Postmortem Actions to Increase Estate Liquidity and Reduce Estate Taxes

REDUCING CASH NEEDS OF THE ESTATE	INCREASING CASH AVAILABLE TO THE ESTATE
Reduce gross estate: • Lifetime gifts • Special-use valuation • Valuation discounts	• Sale of illiquid assets • Buy-sell agreements for business interests • Section 303 redemption of closely held stock
Reduce taxable estate: • Alternate valuation date • Marital deduction • Charitable deduction • Qualified disclaimers • Election against the will • QTIP election	• Life insurance
Reduce estate tax payment: • Installment tax payments • Section 303 redemption	• IRA and retirement plan benefits available to the estate
Reduce probate and administration costs: • Living trust • Will substitutes • Avoid ancillary probate • Postmortem elections and actions	• Loans • Irrevocable life insurance trust (may make loans to or buy assets from estate)

Postmortem Actions to Reduce Income Taxes

ACTION	OPTIONS
Medical expense deduction	May be taken on: • Estate tax return or • Decedent's final income tax return
Estate administration expense deduction	May be taken on: • Estate tax return or • Decedent's final income tax return
Waiver of executor commissions	Avoids reporting and being taxed on income that will be received as a bequest
Selection of fiscal year for estate	Income can be spread over more years potentially benefiting heirs and legatees
Reporting interest on U.S. savings bonds	May be reported on: • Decedent's final income tax return or • Estate tax return

LIFE
INSURANCE

CHAPTER 58

Who Has an Insurable Interest?

MARTY BURBANK (Fullerton, California)

In 2006, I came home to find my next door neighbor's house was, for the most part, lost in a fire. The same thing had happened to another friend of mine in 2003. They had insurance and rebuilt their homes. It would have been nice if I also had insurance policies on their homes. I could have called up the insurance company and had them send me my check too. Unlike my friends, I would not have to rebuild my home, so I could just take the money and go buy that new airplane I've been wanting.

Of course, I did not have insurance on their homes, and I would not have been able to buy any even if I wanted to.

The reason why is that I lacked any insurable interest in either friends' home. What is an insurable interest? Generally one has an insurable interest if he or she has a risk of economic peril. For example, merchants and shipowners in the 16th century experienced great risk that their ships would be lost to storms and pirates. Today, a business owner has a risk that his business will be sued by an injured customer. These are interests that are insurable.

So why do we care, and what does it matter whether I have any economic risk in my neighbor's house. One reason is that it would create a moral hazard. For example, assume that I am home on the day of my neighbor's fire and I smell smoke. My normal reaction would be to try to put out the fire or at least call 911. I might react differently if I owned an insurance policy on my neighbor's house. My mind might not work that same — "what was that number…119?"

With life insurance, however, some people have an insurable interest even if they do not have a risk of economic loss. For example, a sibling, parent, child, or spouse has an insurable interest without having a risk of economic loss. But quite often, life insurance is purchased by others and they generally need to show some economic interest in the life of the insured. Non-family members often have an insurable interest in the life of another. But the non-family member must have some economic dependency on the life of the insured.

One of the most common areas for non-family member owned life insurance is in partnerships and other small business arrangements. A business partner will often want to have an insurance policy on the life of his or her other partners. Life insurance is often used to fund a buy-sell agreement between partners. These types of arrangements can be very beneficial, not only to the surviving partner, but also to the decedent partner's family. If a partner dies and there is insurance payable to the surviving partner (or the entity) then those funds provide the liquidly for the survivor to buy the decedent's interest from the family. This will ensure the family has cash and the surviving partner can run the business without interference from his or her partner's family.

Other arrangements where non-family members have an insurable interest include key employees of an organization. Keyman insurance can save a business when a key employee dies. But it is important that there be some risk that if the employee dies the company would suffer an economic hardship. It is hard to argue that the death of a rank-and-file employee would have a significant economic impact. For several years, Wal-Mart had the practice of obtaining insurance on most, if not all, of their employees, allegedly without always letting the employees know. Most states have laws requiring companies to advise their employees and seek their consent before purchasing the policies, but six states; Delaware, Georgia, New Jersey, North Carolina, Pennsylvania, and Vermont, allow companies to take out life insurance policies on their employees without notice to the employee. Wal-Mart has paid some very large settlements to the families of employees who sued when they learned of the policies.

The world of sports and entertainment is another area where key people are often insured by non-family members. For example, a movie producer or investor planning to make a movie would have an insurable interest on the lives of their lead actors. Professional sports teams have taken out large policies for both life and disability on some of their key players. The St. Louis Cardinals had a $12 million policy on Mark McGwire. But while one team may have an insurable interest in its players, another may not. The Seattle Mariners insure none of their players, as their draw is more dependent on fan loyalty than on superstars.

From time to time, news headlines read of someone who purchased insurance on a person's life and then killed the person. It sounds like a movie pitch, but there is a famous case of the "Blue Eyed Six" who bought a life insurance policy on Joseph Raber and then drowned him in 1878. As recently as April 18, 2008, two women in their 70s were convicted in Los Angeles for taking two separate homeless men off the street, purchasing life insurance on their lives, and killing each of them in separate hit and run "accidents." Clearly, in these cases there was no insurable interest in the victims.

Unlike casualty insurance, for life insurance, an insurable interest need only exist at the time the life insurance is purchased. The Supreme Court has determined that people who own life insurance have a property right interest and are able to sell that property right. Currently, there is great debate on how this might be done. The controversy does not exist when there is a good faith purchase of life insurance which is later re-sold. This is what happens in viatical settlements (for the terminally ill) and life settlements (for those with no impending health issues).

It is common for people to buy insurance with the idea that if the insured dies while the policy is in place, the money will take care of those who are left behind. However, sometimes the need for the insurance is no longer a concern. For example, if a parent purchases life insurance to cover his or her child's educational costs in the event of the parent's premature death, and the child is now grown and educated, or when a spouse has been predeceased by the spouse for whom the insurance proceeds were intended. In these cases, the sale of the death benefit in the insurance can provide a much better outcome than cashing out with the insurance company for the cash value of the policy.

Several programs have evolved over the last few years which give people incentives to purchase unneeded life insurance and then immediately sell the policy to an investor. This seems to run afoul of the insurable interest rules. Currently, however, many people are participating in these types of investments. Many insurance companies would like to see a stop put to these investments and they have been somewhat successful in some states. But in many other states, these transactions are common and account for millions of dollars of insurance sales and commissions every year.

In the Navy Hospital, Marty Burbank cared for heroes of WWI, WWII, and Korea; today he is proud and blessed to serve that same generation, and their families.

Estate Liquidity Worksheet

LIQUID ASSETS AVAILABLE

Life insurance proceeds $_____

Checking and savings accounts $_____

Money market accounts and funds $_____

Certificates of deposit $_____

IRC Section 303 redemption proceeds $_____

Other liquid assets $_____

Total Liquid Assets Available $_____

CASH REQUIREMENTS

Living expenses for family members $_____

Administration expenses $_____

Funeral and cost of final illness $_____

Debt retirement $_____

Personal income and excise taxes (Federal and state) $_____

State death and/or inheritance taxes $_____

Federal estate and generation-skipping transfer taxes $_____

Specific cash bequests $_____

Expenses of family business $_____

Educational costs for child or spouse $_____

Other: _____ $_____

Other: _____ $_____

Other: _____ $_____

Total Cash Needs   ($_____)

Surplus (Deficit) of Cash Available $_____

CHAPTER 59

Tax Issues Associated With Life Insurance

DENNIS CULLEN (Lemoyne, Pennsylvania)

Most everyone believes life insurance is tax-free. However, technically, the Internal Revenue Code deems life insurance to be an exception to the income tax provisions, and as with every legal rule, there are exceptions to the exceptions. Thus, it comes as a surprise to some people when they find out life insurance proceeds are not always tax-free. Unfortunately, most people do not discover this until after a death, in which case it is too late to avoid the tax.

Below are five tax issues to be cognizant of when you are dealing with life insurance.

1. ESTATE TAX

In certain situations, life insurance proceeds may be subject to federal estate tax as well as possibly state tax. The general rule is that if the life insurance policy is owned by the decedent or if the decedent had "incidents of ownership," the life insurance proceeds are included in the decedent's gross taxable estate. Examples of incidents of ownership include a person maintaining the right or an interest in the policy such that they can modify the policy, borrow cash value from the policy, or benefit from the proceeds of the policy.

For example, a life insurance policy is owned by Peter, the life insured is Peter's, and the beneficiary of the policy is Peter's brother, James. Even if there is no state tax, for federal estate tax purposes the life insurance proceeds are includable in Peter's taxable estate. This is significant because if the other assets Peter owns at his death place him close to or above the federal estate tax applicable exclusion amount, the life insurance proceeds may cause, or significantly increase, federal estate taxes due upon Peter's death.

To enhance this example, if the life insurance policy on Peter's life was to pay $1.5 million in proceeds and the other assets in Peter's estate totaled $3 million, for federal estate tax purposes Peter's gross taxable estate would be $4.5 million. If Peter were to die in 2009, $1 million would be subject to federal estate tax in the amount of $450,000.

2. INCOME TAX

Believe it or not, sometimes life insurance proceeds may be subject to income tax as well. If there are any lifetime distributions of the policy's cash surrender value greater than the owner's basis in the policy, the amount of money received above that basis is taxable income. The basis in a policy is the amount of money paid for the premiums and any other consideration paid to purchase the policy. Therefore, any distributions made by the life insurance company to the owner of the policy that exceed the owner's basis are potentially subject to income tax.

For example, Peter owns a life insurance policy with a cash surrender value of $30,000. Since the inception of the policy, Peter has paid premiums equaling $10,000, which is Peter's basis. If Peter were to receive distributions from the life insurance company equal to $20,000, Peter would pay income tax on the $10,000 above his basis.

3. FORGIVENESS OF LOAN

Keeping the previous example in mind, income tax is often avoided by having Peter sign a promissory note to repay the $10,000 loan, the amount above Peter's basis. If Peter then cancels the policy and the life insurance company forgives the $10,000 loan, the forgiveness of the loan has provided Peter with something of "value," which is the elimination of Peter's obligation to repay the loan. Since Peter has received something of "value," he has essentially received $10,000 of income which will be subject to income tax.

4. GIFT TAX

In certain circumstances, life insurance proceeds may be subject to gift taxes. If the owner of a life insurance policy is Peter's daughter, the insured is Peter, and the beneficiaries are Peter's daughter and son, a gift tax would apply to the proceeds received by Peter's son.

This arrangement often occurs when people try to avoid having the insurance proceeds included in the parent's taxable estate. If Peter provided his daughter with the money to pay for the premiums of the policy and the amount is less than the annual gift exclusion, he avoids any gift tax while he is alive. However, when Peter dies, the fact that his daughter owns the policy and she names her brother as a beneficiary will cause the IRS will treat her brother's receipt of proceeds as a taxable gift to her because it comes from his sister who is now the donor.

5. TRANSFER FOR VALUE RULE

The tax-free status of life insurance can be defeated if you run afoul of the "transfer for value rule." In essence, the transfer for value rule was imposed by the IRS to prevent people from speculating on human life where persons with no "insurable interest" would receive insurance proceeds at the death of another. People who have an insurable interest generally include a spouse, children, parents, and co-shareholders in a closely held business. Nevertheless, there may be situations where you transfer the ownership of a life insurance policy for value to a party with no insurable interest in your life, and in doing so, income tax is paid by the beneficiaries. As you can imagine, there are exceptions to this exception which will be explained in more detail in another section. However, below is an example of a transfer for value situation that would defeat the tax exemption of life insurance.

Assume Peter is the owner of a $1 million life insurance policy. Peter is the insured, and the beneficiary is Peter's son. If Peter sells his life insurance policy to his friend, James, for $25,000 and James acquires the right to name himself as the beneficiary, a transfer for value has occurred. James is not related to Peter, and James is not associated with Peter in some business manner. After Peter dies, James collects the life insurance proceeds of $1 million. However, that $1 million is taxed as income to James because of the transfer for value rule.

CONCLUSION

As you can see, it is extremely important for you to consult with an attorney to determine if your life insurance will be received tax-free by your beneficiaries. Each situation has its own facts and, by consulting the appropriate professionals you can minimize or avoid taxation of proceeds.

Our firm focuses on protecting the wealth of individuals, professionals, and businesses via estate planning, asset protection, business organization, succession planning, and litigation defense should a lawsuit be filed.

CHAPTER 60

Irrevocable Life Insurance Trusts

BRUCE G. KAUFMANN (Clearwater, Florida)

HOW TO HAVE YOUR CAKE AND EAT IT TOO

Iam Taxpayer and his wife, Ima Taxpayer, have a serious problem. They started a family business on a large parcel of inexpensive land many years ago. The children, who are looking forward to transitioning into positions of ownership and control, are involved in the business. The Taxpayers have acquired other valuable but non liquid assets. What is the problem? The family business is very successful and very valuable. The land upon which the business sits has become very valuable due to the the discovery of mineral-rich deposits and the subsequent growth of a community to service the mines and related industries. The problem is that the Taxpayers are non-liquid asset "rich" and for estate tax-paying purposes, cash "poor."

The Taxpayers have not considered the estate tax consequences of such valuable assets. Iam, being the husband, the male, and the older of the two, is expected to die first. Iam can pass his share to his wife without significant estate tax consequences because of the unlimited marital deduction. However, upon Ima's death, the entire estate will be heavily taxed because it will all be in Ima's estate. However, the business and the land, while very valuable, will not be easily liquidated. Therefore it will be difficult for their beneficiaries, their children, to pay the impending federal estate tax. The business, or the land, or both, will have to be sold in order to pay the expected 45% estate tax.

What is the estate tax solution? The Taxpayers should consider an irrevocable life insurance trust (ILIT). The Taxpayers should consider their potential estate tax burden and then increase it based upon expected asset appreciation and their life expectancies. One or both should apply for life insurance in death benefit amounts sufficient to pay for the cost of the anticipated estate tax liability.

Assuming they are insurable, they should then create the ILIT. There is no need to create an ILIT if the Taxpayer(s) are not insurable. The ILIT must be irrevocable in order to avoid having the death benefit included in the value of the estate at the time of the Taxpayer's death, thereby increasing the taxable estate and the estate tax liability. Irrevocable means that once the trust is put in place and funded the trust cannot be changed. Therefore, it is wise to think through the selection of trustee and successor trustee(s), and also to consider including provisions for a trust protector, who, among other things, can remove and replace trustees. It is also important to think through the selection of beneficiaries and the terms of the ILIT.

The Taxpayers can then fund the ILIT by:

1. Transferring an existing life insurance policy into the ILIT;

2. Transferring enough money into the ILIT to fund a new single premium paid up endowment life insurance policy;

3. Transferring money into the ILIT bank account set up by the trustee with the new taxpayer identification number for the ILIT, which the trustee will use to pay the initial premium for the purchase of a new life insurance policy and making arrangements to fund the annual premium payment each year with further gifts; or

4. The trustee can arrange a premium financing plan to purchase a new life insurance policy.

However, if the Taxpayers want to put an existing life insurance policy into the ILIT the Taxpayers must transfer the ownership of the policy into the name of the trustee, and the beneficiary must be the ILIT. The transfer of ownership must be irrevocable. The Taxpayers must not be able to borrow on the existing life insurance policy or the life insurance policy will still be considered a part of the taxable estate upon the death of the Taxpayer. The Taxpayer must then live for a minimum of three more years for the life insurance policy, its cash value, and/or its death benefit to be excluded from the Taxpayer's estate. It is important to note that the transfer of cash value to an ILIT may trigger a gift taxable event and/or cause the use of some or all of your lifetime gift tax exclusion. This gift tax complication and the three year "wait and see" rule is the reason why many ILITs purchase new life insurance policies.

The Taxpayers must give enough money to the trust bank account for the trustee to pay the policy premium(s). Using the ILIT concept as soon as possible is important for timing and funding purposes. Life insurance becomes more expensive the older an insured person becomes. The more money that has to be transferred into the trust bank account to fund the life insurance policy premium, the more likely that a taxable gift event will occur, or that the lifetime gift tax exclusion will be used.

The Taxpayers will need to put a plan in place to gift money to the trust bank account so that the trustee can pay the life insurance premiums on behalf of the trust. If the amount needed is substantial, it may be necessary to consider the use of a "Crummey" trust. The "Crummey" trust refers to a situation where the Taxpayers gift money to the trust for the benefit of the beneficiaries, their children, with the idea that the beneficiaries will benefit from the life insurance policy being in place and pay the proceeds to the beneficiaries on the death of the Taxpayers. However, the beneficiaries have to be given notice and a reasonable time in which to take the gift out of the trust before it is used to pay the life insurance policy premiums.

The Taxpayers need to be sure that the beneficiaries, their children, understand the purpose of the ILIT so that they will decide not to exercise their "Crummey" powers and take out the gift. After the beneficiaries have been notified of the gifts and their right to exercise their "Crummey" powers and take out the gifts, and the time (e.g., 30 days) has expired for those rights to be exercised and the beneficiaries have not exercised their rights, then the trustee has the necessary money to pay the annual premium.

The value of the death benefit is paid to the ILIT. The trustee then takes the policy proceeds and performs the trustee's duties according to the terms of the ILIT. One of the terms of the trust should be the power to pay estate taxes due on the deceased Taxpayer's estate. Paying estate taxes with the assets of the ILIT frees up the non-liquid assets (i.e., the land and the family business). Now the children of the deceased Taxpayers do not have to sell the land or the business to pay estate taxes.

The trustee could also utilize the idea of an over-funded premium financed life insurance policy. This concept requires the trustee to borrow a large enough amount of money to overpay the premium into a life insurance policy on the life of the Taxpayer. The excess cash value then increases with the underlying investment and pays the annual premiums. After several years, the increased cash value is used to pay off the loan and the remaining cash value continues to pay the premiums on the life insurance policy. If the Taxpayer dies before the loan is paid off, then the policy death benefit is used to pay off the loan and the remaining death benefit is paid to the ILIT. Once again, properly calculating the expected estate burden and policy loan so that the life insurance death benefit is sufficient to meet all the ILIT's purposes is very important.

Ultimately, utilizing an ILIT allows Iam Taxpayer and Ima Taxpayer to keep their land and family business intact for their children and still pay the estate tax burden to the government. This is like having your cake and eating it too.

Bruce G. Kaufmann, J.D., P.A. of Clearwater, Florida, has been assisting clients in handling their complicated estate planning and tax-paying issues with unique creative legal solutions for nearly 30 years.

Life Insurance Trusts Compared

	IRREVOCABLE	REVOCABLE
Grantor can select trustee to manage insurance proceeds.	X	X
Insurance proceeds are removed from the insured's estate.	X	
Grantor can determine under terms of the trust when beneficiaries receive proceeds.	X	X
Assets in the trust are not subject to probate.	X	X
The trust is ignored for income tax purposes.		X
Grantor loses the ability to control the trust's assets.	X	
Terms of the trust can be altered or amended to fit the grantor's changing circumstances.		X
The trust must have special provisions (Crummey) in order for gifts to the trust to qualify for the annual gift tax exclusion.	X	

Avoiding Tax on Life Insurance Distributions Before Death – Life Settlements and Viatication

NEIL COVERT (Clearwater, Florida)

GETTING CASH OUT OF YOUR LIFE INSURANCE POLICY

You may find yourself needing cash from your life insurance policy. This might occur if you need money for living expenses, educational expenses for children or grandchildren, or for general investment purposes. If you have a life insurance policy with cash value inside of the policy, you may be able to access that cash.

There are generally two methods of accessing cash from your life insurance policy. First, you could keep your existing policy and borrow or withdraw the cash from the policy. Second you could either surrender or sell your policy in exchange for cash. Each method of accessing this cash may result in what is known as a taxable transaction, meaning you may have to pay either income tax or capital gains tax.

WITHDRAW OR BORROW

If you have a cash value type policy, such as a whole life, universal life, or variable life policy, you may be able to withdraw or borrow cash from your policy. The amount of premiums you have paid into your policy generally represent what is called your basis in your policy. If you wish to take this money out, you can withdraw it tax-free, meaning you pay no income or capital gains taxes. However, any amounts withdrawn in excess of your basis are taxable to you as ordinary income.

You can also borrow money from your cash value life insurance policy. You will be required to pay back this loan to the insurance company, and you will usually not be required to pay any income taxes on this loan. One exception to this rule is if your policy is classified as a modified endowment contract, or a MEC. But if you have been paying premiums into your policy over time, your policy is probably not a MEC.

SELL OR SETTLE YOUR POLICY

The other method of obtaining cash from your life policy is to sell or settle the policy. If you find yourself wanting to terminate your permanent life insurance policy (or a term insurance policy that permits you to convert to permanent insurance), then there are essentially two markets to turn to: the life insurance company that issued the policy to you; or the secondary market.

If you contact your life insurance company to see what your policy is worth, it will have a price at which it will permit you to surrender the policy. This is generally referred to as the cash surrender value. This cash surrender value of the policy is determined by your insurance company and is usually based upon how much excess cash has accumulated or has been invested by the insurance company inside of your policy.

A cash surrender value is thought to be significantly less than a true market value of the same policy. This is because death is certain; and if death is certain, and if a policy will pay a contractual amount at a time in the future, the certainty of this event has value. The value is determined by the amount of the death benefit and the likelihood of the death. Therefore, for example, if your health has declined since the issuance of the policy, you may not likely live to your actuarial life expectancy. This means the policy will pay off sooner and the policy will therefore have greater value.

The cash surrender value of your policy in the eyes of your life insurance company is far different than the market value for your policy. The true market value of your policy may be three to six times the cash surrender value your life insurance company may be willing to pay. This difference, in recent years, has become attractive to policy owners. Indeed, the stark difference may seem unfair. Imagine being required by contract to sell your home back to your builder for less than its true market value. No one would agree to that. Similarly, as insureds are becoming more aware of a life settlement secondary market, they are now turning to it to sell their policies rather than back to the original issuing company.

TAXATION OF LIFE SETTLEMENTS AND VIATICALS

If you keep your life insurance policy until your death, the death benefit proceeds of the policy are usually paid to your beneficiaries listed in your life insurance contract free of income tax. If you instead sell your policy to a third party under a life settlement or viatical settlement, that sale will be considered a taxable event. A viatical settlement is one where death is imminent, and historically was used to help people pay for the cost of their medical expenses. A life settlement is a sale of your policy to a third party where death is not imminent.

Since the advent of the life settlement industry, there have been no reported tax court cases or other case law that describe in detail exactly how a life settlement will be taxed. Although there has been one private letter ruling from the Internal Revenue Service, there is still some controversy among tax experts as to how a life settlement will be taxed.

When we speak of taxation in this context, we are generally talking about two types: 1) ordinary income taxation; and 2) capital gains taxation. Ordinary income tax rates are higher than capital gains tax rates. Therefore, if we are to pay taxes on the sale of our policy in a life settlement transaction, we would rather pay capital gains taxes instead of the higher ordinary income taxes.

Most experts agree that taxation of life settlements and viaticals will consist of three component parts. Please refer to the diagram below.

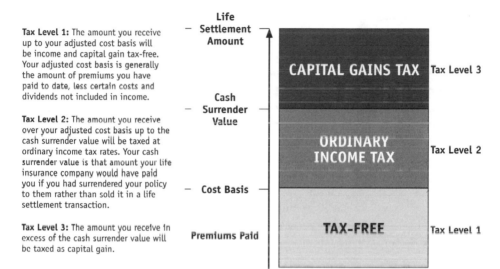

Tax Level 1: The amount you receive up to your adjusted cost basis will be income and capital gain tax-free. Your adjusted cost basis is generally the amount of premiums you have paid to date, less certain costs and dividends not included in income.

Tax Level 2: The amount you receive over your adjusted cost basis up to the cash surrender value will be taxed at ordinary income tax rates. Your cash surrender value is that amount your life insurance company would have paid you if you had surrendered your policy to them rather than sold it in a life settlement transaction.

Tax Level 3: The amount you receive in excess of the cash surrender value will be taxed as capital gain.

CONCLUSION

If you find yourself in need of cash, you may wish to consider borrowing or withdrawing cash from your life insurance policy, or, in the alternative, selling your policy on the life settlement market for its true fair market value.

Neil Covert's firm limits its practice to asset protection planning, estate planning, and business planning.

CHAPTER 62

Transfer for Value Rule

CHRISTOPHER D. SOTO (Tempe, Arizona)

Life insurance is an important estate and financial planning tool. Life insurance is an extremely efficient way to meet cash and liquidity needs that arise when someone dies. One of the most attractive aspects of life insurance as an estate planning tool is the tax treatment of the proceeds. As a general rule, proceeds a beneficiary of a life insurance policy receives when the insured dies are entirely income tax-free. However, an easily missed tax trap known as the "transfer for value rule" can cause some or all of your life insurance policy proceeds to become income taxable. In order to ensure life insurance proceeds will be fully available to your beneficiaries, it is critical that you avoid triggering the transfer for value rule.

As the name implies, the transfer for value rule is triggered when there has been a transfer of a life insurance policy (or an interest in the policy) and valuable consideration is given in exchange for that transfer. Transfer for value rule issues often arise in connection with buy-sell agreements where business owners are using life insurance proceeds to buy out a co-owner's interest on the death of the co-owner. Consider the following example: Andrew and John are the shareholders of their closely-held corporation. Andrew buys a $1 million policy on John's life. When John dies, Andrew collects the life insurance proceeds and intends to use those proceeds to buy out John's ownership in the corporation. If Andrew bought the life insurance policy from John, the proceeds will be subject to ordinary income tax, which could result in an income tax bill of over $300,000, leaving a fraction of the proceeds available to buy out John's shares. However, if instead of buying a policy transferred from John, Andrew purchased $1 million in insurance on John's life directly from the insurance company, the $1 million in life insurance proceeds would go to Andrew completely income tax-free and leave the full $1 million available to fund the buyout of John's shares.

It is also important to understand the transfer for value rule can arise any time economic benefits of a life insurance policy are transferred in return for valuable consideration — even if there is no transfer of ownership of the policy. As an example, if Steve makes his friend, Jim, the beneficiary of a policy on Steve's life in exchange for Jim's transfer of ownership of his houseboat, there has been a transfer for value. Therefore, if there is a transfer — even of a mere interest in a policy —

and that transfer is made in exchange for any type of economic consideration, the transfer for value tax trap is set.

Fortunately, the tax laws contains several exceptions to the transfer for value rule. A beneficiary can continue to receive insurance proceeds income tax-free, even if there has been a transfer for value, in each of the five following circumstances:

1. A transfer to the insured;

2. A transfer to a partner of the insured;

3. A transfer to a partnership in which the insured is a partner;

4. A transfer to a corporation in which the insured is a shareholder or officer; and

5. The transferor's basis exception.

Following are some examples of transfers which fall within the exceptions outlined above:

- If a corporation owns a life insurance policy on the life of a key executive, Jim, and the corporation transfers the policy to Jim for valuable consideration, the life insurance proceeds will remain income tax-free when Jim dies, because Jim was the insured and the transfer falls within the transfer to the insured exception.

- Joe and Al are partners in a partnership. Joe sells Al a policy on Joe's life in exchange for a cash payment. Because it is a transfer to a partner of the insured, this transfer is an exception to the transfer for value rule, and Al's receipt of the policy proceeds will be income tax-free.[1]

- Similarly, if Al sold a policy on his life to the partnership in exchange for financial consideration, this falls within an exception and the partnership will receive the proceeds income tax-free.

These exceptions to the transfer for value rule provide you and your advisors with a number of creative opportunities and tools to transfer interests in life insurance policies while keeping the life insurance death proceeds completely income tax exempt.

In summary, if the IRS determines you have made a transfer of an interest in a life insurance policy that triggers the transfer for value rule, it could have devastating income tax ramifications to the beneficiary, and could have a potentially catastrophic effect on the objectives for which the insurance was purchased. Therefore, it is critical you and your advisors carefully analyze any potential transfer of an interest in a life insurance policy to determine whether the transfer for value rule applies. Proper navigation of the transfer for value rule and proper coordination of policy ownership and beneficiary designations can literally allow you to leave an unlimited amount of life insurance proceeds to your beneficiaries completely estate and income tax-free.

The Soto Law Firm is dedicated to providing comprehensive, highly personalized estate planning services to couples, families, individuals, and businesses.

1. It is important to note that this exception only applies to partners in a partnership, not to shareholders in a corporation. If instead of being partners, Joe and Al were shareholders in a corporation, this transfer would not fall within the transfer to a partner of the insured exception, and the life insurance proceeds would be income taxable upon Joe's death.

CHAPTER 63

Can You Afford Your Buy-Sell Agreement?

NATALIA KABBE (Naperville, Illinois)

Ernie and Don were the classic, almost archetypical, American success story. Working in their proverbial garage, they came up with a new and exciting game, one that took the market by storm. They formed a private company together and prospered, selling thousands of units, with the games going out their garage door faster than they could stock them. Both of them seemed destined for wild success. Then tragedy struck.

One frozen January morning, Don suffered a heart attack. Unfortunately, he did not survive. Upon Don's death, his half ownership of the company went to his widow. What was a tragic situation for her, turned into a crisis for the successful, but still fledgling, company. Don's widow and Ernie did not get along. While they finally reached an agreement to allow Ernie to buy her out, Ernie seriously overextended himself in the process. Ernie raised money to keep the company going by selling a significant portion of his own shares, leaving him with only a 30% stake in the company.

The new partners, two brothers, pushed Ernie out and proceeded to run the company into the ground. Ernie eventually wrested control of the company away from them, but that did not end his troubles. Out of spite, the two brothers retaliated by selling their shares in the company to Lorraine, a woman who took it as a matter of pride that she had nothing to do with games. Ernie tried to stop the sale in court, but lost. Lorraine continued to run the company into the ground and, in the end, was forced to sell the company herself. But long before that happened, Ernie had sold his shares and left the company, having lost the rights to his game and all desire to work for the company he had built.

Does this scenario sound unlikely? It shouldn't. The game in question was Dungeons and Dragons, and Ernie's full name was Ernest Gary Gygax. This hypothetical was all too real. But it could have been avoided had Ernie taken a few vital steps back when he was first forming his company.

It is not surprising Ernie and Don did not plan for their deaths. When first starting a business, the prospect of a partner dying is probably the farthest thing from your mind. There are too many other things to worry about, like designing products and selling to customers. You aren't thinking about how to get rid of your business, but how to grow it.

You, like Ernie, face two potential problems as a part owner of a closely held business, be it a partnership, corporation, or limited liability company. The first problem is how to deal with a situation where the shares of a partner may pass to someone else, whether through tragedy, such as death or disability, a falling out, or simply a decision by a partner to move on to other things. As Ernie learned, a new partner can cause conflict and deterioration of the business. A buy-sell agreement can protect the remaining partners — and the company — by allowing the other partners (or the company as a whole) to buy the shares of the departing or deceased partner. The buy-sell agreement also protects the heirs of a deceased partner, by setting a value for the partner's interest in the company. Unlike Ernie and Don, many business owners have taken this first step. But their plans may still fail due to the second problem.

The second problem, as Ernie found out, is how the remaining partners will pay for the shares. Even though Don's widow was willing to sell, Ernie lacked the finances to buy. As a result, Ernie still ended up with unwanted partners. What could have saved Ernie, and what can save you in the event of a partner dying, is life insurance specifically set up to cover the cost of acquiring your deceased partner's share of the company.

There are two basic ways to set up a life insurance policy to fund a buy-sell agreement. The first option is for each partner to take out a life insurance policy on every other partner. The life insurance proceeds are used by the partners to fund the purchase of their pro-rata portion of the deceased partner's shares. One of the biggest disadvantages of this arrangement is that it can get very complicated if there are more than a few partners because each partner must purchase a policy on the life of each other partner. Another downside is that some partners may pay more for their policies than others because the cost to insure each partner will likely vary based on age and health. The extra complication can be worth it, though, because the shares purchased by the surviving partners are valued at their purchase price for tax purposes (stepped-up cost basis).

The second option is for the company itself to take out a single life insurance policy on each partner. If a partner dies, the company buys the deceased partner's shares with the proceeds of the life insurance. The company can then either keep the shares, reducing the number of outstanding shares, or distribute the shares proportionally to the surviving partners. Having the company buy the policies is the simplest solution because only one policy is purchased for each partner. Also, because the company pays for the policies, no partner pays more than his or her fair share of the policy premiums. But this simplicity comes at a cost. The shares purchased by the company do not receive a stepped-up cost basis.

Don't find yourself in Ernie's situation. Make sure you have a buy-sell agreement in place and then properly fund the agreement with life insurance.

Natalia Kabbe is the founder of The Law Offices of Natalia Kabbe, LLC, a boutique estate planning law firm in Naperville, Illinois, serving business owners, executives, and high-net-worth individuals.

RETIREMENT PLANS

CHAPTER 64

The Tax on Income in Respect of a Decedent – an Estate Tax for Everyone

NATALIA KABBE (Naperville, Illinois)

There is a tax applicable to estates even your CPA might miss. This tax could hit you for up to 35% and potentially applies to any estate, not just those over a certain amount. This is a tax on what is referred to as Income in Respect of a Decedent (IRD).

What is IRD? Simply put, IRD is any income owed to the decedent that was not collected by the decedent before death. An example of IRD is a paycheck paid for the last days the decedent worked but not actually sent until after the date of death. Another example of IRD are the proceeds of a contract entered into by the decedent in selling a car. A final, and very significant example of IRD, is a tax-deferred retirement account, such as an IRA.

Because IRD isn't collected during the decedent's life, it is not included — and, therefore, not taxed — on the decedent's last income tax return. Instead, IRD is taxed as income to whomever receives this income after the decedent's death. This means the decedent's heirs pay the tax. If your heirs aren't expecting to pay this tax — for instance, if they cash out your IRA, planning to enjoy it as tax-free inherited income, they could be in for quite a shock months later when their income taxes become due. But being unaware of the potential for this trap on smaller estates is not the most serious problem. It is even worse for estates large enough to be subject to estate taxes.

The most serious problems occur when the estate exceeds the federal estate tax exclusion and has most of its liquid assets in an IRA or other tax-deferred retirement account. It is not uncommon for a taxable estate to consist primarily of some real estate, an IRA or 401(k), and a checking or savings account. When this happens, you are hit with a double-whammy. First, even though income taxes will be owed on the IRA withdrawals (as IRD), the IRA still counts in the total size of the estate when calculating the estate tax. If your heirs do not want to sell your home, that leaves them with the IRA as the primary source of funds with which to pay the estate tax. Unfortunately, withdrawing funds from the IRA to pay taxes triggers the second whammy, income taxes on IRD. With no other liquid assets to cover the income taxes, the IRA would need to be further cashed out to cover the additional taxes.

That further cashing out would trigger yet more taxes on IRD, leading to a cascade of withdrawals that could very quickly eat up upwards of 80% of the IRA, just in taxes. Fortunately, there are steps you can take to ameliorate this problem.

First, even if you only find out about the IRD problem after cashing out the IRA to pay estate taxes, there is some relief offered by the IRS. The IRS allows a tax deduction based on the amount of the estate taxes attributable to the IRD. The deduction can only be taken when the IRD income is actually received, for example, when money is withdrawn from an IRA — and is prorated based on the total amount of the IRD.

> **EXAMPLE:** Robin passed away leaving three properties worth a total of $3,750,000 and an IRA worth $750,000. Her other assets are negligible. Assume the federal estate tax rate is 45% and applies to any assets over $3,500,000. Robin's estate will owe estate taxes of $450,000. Without including the IRA, Robin's estate would owe only $112,500. The IRD income tax deduction for Robin's IRA is $337,500, the difference between those two amounts. For each $750 withdrawn from the IRA, the recipient will qualify for a $337.50 IRD deduction. The deduction will not completely offset the taxes paid, but it lowers the worst case scenario from an 80% combined tax to a 60% combined tax.

One way of ameliorating the tax net is to purchase life insurance to cover estate taxes when the estate contains few liquid assets except for an IRA or another tax-deferred retirement account. Paying estate taxes with life insurance proceeds allows the IRA to remain untouched and to continue to do what it does best, grow your money tax-free (until it is withdrawn). This strategy can be combined with the IRD deduction, minimizing the taxes owed when IRA distributions are made.

Ultimately, you want to be prepared for the taxes on IRD in your estate. That means informing your beneficiaries about taxes on IRD and having sufficient liquid, non-IRD assets available to cover the full cost of your estate taxes. With IRAs becoming an ever larger share of estates, appropriate planning to handle the taxes on IRD is of supreme importance. You want to leave your heirs the fruits of your estate, not a tax headache. Don't get caught off guard. Start tax-proofing your estate today.

Natalia Kabbe is the founder of The Law Offices of Natalia Kabbe, LLC, a boutique estate planning law firm in Naperville, Illinois, serving business owners, executives, and high-net-worth individuals.

CHAPTER 65

Planning Strategies to Avoid Income in Respect of Decedent (IRD)

RANDY GARDNER (Leawood, Kansas) and BOB KEEBLER (Green Bay, Wisconsin)

Figuring out how to avoid the double tax on Income in Respect of a Decedent (IRD) assets is perplexing. Here are steps to help you through the analysis:

Identify who is going to pay the estate tax.

If there is no will or the will is silent on the issue, many states require that the distributed assets bear their burden of estate tax. Most wills direct debts and taxes to be paid from the residuary share. If the recipient of the IRD asset and the residuary are the same, there is no problem. However, if the recipient of the IRA is a child and the taxes are to be paid from the surviving spouse's residuary share, the surviving spouse may be surprised by the small amount received after paying the debts and taxes attributable to other properties in the estate.

Do not forget to claim the income tax deduction for the estate taxes paid.

If the estate tax is paid from the residuary and not from the property itself, this deduction is often overlooked.

If possible, defer the payment of income tax on the IRD by postponing the receipt of IRD income.

Normally heirs want to collect accounts receivable as soon as possible and installment payments when they are due, but retirement plan distributions can usually be stretched over the life expectancy of the designated beneficiaries. Although postponing collection of income also means postponing the deduction for estate taxes paid, breaking the payments into smaller pieces at lower marginal income tax rates and taking advantage of the time value of money by paying the income tax in the future rather than today support deferring the receipt of income. The benefit of this approach is enhanced if the IRD asset is growing tax-free as a retirement account likely is.

Retirement accounts left to multiple beneficiaries generally must be distributed over the life expectancy of the oldest beneficiary. PLR 200537044 added a beneficial twist to the strategy of trying to reduce the marginal rates of tax on the distributees by allowing multiple IRAs within trusts to be named as beneficiaries. The ruling allowed each beneficiary to receive the assets over his or her own life expectancy, rather than the life expectancy of the oldest beneficiary.

If the decedent has a lower marginal income tax rate than the beneficiaries, execute a Roth conversion or distribute the IRD asset to the decedent before death.

The decedent might have a lower tax rate because: the decedent's marginal income tax rate is lower than the tax rates of the estate or heirs; the decedent's anticipated time of death is early in the year, before much income has been earned; or the IRD asset is eligible for special income tax treatment, such as lump sum distribution averaging, pre-1974 capital gain treatment, or the benefits of net unrealized appreciation on employer stock.

Avoid estate tax by transferring the IRD asset to the surviving spouse.

The first spouse to die typically designates the surviving spouse as the beneficiary. This transfer qualifies for the marital deduction and usually has the added advantage of spreading the distribution of the income at lower marginal tax rates over the life of the surviving spouse. Surviving spouses have the discretion to: withdraw the retirement plan assets when needed, stretch the distributions over their life expectancies; or treat the retirement accounts as their own by rolling the assets over to their own IRAs. Under the Pension Protection Act of 2006, nonspouse beneficiaries can now transfer retirement plan assets and IRAs to their own accounts, but they do not have the option of postponing distributions until 70½ as a spouse does.

Revenue Ruling 2006 — 26, 2006-22 I.R.B. 1 addresses the issues of holding an IRA in a qualified terminable interest property (QTIP) trust. QTIP treatment allows the first spouse to die control over the ultimate disposition of the trust property after the death of the second spouse, yet still receive a marital deduction. In order to qualify for the marital deduction, the QTIP trust must distribute its income annually to the surviving spouse. What is the income of an IRA that produces income, but is also required to make required minimum distributions (RMD)? For a spouse who can compel the IRA custodian, through the trustee, to invest in productive assets, the Ruling holds that the IRA must distribute to the spouse the higher of the RMD or IRA income. After distribution from the IRA to the trust, the amount is distributable to the surviving spouse.

Avoid estate tax by transferring the IRD asset to charity.

Another effective way to avoid the two layers of tax on IRD assets is to take advantage of the estate tax charitable deduction. Charitably-inclined clients can transfer IRD assets to charity while transferring assets which receive a step up in basis and have minimal income tax impact at the beneficiary level to the estate and heirs.

Unless the will provides otherwise, some states require that a decedent's estate be distributed pro rata to the estate beneficiaries. In other words, if an estate has three beneficiaries — two children and one charity — and three assets — $1 million in securities, a $1 million residence, and a $1 million IRA — the executor might be required to transfer a ⅓ interest in each of the assets to each of the beneficiaries. If the will provides for specific bequests or gives the executor discretion regarding how to divide the assets among the beneficiaries, the IRA could be transferred to charity and the house and securities could be transferred to the two children.

To summarize, the estate tax portion of the tax on IRD can be avoided by making marital or charitable transfers. The income tax portion can be minimized by postponing distributions of IRD and spreading the distributions among beneficiaries.

Randy Gardner, LLM, MBA, CPA, CFP®, is the Director of Education for WealthCounsel, LLC and also a Professor of Tax and Financial Planning and Director of the Certificate in Financial Planning Program at the University of Missouri – Kansas City.

Robert S. Keebler, MST, CPA, Partner, Virchow Krause & Company, LLP, focuses his practice on family wealth transfer and succession planning, retirement distribution planning, estate administration, and IRS representation.

CHAPTER 66

Retirement Plans – Beneficiary Designations

GUY GARNER (Arlington, Texas)

Retirement plan accounts, such as Individual Retirement Accounts (IRAs), 401(k), 403(b), and 457 plans, just to name a few, are types of assets most Americans will own at the time of their death. Retirement plan assets are often one of the largest assets individuals own at the time of their death, at times exceeding the value of their residence and their life insurance death benefits. Retirement plan assets, unlike all of the other assets you own, require special attention when you are planning your estate. This chapter will discuss some of the basic rules and principles applicable to your retirement plan accounts. If you follow these rules, your retirement plan assets can become a fortune. If you fail to follow the rules discussed in this chapter, your retirement plan account balances will most likely suffer a devastating loss of value after your death.

RETIREMENT PLAN RULES AND PRINCIPLES

Your retirement plan accounts need their own special "Will," separate and apart from your other Last Will and Testament or revocable living trust.

This special "Will" for your retirement accounts is called a "beneficiary designation form," which you must create to ensure your retirement plan benefits pass to whom you want, when you want, and in the manner you want, after you die. The terms and provisions of your Last Will and Testament or revocable living trust will not, and cannot, dictate where your retirement plan account assets will go after you die. You must have completed and signed a beneficiary designation form for each and every retirement plan account you own if you want to control the distribution of your retirement plan assets when you die.

If you have an IRA at Vanguard, an IRA at Fidelity Investments, and a 401(k) plan with your employer, you will need to complete and sign three different beneficiary designation forms in order to control the distribution of the assets in each of these accounts at the time of your death.

If you fail to complete and sign a beneficiary designation form for a retirement plan account you own, then the terms of what is called the "custodian agreement" or "plan agreement" will dictate by default where and how your retirement plan benefits will be distributed when you die. Every retirement account you own will have, in addition to the beneficiary designation form, a contractual agreement between you and the entity that is responsible for holding and, in some cases, managing your retirement plan assets.

These custodial or plan agreements specify who will receive your retirement plan assets when you die if you fail to have signed a beneficiary designation form. Suffice it to say, if you let your retirement plan agreement decide who will get your retirement benefits when you die, there is a very good chance that the "default" beneficiary named in your retirement plan agreement will be your "estate."

Typically, if your estate is the primary beneficiary of your retirement plan when you die, the entire value of the retirement plan account will be subjected to federal income tax and state income tax (if you live in a state with state income tax). As a rule of thumb, whenever your estate is the beneficiary of one of your retirement accounts, at least ⅓ of that retirement plan account balance at the time of your death will be lost due to income taxation of your entire retirement account balance. This tragic loss can be easily prevented simply by making sure you have completed and signed proper beneficiary designations for every retirement account you own prior to your death.

> **EXAMPLE:** John rolled over his 401(k) plan from a previous employer into an IRA account at his bank. John's personal banker, Sally, told John he would need to stop by the bank to sign the "paperwork" on his new IRA account. John was divorced and had two adult children, John Jr. and Jean, whom he had named as his primary beneficiaries on his 401(k) plan.
>
> In spite of Sally's pleas for John to come in to complete his IRA beneficiary designation form, John kept procrastinating and did not stop by the bank. On his way home from work one night, John's car was struck head-on by a drunk driver, and John was killed. John's Last Will and Testament left his entire estate to John Jr. and Jean equally. John had $300,000 in his IRA account when he died.
>
> Because John had never completed a beneficiary designation form for his new IRA with his bank, the default provisions of John's IRA custodian agreement controlled whom John's beneficiaries would be on his death. In this case the default primary beneficiary of John's IRA account was John's estate. Because John's estate was not a "designated beneficiary" (meaning a person, or a special type of trust called a "qualifying trust"), the entire amount of John's IRA had to be distributed in one lump sum when John died and income tax was due on the full $300,000 IRA distribution, approximately $100,000.

If John had completed his IRA beneficiary designation form before he died, naming his two children as beneficiaries of his IRA account, they would have ended up with an extra $100,000! That is a huge, unnecessary waste.

Seek the help of a qualified estate planning professional to assist you in preparing all of your beneficiary designation forms.

Nationally renowned CPA and retirement account planning expert, Robert Keebler, began his retirement benefits estate planning course with the following statement: "All retirement plan estate planning begins at the beneficiary designation level."

If you will memorize and utilize this one rule, and follow the advice that follows, you will optimize the uses, benefits, and increases in the value of your retirement plan benefits after you die.

How to properly prepare and complete your individual retirement plan beneficiary designations is beyond the scope of this chapter. There are many ways to complete your retirement beneficiary designations depending on your estate planning objectives. Questions such as: "Whom do you want to receive your retirement plan death benefits when you die? When and how do you want your retirement plan benefits distributed to your beneficiaries?" must be addressed in your retirement plan beneficiary designation forms.

You and your loved ones will best be served if you consult with a qualified estate planning attorney for assistance in reviewing and drafting all of your retirement plan beneficiary designation forms. There are many legal and tax considerations that go into designing the best possible beneficiary designation for your needs. Remember, just because an advisor is sincere doesn't mean his or her advice is correct; he or she could be sincerely wrong.

> **EXAMPLE:** Frank had $500,000 in his IRA account. Frank's two adult children, Mary and Jane, were poor money managers and spent everything they got their hands on. Frank had read a book about "stretching IRA benefits" for adult children upon a parent's death. Frank decided he wanted an IRA stretch for his IRA so that Mary and Jane wouldn't take a lump sum distribution when Frank died and lose a substantial amount to the IRS in income taxes.
>
> Frank told his IRA account broker that he wanted to make sure his daughters would have "stretch IRAs" when Frank died. Frank's broker said Mary and Jane would have a stretch IRA merely by putting their names on Frank's IRA beneficiary designation. Frank followed his advisor's advice and named his daughters as the primary beneficiaries on his IRA. When Frank died one year later, both of his daughters requested and received lump sum distributions of Frank's IRA account. In the process, Mary and Jane ended up paying over $166,000 in federal income tax!

What went wrong? What Frank's advisor told Frank was correct. His daughters had the opportunity to stretch out Frank's IRA if they chose, but they were not required to do so. If Frank had worked with an estate planning attorney experienced in drafting IRA Trusts, Frank could have legally forced his daughters to stretch his IRA over their lifetimes. If he had done so, Frank's IRA would have ultimately distributed several million dollars to Mary and Jane over their lifetimes.

Keep a copy of every retirement plan beneficiary designation you have in a safe place, and have your retirement plan beneficiary designations reviewed by your estate planning attorney on a regular, ongoing basis.

Keep a copy of all of your retirement plan beneficiary designations in a safe place.

Never assume the companies and financial institutions serving as your retirement plan's custodian or administrator have on file a copy or the original of the beneficiary designation form you signed. Retirement account beneficiary designation forms do get lost, misplaced, or are sometimes inadvertently destroyed. The IRS has taken the position that if one of your retirement plan beneficiary designation forms cannot be retrieved after your death, it will be assumed you died without having completed a beneficiary designation form! In that case, the default provisions of your retirement plan contract will dictate who your primary beneficiary will be. If the default primary beneficiary happens to be your "estate," your entire retirement plan account balance will be taxed as ordinary income in the year of distribution, and most likely ⅓ of that account's value will be lost before your loved ones receive a penny!

Estate planning should be an ongoing process rather than a onetime transaction. Laws change, family situations change, wants and needs change, and your net worth can change. Schedule an appointment to meet with your estate planning attorney at least every couple of years and have your retirement plan beneficiary designations periodically reviewed along with your estate planning documents.

When it comes to estate planning involving your retirement plan accounts, there is no substitute for qualified professional assistance. Being informed yourself should also be a priority, because proper estate planning is really a joint effort between you, your estate planning attorney, your accountant, and your financial advisors.

The author recommends the following books written by CPA and author Ed Slott as excellent sources of information about retirement plans and estate planning, as well as the topics discussed in this chapter: *The Retirement Savings Time Bomb... and How to Defuse It; Parlay Your IRA into a Family Fortune;* and *Your Complete Retirement Planning Road Map —The Leave-Nothing-to-Chance, Worry-Free, All-Systems-Go Guide.*

Guy B. Garner, III, P.C. offers customized estate and asset preservation planning services to individuals and families wanting superior service and "state of the art" legal representation.

CHAPTER 67

Required Minimum Distributions and Stretching

PATRICK B. CASEY (Bonita Springs, Florida)

While numerous benefits derive from saving for retirement using IRAs and Qualified Plans, one of the more significant is tax deferral. Money inside an IRA or Qualified Plan is not subject to income tax until it is distributed from the plan (IRC §402). For an example of how this works, assume that an IRA with a beginning balance of $1 million accumulates tax deferred at a 10% rate of return for 20 years. With no further contributions, the IRA will grow under such conditions to $6,727,500. However, if the IRA is taxed at 29% as it grows, the end result is $4,222,590. Because of the effect of tax deferral, you would keep your money invested in IRAs indefinitely if you could. However, the Government never intended to wait forever to tax your money. So Congress passed rules to serve the Government's interest. In general terms, these rules govern when and how funds must be distributed from IRAs and Qualified Plans.

WHEN THE MONEY MUST START COMING OUT – REQUIRED BEGINNING DATE (RBD)

When the money must begin coming out of an IRA or Qualified Plan depends on the type of IRA or Qualified Plan. As a general rule, funds must begin coming out of the IRA or Qualified Plan by April 1st of the year after the participant turns age 70½. Unless the IRA custodial agreement or Plan Agreement provides otherwise, follow the distribution rules in the chart at the end of this chapter (Treas. Reg. §1.401(a)(9)-4).

If withdrawals do not begin by the RBD, a penalty equal to 50% of the amount that should have been withdrawn, but wasn't, will be incurred. Keep in mind that the RBD date is mandatory date by which the plan participant/IRA owner must begin withdrawing from the account. This does not mean withdrawals cannot occur earlier. In fact, withdrawals can occur as early as the plan participant/IRA owner turning age 59½. Withdrawals occurring prior to age 59½ will be penalized at 10% on the amount withdrawn.

HOW THE MONEY MUST COME OUT – REQUIRED MINIMUM DISTRIBUTIONS (RMDS)

Required Minimum Distributions are the annual amounts the plan participant/ IRA owner must withdraw from the Qualified Plan or IRA to avoid penalty. The

RMD rules apply to all Qualified Plans, IRAs (including Roth IRAs held by beneficiaries), Deferred Compensation Plans, and IRC section 403(b) plans. RMDs are a function of two variables:

1. The maximum period over which distributions can occur without penalty; and

2. The amount of money in the plan or account.

MAXIMUM DISTRIBUTION PERIOD – LIFE EXPECTANCY

The longest period over which distributions can occur without penalty is the life expectancy of the Qualified Plan or IRA beneficiary. Life expectancies are set by Tables published by the IRS. See Treas. Reg. §1.401(a)(9)-9. Three tables are published:

1. Single Life Table — used for determining the life expectancy of a single individual;

2. Uniform Life Table — sets forth the life expectancy of a married plan participant or IRA owner whose spouse is not more than 10 years younger than he or she is; and

3. Joint and Last Survivor Table — provides the life expectancy of a plan participant or IRA owner whose spouse is more than 10 years younger than he or she is.

As long as the plan participant or IRA owner is alive, determining life expectancy is straightforward. One simply goes to the appropriate table and finds his or her age in the year the distribution is to occur and selects his or her life expectancy from the Table. Things get more complicated if the plan participant/IRA owner dies before his or her interest in the Qualified Plan or IRA is entirely distributed. In such a case, the maximum distribution period will depend on whether the plan participant/IRA owner died before or after the required beginning date and whether he or she named a designated beneficiary for the remainder of the interest.

Life Expectancy if Death Occurs Prior to Required Beginning Date

The maximum distribution period if the plan participant/IRA owner dies before reaching age 70½ depends on whether a Designated Beneficiary was named to receive the balance of the interest. For these purposes, the term "Designated Beneficiary" is a term of art.

Under IRC §401(a)(9)(E) and the regulations thereunder, Designated Beneficiaries are only *individuals* who are entitled to a portion of the plan participant or IRA owner's benefit upon the death of the participant/owner, or other specified event. In some cases, a properly crafted trust will qualify as a Designated Beneficiary. If anyone other than an individual or a qualified trust is named as a beneficiary, the participant/owner will be treated as having no Designated Beneficiary, even if individuals are also named.

In the absence of Qualified Plan or IRA provisions to the contrary, the balance of the plan participant/IRA owner's interest can be distributed over the Designated Beneficiary's life expectancy if death occurs prior to the Required Beginning Date. If there are multiple Designated Beneficiaries, the shortest life expectancy (that is, the life expectancy of the oldest beneficiary) is used in the absence of separate accounts.

If there is no Designated Beneficiary, the balance of the plan participant/IRA owner's interest must be distributed in full by December 31 of the fifth year after his or her death. This is commonly referred to as the Five Year Rule.

Whether a life expectancy or the Five Year Rule is used, RMDs must begin by December 31 of the year after the plan participant/IRA owner dies. Surviving spouses receive special consideration. When spouses are named as Designated Beneficiaries, they have a choice: 1) they may defer taking RMDs until December 31 of the year the plan participant/IRA owner would have turned 70½; or 2) they may follow the general rule and begin taking RMDs by no later than December 31 the year after the plan participant/IRA owner died.

Life Expectancy if Death Occurs After Required Beginning Date

If the plan participant/IRA owner dies after his or her required beginning date, the maximum period over which the remaining balance can be distributed will again depend on whether there is a Designated Beneficiary. If there is a Designated Beneficiary, distributions can occur over the life expectancy of: 1) the plan participant/IRA owner; or 2) the Designated Beneficiary, whichever is longer. If a Designated Beneficiary is not named, distributions may occur over the theoretical life expectancy of the plan participant/IRA owner for his or her age as of the year he or she died had he or she lived. For obvious reasons, this is commonly referred to as the "Ghost Life Expectancy."

MINIMIZING RMDS – THE STRETCH

The power behind Qualified Plans and IRAs is tax deferral. For this reason, plan participants/IRA owners would leave the money in the Qualified Plan/IRA forever if they could. However, the government wants its due and has promulgated rules that force the money out from under the umbrella of tax deferral. Carefully applied, however, the rules allow us stretch distributions over a period of time, thereby preserving the tax deferral (at least for a while). The key to preserving tax deferral then is to maximize the stretch afforded by the rules; the key to maximizing the stretch is the Inherited IRA.

THE INHERITED QUALIFIED PLAN/IRA

Just like the term "Designated Beneficiary," the phrase "Inherited Qualified Plan/ Inherited IRA" is a term of art. A Qualified Plan or IRA is inherited if the person for whom it is maintained acquired his or her interest because of the death of the original owner. Two key elements make this work. The first is the beneficiary designation form.

The beneficiary designation form is provided to the original owner by the plan administrator/IRA custodian and is used to name who will receive what remains of the original owner's interest when he or she dies. In other words, the form names the Designated Beneficiary. The trick to the beneficiary designation form is to ensure it is completed before the original owner dies and that it names only beneficiaries who qualify as Designated Beneficiaries. In a perfect world, these forms are drafted by legal counsel. Why? Because it is the beneficiary designation form and not the will, trust, or other estate planning document that controls the disposition of the plan/IRA interest upon the original owner's death. Therefore, to achieve the original owner's estate planning goals, the beneficiary designation form must be consistent with the architecture of the overall estate plan. The second key to Inherited Qualified Plans/IRAs is how the interest is titled after the death of the original owner.

In the world of Inherited Qualified Plans/IRAs, re-titling what remains of the original owner's interest in the name of beneficiaries is fatal. Doing so is deemed a lump-sum distribution to the named beneficiaries. If the interest is deemed distributed in its entirety, it is not possible to distribute it over a beneficiary's life expectancy, so the stretch is destroyed. The proper way to retitle a Qualified Plan/IRA after the death of the original owner is essentially "John Doe, deceased (09/01/08), FBO Fawn Doe, beneficiary."

Spouse as Designated Beneficiary

Surviving spouses receive preferential treatment if named as Designated Beneficiary of an Inherited Qualified Plan/IRA. First, they can elect to defer taking RMDs until the original owner would have reached 70½. Second, they can use a method of determining life expectancy that recalculates life expectancy each distribution year. Most important, however, is the surviving spouse's ability to roll the Inherited Qualified Plan/IRA into his or her own Qualified Plan/IRA. This is commonly referred to as the "Spousal Rollover." The Spousal Rollover is available only to surviving spouse Designated Beneficiaries.

As with most options, there is an upside and a downside to Spousal Rollovers. On the upside, by rolling over an Inherited Qualified Plan/IRA, the new account is treated as the surviving spouse's own account, subjecting the surviving spouse to all the "normal" rules applicable to an account owner and entitling the surviving spouse to all the rights and incidents of ownership, including the right to name beneficiaries. On the downside, if a spouse is younger than 59½, he or she won't be able to get to the money without incurring the 10% early withdrawal penalty. This is commonly known as the "Spousal Rollover Trap."

Another consideration is who will receive the funds remaining upon the death of the surviving spouse and how those beneficiaries will receive them. While the

Internal Revenue Code and the Regulations thereunder provide rules permitting the use of successor beneficiary life expectancies, the Qualified Plan or IRA Custodial agreement may not. Since the Qualified Plan or IRA Custodial agreement controls, the longer life expectancies permitted by the tax rules may not be available. Consequently, an upside to a Spousal Rollover is the ability to add certainty to the life expectancy that can be used upon the death of the surviving spouse.

For the foregoing reasons, there is a tension between the surviving spouse rolling and not rolling over an Inherited Qualified Plan/IRA. Relief lies in the fact that a surviving spouse can effect a Spousal Rollover any time after the death of the original owner. If the surviving spouse is under age 59½ and the goal is to give the survivor penalty-free access to the funds while ensuring the maximum stretch, he or she should maintain the account as an Inherited Qualified Plan/IRA until age 59½. After reaching age 59½ the surviving spouse can roll over the account in order to avail himself or herself of the incidents of ownership.

Multiple Designated Beneficiaries

It often suits the account owner's purpose to name multiple Designated Beneficiaries. For example, the beneficiary designation form may read something to the effect of "equally to my brother and three nephews." For purposes of "stretch" planning, however, naming multiple beneficiaries can produce unintended and unfortunate results. The reason for this is that the law looks at the population of all Designated Beneficiaries, selects the one with the shortest life expectancy, and imputes that life expectancy to all the others. In other words, a single life expectancy is used for all beneficiaries, irrespective of their actual ages. If there is a large disparity in the ages of the beneficiaries, this outcome is disastrous as the younger beneficiaries are stuck taking their RMDs over the life expectancy of the oldest.

All is not lost, however. Under appropriate circumstances, the law allows an Inherited IRA to be divided into separate accounts, one for each of the Designated Beneficiaries. As long as the division occurs by December 31 the year following the original owner's death, each beneficiary can use his or her own life expectancy in determining RMDs. Disaster is avoided.

USE OF DISCLAIMERS

No discussion about stretching IRAs is complete without mentioning Qualified Disclaimers. A Qualified Disclaimer is a legal "no thank you." In other words, a Designated Beneficiary legally declines to accept what he or she is otherwise entitled to. A Designated Beneficiary who disclaims an interest is treated as if he or she predeceased the original owner. In this event, his or her interest passes to the next Designated Beneficiary in line. By coupling Qualified Disclaimers with skillful naming of contingent Designated Beneficiaries, significant flexibility is added to the planning.

Qualified Plan/IRA Distribution Guidelines

Traditional IRAs, including SEPs and Simple IRAs	Distributions must begin by April 1 of the year after the owner turns 70½
Qualified Plan participant (including 403(b) plans) owning more than 5% of the plan sponsor	Distributions must begin by April 1 following the later of: 1) the year the participant turns 70½; or 2) the participant's retirement from the company
Qualified Plan participant who owns 5% or less of the plan sponsor	Distributions must begin by April 1 of the year following the year the participant turns 70½
Qualified Plan participant with a TEFRA 242(b) election in effect	Date of retirement
Roth IRAs	No RBD as to the original owner

Patrick B. Casey, JD, CPA, focuses exclusively on the design and implementation of wealth transfer, asset protection, and value preservation strategies for persons wishing to pass along legacies as opposed to mere inheritances.

Effect of Beneficiary Designations:
Participant Dies Before Required Beginning Date

DESIGNATED BENEFICIARY	OPTIONS
Spouse	1. RMDs postponed until later of: Year following participant's death; Year participant would have attained 70½; or End of the 5th year after the participant's death, if the plan permits and the surviving spouse elects. 2. RMDs over spouse's life expectancy (unless 5-year rule is used). 3. Rollover available.
Nonspouse	1. RMDs over single life of designated beneficiary beginning in year following death. This factor is reduced by one for each year thereafter. Otherwise, distributions must be completed by end of 5th year following participant's death. 2. Rollover available if made as a direct transfer to an inherited IRA.
Trust	1. RMDs over life of oldest trust beneficiary beginning in the year following death if trust qualifies as designated beneficiary. 2. If trust does not qualify as designated beneficiary, RMDs must be completed by the end of the 5th year following participant's death. 3. Rollover available for a qualified trust if made as a direct transfer to an inherited IRA on behalf of the trust, with the trust identified as the beneficiary. 4. Eligible for spousal rollover if the trust is a qualified trust and all distributions from the plan are payable to the spouse during his or her life.
No Beneficiary (Estate or Charity)	1. Distributions must be completed by end of 5th year following participant's death. 2. Spousal rollover may be available if the surviving spouse has the right to receive all plan assets and can cause plan benefits to be distributed to himself or herself.

Effect of Beneficiary Designations:
Participant Dies After Required Beginning Date

DESIGNATED BENEFICIARY	OPTIONS
Spouse	1. Distributions can be made over the spouse's single life expectancy recalculated annually. At spouse's death, RMDs are made over spouse's remaining single life determined in year of death and reduced by one for each year thereafter. 2. Rollover available.
Nonspouse	1. RMDs over the beneficiary's single life expectancy. 2. Rollover available if made as a direct transfer to an inherited IRA.
Trust	1. If trust qualifies as designated beneficiary, RMDs over the life expectancy of the oldest beneficiary. 2. If trust does not qualify as designated beneficiary, RMDs over the owner's life expectancy. 3. Rollover available for a qualified trust if made as a direct transfer to an inherited IRA on behalf of the trust, with the trust identified as the beneficiary. 4. Should be eligible for spousal rollover if the trust is a qualified trust and all distributions from the plan are payable to the spouse during his or her life.
No Beneficiary (Estate or Charity)	1. RMDs over the owner's life expectancy. 2. Spousal rollover may be available if the surviving spouse has the right to receive all plan assets and can cause plan benefits to be distributed to him or herself.

CHAPTER **68**

Using Standalone Retirement Distribution Trusts

STEPHEN T. O'NEILL (Providence, Rhode Island)

In the preceding chapter, you learned about the income tax-deferred "stretchout" available under Treasury Regulations for your IRAs and qualified plans. You also learned that this stretchout is available not just to you and your spouse, but also to your children or other beneficiaries whom you designate to receive these retirement assets after your death.

You also learned that a trust designated to receive retirement assets after your death may qualify for the same stretchout as an individual beneficiary, the length of the stretchout being based upon the life expectancy of the oldest trust beneficiary. In this chapter, you'll find out whether it makes more sense to have retirement assets payable to a living trust or to a "standalone retirement distribution trust."

Regarding your estate in general, the types of beneficiaries for whom a trust is advisable include a beneficiary who is financially irresponsible, a beneficiary with special medical needs, or a beneficiary with a developmental disability. Perhaps less clear-cut is a beneficiary who has a troubled marriage, a beneficiary who is in a high-risk profession, or a beneficiary whose own estate taxes can be reduced by placing all or part of his or her inheritance in a trust.

As to retirement assets in particular, a trust may be advisable to prevent a beneficiary from unwisely deciding to cash in your IRA or qualified plan right after your death so that it becomes immediately and fully income-taxable. But let's assume you're certain your beneficiaries will wisely opt to stretch out distributions over their life expectancies. Even so, unless your retirement assets are made payable to a trust, the benefits may wind up with someone whom you wouldn't have chosen as a beneficiary, because your beneficiary may not live a full life expectancy, and he or she gets to designate his or her own death beneficiary for any undistributed amounts.

Whatever the reason, if you're naming a trust as beneficiary of retirement assets, additional rules and strategies apply:

- If your trust has charitable beneficiaries who aren't "cashed out" by

September 30 of the year following the year of your death, your trust and its beneficiaries won't be entitled to any stretchout.

- If your trust has a contingent beneficiary who is older than the trust's primary beneficiary, unless your trust has appropriate provisions stating that it is a mere "conduit" for IRS required minimum post-death distributions, or unless each such contingent beneficiary disclaims his or her interest in the trust by September 30 of the year following the year of your death, the oldest contingent beneficiary's life expectancy will determine the stretchout period for your retirement assets.

- If your trust gives your primary beneficiary the power to "appoint" the trust at death among a group which might include older persons or charities, again, unless the trust has appropriate provisions stating that it is a mere "conduit" for IRS required minimum post-death distributions, the retirement assets may have a shortened stretchout or possibly no stretchout at all.

- If upon your death your trust splits into subtrusts for several beneficiaries, unless your IRA or qualified plan beneficiary designation form directly designates the subtrusts as beneficiaries of specified shares of the IRA or qualified plan, it is likely that the life expectancy of the oldest of all your trust's beneficiaries will be the stretchout period for that particular IRA or qualified plan.

By the way, qualified plan assets, unlike IRA assets, don't automatically qualify for stretchout by a nonspouse beneficiary. Each plan document must be checked in this regard.

As indicated above, if your trust is a mere "conduit" for IRS required minimum post-death distributions, it will qualify retirement asset distributions for stretchout over the life expectancy of the trust's (or its subtrusts') primary beneficiary, regardless of the identity of any contingent beneficiaries or of any potential appointees under powers of appointment.

But maybe you don't want your trust to be a mere conduit. Maybe you'd like to give your trustee the power to decide whether to distribute or accumulate the required minimum distribution amounts, for example, when you have an incapacitated beneficiary. If your trust confers such a power, it will only qualify for the desired stretchout if there is no possibility under the trust of there ever being a contingent beneficiary or a beneficiary of a power of appointment: 1) with no life expectancy (a charity); or 2) who may be older than the primary beneficiary. But eliminating all these persons as possible beneficiaries might thwart your intentions, so it is not always a simple decision.

Significantly, the IRS ruled in PLR 200537044 that where powers are given under a trust to a fiduciary to "toggle" a trust between being a "mere conduit trust" or a "distribute or accumulate trust," and to delete or modify contingent beneficiaries and/or powers of appointment as needed to assure such "toggling" won't prevent the intended stretchout, full stretchout of an IRA over the separate life expectancy of the primary trust beneficiary is available. The ruling (and the trust) also stated that these powers had to be exercised by September 30th of the year following the year of the IRA owner's death. This ruling provides additional planning flexibility, but its use in your estate plan requires careful drafting.

Due to the complex rules and strategies in this area, many advisors believe a standalone retirement distribution trust is far preferable to a living trust as beneficiary of retirement assets. The reasons for this include:

- It is easier for your trustee and advisors to comply with the stretchout rules.

- Your living trust is simpler and easier to understand.

- Your living trust can name older and/or charitable beneficiaries, use normal marriage and adoption provisions, contain broad limited and/or general powers of appointment, and have broad spendthrift, in terrorem, incentive/disincentive, and similar payout-curtailing clauses. Such provisions, prone to being a stretchout-defeating minefield, are more easily avoided in a trust dedicated to receiving retirement distributions.

Stephen T. O'Neill, an estate planning attorney for 33 years, is admitted to practice in Rhode Island and Massachusetts. He is a Fellow of the American College of Trust and Estate Counsel.

CHAPTER 69

The IRA Designated Beneficiary Trust – Saving Your Family Millions

STUART KALB (Denton, Texas)

THE PROBLEM

Due to certain income tax rules enacted several years ago, your IRA, when inherited, may be the largest asset your loved ones receive from you. However, if you are not careful, your family will face significant income and estate taxes on this asset. Moreover, this asset can be completely lost to your beneficiaries' judgment creditors, divorce, inadvertent planning, financial irresponsibility, and the like. Therefore, it is incumbent upon you to consider all available alternatives to minimize income and estate taxation generationally while maximizing asset protection. One of these alternatives involves the use of a dynamic technique known as the IRA Designated Beneficiary Trust (DBT).

IRA beneficiaries who take advantage of deferring or "stretching-out" the taxable, required minimum distributions (RMDs) over their own life expectancies may compound income tax-free for a much longer period than you (as the IRA owner) would be able to — allowing the IRA to grow to be worth millions of dollars. The problem is that this stretch-out does not happen automatically.

If you are like most people, you will name your children or other individuals as beneficiaries of your IRAs. Unfortunately, they may not necessarily obtain the income tax stretch-out, costing them and their heirs potentially millions of dollars. This outcome may happen because your beneficiaries are not aware of the tax and the timetables involved and their alternatives regarding distribution. Or, they may just get improper advice. Sometimes, beneficiaries are unduly influenced by a spouse or some unscrupulous third party with a hidden agenda.

All too often, IRA beneficiaries access the cash immediately, and in many cases, cash out the entire account immediately, only to foolishly spend the balance. They do this before they consult with family members, a financial consultant, or other advisor. Unfortunately, the IRA custodian does nothing more than offer a payment to the beneficiary, which results in financial disaster from the standpoint of tax-free compounding.

But even if your beneficiaries do correctly attempt to maximize the income tax stretch-out of the IRA, the inherited IRA may still be seriously exposed to additional risk of loss by virtue of: 1) an unintended beneficiary inadvertently inheriting the IRA; 2) estate taxation at the maximum rate; 3) your beneficiary's divorce; 4) poor money management skills (particularly if some of the IRA monies eventually pass down to your grandchildren or others who are young or financially inexperienced, or are spendthrifts); and 5) creditors of your beneficiaries seizing all of your IRA assets after your death.

THE SOLUTION

The obvious solution that comes to mind is to create a trust to be the beneficiary of your IRA. With a trust, a trustee can assure the beneficiaries properly withdraw the annual required minimum distribution. Another benefit of a trust is that it may protect against a beneficiary's poor spending habits or poor money management skills.

A trust can also preserve your beneficiary's needs-based government benefits, if applicable. This is not about Social Security or Medicare. Rather, it involves benefits such as supplemental or disability income or Medicaid, where need must be proved. If your beneficiary were to receive an inheritance from you, this could jeopardize his or her qualification for these benefits and possibly cut off your beneficiary's inheritance. Also, the IRA asset may be looked to for reimbursement of benefits provided during your beneficiary's life. A trust, properly structured, can allow your beneficiary to utilize the IRA account to supplement these other government benefits, rather than losing them or having them subject to reimbursement.

Also, a trust can ensure the right people will eventually inherit your IRA assets, rather than simply allowing either your surviving spouse, or more often, the beneficiary's surviving spouse, to then pass that IRA to a new spouse, or to children of another marriage. Additional trust provisions can be drafted to protect your child if he or she is in a high-risk profession, has known substance-abuse challenges, or has a troubled marriage.

Finally, a properly structured trust can provide you what is called "generation-skipping" for estate tax purposes. This means that when your child passes away, whatever remains in the trust will not be taxed again in your child's estate for federal tax purposes before it goes to your grandchildren.

But even if your family is highly educated and understands the consequences of cashing out the IRA account prematurely, there are still some very good estate and financial planning reasons for having a trust named as the beneficiary of your IRA account (either the primary beneficiary or a contingent beneficiary if you are married). As noted above, a trust can provide your beneficiaries with greatly enhanced protection against risk of loss of the IRA account due to lawsuits, creditors, divorce, and so forth.

Naming your traditional family living trust as the beneficiary of your IRA, however, will not work to minimize all of these problems and qualify for the maximum stretch-out of income taxes. Unfortunately, under the final IRS Regulations, a trust named as a beneficiary must pass a number of legal tests for the required minimum distributions in order to obtain the maximum stretch-out over the lifetime of the beneficiaries of the trust. There are numerous traps that are often unavoidable or overlooked when using a trust drafted for other purposes. See Internal Revenue Code (IRC) Section 401(a)(9); Treas. Reg Section 1.401 (a)(9)-4, Q&A 1. (Note that in 2005, IRS private letter ruling 200537044 clarified this area of the law and gave rise to an increased use of a standalone trust as a beneficiary of an inherited IRA.)

The required special IRA trust provisions set forth in the IRC and correlated Regulations allowing stretch-out contradicts many provisions in a traditional family living trust. If your retirement account is made payable to a non-qualifying trust, a tremendous amount of tax-deferred growth will be lost. Most traditional living trusts that are drafted for other purposes do not meet one or more requirements to be classified as a designated beneficiary. To ensure your estate planning goals are met without the loss of tax deferral, a "standalone" or separate trust should be implemented when making a retirement account payable to a trust. Moreover, from a practical standpoint, this separate DBT alerts your beneficiary to the different income tax treatment of your IRA after your death. This point is extremely effective in keeping your beneficiary from going in the next day and withdrawing the balance. It also makes it easier for the custodian to properly administer your beneficiary's IRA account.

A skilled estate planning attorney (experienced in the area of retirement planning) should be used to carefully draft a trust complying with the complex income tax regulations to qualify the trust as a qualified designated beneficiary — hence the name IRA "Designated Beneficiary Trust." Each trust share for each of your beneficiaries must be artfully drafted to afford the beneficiary a subtle blend of flexibility, control, and asset protection. Numerous planning issues need to be addressed, such as deciding: 1) whether or not the DBT should be the primary or contingent beneficiary; 2) the proper wording for the beneficiary designation form; 3) the degree to which assets of the trust share can be accessed by your beneficiary; 4) whether or not more than one DBT must be used; 5) how to address the sometimes conflicting needs of a surviving spouse and children born of another marriage; 6) the degree to which the DBT will adapt to the conditions existing at the time of your death; 7) whether to have all IRA distributions flow over into your DBT and then be immediately distributed out to your beneficiary, or whether to allow IRA distributions to flow to your DBT, but accumulate in the trust with distributions made to your beneficiary at the discretion of the trustee (see Example 2 of Treas. Reg 1.401 (a)(9)-5, A-7(c)(3); Treas. Reg. 1.401(a)(9)-5, A-7(s); See also PLR's 199931033 and 20010646); 8) how to implement the distribution provision and accumulation provision when needed and flipping over from one to the other depending upon your beneficiaries' needs; 9) how to provide for separate share treatment for your beneficiaries so each may use his or her own life expectancy for stretch-out purposes as opposed to using the life expectancy of the oldest beneficiary, thus maximizing tax deferral within the retirement account; 10) who to name as trustee(s); and 11) whether to have the DBT act as a credit shelter trust (otherwise known as a family trust or bypass trust) — just to name a few.

In summary, the IRA designated beneficiary trust (when drafted and implemented properly) is a solution that should be considered by anyone with an IRA of at least $200,000. It can certainly be an extremely powerful tool, combining wealth accumulation through income tax savings and asset protection at the same time.

The Law Offices of Stuart B. Kalb concentrates in estate and retirement planning to include asset protection, business, and tax planning through correctly implemented strategies and techniques.

BUSINESS AND INVESTMENT INTERESTS

Business Succession Planning

JOHN R. WINDSOR, JR. (Memphis, Tennessee)

This chapter is designed to provide a broad overview of the business succession planning process, familiarize you with some of the terminology, and discuss general considerations in the planning process.

Businesses change ownership for a number of reasons, including unexpected health problems, death, divorce, sale, or retirement. Each of these circumstances presents different challenges to successfully plan for business ownership transition, but a proactive approach to the planning will help maximize the proceeds to the seller and the profitability of the company.

Owners of companies valued below $10 million, who wish to transfer their business to family members, unrelated key employees, or outside third parties, should consider one or more of the possibilities discussed in this chapter and beyond to meet their needs and the needs of the business.

In a study by the National Federation of Independent Businesses, 40% of small business owners are age 55 or older[1]. Anecdotally, this means that many businesses will experience a transition in ownership, whether there is a plan to do so or not. Just as studies show that only 30 to 40% of individuals die with a Will in place, many won't engage in this type of business succession planning[2]. However, those who do can not only ease the burden on their family, employees, and their business, they can maximize the amount received for their business interests.

There is little doubt that a substantial number of small businesses will change hands, just as the population "bubble" of the baby boomers continues to age. One can reasonably conclude that, as we are told, there are a large number of individuals who will die in the next 20 or 25 years. Many of these individuals own businesses. Those ownership interests will transfer during this period; some interests will transfer multiple times.

The primary tools for business succession planning are:

- buy-sell agreements;
- stock bonus plans[3];
- deferred compensation plans[4];

- qualified retirement plans, including employee stock ownership plans ("ESOP");

- non-compete agreements;

- consultation contracts; and

- death transfers using wills or will substitutes, such as living trusts.

Each of these tools can be potentially useful, based on the goals and circumstances of the owner and company. These options should be carefully considered and crafted to form a plan that becomes a successful business succession plan.

In order to determine which combination of tools to implement, information must be obtained about the company, its value, employee make-up, the owner's family circumstances, and ultimately the owner's personal objectives.

QUESTIONS FOR THE OWNER

The business owner will make several decisions prior to beginning the planning process, whether he or she is aware of it or not. Such decisions will include: what advisors to hire; what process the owner will pursue; the pricing of these services; and the timing for hiring, paying for, and implementing this type of plan.

We have found that the team employed is critical, and there must be rapport among the team of advisors and the owner. The team typically consists of an insurance/financial advisor, certified public accountant, valuation analyst, and attorney. The team may consist of more than one of any, or several, of the team members listed. It is crucial to have members who understand the various roles and tools at their disposal to implement a plan effectively.

To begin the planning (Business Succession, Exit, Transition Planning, as it is variously known), some questions are in order. The answers to these questions are required in order to begin crafting a plan for the transition of ownership under various circumstances.

- When do you want to exit your business, or how much longer do you want to remain active in your business?

- How much money do you need in order to allow an exit (taking into consideration the impact taxes will have on what you get)?

- Under what terms do you want to transfer the business — payment over time such as an "earn out" (payments contingent on future business performance), or an outright sale receiving a lump sum payment?

- Whom do you want to receive the ownership interest — family member, non-family insider, third-party?

- When are you willing to become committed to the planning process?

Although not discussed as regularly as the foregoing issues, given the focus on the benefit being conferred on the transferee, the current owner must consider which structure gives the company the best chance of being successfully paid for and continuing to prosper as a business.

FAMILY MEMBER TRANSFEREES

Just as those who have a family should engage in estate planning to smooth the transition at death, minimize potential disputes, consider and plan for any federal estate and state inheritance taxes, and provide a clear map of the wishes of the Testator, these issues are magnified when a closely held business interest is part of the estate. Most estate plans involve dispositions of assets to surviving spouses, either outright or in trust for their lifetimes, as compared to the state statutory scheme in some states which have children inheriting a percentage of the estate outright. Without a Will, both a surviving spouse and one or more children may become the new owner or partner with a surviving partner. With a Will, the surviving spouse may be a partner in effect, but the children wouldn't be, unless it was the desired outcome.

A thoughtful plan for business succession incorporates estate planning for the various owners and key employee(s), or children who will run the business after transition. With a business succession plan, the spouse, unrelated key employee, or children can be a part of the company, but it occurs by design, rather than by accident. The plan frequently contemplates several options so that if the spouse and/or family is not to be involved in the business, they receive a predetermined value for the interest and are not burdened with continued involvement in the business.

As is done in estate planning for families involving children from previous marriages and the potential to disinherit one "branch" of the family following the death of the natural parent, equalizing the inheritance of a non-participating child with the inheritance of a child who ends up with some or all of the business interest must be addressed. In many estates that include ownership of a small business, a major portion of the estate's value may be comprised of this business interest.

While ownership may provide adequately or even handsomely for the child who inherits the ownership, it may otherwise mean substantially less value passes to children not involved in the business. Simply leaving the non-active child some ownership in the small business, without a paid position within the company, is often, at best a Pyrrhic victory[5]. Few small companies, as a practical matter, pay dividends to shareholders, nor are they required to in most circumstances.

Of course, the actual transfer can take the form of a bequest at the death of the owner to one or more family members. If the needs of a surviving spouse must be addressed, and the business is the primary asset of the Testator, then a buy-sell agreement between the Testator/Owner and the family member might be implemented. Assuming compensation reasonableness can be maintained, a "stock bonus" plan that transfers partial interest in given years to the transferee can be implemented during the life of the owner. The effect on the other heirs, who would inherit either a portion of the business interest or an equivalent value, must be considered in this context.

NON-FAMILY TRANSFEREES

What if there are no family members working inside the business? Or, what about situations where there are family members working in the business, but none are interested in taking over the company in the future?

Most likely, the owner will not be inclined to make a gratuitous transfer to non-family members if you exclude bonus type arrangements. Thus, the planning must address transferring the ownership interest over time or at a specific point to the "key" person transferee. If the company is of sufficient profitability and has a large enough eligible payroll, an ESOP may meet the various needs of the owner and company. An ESOP allows tax-advantaged proceeds to the current owner[6] and transfers ownership to management via tax deductible contributions[7].

Various agreements, either alone or in combination, might be used.

- Stock bonus to transfer stock over time to a transferee;

- Buy-sell agreement to transfer stock under predetermined conditions at a "trigger point" in the future, often coupled with life insurance (and/or disability insurance) to provide the funding at the needed time to pay for the interest in the company;

- Non-qualified deferred compensation can be used to "fund" the eventual purchase of the interest without transferring cash or stock today to the potential transferee; and/or a

- Promissory note, with the company assets or stock being used as security for a stream of payments.

VALUATION

It may seem contradictory, but a valuation of the business, commonly called "the lowest supportable value" may be in your and your family's best interests. Why? Because it allows the outright transfer to family members via annual gift tax exclusions or via transfers of limited partnership interests at substantially greater values than might otherwise be thought possible.

A valuation, whether low or high, when selling to an insider is not nearly as important as the cash flow of the "deal" after the owner departs and the buyout begins. The future cash flow of the transaction and lower tax burden are more important. By lowering the tax burden, the cash flow of the business is enhanced, allowing greater access to cash flow to fund the transfer.

TAX CONSIDERATIONS

Estate tax considerations in an owner's estate plan must be considered in light of the current and forecasted value. The transfer of the interest will impact the net amount received by a seller and the total amount earned in order to fund a buyout of the business.

The income tax effects on the net proceeds to the seller must also be considered in structuring the plan. For each increase in payment to the seller, the buyer of the company must earn an even greater amount (before taxes) to fund the payment. Additionally, capital gains treatment to the seller reduces the total needed to meet his or her goals in selling the business.

Under the right circumstances, the benefit to the seller is increased and the burden on the purchaser is reduced if an ESOP or other tax advantaged tool is used. This is because an ESOP permits tax-deductible company contributions to be used to fund the purchase of the stock and potential favorable tax benefits to the seller. Other qualified retirement plans can be useful in transferring funds to the seller in satisfaction of the payment. For example, a qualified retirement plan in which the seller and purchaser are both participants and "highly compensated employees," can be structured to benefit one to the exclusion of the other. Because, these contributions are also, within limits, tax deductible, it reduces the total burden on the company to fund.

BUSINESS SUCCESSION CANDIDATES

Small businesses are categorized in a number of ways, but businesses that engage in this type of planning are generally those with a motivated owner who recognizes the benefits of such planning, and the economics justify implementation of the plan. The "efficient" horizon for this planning depends on the overall value of the business, but the type of business affects this horizon. For example, the feasibility of planning for a service company, which is valued at $1 million may very well be more valuable than a manufacturing company of the same value, due to the additional cash flow of the service business.

Of course, this begs the question, why plan the transfer of ownership of a business?

Are you like many business owners?

- A majority of closely held and family owned businesses will change hands within the next five years[8]; but

- Many business owners may not have taken active steps to transition out of ownership.

Again, if you are like many of business owners, the reasons for failing to plan may be:

- You may have simply been too busy working in your business to be working on it.

- You may be unsure of how to begin succession planning, whom to use, or even where to begin.

Proper knowledge and preparation can possibly mean millions of dollars to you when you ultimately leave your company. If you start succession planning today you can help to avoid the sad (but too common) fate of owners who don't plan — those whose delays cause additional burdens to their families, reduce the amount ultimately received for their business, and may jeopardize the continued success of the business. Your plan will begin to take shape as you answer each of the following questions:

1. What are your retirement goals, and what level of assets will this require?

2. What is your business worth, in cash, today?

3. What options are available, and what is the best way to increase the income generated by the transfer of your ownership interest?

4. What method(s) of transfer will allow for lower taxes when transferring your business to family members, co-owners, or employees, while lowering taxes?

5. Is there a plan for continuity if something happens to you? Does it include your family's needs?

Creating and implementing your succession plan is an important business decision and may be your most important lifetime financial event.

The Windsor Law Firm, PLC uses compensation, tax, and estate planning expertise to assist small businesses meet their succession planning and legacy objectives for employees and family.

1. Volume 5, Issue 3, 2005, William J. Dennis, Jr., NFIB Research Foundation

2. Fifty-seven percent (57%) of Americans do not have a will, according to a 2004 study by Findlaw.com. In a 2004 AARP survey, it is reported that sixty-percent (60%) of those over age 50 have a Will.

3. Used here more generally to refer to any one of a number of stock or equity based plans including: §83(b), stock purchase, Stock Option (including incentive and non-qualified stock option) plans.

4. Those plans involving crediting an amount to an employee participant in such a plan, but the employer receives no deduction until such time as the employee includes the amount in compensation. Until that time the funds remain the asset of the employer, subject to the claims of the employer's creditors.

5. A Pyrrhic Victory is a victory with devastating cost to the victor. A Pyrrhic victory is so called after the Greek king Pyrrhus, who, after suffering heavy losses in defeating the Romans in 279 B.C., said to those sent to congratulate him, "Another such victory over the Romans and we are undone." Source: www.dictionary.com

6. §1042, qualified replacement property, for so called "C" corporation stock, it excludes subchapter "S" stock from this favorable treatment. The plan must hold at least thirty-percent (30%) of the stock immediately after the sale.

7. §404(a)(9). Limits vary depending on whether a loan is present to allow the purchase of the stock and the percentage of stock of the company purchased by the ESOP. Additional contributions are allowed for so called "leveraged" ESOPs where there is a loan to purchase the stock.

8. Winsby, Roger. Axiom Valuation, 2003

Estate Planning, Business Succession Planning, and Exit Planning – How Can (or Do) They Fit Together?

DANIEL B. CAPOBIANCO (Boston, Massachusetts)

INTRODUCTION

Previous chapters of this book have explained various concepts and techniques used in estate planning. When a closely held business is involved, there are many more issues that need to be addressed. Often times, the closely held business comprises approximately 80% of a family's wealth, and unless sold, is also a relatively illiquid asset. Typical forms of ownership of family-owned businesses are the S Corporation, C Corporation, LLC, and limited partnership. The design and implementation of any estate plan in which a closely held business is a major asset must, by necessity, focus on the succession plan of the business and/or the exit of the owner(s) from the business. Sometimes they are mutually exclusive, sometimes they overlap.

The succession plan focuses on who will run your company, either upon your retirement or upon your death. In other words, this is a management issue. If your spouse and children are already in the business, the succession plan will address how the company will continue to run. If your family does not want to (or cannot) continue to run the business upon your death or retirement, but nevertheless desires to keep the business in the family, then the succession plan must address the location, hiring, and retention of a quality management team.

The exit plan concerns the owner's sale of the business, either during life or upon death. The potential buyers of the family members typically fall into three groups:

- The owner's children
- Key employees
- Third-party buyer

Complicating any such sale is the fact that the closely held business is by its very nature, a non-public company, not easily valued. There is typically no ready market for the business.

THE TECHNIQUES

A common thread running through most estate plans involving a closely held business is, how can we retain control of the business and enjoy the benefits of ownership (that is "cash flow") yet remove some or all of the business from our estate? The solution is the sophisticated use of trusts and integrating and layering multiple planning solutions.

EXAMPLE 1

Family business is owned 100% by one or both parents. The goal is to transfer the business to future generations, provide creditor and/or divorce protection for children and grandchildren, retain cash flow from the business, and control management of business for at least the next few years, while excluding all future appreciation of the business from the parents' estates. The combined family estate exceeds the estate tax exemption amounts.

If the business is owned by a C Corporation, then make the S corporation election. This is important for pass through tax treatment.

If there is only voting stock outstanding, the next step is to recapitalize the corporation so there is voting and non-voting common stock. This will not violate the S corporation rules as long as there is only one class of stock (that is, common stock).

Establish an irrevocable trust. With careful drafting, this irrevocable trust will be "invisible" for income tax purposes yet be respected as a legal person separate and distinct from the grantor or its beneficiaries. This is what is known to estate planners as an intentionally defective grantor trust. The intentionally defective grantor trust is a valid S Corporation shareholder (note — only certain types of trusts are permitted shareholders, otherwise the S election becomes void).

Because this trust is also designed to benefit children and multiple future generations, it is also sometimes referred to as a "dynasty trust." Again, careful drafting is essential to ensure the trust is insulated from the application of the generation-skipping transfer tax.

Finally, some or all of the non-voting stock is gifted and/or sold to the trust. If the stock is sold to the trust, usually it will be for an interest only "balloon" promissory note or in exchange for a self-canceling installment note. Because the trust is a defective grantor trust, the owner will not pay income tax on the sale. Because the grantor is retaining ownership of the voting stock, the owner maintains control.

The annual earnings from the S Corporation attributable to the stock owned by the trust will flow to the trust. Because the trust is a grantor trust, the grantor will be responsible for tax on the earnings, even though the distributions are made directly to the trust (because it is the true shareholder). The tax payments on those earnings are, in effect, a non-taxable gift to the trust. The cash received by the trust is used to pay interest to the grantor and make any principal distributions, if desired. The trust can also purchase life insurance on one or both of the parents using the cash received from S corporation shares.

On death of the grantor, only the value of the unpaid promissory note is included in the grantor's estate. Any appreciation in the S corporation's stock value will be outside the grantor's estate, not included in the estates of the children and grandchildren, and exempt from generation-skipping transfer taxes. Further leverage is achieved through an expert appraisal of the business before transferring it into the trust. The non-voting stock will be subject to a discount, which will further enhance the estate and generation-skipping transfer tax savings.

EXAMPLE 2

Assume the same facts as above, except instead of selling shares to an intentionally defective grantor trust, the parents establish a Grantor Retained Annuity Trust (GRAT) which will hold the non-voting S corporation stock. The length of the GRAT will be determined by how much annual cash flow is desired by the parents and by the published IRS interest rate for the GRAT calculation. At the end of the GRAT term, the S corporation stock is then distributed from the GRAT into an irrevocable dynasty trust for the benefit of children and future generations with no gift tax consequences (assuming the GRAT was "zeroed-out" at inception).

EXAMPLE 3

Assume the same facts as above, except the "exit" strategy is to seek a buyer of the business. In working with consultants, the family has determined a three-year time horizon is realistic.

Since the actual sales price three years from now is, in all likelihood, greater than the value today, the GRAT is an ideal technique to push substantial value out of the parents' estates and into a dynasty trust similar to the previous examples. Today's value is established by an expert appraisal before contributing shares to the GRAT. The annuity from the GRAT remains the same whether the stock sale occurs inside the GRAT or after the GRAT terminates, in which case the sale is made by the dynasty trust.

This is a powerful technique in almost any situation where there is a vision of selling some or all of the family business, or where a public offering is planned. Since the time frame for any public offering of closely held stock is usually several months, placing some or all of the stock to be sold into a GRAT can achieve substantial estate and gift tax savings, while permitting the parents to retain a substantial portion of the profit from the sale of their business.

EXAMPLE 4

Often in very large estates, life insurance is a critical component to provide funding for future estate tax liability. However, the larger the potential estate tax, the larger the premium. The larger the premium, the more likely the annual premiums will exceed the "Crummey" gift exclusions. Once the annual Crummey gift exclusions are used, the life insurance premiums will begin to erode the lifetime gift exclusion of $1 million. Then, the issue becomes, how do we get the funds for premium payments into the trust without incurring additional gift taxes once the lifetime exclusion is used up? One solution is as follows.

All future gifts into the trust that exceed the lifetime exemption (and annual Crummey exclusion) will be treated as "loans" from the grantor. The loans must carry the prescribed IRS interest rate. This interest can be paid annually or accrued. A GRAT is then established with potentially highly appreciating assets such as real estate, closely held business stock, low basis investments, or similar assets. At the end of the GRAT term, the assets inside the GRAT are distributed to the life insurance trust free of gift taxes. The life insurance trust then repays the loans plus any accrued interest.

This same technique can be used to repay loans made by third party lenders. There are some institutions that will lend the life insurance trust money to pay insurance premiums. In this manner, an unrelated financial institution can provide the funding so the grantor/insured doesn't have to lend money to his or her insurance trust.

SUMMARY

The foundation for any of the foregoing applications is the skillfully drafted irrevocable trust, one or more GRATs, perhaps an FLP, and an attorney specializing in estate planning. This is not "form book" planning since it requires mastery of several different techniques and the ability to determine which techniques can be integrated with others.

Daniel B Capobianco specializes in domestic and international taxation with emphasis on complex integrated estate plans with multiple tax strategies, charitable planning, and business succession planning.

CHAPTER 72

Valuation Discounts and Premiums on the Transfer of Business and Investment Entities

RON FEINMAN (Lynchburg, Virginia)

INTRODUCTION

In addition to providing for the orderly transition of management and ownership of a business as it is passed on to your children or other heirs, the use of entities such as Family Limited Partnerships and Limited Liability Companies afford an additional way to reduce estate and gift taxes that might be due when ownership of these entities is transferred. In this chapter we will discuss the transfer of interests in these types of entities solely focusing on limited liability companies (LLCs), but the concepts explained apply to partnerships as well.

As discussed in prior chapters, not counting annual exclusion gifts, if an individual dies and transfers more than the estate tax exemption amount ($2 million in 2008, and 3.5 million in 2009), the excess amount transferred will be subject to a gift or estate tax of approximately 45% or more. You must remember that of the total exemption amount, only $1 million per person may be utilized during lifetime. This $1 million is the lifetime gift tax exemption amount; the remaining exemption amount is applied to the estate of the donor at his or her death.

The IRS Regulations provide that a gift is valued for gift tax or estate tax purposes at its fair market value, the price for which it "would change hands between a willing buyer and a willing seller, neither being under any compulsion to buy or to sell and both having reasonable knowledge of relevant facts." In other words, what the asset would really be worth if you were to sell it on the open market.

An important distinction to keep in mind is the different way assets are valued for lifetime gift tax exemption purposes versus the way they are valued for estate tax purposes at death. For lifetime gifts, the value of each individual gift of an entity ownership interest is considered separately, no matter how many other similar gifts are made at the same time. As you will see below, treating each gift separately creates a very powerful benefit for our lifetime gifts. The business ownership interests remaining in one's estate at his or her death, however, are all combined or aggregated together before considering their fair market value. We will consider an example of this below.

TRANSFER ENTITY OWNERSHIP INSTEAD OF ASSETS DIRECTLY

The first way we are able to reduce gift or estate taxes comes from having special terms included in the legal documents setting up the LLC. These special terms affect who controls the operation of the LLC and how and when its ownership interests can be transferred to others. The effect of having these special terms is that they create valuation discounts for an interest in the entity when it is transferred.

Here is how this works: You first contribute the property you want to pass on to your heirs to the LLC in exchange for ownership interests in the entity, the same way a stockholder gives a corporation money in exchange for shares of its stock. For example, a husband and wife might contribute a portfolio of securities and other assets having a fair market value of $2 million to their brand new LLC in exchange for 100% of the ownership interests in the LLC.

Assuming there are no hidden liabilities, we would now assume the new LLC is worth about $2 million and that if you wanted to sell, say, 25% of the LLC to another, it would command a sales price of about $500,000. But what if the LLC documents were drawn so that even if you sold a partial ownership, you still had complete control over the management of the LLC and got to make all investment decisions? You also retained full control to decide when (and if) any distributions would be made from the LLC to its owners.

What would a reasonable person pay for a 25% ownership interest in such an LLC? What would you pay for an ownership interest in a company where someone else made all the investment decisions, and you couldn't ever get any earnings back without someone else's permission? At this point we can safely say the value of a 25% interest would definitely be less than $500,000. We call this reduction in value a lack of control discount.

Let's suppose that in addition to you retaining control over the management of the LLC, the new purchaser cannot sell or transfer his or her 25% share without your permission. Not only that, but he or she cannot even use the ownership interest in the LLC as collateral for a loan. In other words, the purchaser is dependent on you to get his or her money, including any earnings, out of the LLC; it has become a very illiquid investment. Now how much would you pay for such an interest? As with the lack of control restrictions, these provisions would clearly reduce the amount someone would be willing to pay for partial ownership in the LLC. We call this reduction in value the lack of marketability discount.

The size of these discounts is determined by using a qualified independent appraiser to examine the LLC documents, the underlying assets of the LLC, the state laws governing LLCs, and the current market for such interests. After this review, the appraiser will assign a value to the various discounts as they apply to the interests in the LLC. Applying these discounts will reduce the amount of the underlying value of the assets recognized for our gift tax calculations upon transfer.

Returning to our example, the appraiser might assign a discount of 25% for the lack of marketability discount and a 15% discount for lack of control. The discounts are applied sequentially, resulting in a cumulative discount of 36.25%. Here's how the value of our 25% interest in the LLC is now computed:

Underlying asset fair market value:	$500,000
LESS 25% marketability discount ($500,000 x .25)	-125,000
	$375,000
LESS 15% lack of control discount ($375,000 x .15)	56,250
VALUE after both discounts	**$318,750**

The cumulative discount is $181,250 ($125,000 + $56,250), which is 36.25% percent of the underlying value of the assets ($181,250 ÷ $500,000 = .3625).

THE SAVINGS

Assuming you have a taxable estate, what are the real benefits to you if you make use of these discounts for gifting to your children? There are several:

1. You can transfer more value during your lifetime. Instead of only being able to transfer $1 million in value with your $1 million lifetime gift tax exemption amount, you can now transfer approximately $1,568,000 of value.

2. As with any gift made during life, you have removed all future increases in value from your estate. So if the $1,568,000 were to double in value by the time of your death, the total amount transferred at that time would be $3,136,000 — all from just using your $1 million lifetime exemption amount!

3. The estate and gift tax savings, assuming the value doubled, and using the 45% transfer tax rate, would amount to $774,300! ($2,136,000 x .3625 = $774,300).

   But what about the restrictions? In most cases they actually provide another benefit:

4. The value of the gift is transferred to your children, but you remain in charge of all the important decisions concerning the underlying assets. You maintain control over how they are invested, and when any distributions are made to the children. The lack of marketability restriction assures you a child can't sell the assets to a stranger. The restrictions allow you to protect your children from taking improvident actions until you feel comfortable they are mature enough to do so.

5. Additional special planning techniques can be combined with LLCs and similar entities to provide even more benefits, such as preserving a step

up in basis at death for the ownership interests transferred, or even additional transfer tax savings by combining techniques to achieve multiple discounts above those discussed here.

THE CONTROL PREMIUM

One final note: In the same way the restricted interests receive a discount because of lack of control and lack of marketability, the ownership interest you retain will actually receive an increase in value, known as a control premium, reflecting your authority over all the interests in the LLC. This may range from 15% to 40%[1]. A method to reduce the impact of this increase in value is to make sure only a small percentage of ownership represented by interests with a control premium is retained by you. For example, if the underlying assets are valued at $1 million and you retain a 1% controlling interest with a 35% premium, this 1% would be valued at $13,500 instead of $10,000, a relatively minor adjustment in the overall scope of things.

A SKILLED PROFESSIONAL ADVISOR TEAM IS VERY IMPORTANT

The foregoing techniques involve sophisticated planning with many tax and other legal traps. As you would expect, ensuring you employ a skilled attorney to draft the proper documentation, utilizing a knowledgeable and competent appraiser, and preparing proper accounting and tax filings is of tantamount importance.

Attorney Ron Feinman graduated from UVA Law School in 1979 and has a nationwide practice centered in Lynchburg, Virginia, in estate, business, and legacy planning, elder law, and asset protection.

---

1. In other circumstances where control is exercised by a majority interest, a relatively small ownership percentage may also receive an increase in value. For example, if three individuals own 48%, 48%, and 4% of the ownership interests, the 4% owner can decide who controls the entity by choosing with which of the other owners to vote his interest. This ability is known as a swing vote premium, and his interest would be valued at more than 4% of the underlying assets.

CHAPTER 73

Family Limited Partnerships

MICHAEL BURSTEIN (Los Angeles, California)

Family limited partnerships (FLPs) are one tool in the estate planning attorney's toolbox and are primarily used by people with estates large enough to be subject to federal estate tax. If you have such an estate and have a desire to retain control over your assets for the remainder of your life, as most do, it is something to consider.

One way to obtain a quick understanding of the benefit of an FLP as an estate planning tool is to imagine you owned a painting by Pablo Picasso worth exactly $10 million. You were about to sell it for that amount. Then the evening before the sale, the bottom right corner of the painting was cut off. It was a small cut, amounting to less than 3% of the painting. Obviously, the painting would no longer be worth $10 million. It is highly unlikely that the painting would sell for $9.7 million, which is 3% less than $10 million.

What would be the value of the painting now? While we are not certain what someone would pay for it, one thing that we do know is that it would be worth substantially less than $10 million. It might be worth $8 million, which is 20% less, or $7 million, which is 30% less, or maybe $6 million, which is 40% less. Similarly with an FLP, because you have family members who are limited partners and you no longer own 100% of the assets, the value of your interest is reduced by more than the amount owned by the other family members and therefore the value of your estate is decreased. Discounts for FLP interests are typically based on lack of marketability and lack of control of the partnership interest.

WHAT IS AN FLP?

Just as the name implies, an FLP is a partnership entered into between at least one general partner and at least one limited partner. Frequently the general partner is the person who owns the assets, but it can be a limited liability company, a corporation, a trust, or someone else in the family. The law requires that the partners in an FLP be family members and that includes spouses, ancestors, lineal descendants, and trusts for such family members.

The general partner has complete control over the partnership and is actively engaged in the management of the partnership. As such, if you serve as general partner, no one can order you to do anything. While your limited partners are your financial partners, the FLP agreement provides them with no ability to manage the underlying business. This can be of benefit to the limited partners in that they have limited liability for the acts of the partnership.

The major drawback to serving as the general partner is that you have unlimited liability. That means that you are exposed to being sued personally. For those concerned about personal liability, one alternative is to have a limited liability company of which you are a member, serve as the general partner.

WHY ENTER INTO AN FLP?

The primary reason people enter into FLPs is to reduce the size of their estate and therefore reduce estate taxes. This is done because of what is known as valuation discounts. To put it as simply as possible, and as the Picasso painting example illustrates, the value of all of the partnership interests in the partnership always add up to less than the value of the underlying asset(s).

However, there are a variety of other reasons to create an FLP. These reasons include protecting and conserving your family's assets and investments, protecting your children's property and inheritance from loss to a divorce or creditors, maintaining control of your assets, and creating a succession plan for the family business.

HOW DO FLPS WORK?

Jack Johnson is a 73 year old widower. He has four children and five grandchildren. Jack is concerned about maintaining family ownership of what he has worked hard to acquire. He receives a pension from work in the amount of $7,500 per month with cost of living increases, and also collects social security, and lives very comfortably on his income from those two sources. He has the following assets, all of which are in his living trust except for his IRA:

Banks Accounts and Certificates of Deposit	$ 375,000
IRA	$ 925,000
Mutual Funds/Marketable Securities	$ 800,000
Apartment Complex	$ 1,500,000
Additional Rental Real Estate	$ 700,000
Personal Residence	$ 700,000
Total	**$5,000,000**

Mr. Johnson's estate planning attorney suggests an FLP. Mr. Johnson agrees and decides to take an aggressive approach to funding the partnership. He places the real estate (other than his residence) and his securities/mutual funds into the FLP so that the FLP contains assets valued at $3 million. Mr. Johnson receives a 1% general partnership interest and the Jack Johnson Living Trust receives a 99% interest.

About six months after creating the FLP, Mr. Johnson gifts 12.5% limited partnership interests to each of his four children. To determine the value of the underlying gifts, Mr. Johnson hires a qualified appraiser to perform a qualified appraisal to determine valuation discounts. The appraiser determines that a 33.33% discount should be applied for lack of control and lack of marketability.

Mr. Johnson is therefore able, by applying the discount to the proportionate value of FLP assets, to give limited partnership interests valued at $250,000 instead of $375,000 to each of his children. Assuming Mr. Johnson has 100% of his lifetime gift tax unified credit of $1 million available, there is no gift tax required.

Shortly thereafter, Mr. Johnson dies before any appreciation of the assets in the FLP, and prior to having an opportunity to do any additional gifting. The appraiser determines a 20% discount should be applied to his general partner interest and a 30% discount should be applied to his limited partner interest on the estate tax return. Had Mr. Johnson died without an FLP, all $3 million of the assets transferred to the LLC would have been included in his estate. However, by utilizing an FLP, his taxable estate was reduced by approximately $445,000. Assuming a 45% estate tax rate, $201,000 in estate tax is saved.

The estate tax savings would have been significantly larger had Mr. Johnson lived longer, made annual gifts to his children and grandchildren, and had the assets in the FLP appreciated.

WHAT ARE THE DISADVANTAGES OF FLPS?

One of the most significant disadvantages of an FLP is that for highly appreciated real property, the gifted limited partnership interests do not receive a step up in basis. Rather, they have a carry over basis. Therefore, there may be capital gains taxes that would have been avoided had, for example, Mr. Johnson's children been beneficiaries of the real property at Mr. Johnson's death rather than gifted with the property during his lifetime.

Moreover, in certain states, including California, care must be taken so that real estate transferred to the FLP is not reassessed for property tax purposes. In other states, documentary transfer taxes may be an issue to consider.

The financial costs associated with an FLP include the initial fees paid to the attorney to create the partnership, state filing fees, appraisal fees, and the cost for preparing a tax return every year the FLP is in existence.

CONCLUSION

A Family Limited Partnership is a great estate planning tool that not only reduces estate taxes, but is also an asset protection tool, promotes family harmony, and may provide a business succession plan. Each person's situation requires an analysis of different factors, so working with an experienced estate planning attorney is therefore extremely important.

Michael Burstein's practice is focused on estate planning, elder law, estate administration, and probate. He has prepared more than 3,000 estate plans and probates 50+ estates per year.

Family Limited Partnerships: Advantages and Disadvantages

ADVANTAGES	DISADVANTAGES
Income tax advantages	Administration expenses
Estate freeze	"Real" discounted value
Estate and gift tax valuation adjustments	Potential family disharmony
Some degree of control over assets	IRS scrutiny
Facilitate family gifting	Reduced fringe benefits
Management flexibility	Restrictive income tax rules
Avoiding probate	Difficult trust administration
Avoiding fractionalization of title	Loss of basis step up
Creditor protection	Underfunded marital deduction
Some degree of control over donees	Liquidity concerns
Economies/diversification investments	Potential legislation
Keep assets within family	S corporation incompatibility
Flexibility to adapt	Uncertain estate tax implications
Dispute management	Investment company rules
Avoidance of guardianship	Maintain partnership formalities
Family communication in harmony	
Certainty of income tax treatment	

CHAPTER 74

Limited Liability Companies

JAMES K. BURAU (Incline Village, Nevada)

Anyone who owns or operates a business should consider the advantages of doing business within a Limited Liability Company (LLC). The LLC is a very flexible form of business entity, incorporating elements of both corporations and partnerships. Because owners of an LLC, who are called "Members," are generally not liable for its debts, the LLC also offers superior asset protection advantages compared to partnerships and corporations. This freedom from personal liability, or "limited liability" is what the name implies.

Ownership interests in LLCs are usually characterized as Membership Interests, expressed either as shares or percentages of ownership. Since the LLC was first adopted by Wyoming in 1977, its popularity has spread, and LLCs, even single-Member LLCs, are now allowed in all 50 states and the District of Columbia. Although corporations are still popular for business owners who anticipate selling stock to attract investors, or who wish to distribute stock to employees, for most small businesses, the LLC is the preferred form of business entity.

FORMATION OF THE LLC

An LLC must have at least one Member who owns the business interest. The Member may be a natural person, another business entity such as a corporation or partnership, or a trust. Forming an LLC in most states is simple, requiring only the filing of form Articles of Organization in the LLC's home state, and appointing an Agent in the state for service of process on the entity. Annual filing fees to maintain an LLC in most states are also generally low.

OPERATION AND TAXATION

In addition to the freedom from personal liability for its Members, LLCs are also popular because of their flexibility in organization and administration. An LLC can be managed either by the Members or by one or more Managers who may, but need not be, Members. The choice is generally determined in the Articles of Organization or in a written agreement of its Members, called an "Operating Agreement." Most business owners want to actively participate in the business, so most LLCs are managed by the Members. Sometimes, however, Members are merely passive investors in the business and do not want to participate in its management, and in these situations the Manager-managed LLC may be more appropriate. The choice does not affect the liability of the Members, whether they participate in the management or not, because they will all enjoy limited liability within the limits afforded by statute and applicable case law.

Although LLCs generally must, at least annually, file a basic informational document with the Secretary of State in its home state, most states do not require LLCs to hold meetings and prepare minutes. Accordingly, the record-keeping requirements for LLCs are generally less burdensome than for other business entities. Still, to ensure the separate legal existence of the company in the event it is audited or sued, it is a good practice to document and maintain records of important actions which affect the company, such as appointing and replacing Managers, adding and substituting Members, acquiring or disposing of significant company assets, etc.

An LLC can elect to be taxed as a corporation, either as a traditional C corporation or as an S corporation, or it can elect to be treated as partnership for income tax purposes. In the former case, the LLC will pay tax at the entity level and a separate income tax return will be filed. In the case of a partnership or S election, an informational return will be filed for the entity and all profits and losses will pass through to the Members on a K-1 and be reported on Schedule E of their individual income tax returns. In the case of a single-Member LLC (or an LLC owned by a husband and wife who live in a community property state), the Member(s) can elect for the entity to be disregarded as an entity separate from its owners for income tax purposes, in which case no income tax return is required to be filed for the LLC, and all profits and losses are reported by the Members on Schedule C of their individual income tax returns.

VOTING AND NON-VOTING INTERESTS

The Operating Agreement spells out the rights and duties of the Members and the Manager, including voting rights and restrictions on the transferability of Membership Interests. Like Limited Partnerships and Corporations, LLCs can have voting and non-voting interests. The Members can also decide whether to divide profits and losses among the Members equally, according to their capital interests, or unequally, according to other criteria. In the absence of an Operating Agreement these rights and duties are covered by state law.

LIMITS ON THE LIMITATION OF LIABILITY

While a Member of an LLC is generally not personally liable for the actions and obligations of the LLC, this protection is not absolute. A Member is at risk for the obligations of the LLC if the Member personally guaranteed them or offered the Member's own assets as security for the company's obligation. A Member is also at risk for his or her actions that cause injury to others, typically tort liability to injured third parties, such as if the Member operated a vehicle recklessly and caused injury to another person, but the LLC will generally preclude the other Members from incurring liability for the actions of the Member who caused the damage or injury. A Member or a Manager can also be liable for breach of a duty of care owed to the company or to those with whom the company does business

Recently, some states, borrowing from the law of corporations, have allowed the "veil" of LLCs to be "pierced" and personal liability imposed on the Members when business formalities were not observed and Members failed to maintain the LLC's separate existence.

VARIATIONS ON THE THEME

Professional Limited Liability Company (or PLLC) is an LLC formed to provide professional services, such as legal services or accounting. Generally, the Members are not liable for the debts of the business or for the negligent or intentional acts of the other professional Members. However for public policy reasons, the professional remains liable for his own negligence. A variation on the PLLC is the Registered Limited Liability Partnership or RLLP.

Series LLCs allow a single LLC to separate assets of the LLC into separate "series" that may have separate Members and Managers, or different allocations of profits and losses between the separate series. The Series LLC generally protects the Members against liability generated within one series from carrying over to any other series. Series LLCs are popular, for example, for the client who owns multiple parcels of investment real estate and wants to segregate the assets for liability purposes without requiring a separate LLC for each parcel.

Family Limited Liability Companies, or FLLCs, are estate planning tools which, through the Operating Agreement, restrict the ability of Members with minority interests from participating in the management and control of the business, or restrict the free transferability of the Membership Interests. These restrictions require the value of a Member's interest to be discounted, which reduces taxes on eligible transfers during life or at death. FLLCs are similar to Family Limited Partnerships, but because there is no General Partner for a FLLC, all of the Members enjoy limited liability to the extent allowed by law.

Close LLCs — Many states have modified their statutes to permit "Close LLCs" which even further simplify the administration of the company. In a Close LLC, Members are generally prohibited from selling their membership interests without first offering them to the other Members, and certain record-keeping requirements are relaxed or eliminated.

Mr. Burau's practice focuses on wealth preservation planning for higher net worth clients. He has counseled hundreds of clients in regard to their estate and small business planning needs.

CHAPTER 75

Grantor Retained Annuity Trusts

HENNA SHAH (Fort Lee, New Jersey)

A grantor retained annuity trust (GRAT) is an advanced planning technique that can transfer significant wealth with little or no federal gift tax consequences. A GRAT can also reduce potential estate tax liability because it freezes the value of contributed property upon its transfer to the trust, thereby removing future appreciation on that property from the estate. GRATs are created by statute and have little risk of not being recognized by the IRS.

HOW GRATS WORK

A GRAT is an irrevocable trust to which a grantor contributes assets that are likely to have significant earnings or appreciation and in which the grantor retains a qualified annuity interest (in compliance with Internal Revenue Code Section 2702) payable at least annually for a specified term of years. Assets that are suitable for contribution include business interests, securities, real estate (subject to local real estate transfer tax issues), and other investments. The annuity amount is calculated by reference to an interest rate published monthly by the IRS (the Section 7520 rate). A key factor is deciding the GRAT term — usually based on the grantor's life expectancy and the time frame in which the contributed assets are expected to achieve optimum performance.

In order for a GRAT to be successful, GRAT assets must outperform the Section 7520 rate. Accordingly, GRATs are generally more attractive when the Section 7520 rate is low. If GRAT assets earn and/or appreciate at a rate that exceeds the Section 7520 rate, there will be assets available for distribution to beneficiaries of the GRAT upon the expiration of the GRAT term. If GRAT assets fail to outperform the Section 7520 rate, beneficiaries will not receive anything at the end of the GRAT term and the grantor will be in the same position as if the GRAT had never been created (less funds expended in forming and administering the GRAT). If the grantor dies before the end of the GRAT term, the grantor's estate will include the amount of GRAT assets necessary to produce the annual annuity without reducing or invading principal, as determined using the Section 7520 rate in effect on the date of death or on the alternate valuation date.

If GRAT assets have not achieved their full potential upon the expiration of the GRAT term, the grantor can contribute those assets to a newly formed GRAT. Alternatively, the grantor may wish to establish several GRATs funded with different types of assets in order to optimize the appreciation potential of each unique asset.

> **EXAMPLE 1:** Assume you own 25,000 shares of XYZ Company stock valued at $40 per share, for a total fair market value of $1,000,000. You believe the stock is likely to appreciate within the next two years. You form a GRAT with a two-year term for the benefit of your child and transfer all 25,000 shares of XYZ Company stock to the GRAT when the Section 7520 rate is 4%. Based on these facts, your optimum annual annuity payout amount is equal to 53% of the value of the initial asset contribution, or $530,000. (In order to zero out the gift, the payout percentage must be 53.01943%. Rounding the payout percentage down to 53% results in a nominal taxable gift of $367). If the value of XYZ Company stock increases by 10% annually, at the end of the GRAT term, you will have received back $1,060,000 and $97,000 will be available for distribution to your child tax-free.

> **EXAMPLE 2:** Using the same facts as in Example 1, assume instead that the value of XYZ Company stock increases by 20% annually. At the end of the GRAT term, you will have received back $1,060,000 and there will be $274,000 available for distribution to your child.

> **EXAMPLE 3:** Using the same facts as in Example 1, assume instead that the value of XYZ Company stock increases by 3% annually. At the end of the GRAT term, you will have received back $1,045,000 and no funds will be available for distribution to your child. This result stems from the fact that the appreciation in the value of the stock did not exceed the Section 7520 rate of 4%.

> **EXAMPLE 4:** Using the same facts as in Example 1, assume instead that the value of XYZ Company stock decreased over the period of the GRAT term. You will receive back your initial contribution amount, reduced by the decrease in the value of the stock, and no funds will be available for distribution to the beneficiaries.

TAX CONSEQUENCES

Gift Tax: GRATs are designed to take advantage of the rule that imposes a gift tax on transfers to the extent that the fair market value of the property transferred exceeds the value of the grantor's retained annuity interest. By providing for the grantor's retained annuity interest amount to be equal or close to the value of the contributed assets (as adjusted by the Section 7520 rate), the taxable gift can be zeroed out or at least minimized. Future appreciation on the contributed assets is not included in determining the value of the taxable gift.

Income Tax: For income tax purposes, the grantor is treated as the owner of all of the assets in the GRAT during the GRAT term. Accordingly, income earned on any GRAT asset during the GRAT term is taxable to the grantor. Any transfers between the grantor and the GRAT (such as when assets are contributed to the GRAT or annuity payments are made to the grantor) during the GRAT term are not taxable for income tax purposes.

CONCLUSION

GRATs are an excellent tool for freezing the value of assets and transferring appreciation out of a grantor's estate with minimal federal transfer tax consequences. Additionally, GRATs can be combined with other estate planning techniques to result in even greater tax savings.

Shah Law is a boutique estate planning firm focusing on family wealth transfer, asset protection, tax minimization, and business succession matters.

Grantor-Retained Interest Trusts

	GRAT	GRUT	QPRT
Grantor's Retained Interest	Fixed % of the initial value of the assets for a term of years.	Fixed % of assets as valued annually for a term of years.	Use of a personal residence retained for a term of years.
Value of the Gift	Remainder interest after deducting the value of the retained annuity.	Remainder interest after deducting the value of the retained unitrust.	Remainder interest after deducting the value of the retained use interest.
Annual Exclusion Amount	None. Remainder is a future interest.	None. Remainder is a future interest.	None. Remainder is a future interest.
Amount Included in Grantor's Gross Estate	Grantor survives the term of the trust: None. Grantor dies during term of the trust: A portion of trust assets.	Grantor survives the term of the trust: None. Grantor dies during term of the trust: A portion of trust assets.	Grantor survives the term of the trust: None. Grantor dies during term of the trust: Full amount of trust assets.

CHAPTER 76

Qualified Personal Residence Trusts

ERIN M. THRASH (Austin, Texas)

Tom is in his late 50s, healthy, divorced, with five adult children. His best friend, Doug, passed away several years ago. Finally, after three years of legal work and an IRS audit, Doug's estate was distributed. However, because Doug only had a simple will and no other estate planning in place, his estate was taxed at a devastating 45% tax rate. As a result, Doug's girlfriend and children received less than 50% of the original estate value. Tom, realizing current estate tax rates may sunset and return to an even higher federal estate tax rate of 55% in a few years, is determined to protect his children. Tom meets with his estate planner to put planning into place for his large estate. Part of his estate includes a ranch in Texas where he spends part of the year, and a condominium in Florida where he spends the remainder. His Florida condominium is valued at $1.8 million and his ranch is valued at $2.5 million. His estate planner suggests a Qualified Personal Residence Trust, commonly referred to as a "QPRT" (Q-pert), for the Florida condominium. Tom is interested but wants to know how a QPRT works.

A QPRT is an irrevocable grantor trust in which the "Grantor" (Tom) contributes a "personal residence" to the trust, and receives the right to "use" the personal residence for a term of years (the "term"). This contribution counts as a gift to the trust subject to gift tax. However, because the Grantor retains the right to live in the personal residence for a term of years, the value of the gift is "discounted" based upon the length of the term retained by the Grantor. At the end of the term, the trust property passes to the beneficiaries of the trust (Tom's living children). During the term, the Grantor continues to pay the expenses and taxes. If, at the end of the term, the Grantor chooses to continue to reside in the personal residence, then the Grantor can "rent" the residence from the trust at fair market rental value. The rent passes through the trust to the beneficiaries. The Grantor may also choose to serve as the Trustee of the trust during the term, enabling him or her to make all decisions regarding the personal residence. If the Grantor/Trustee decides to sell the condominium during the term, the proceeds of the sale belong to the trust. However, the Grantor/Trustee can use the proceeds to buy another residence on behalf of the trust. The key impediment to a QPRT is that the Grantor must survive to the end of the term for the QPRT to work. If the Grantor does not survive, then the QPRT fails and the personal residence is included in Grantor's estate.

Although a QPRT appeals to Tom he still has the following questions:

Is the Florida condominium better suited for a QPRT than the Texas ranch?

Yes. The IRS definition of a personal residence is restrictive and may disqualify the QPRT if the property fails to qualify. In Tom's case, because the ranch includes a portion of acreage which is used for raising cattle, his planner is concerned it may fail to meet the criteria. Therefore, if Tom chooses to do a QPRT for the ranch, his planner suggests the ranch be divided into a "residence" share and a "ranch" share.

If Tom sells the residence will there be any capital gain/income tax issues?

The capital gain exclusions ($250,000 for an individual, and $500,000 for a couple) are applicable to the proceeds. Tom should be aware, however, that transferring the property to his children by way of a QPRT, rather than having them inherit the property at his death, will result in his children assuming Tom's cost basis in the property rather than the stepped-up basis they would otherwise receive at Tom's death.

Will Tom have to pay gift tax?

It depends. Because the contribution of the personal residence to the trust is a "gift" there will be a gift tax return (IRS Form 709) filed. The plan is to make the term of the trust sufficient to keep the value of the "gift" under the lifetime exclusion (currently $1 million).

If at the end of the term of the QPRT the property is worth double the value from when I contributed it, will Tom's children have to pay additional gift taxes?

No. Assuming Tom survives the term, the property is valued and taxed at the contribution date. The property is out of the estate at that original value.

How does Tom contribute the property to the QPRT?

By a deed, just as he would any other transfer of real property.

Will Tom lose his homestead and other property tax exemptions?

Generally no, but these exemptions are local. The answer should be investigated by the estate planner with the local taxing authority before transferring the property to the QPRT.

Does a QPRT provide asset protection?

Because a QPRT is an irrevocable trust, people often assume it provides asset protection. However, Tom's life interest in the property is attachable by creditors, meaning a creditor can rent out the property for the term of the QPRT.

Tom decides to implement the QPRT but wants to know what kind of gift he will be making. His estate planner provides him with this illustration using the following values:

Present value of the property: $1.8 million

Term of the QPRT: 15 years

Assume 7520 rate: 3.6%

The illustration reflects that the value of Tom's retained right to use the Florida condo is $1,100,000, which leaves the discounted value of the gift to the trust equal to $700,000. The gift tax reported is approximately $280,000 (assuming a 45% gift tax rate), and is well within Tom's $1 million lifetime exclusion.

Compare this to the $720,000 gift tax Tom would incur if he gave the Florida condominium outright to the children. So by using a QPRT, there is a tax savings of $440,000. If we assume a 4% growth rate for the Florida condo and a term of 15 years, the condo will be worth $3,250,000. At the current tax rate, the tax savings are $1,200,000!

This illustration does not take into account the rent Tom would pay if he lived an additional ten years (his life expectancy) after the end of the QPRT. Rental payments will further reduce Tom's estate.

If Tom were married, both he and his spouse could create separate QPRTs for their respective shares of ownership of the personal residence, which would increase the chances that one of the Grantors would survive the term. This strategy is especially effective when Grantors had significantly different life expectancies.

Tom believes a QPRT is a valuable technique in his situation and adds it to his estate plan.

QPRTs can be a valuable tool in an estate planners "tool box." However, it is important for a planner to not only take into account what value a QPRT will provide for a client, but also the very strict criteria for contributions, definitions of a personal residence, the size of an estate which will benefit from a QPRT and the age, life expectancy and health of the client(s).

Erin M. Thrash, Principal, Thrash Law Firm, located in Austin, Texas, focuses on family wealth planning and preservation through business succession planning, advanced estate, family and charitable planning, and asset protection.

CHAPTER 77

Corporate Recapitalization

BETH K. RAUTIOLA (Irvine, California)

WHAT IS CORPORATE RECAPITALIZATION?

Acorporate recapitalization is the reorganization of a corporation's capital structure. The capital structure includes stock ownership and the rights associated with each class or type of issued stock.

For shareholders of a closely held business, recapitalization is a succession strategy. Recapitalization, also referred to as "reorganization," is a division of rights associated with corporate stock. There are many ways to use a recapitalization. It is a valuable tool when combined with other strategies, such as gifting programs, structured sales, or an Intentionally Defective Grantor Trust (IDGT).

The most common way to recapitalize a corporation is to arrange the stock rights to imitate a Limited Partnership structure. After the recapitalization, all voting control is held by a limited number of shareholders (just like the General Partner in a Limited Partnership) and the bulk of the ownership is held by non-voting shareholders (like Limited Partners in a Limited Partnership).

For comparison, think of your business as a television and remote control. A recapitalization allows you to separate the ownership of the television from the remote control. It allows you to transfer ownership of the television, but keep the remote control. The remote control is the voting stock and the television is the non-voting stock.

HOW DOES A RECAPITALIZATION WORK?

The recapitalization is simple in theory. It is always finely tailored for each set of circumstances. A typical corporate recapitalization will require the issuance of a new class or type of stock that is either non-voting or is one with different ownership interests than those previously owned by the shareholders.

There are several ways to structure a recapitalization to meet each corporation's specific needs. A general recapitalization is outlined in the following example.

> **EXAMPLE:** Assume you own a corporation with your friend, Shareholder X. Corporation has 100 shares of stock outstanding (issued) and 1,000,000 shares authorized. You own 75% and Shareholder X owns

25%. You decide you would like to recapitalize the corporate stock. See Diagrams 1 and 2.

Diagram 1. 100 Shares Outstanding

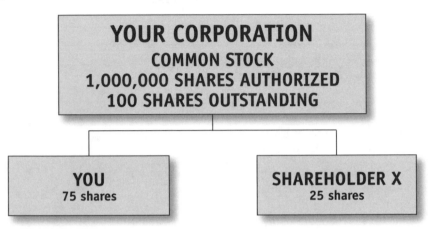

To recapitalize, you decide to issue non-voting common stock. The non-voting stock is issued in the selected ratio based on your specific goals, needs of the corporation, and shareholders.

> **EXAMPLE:** The new issuance ratio is 9:1. Nine new shares of non-voting stock are issued for each share of common (voting stock) currently held by each shareholder. Immediately after the recapitalization, you still own 75% of the corporation and Shareholder X owns 25%. See Diagram 2.

Diagram 2. 9:1 Ratio Recapitalization 1,000 Shares

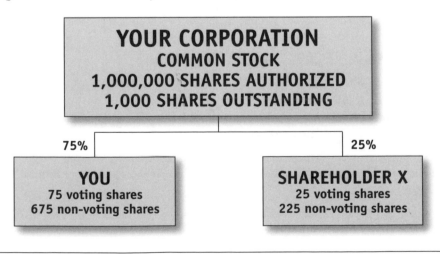

The ownership percentages remain the same. You own 75% and Shareholder X owns 25%. However, the stock or capital structure has changed.

The split of voting and non-voting ownership affects the valuation of stock for lack of control discounts.

EXAMPLE: After the reorganization, assume you give all of your non-voting stock to your grandson. This is where you separate the television from the remote control. Your grandson now owns 67.5% of the corporation. Due to the non-voting nature of grandson's stock, it is not a controlling interest. The non-voting stock has a lower monetary value because of its "lack of control." After your gift, you own 7.5% of the Corporation, but you still have voting control of the Corporation. You give your grandson the television and you retain ownership of the remote control. See Diagram 3.

Diagram 3. Gift of Non-Voting Stock to Grandson

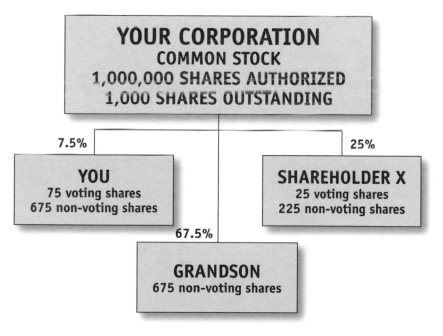

WHY RECAPITALIZE?

As part of your business and succession planning corporate recapitalization is an important step. It is not necessary for every corporation to recapitalize its stock. However, it provides the framework for several advanced planning techniques. In addition, when done properly, recapitalization triggers valuation discounts.

Your attorney should consider corporate recapitalization prior to any IDGT transaction involving corporate stock. The recapitalization enables you to transfer the non-voting interests to the IDGTs, while you retain control of your corporation until you decide otherwise.

Another reason to consider recapitalization is to accommodate new shareholders or investors. You may want to gift or sell your non-voting stock to your family or key employees today. Particularly if you have children or grandchildren working in your business, a transfer of non-voting stock is a very important incentive and an aid to your tax planning. If you consider new equity investors, each investor will have its own criteria for recapitalization.

Beth K. Rautiola of Brown & Streza, LLP in Orange County, California, practices in the firm's business department planning and coordinating business transactions, including mergers, acquisitions, and other business succession plans.

CHAPTER 78

Using Section 6166 to Assist With Payment of Estate Taxes

VANESSA GREGOR (Irvine, California)

The Internal Revenue Code (IRC) provides a method of assisting business owners or farm owners with the payment of estate taxes. The method allows for: 1) a special extension of time to pay; 2) a special payment schedule; and 3) a low interest rate. The IRC Section is 6166 and therefore an extension of time to pay using this method is commonly referred to as a "6166 extension."

DUE DATE FOR ESTATE TAX PAYMENT

The estate tax is due exactly nine months from the date of death. If you do not have enough cash to make all or part of the estate tax payment, you can request an extension of time to pay. Usually the IRS will grant this extension for one year to allow the estate to obtain the needed cash. The IRS will charge interest on the unpaid tax beginning on that nine month date, continuing until the estate tax is paid.

Although this one year extension can be very helpful to an estate, the interest charges can be expensive, and if a family business is a large part of the estate and the family wants to keep the business in the family, this additional year may not allow the family enough time to obtain enough cash to completely pay the estate taxes. Section 6166 allows your family to pay the estate taxes in installments, by either extending the period for payment so your family can obtain needed cash without upsetting business operations, or by making tax payments out of the earnings of the family business each year.

Following are highlights of the provisions of Section 6166:

Special Extension of Time

Section 6166 allows a special extended extension of time for payment of estate taxes related to a family-owned business. Instead of only one additional year to pay the estate tax, Section 6166 allows payments to be spread out over as long as 14 years.

Special Payment Schedule

There are two parts to the 6166 payment schedule allowed for the total of 14 years.

For the first four years you only have to pay the interest due on the unpaid estate taxes. The first of the four interest payments is due nine months from the date of death.

After the first four years, beginning on the fifth anniversary of the original estate tax due date, you make installment payments of the estate tax itself each year, plus interest. The installment agreement can allow payment of as few as two payments made in each of two years or up to as many as ten payments made in each of ten years. You are allowed to pay the entire amount of tax early any time you want, but if you stay on the maximum ten payment schedule, the taxes will be completely paid off in ten years.

Low Interest Rate

Section 6166 also allows you to pay a low interest rate on a large portion of the business-related estate taxes while you use the 14 year extension. The interest rate is only 2% a year. The interest rate can be even lower than 2% in a low interest rate economy. The IRS sets the interest rate charged on unpaid taxes four times a year. So, the 6166 interest rate you pay over the 14 year extension time may change, but should not be higher than 2%.

BUSINESSES THAT QUALIFY FOR THE 6166 EXTENSION

The 6166 extension is designed to help active family businesses stay in business by giving family members an extended period of time to pay the estate taxes related to the value of the business. Many types of family businesses qualify for this tax extension, including retail stores, service companies, manufacturing companies, companies active in management of real estate, and lending and financing businesses. Merely investing in the stock market or holding cash is not considered a business for purposes of Section 6166.

The family business can be owned directly as a partnership, a limited liability company, or as a corporation. If it is a partnership, you must own at least 20% of the partnership at the time of your death to qualify for the 6166 extension. If it is a corporation, you must own at least 20% of the voting shares. A partnership or corporation must also have 45 or fewer owners of the business to qualify. In addition, the portion of the business you own must be valued at your death at 35% or more of your total estate value. You can add together the value of two or more businesses to cross this 35% threshold as long as you and your spouse together own at least 20% of each business.

Example of estate tax payment, death of a single taxpayer in 2008:

$4,000,000 adjusted gross estate
Business with less than 45 owners

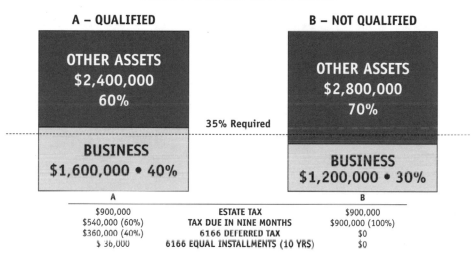

A	ESTATE TAX	B
$900,000	ESTATE TAX	$900,000
$540,000 (60%)	TAX DUE IN NINE MONTHS	$900,000 (100%)
$360,000 (40%)	6166 DEFERRED TAX	$0
$ 36,000	6166 EQUAL INSTALLMENTS (10 YRS)	$0

PLANNING TO MAKE SECTION 6166 AVAILABLE FOR YOUR ESTATE

Your estate and family can use the 6166 estate tax payment extension if you need extra time to make the business-related estate tax payment. Remember, however, that Section 6166 does not reduce estate taxes for your family. It merely helps your family make payments over a longer period of time.

During your life, you can make planning choices to leave Section 6166 available as a payment option for your estate as a part of your overall estate plan. If there are more than 45 owners of the business, you can keep at least a 20% ownership in the business instead of selling it all or giving it away during your lifetime. You may also choose to sell or give away different assets in order to increase the percentage the family business bears to the overall value of your total estate in order to meet the 35% test.

After your death, your family members and your business managers have requirements they must follow to allow the 6166 extension to continue for the full 14 years. Restrictions will be imposed on their ability to transfer or sell more than 50% of the business and the amount of cash that they can remove without using the cash to make an estate tax payment. If these restrictions are broken, for example, if the family sells the business to an outside buyer, then the full amount of unpaid estate taxes becomes due and payable.

Vanessa Gregor, Brown & Streza, LLP, is a Certified Specialist in Estate Planning, Trust and Probate Law and focuses on estate administration, estate and gift tax compliances, and estate and income tax.

ASSET PROTECTION

CHAPTER 79

Asset Protection Case Studies

WILLIAM R. BLACK (Wilton Manors, Florida) and JOSEPH STRAZZERI (San Diego, California)

CLIENT #1

J ohn and Mary Smith have not yet implemented any estate planning. John, age 46, is a CPA who audits SEC filings for mid- to large-sized corporations. Mary, 40, is a homemaker. They have two children, John Jr., age 12, and Jennifer, age 14. They are residents of Florida.

John's assets include his accounting practice, a professional S-corporation. The corporation employs four other CPAs and a number of support staff. John values his practice at approximately $4 million. John and Mary own a home worth approximately $1.7 million, with an outstanding balance on their mortgage of less than $800,000. John and Mary own three parcels of commercial real property, all located in the state of Florida. The combined value of these properties is approximately $2.2 million, with combined outstanding mortgages of $1.6 million. John and Mary have joint accounts (bank, savings, and brokerage accounts) valued at approximately $3.5 million. Mary has a separate brokerage account, an inheritance from her grandparents, valued at $750,000. John has a deferred compensation plan valued at approximately $2.5 million and a 401(k) plan valued at $550,000. John has a universal life insurance policy with a face value of $500,000 and a $100,000 cash surrender value, and a $1 million term policy insuring his life. Mary has no life insurance. John and Mary have no credit card debt and John's income from his business is more than enough to meet their day-to-day requirements.

John recently became concerned that the work he does made him vulnerable to lawsuits, as he learned the SEC had changed its policy regarding sanctioning individuals for errors committed. Whereas in the past the SEC had only held the firm liable, they now intended to hold individual CPAs liable. John's concern is that the SEC may qualify as a "super creditor" in the event they should levy a sanction against him.

Florida's Constitution protects the homestead from claims of creditors. This protection is generally unlimited, except that recent U.S. Bankruptcy Court rules have limited the equity the bankruptcy court is willing to protect to $500,000. Florida also has tenancy by the entireties (TBE). TBE generally protects accounts that are in the name of husband and wife from claims of creditors of either the husband or wife, but not both.

The choice John and Mary face is how complicated they want to make their lives in order to protect their assets. John and Mary decide that, for the time being, it is more important to them to protect their assets, at least until John retires (probably in the next ten years), than to worry about the complexity. Mary is sure she and John can handle the changes.

An estate planning attorney's goal is to provide a reasonable level of protection to clients without unduly burdening them.

Recommendations:

1. Prepare and execute basic estate planning documents: Revocable Living Trusts; Pour Over Wills; Durable Powers of Attorney; Health Care Documents (Health Care Surrogates, Living Wills, and HIPAA Releases); and Designation of Pre-Need Guardians for their minor children.

2. Asset Protection Planning: Prepare and execute an Alaska Family Limited Partnership (FLP). Prepare and execute two Delaware Self-Settled Spendthrift Trusts. Ownership of the FLP will be held in the name of the Delaware Self Settled Spendthrift Trusts. The ownership distribution will be 1% to the Management Trust (General Partner of the FLP), 80% to Mary's Delaware Trust, and 19% to John's Delaware Trust.

3. Have John and Mary obtain a line of credit against their home equity in an amount sufficient to bring the equity below the $500,000 homestead amount. In the event they are sued, this line of equity can be used to fund their defense.

4. John and Mary will re-title all personal checking accounts in the name of their individual Revocable Living Trusts.

5. Create three Limited Liability Companies (LLCs). These are single member LLCs, the only member being the FLP. These LLCs will be treated as disregarded entities for income tax purposes. The three commercial properties will be deeded to these LLCs. This will allow them to isolate the individual properties, thereby protecting the equity in the properties from claims against the other properties.

6. The savings and brokerage accounts are re-titled into the name of the FLP.

7. John needs to reorganize his business affairs. John needs to keep his professional S Corporation but he needs to establish a separate LLC for his business. He then should enter into an employment contract with the new LLC to hire him as a CPA. He should do this with all of the other CPAs who work for the firm as well. Each CPA should be required to

maintain Errors and Omissions coverage. The LLC should then have a blanket policy for all of them.

8. John's firm should obtain a line of credit against the Deferred Compensation Plan. An advance against the Line of Credit can be used to fund a Corporate Owned Life Insurance Policy on John's life.

9. John's 401(k) is an ERISA plan that meets all the qualifications for creditor protection both under ERISA and Florida Statute 222.

10. Mary's inheritance should be maintained in a separate account in her name. In addition, Mary should invest the money in creditor-proof investments. Florida protects funds invested in annuities and life insurance from the claims of creditors. Mary can also use part of this money to fund a 529 plan for her children. We recommend that the 529 plan be owned by an irrevocable trust with someone other than Mary as the trustee.

11. Finally, John and Mary need additional life insurance coverage — an additional $2 million on John, $1 million on Mary, and a $2 million survivorship policy. These new policies should be owned by an Irrevocable Life Insurance Trust.

12. The cost to John and Mary to set up this plan including the creation of all the entities, filing fees, document stamps, and attorney fees can approximate $60,000.

What has been accomplished? John's and Mary's primary assets are now owned by a partnership. The terms of this partnership are that John and Mary will have no right to income, no right to the principal in the FLP, and no right to dissolve the entity. John, through his Delaware Trust, will only own 19%. If John were sanctioned by the SEC or sued, this would be the maximum extent of his exposure. The line of credit against the Deferred Compensation Plan will protect it from other creditors. Mary's inheritance is protected in the event she is sued. If either John or Mary should die unexpectedly, they have protected their assets and have the necessary liquidity to see the survivor through.

The last bit of advice is that each of them own or lease and drive their own car. This prevents them from being drawn into a lawsuit over a traffic accident involving the other.

CLIENT #2

Bob is a very successful plumbing contractor, having developed and marketed a new plumbing system for high-rise buildings. Bob's business is an LLC. Bob is the manager and an 80% owner, with Bob's father owning the remaining 20%. Bob's business is worth approximately $15 million. Bob's business provides him with more than adequate income to meet his personal obligations. Bob has been married for 17 years and has two teenage sons. Bob's marriage has been shaky for a couple of years and he feels there is a high probability he will be going through a divorce in the next couple of years. In addition to his business, he has a brokerage account worth approximately $5 million. Bob has always maintained this account in his individual name. However, it would undoubtably be considered a marital asset in the event of a divorce. Bob has no life insurance. Bob's primary concern is that he not be forced to sell his business to comply with a property settlement agreement in the event of divorce.

Bob's case presents some interesting problems. First, Bob believes his wife would not want to participate in the planning and if she did, she would want a separate attorney. Under the circumstances, an estate planning attorney should not represent both because their interests are adverse to one another. At the same time, Bob needs to implement some estate planning and asset protection planning. Bob has a Will that was drawn up by an attorney when his children were small. It names his wife as personal representative, leaves all his assets to her, and if something happens to her, has the assets go to the children. The problem with the Will is that it gives everything outright to the wife, does not have provisions for estate taxes, provides no creditor protection, and does not have any provisions regarding divorce or remarriage. In all respects it is a very simple Will for a very complex estate.

Recommendations:

1. Have Bob sign a Revocable Living Trust. The terms of the trust are such that at his death, everything will go to his wife, unless divorce proceedings have been filed by either of them. In that case, she will be limited to the statutory "elective share" and the balance will go in trust to his children. If the divorce is final at the time of his death, she is to be treated as though she predeceased him.

2. The next issue is the property settlement agreement in the event of divorce. Bob's business depends heavily on him as the proprietor, and for that reason, his estate planning attorney advises him to purchase a universal life insurance policy with a face value of $10 million to provide for Bob's wife and children if he dies before a divorce were filed. Although it is important to Bob to try to keep his marriage intact, Bob knows it is a difficult challenge.

3. With regard to Bob's business assets and his brokerage account the estate planning attorney sets up a Family Limited Partnership (FLP), re-titling Bob's membership interest in the plumbing business and his brokerage account in the name of the FLP. It is hoped that as time goes by, and no divorce is filed, that the transfers will not be a problem.

4. The estate planning attorney establishes two Granter Retained Unitrusts (GRUTs), one for each of Bob's sons. The terms of these GRUTs are 20 years and they are to be funded with 30% of Bob's FLP interest. This leaves Bob with a 40% interest in the FLP. At this point, the estate planning attorney obtains the consent of Bob's wife to fund the GRUTs, so she

is provided with draft copies the GRUTs to take to her attorney for review. In addition, she is named as the successor trustee in the event something happens to Bob. She consents to the funding.

Two years later, Bob's wife files for divorce. The court rules that the transfers to the FLP were all part of Bob's estate planning and that she still had an interest in Bob's interest in the FLP as marital property. The wife attempts to have the transfers to the GRUTs reversed but the court rules that she agreed to the transfers, the transfers were designed to benefit their children, and Bob did not benefit from the transfers. The wife is awarded 20% of the FLP, an equitable share of Bob's 40% interest in the FLP. Bob as the trustee of the Management Trust, General Partner, tenders a fair market value offer to purchase her share, which she accepts. The net result is that Bob saves his business and provides for his children. Bob still is required to pay child support and alimony but is (somewhat) happy to do so because he has retained his business.

William R. Black received a JD from Nova University, Ft. Lauderdale, Florida, a BS in Management from the University of West Florida, an MBA from Golden Gate University, and a Masters in Estate Planning from the Esperti Peterson Institute.

Joseph J. Strazzeri, Law Firm of Strazzeri Mancini, LLP, San Diego, California. By combining your family's legal, financial, tax, and business affairs into a unified plan, Strazzeri Mancini, LLP, can enable you to pass your values to your heirs while substantially reducing taxes.

CHAPTER 80

Asset Protection Utilizing Asset Protection Trusts and Limited Liability Companies

JEFFREY R. MATSEN (Costa Mesa, California)

INTRODUCTION AND OVERVIEW

Corporate Shield of Liability

For centuries, business structures have been utilized for asset protection planning. A corporation is normally a very effective way to shield one's personal assets from liability resulting from the operation of a business. Normally, the shareholders of the corporation are only liable to the extent of their investment in the corporation. However, officers, directors, and employees can be personally liable for their conduct relative to the operation of the business and, therefore, may want to consider other alternative means of asset protection with respect to their personal assets. Over the last few decades, expanding theories of liability and the proliferation of litigation has given increased emphasis to asset protection planning above and beyond the corporate shield of protection. Potential liability is a major concern to doctors, dentists, other professionals, and persons of high net worth engaged in business or real estate activities.

Inside and Outside Debts

1. Inside creditors are those creditors whose claims are directed against the business operation or real estate which is operated and owned inside of a business entity.

2. Outside creditors are those creditors whose claims arise outside the purview of the business entity and are generally asserted against the professional, business, or real estate owner personally.

3. Corporations protect against inside debts against the business, as do limited liability companies (LLCs). LLCs are state chartered entities that provide a shield of protection similar to the corporate shield, but are treated for tax purposes as either a sole proprietorship or partnership. LLCs are extensively used to hold real estate assets because they combine the protection aspects of a corporation with the tax benefits of a partnership or proprietorship. Because of the tremendous liability potential of real estate activities, serious consideration has to be given to holding real estate (especially income-producing real estate) in LLCs.

4. Although corporations and LLCs protect against inside debts, we have already

indicated that many professionals, business owners, and real estate owners are concerned about outside debts or personal debts such as malpractice claims, negligence claims for accidents, and other kinds of personal liability claims engendered by aggressive plaintiffs' lawyers. The question then becomes, how do we protect against the outside claims (personal liability claims)? This is where the combination of an LLC with an asset protection trust can be a very beneficial strategy.

The LLC and the Charging Order

The basic remedy for a creditor of a member or owner of an LLC is to obtain a charging order against that member. The charging order prevents the creditor from reaching the LLC assets. The creditor is limited to a court order charging the interest of the member/debtor so that if any distributions are made from the LLC to the member, they have to be distributed to the creditor. Normally, the creditor gets only the economic rights to the distributions, not the voting rights or other non-economic rights of the LLC member. The application of the charging order in any particular case will depend on the state's statutory provisions and case law treating the charging order subject. The benefit of the charging order remedy to the owner of the LLC is that the assets within the LLC are protected from outright seizure by the creditor who is limited only to distributions that may not be made pursuant to the discretionary right of the manager to withhold such distributions. In other words, assets that would otherwise be attractive to a judgment creditor become much less attractive if they are held within a LLC where a charging order is the exclusive remedy.

Domestic Asset Protection Trusts

1. The general rule in most states is that creditors can reach the interest of the trustor (the maker of the trust) of domestic self-settled trusts. However, several states have recently adopted legislation somewhat similar to various offshore jurisdictions that provide, by statute, various degrees of asset protection for a trustor's interest as a beneficiary of a self-settled trust. Alaska, Delaware, South Dakota and Nevada seem to have the best laws in this regard.

2. If properly set up and maintained, the domestic asset protection trust is a significant barrier to creditors and will afford significant leverage to the debtor with respect to his or her negotiations with the creditor. This is especially true if the assets of the trust needing protection are domiciled in a state which is a domiciliary of the asset protection trust.

3. The problem is that the courts of the non-domiciliary states may not give effect to the asset protection features of the trust. However, there is no question that a significant degree of protection is afforded by using the domestic asset protection trust, especially when it comes to negotiating for a settlement with the creditor.

Foreign Asset Protection Trusts

1. A foreign asset protection trust is a trust that is set up in an offshore jurisdiction which has enabling trust legislation providing for substantial protection against

creditors of the trust. One of the greatest advantages of the foreign asset protection trust is the fact that by its very nature, any legal attack against its assets is transferred abroad to a different legal system. Normally, a foreign trustee is necessary for the efficacy of the foreign asset protection trust. The biggest advantage in utilizing the foreign asset protection trust is that assets can be placed offshore beyond the jurisdiction of U.S. courts. Some of the principal advantages of offshore trusts are as follows:

- Most foreign jurisdictions do not recognize U.S. court decisions as judgments. This may force a new trial on the merits in the foreign situs country.

- Some foreign situs jurisdictions require a much more difficult burden of proof for a creditor to challenge asset transfers to foreign asset protection trusts.

- Some jurisdictions have a statute of limitations for challenging asset transfers to a foreign asset protection trust that begins to run on the date of transfer.

- Fees and expenses in litigating in the foreign jurisdictions are going to be substantial, thereby serving as a strong deterrent to foreign litigation.

Modular Structuring

One of the best asset protection strategies is to combine the utilization of the domestic asset protection trust (DAPT) or foreign asset protection trust (FAPT) with an LLC. Basically, the member interest of the owner of the LLC is transferred to the DAPT or FAPT, which holds the interest more or less as a custodian. For example, a husband or wife can be a trustor or the maker of a DAPT or FAPT. An LLC can then be set up to hold real property and the member interest can be transferred to the DAPT or FAPT. Another LLC can be set up to hold liquid investments and, again, the member interest can be transferred to the DAPT or FAPT. It is recommended that a third party own at least 5% of the LLC because the efficacy of the charging order is greatly reduced and even eliminated when the LLC is a single member LLC. A diagram of the structure is set forth below:

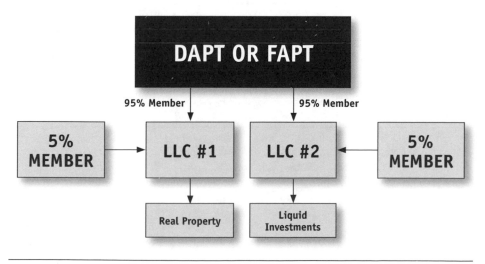

Divided You Stand, United You Fall

If an individual owns everything in one company, or in his or her own name, one lawsuit can result in the individual losing everything he or she owns. However, if assets are spread around into different liability-protected entities, then only the entity involved in the suit may be at risk. What this means is that most valuable assets should be segregated into separate LLCs (i.e., real estate parcels in separate LLCs and business equipment and/or liquid investments in other LLCs).

> **EXAMPLE:** John Smith and his wife, Jane own two income-producing properties and several percentage investments in other real estate projects. John is a building contractor and developer, and is not only worried about liability for his real estate and business interests, but also has concerns about personal liability. He and Jane set up a DAPT and place their income-producing properties in separate LLCs, and some of their investments and liquidities in other LLCs. John's sister, Joan is given a small interest in some of the LLCs, and Jane's sister, Jenny is given a small interest in some of the other LLCs. If creditors try to assert personal liability against John and are successful in obtaining a judgment, they will have to try to enforce the judgment by going against the DAPT as well as the various LLCs, where they may be limited only to a charging order remedy. The example is diagrammed below:

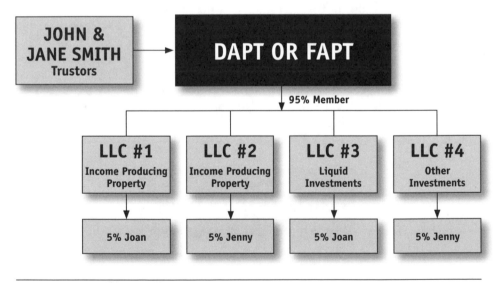

*Jeffrey R. Matsen, Wealth Strategies Counsel, has been designated by **Worth Magazine** as one of the "Top One Hundred Attorneys" in the country. His firm provides estate, asset protection, and business planning.*

CHAPTER 81

Multiple Business Entities as an Asset Protection Tool

ROBERT VAKSMAN (Las Vegas, Nevada)

It is common to see a business accumulate various assets (cash, real estate, securities, etc.) not related to the direct operation of the business. Aside from other potential issues and/or risks, doing so subjects all of the assets to the vulnerabilities of each individual asset. Imagine an ice cream company so popular that it has enough profits to invest in apartment buildings. One day, an accident occurs in the boiler room of one of the apartment buildings and a maintenance worker is severely injured. A lawsuit is filed and a judgment is entered in favor of the worker. Unfortunately, the accident leaves the maintenance worker paralyzed for life, with significant damages as a result. Presumably, he will seek recovery from the building's insurance carrier but, alas, the building is underinsured for such a catastrophe. Where else will the worker look to recover the remaining damages? As owner of the apartment building, the ice cream company is liable and will potentially lose all of its assets, including its ice cream inventory.

One possible solution is to simply remove the assets from the business by distributing them to the owners. However, this approach simply shifts the risk from the business to the owner. In other words, while the assets are in the business, they are subject to the business's creditor claims, and when distributed to the owner, the assets are subject to the owner's creditor claims. A comprehensive approach to asset protection must address both of these competing interests.

Fortunately, there is a relatively straightforward solution to this dilemma.

The business owner should consider establishing multiple divisions of the company. In its basic form, this means creating an operating company and a holding company. The holding company (also known as the management company) manages the other divisions (i.e., other companies) and receives compensation for its efforts. Additionally, the holding company owns most, if not all, of the assets, and loans those assets to the operating company.

It is important to ensure only the operating company contracts with any outside vendors and customers. This way, only the operating company is subject to risk of loss due to vendor and customer claims and lawsuits. Even in the case of a potential claim or lawsuit, because the operating company does not own any assets (rather, it leases assets provided by the holding company), the operating company has no assets to lose. Notably, the operating company will have recurring cash flows and receivables that may be subject to creditor claims, but most of these funds (minus operating expenses, of course) should be consistently paid to the holding company in the form of management fees.

ILLUSTRATED EXAMPLE: Business One "A1" owns its own assets, and contracts directly with its customers and vendors; thereby subjecting itself to creditor risk. Business Two holds its assets in "B1" and contracts with vendors and customers through "B2"; thereby limiting its liability only to those assets within "B2."

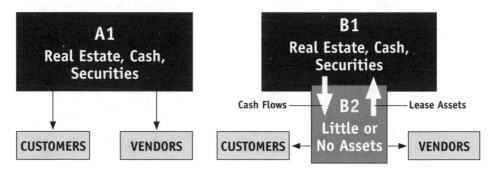

Utilizing this strategy will, admittedly, cause additional administrative, accounting, legal, and logistical difficulties. Yet, for a company with substantial assets, it is easy to see that the asset protection benefits quickly outweigh the burdens. For those for whom the benefits don't (yet) outweigh the burdens, there is another solution: Series LLCs.

For our purposes, suffice to say that although LLCs are relatively young in comparison to other business forms, they have quickly become the top entity choice for businesses, based upon their easy manageability and asset protection capabilities. LLCs are especially ideal for the multiple entity approach explained earlier. However, while they may be the ideal entity choice for our strategy, maintaining multiple LLCs does not deal with the problem of added administrative, accounting, legal, and logistical burdens.

In 1996, Delaware became the first state to enact a series limited liability company statute and, since then, a handful of states have developed similar statutes. A series limited liability company provides limited liability to the owners (members, in the case of LLCs) of each entity in the series. Each series of an LLC is essentially its own separate entity, with distinct assets, liabilities, managers, and members.

This structure is similar to the multiple entity approach explained earlier, but different in a few important respects. The primary difference is that a single operating agreement can be used to easily establish (and terminate, if need be) multiple and separate LLCs. This feature, at least partially, lessens the added cost and administrative burdens of the multiple entity approach. However, because very few statutes and very little case law and administrative guidance exists on the use of series LLCs, it is especially important to seek advice from a knowledgeable attorney.

Robert B. Vaksman, Esq., LL.M is among a small group of our country's most distinguished tax and business law practitioners. He dedicates his career to providing comprehensive solutions to families and businesses.

CHAPTER 82

Alaska Asset Protection Trusts

ELLEN GAY MOSER (Naperville, Illinois)

Today more and more lawsuits are being filed, new theories of liability are being developed, and you are more likely to have a jury award punitive damages now than in the past. Asset protection planning is not a new concept, but is now accepted as a necessary objective for you if you own property or a business you want to protect against unexpected risks.

Under federal law, you have some degree of asset protection, as any retirement plan governed by the Employee Retirement Income Security Act of 1994 (ERISA) is exempt from creditors. Individual retirement accounts (IRAs) are protected if necessary to support the owner or his or her dependents. State law may offer additional protections and business owners may limit personal liability by creating business entities, but you must consider that in some cases the courts have "pierced the corporate veil."

POTENTIAL LIABILITY

Some liability comes with the profession; doctors, lawyers, architects, and accountants are targets. If you are an employer, you are liable for the actions of your employees. Accidents happen and you may be subject to claims arising from a company vehicle or your personal automobile. If you personally guarantee a loan to your company, you are personally liable. When you own real estate, as an individual or as a business owner, you face a number of risks.

Your concern for family members may also create the urgency for asset protection planning. As parents, you may plan to protect your young children until they reach a certain age. Trust provisions which restrict your children's access to their trust funds also protect those trust assets from the claims of your children's creditors. You can plan to protect your children from a divorcing spouse by planning your revocable living trust with limitations on distributions to your children and grandchildren. Your estate planning attorney may advise you about asset protection planning for yourself and your loved ones.

ALASKA'S BENEFITS

In 1997, Alaska passed new law authorizing domestic self-settled asset protection trusts (Alaska Trusts). Alaska continues to pass laws protecting individuals, families, and family business entities. A few other states have also passed laws permitting domestic asset protection trusts in response to many American lawyers and clients being uncomfortable with offshore trusts and the laws of a foreign country. Understanding the opportunity to protect assets from creditors, but reluctant to avail themselves of the friendly foreign jurisdiction offshore, a number of people have chosen Alaska as the situs for their asset protection trusts and family limited liability companies.

Unless the transfer of assets to the Alaska Trust is intended to defraud known creditors, or make you insolvent, your assets in your Alaska Trust are not subject to the claims of your creditors.

CREDITOR PROTECTION

Alaska law prohibits all creditors from attaching trust property before distributions to a beneficiary. This includes claims of tort creditors and ex-spouses for alimony or child support. Further, Alaska provides that a beneficiary's interest in a trust is not property subject to division in a divorce or dissolution. An Alaska Trust is an irrevocable trust which allows the grantor to transfer assets to his trust and to be a beneficiary to whom the trustee can distribute trust property. If the trust is not obligated to distribute trust assets to the grantor/beneficiary, the assets will not be subject to his or her creditors' claims.

Before you set up your Alaska Trust, you must sign an "Affidavit of Solvency" and plan with your attorney which assets are to be contributed to your Alaska Trust. A "rule of thumb" among estate planning professionals is that no more than 50% of the grantor's net worth should be contributed to your Alaska Trust. An Alaska Trust may replace a pre-nuptial agreement, may be used for estate freezes, and may be a grantor or non-grantor trust. You may also be able to take advantage of no state income tax assessed on your Alaska Trust.

ALASKA REQUIREMENTS

A trust will qualify as an Alaska Trust if some or all of the trust assets are deposited in Alaska. Part or all of the trust administration must take place in Alaska. At least one Trustee must be an Alaska resident or an Alaska-headquartered bank or trust company. The duties of an Alaska trustee include maintaining books and records of the Alaska Trust, and preparing or arranging for the preparation of trust tax returns.

In conclusion, creditors have made claims against assets held in domestic asset protection trusts, but informally, trustees say these claims have been settled in favor of the grantor. No case has been decided, so the effectiveness of an onshore asset protection trust is not absolute. Your assets may be better protected under the jurisdiction of Alaska in an Alaska Trust.

Ellen Gay Moser counsels individuals and families to: Protect their assets; exit their business; provide for loved ones and obtain peace of mind. Her mission is to "Protect Family Values for Generations."

CHAPTER 83

Planning With Wyoming LLCs

CECIL SMITH (Memphis, Tennessee) and CAROL GONNELLA (Jackson, Wyoming)

Clients who desire a simple and effective strategy to protect their assets from future lawsuits, and to get discounts in value for estate and gift tax purposes should consider incorporating Wyoming Limited Liability Companies into their planning.

Limited Liability Companies are not all created equally. Some states have excellent statutes that provide clients with good asset protection and good discounts for estate and gift tax purposes. Other states have less-effective statutes. You will want your attorney to compare the various state laws to find the state that offers you and your assets the most protection with the least red tape and administration headaches.

In 1977, the State of Wyoming invented the Limited Liability Company in the United States. It gave us another choice for a business entity. Wyoming's legislature blended the best features of a corporation with the best features of a partnership, and called this new entity a Limited Liability Company (LLC). It was five years before other states caught on and began to copy the Wyoming statute. Over the next 20 years, all of the other states and the District of Columbia enacted LLC statutes.

The word "Close" conveys the notion that this new business entity is perfect for a small closely held family business or venture, such as a family investment company or a family real estate company. Compared to the other available choices of business entity, such as the Family Limited Partnership, the Wyoming Close LLC is by design much simpler to set up and administer. When the Wyoming Close LLC statutes are compared with the LLC statutes of other states, it is deemed one of the best in the country for 1) maximum creditor protection, 2) discounting of the value of assets in the LLC, and 3) low fees and administration of the LLC.

Wyoming is tax-friendly to individuals and business entities. Wyoming has no inheritance tax or gift tax. It has no state income tax, inventory tax, use tax, intangibles tax, or ad valorem property tax. Nor does it have a franchise or excise tax (many states do). The Wyoming Close LLC is a flow-through entity like a partnership and Subchapter S Corporation, so it is not taxed at the business entity level.

The Wyoming Close LLC is a known quantity, whereas other planning strategies that may provide similar benefits, such as an offshore asset protection trust, possess certain inherent levels of risk. For example, the offshore asset protection trust requires a connection with the offshore country, such as having a trustee who resides in that country, and the assets are subject to the laws of a foreign jurisdiction.

The Wyoming Close LLC can be coupled with many other tried and tested estate planning strategies to enhance the long-term benefits to a family, such as making gifts or selling units of the LLC at discounted values (see below).

Residents of any state can establish a Wyoming Close LLC. Minimum contacts must be made with the state by having a Registered Agent appointed to represent the LLC in the state of Wyoming. The Registered Agent can be any individual who resides in Wyoming, or it can be a corporation with an office in Wyoming.

FIRST CONSIDER THE FIVE TIERS OF ASSET PROTECTION PLANNING

1. Take advantage of existing laws to protect some of your assets through the use of life insurance, annuities, retirement accounts, and, where appropriate, Tenancy by the Entireties property.

2. Increase your professional liability insurance and/or your umbrella coverage.

3. Domestic Asset Protection Plans (Level I): Form an LLC, such as the Wyoming Close LLC, to protect the assets in the LLC.

4. Domestic Asset Protection Plans (Level II): Form an LLC to protect assets in the LLC *plus* an Asset Protection Trust, such as the Wyoming Asset Protection Trust, to protect the distributed income from the LLC.

5. Offshore Asset Protection Plans.

ASSET PROTECTION FROM INSIDE LAWSUITS

Example of an Inside Lawsuit: Mom and Dad are retired and live off Social Security and the income from a jointly owned rental house. Included in Mom and Dad's $1 million estate is the rental house worth $70,000. They get $350 a month rental income. It's a nice supplement to their Social Security income. There's a fire! A tenant dies in the fire. Whom do you think the victim's family sues? The owners of the rental house, of course. Who are the owners? Mom and Dad. There is a dispute over who's at fault, so a jury has to decide. If the victim's family wins the lawsuit, and if Mom and Dad's liability insurance is not enough to cover the judgment awarded by the jury, most of Mom and Dad's assets can be seized to satisfy the judgment.

How a Wyoming Close LLC would have protected Mom and Dad's assets from seizure, if an LLC had owned the rental house: This lawsuit against Mom and Dad is known as an inside lawsuit. It's a lawsuit resulting from an accident involving an asset inside the LLC. If the victim's family obtains a judgment against the owner of the rental house, the LLC is the owner — not Mom and Dad. Thus, only the asset owned by the owner (i.e., the rental house) is subject to seizure. Mom and Dad's other assets are not subject to seizure.

Thus, the LLC serves to isolate "hot" assets (real estate, for example) from "cool" assets (stocks, bonds and cash, for example). If a hot asset is inside an LLC and the LLC is sued, cool assets are protected from the lawsuit.

ASSET PROTECTION FROM OUTSIDE LAWSUITS

Example of an Outside Lawsuit: Dad is in an automobile accident. He accidently ran a stop sign. However, a teenage passenger in the other car is now paralyzed from the neck down and will spend the rest of her life in a wheelchair. There is not a dispute about who is at fault. Dad is at fault. It is only a matter of whether Dad's liability insurance will cover the damages. If not, the injured victim will be able to obtain a judgment against Dad. Most of Dad's assets can be seized by the victim to satisfy the judgment she obtains against Dad.

How a Wyoming Close LLC would have protected Dad's assets from seizure, if brokerage accounts, savings accounts, etc. had been owned by an LLC: This lawsuit against Dad is known as an outside lawsuit. It's a lawsuit resulting from an accident outside the LLC.

The law in Wyoming provides that the sole remedy of a judgment creditor is to obtain a Charging Order. This is a court order that charges the managers of the LLC with the duty to pay any income that is being distributed to Dad to his judgment creditor, rather than to Dad. If the judgment creditor actually asks for and obtains the Charging Order, she may only receive the distributions from the LLC to Dad if the manager of the LLC decides to make any distributions. The manager may decide to make no distributions in any given year. Some practitioners feel the judgment creditor still may have to pay income tax on the undistributed income. The reality of this structure is that most judgment creditors will go back to the negotiating table and try to settle within the insurance limits.

FAMILY & BUSINESS REASONS TO FORM AN LLC

There are many reasons to create an LLC beyond creditor protection and discounting of assets for estate planning, however. Just a few of the reasons follow:

1. **Promoting Family Harmony.** The Wyoming Close LLC promotes family harmony by permitting children and/or grandchildren to participate in management of the family wealth as Members of the LLC. However, only Managers of the LLC control the LLC. Thus, although the children and grandchildren are involved as Members, they have no vote. The LLC promotes knowledge and communication about family wealth among all family members who are Members of the LLC.

2. **Management & Control.** The Wyoming Close LLC permits family members to consolidate fractional interests in assets and to provide consolidated management of the assets. The Managers of the LLC control the assets of the LLC. For example, a parcel of real estate owned jointly by parents and children as tenants-in-common so that each owns an undivided interest in the parcel, can be contributed to the LLC to consolidate ownership and to name one or more Members as the Managers of the LLC.

3. **Protecting Family Wealth.** The Wyoming Close LLC protects family wealth by restricting the right of a non-member to acquire an interest in the LLC or in the assets of the LLC. The LLC also provides protection to family wealth by preventing the transfer of a membership interest as a result of a failed marriage. The assets owned by the LLC are protected from future judgment creditors of the Members of the LLC.

4. **Dispute Resolution.** The Wyoming Close LLC provides an orderly buy-sell arrangement between and among the Members of the LLC and their families without fractionalizing assets of the LLC. In addition, the LLC insures that any disputes regarding family wealth owned by the LLC will be resolved privately by mediation or arbitration rather than publicly through the court system.

ESTATE PLANNING REASONS TO FORM AN LLC

1. **Valuation Issues/Discounts.** The Operating Agreement of the Wyoming Close LLC contains the maximum restrictions allowed by Wyoming statutes on Members of the LLC. These restrictions include restrictions on the transfers of membership interests and restrictions on liquidation of membership interests. These are "friendly" restrictions for family members because the approval of the family Member-Managers is all that is required. But a buyer outside the family will not be willing to pay 100% of the fair market value of the assets owned by the LLC because of the restrictions. A professional business appraiser will determine the fair market value of the membership interest, and this will usually result in discounts of 25% to 50%, or greater.

2. **How the LLC Affects Estate Taxes.** At death, the assets in the Wyoming Close LLC are no longer owned by the decedent. The decedent only owned a membership interest in the LLC. During lifetime, the value of the assets owned by the LLC is not reflected on a financial statement. Only the membership interest in the LLC is listed. At death, however, the value of the membership interest must be determined by a qualified business appraiser for estate tax purposes. The discounted value of the LLC membership interest is reported on IRS Form 706 Federal Estate Tax Return, which results in less estate tax owed and increases the amount passing to beneficiaries.

3. **How the LLC Affects Gift Taxes.** In terms of gifting, again, the assets in the Wyoming Close LLC are no longer owned individually; the individual only owns a membership interest in the LLC. If lifetime gifts are made to other family members, trusts for family members, or charities, the value of the membership

interest must be determined by a qualified business appraiser. The discounted value of the LLC membership interest is reported on IRS Form 709 Federal Gift Tax Return, which results in less gift tax owed and increases the amount passing to beneficiaries. More value can be gifted to beneficiaries using only the annual gift tax exclusion amount, currently $12,000 ($13,000 in 2009).

4. **How the LLC Affects Income Taxes.** The Wyoming Close LLC is usually taxed as a partnership, a flow-through entity. In other words, the LLC does not pay income tax. Rather, each member of the LLC must pay his or her pro rata share of the income tax. If a gifting program to children and grandchildren is implemented so that they receive membership interests in the LLC, each child or grandchild who owns an interest in the LLC must pay income tax on his or her pro rata share of the taxable income produced by the LLC. The gift of LLC interests to the children or grandchildren can shift income taxes to family members who are in lower income tax brackets, without fractionalizing the income producing asset.

Illustration of Using Two LLCs (One to protect a Brokerage Account, and one to protect Real Estate)

ACTION STEPS
1. Mom creates and funds LLC-I with her brokerage account.
2. Mom creates and funds LLC-II with real estate (other than her personal residence).
3. Mom creates a Revocable Living Trust (RLT) to avoid probate.
4. Mom transfers her ownership interests in her Investments LLC to her RLT.
5. Mom transfers her ownership interests in her Real Estate LLC to her RLT.
6. Mom then funds her RLT with her other assets. The RLT avoids probate.
* In some cases LLC units are funded after death by TOD (Transfer on Death) provision in order to avoid a state's Franchise & Excise Tax.

SUMMARY OF BENEFITS
- Mom's brokerage account and real estate are now protected from seizure by a judgment creditor. Thus, if Mom has an automobile accident and the other party sues her and obtains a large judgment, the judgment creditor will not be able to take Mom's brokerage account and real estate away from her.
- Mom's assets are not subject to the jurisdiction of the Probate Court. In other words her estate will avoid Probate.
- Mom's brokerage account will be valued less in the LLC than if it had not been in the LLC. It is expected that a discount will be available for estate and gift tax purposes in the range of 25% - 40%.
- Mom's real estate will be valued less in the LLC than if it had not been in the LLC. It is expected that a discount will be available for estate and gift tax purposes in the range of 40% - 55%.
- Family harmony results from the children being involved in the ownership of Mom's assets.
- Mom may later pass management responsibility to kids.
- Mom and the children are illustrated as all being Managers (optional).

Cecil Smith has law offices in Memphis and Nashville, Tennessee. Carol Gonnella has offices in Jackson, Wyoming. Cecil and Carol limit their practices to estate planning, asset protection planning, charitable planning, business planning, and postmortem settlement of trusts and estates.

CHAPTER 84

Estate Planning for Physicians
and Other Professionals

THEODORE G. GUDORF (Dayton, Ohio)

Estate planning clients who are physicians or other professionals (dentists, lawyers, accountants, veterinarians, etc.) are different from the average client. Not only are these individuals typically better educated, but they are in a different life situation and have very different concerns. Professionals earn more money, pay more taxes, and have more exposure to liability. Therefore, not only do they need different advice, they need better advice pertaining to wealth protection.

The first key ingredient for success is the establishment of a collaborative, professional, and focused team of advisors. The team necessarily involves a estate and business planning attorney, investment advisor, and a certified public accountant. The team focuses on asset protection for business and personal assets, while establishing strategies to minimize estate and income taxes, developing practice exit strategies, and creating significant retirement benefits.

Team meetings are mandatory. The client must set the agenda and insist upon a regular schedule. The discourse amongst talented advisors in front of the professional client results in an unparalleled degree of honest advice coupled with the opportunity to analyze strategies under a multidisciplinary lens. This almost always produces a far better economic and legal result. At a minimum, it keeps the client and team on the "same page."

The second key ingredient for success is keeping the team's number one priority focused on asset protection. It is not about hiding or concealing assets. It is about maintaining control while discouraging lawsuits from the outset. For the professional client, there is significant value in shielding assets while achieving other goals. The cardinal rule is that wealth protection has to be tied to wealth creation. Like all tax planning, asset protection should have economic substance.

It must be understood that asset protection has a "Sliding Scale." See the "Asset Protection: 'Sliding Scale'" chart at the end of this chapter. By understanding "no shield" strategies such as general partnerships to "ultimate shields" such as state and federal exemptions, the team will help the professional client protect wealth while building wealth professionally and personally, all without doing any more work!

Professional clients often have large homes and significant brokerage accounts, or other real estate investments. Designing plans to protect these personal assets is essential. The advice may be as simple yet unconventional as to "never pay off your mortgage" to as complicated as combining a domestic asset protection trust with the charging order protection of a Wyoming or Delaware limited liability company. See the "What a 'Charging Order' Means" chart at the end of this chapter.

Estate tax planning is the third key ingredient to success. Every client should assist in the design of a customized revocable living trust which incorporates legacy trusts for their children. Further, for the most part, all life insurance should be owned by an irrevocable life insurance trust. Finally, valuation discount planning, utilizing a Wyoming or Delaware limited liability company in conjunction with an irrevocable grantor trust, will enable the client to minimize, if not eliminate, state and federal estate taxes. See the "Using the FLP or LLC" chart at the end of this chapter.

Benefits planning for the professional is the fourth and final ingredient for success, and often involves unconventional wisdom. For instance, most professionals are familiar with qualified plans. However, many do not realize these can be a tax trap with funds left in the estate at death taxed up to 75% or more. Alternatives such as Section 79 plans or the establishment of a captive insurance company are possibilities that should be explored. These strategies, when combined with sound asset protection and exit strategy planning, will enable the professional client to sleep well at night. Further, if a catastrophic event occurs, such as the disability or the death of a partner or a lawsuit against the client or partner, everyone involved will be protected.

There are many aspects of planning for the physician and other professional clients that are beyond the scope of this article. However the steps outlined in this article provide the basis for the implementation of a sound comprehensive plan.

Asset Protection: "Sliding Scale"

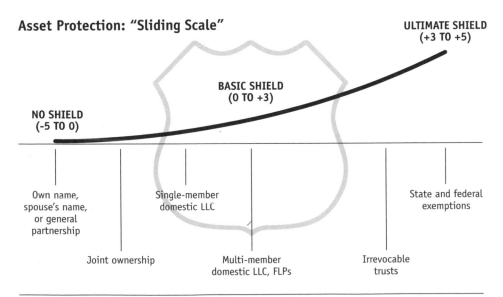

ULTIMATE SHIELD
(+3 TO +5)

BASIC SHIELD
(0 TO +3)

NO SHIELD
(-5 TO 0)

Own name, spouse's name, or general partnership

Single-member domestic LLC

State and federal exemptions

Joint ownership

Multi-member domestic LLC, FLPs

Irrevocable trusts

What a "Charging Order" Means

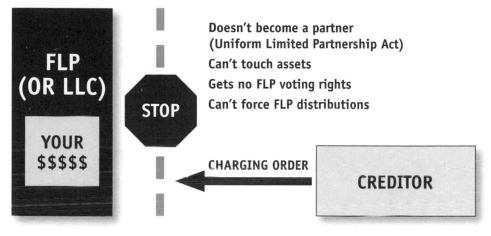

FLP (OR LLC)

YOUR $$$$$

STOP

- Doesn't become a partner (Uniform Limited Partnership Act)
- Can't touch assets
- Gets no FLP voting rights
- Can't force FLP distributions

CHARGING ORDER

CREDITOR

Using the FLP or LLC

FLP/LLC INVESTMENT

HUSBAND	WIFE	KIDS
49%	49%	2%

Will shield assets, reduce taxes,
and allow for estate planning

Our law firm represents professionals such as physicians, dentists, accountants, engineers, lawyers, farmers, and business owners. We focus on asset protection planning in the context of comprehensive estate planning.

OTHER
CONSIDERATIONS
IN ESTATE
PLANNING

CHAPTER 85

State Death Taxes –
Potential Impact and Strategies

JEFFREY L. KNAPP (Basking Ridge, New Jersey)

Is your estate subject to one or more state death taxes? For a quick answer, refer to the chart at the end of this chapter, check the line for each state in which you own property, and see if there are blanks under the "Estate" and "Inheritance" columns. At time of publication, 26 of our states are essentially not collecting any death taxes. But, you should bear in mind that state death taxes are in a state of flux because many are still coupled to the federal estate tax system, which itself is in major flux, and we are referring to 51 separate jurisdictions, all or nearly all of which are consistently operating in deficit mode. Please "stay tuned" if you are considering relocating to, or already own property in one or more states that have either an "Estate" or an "Inheritance" tax listed in the chart. Let us briefly define a few terms and discuss the significance of the numerical entries.

"Estate" taxes are based on the size of a decedent's estate. Historically, few states have had separate estate taxes. More have had "pick-up taxes" tied to the federal credit for state death taxes, which has been phased out. "Inheritance" taxes are levied on one's right to inherit property. Those inheriting are classified by their degree of relationship to the decedent, with different exemptions and tax rates applied to each class. Spouses and children are often exempt from inheritance taxes; while siblings, nieces, and nephews will generally incur an applicable inheritance tax. While Oregon and Tennessee refer only to an "inheritance tax," these two states do not appear to distinguish among classes of beneficiaries, so their taxes are listed under "Estate" taxes in the chart.

You may recognize the figures appearing in the "Estate" column of the chart. In 2001, Congress raised the federal estate tax exemption amount from $675,000 to $1 million, and to $2 million in 2008, before increasing it to $3.5 million for 2009. Most of the states collecting an estate tax currently exempt either the first $675,000, $1 million, or $2 million of the estate. While the states generally publish marginal rates of 5% to 16% on the taxable portions above the exempted amount, it is true that most of these states have effective rates of 37%, 39%, or even 41% on relatively small (approx. $50,000 to $100,000) slices of estates just over the respective exemptions of $675,000, $1 million, or $2 million. This hidden reality creates planning incentives for those with estates that are perhaps 5% to 25% over their state's applicable exemption. Could you, by gifting down to the point of your state's exemption, avoid both the state tax and the need to file any estate tax return?

This is where the concept of "local rule," and the absolute necessity of consulting local counsel, comes into play. For example, you will note that the chart does not capture the intricacies of exemptions under the various "Inheritance" taxes. On the topic of gifting, several states (including Iowa and North Carolina) have separate gift taxes, and several other states (including New Jersey and Oklahoma) have "clawback" provisions that bring gifts made within 36 months of death back into one's estate for state death tax calculations. Some state death taxes exempt life insurance where the beneficiary is a direct relative (New Jersey), and some state death taxes apply to non-resident owners of local real estate (Maryland).

If you have substantial assets, including property in two or more states, you may want to engage local counsel in each of those states in conversations about "domicile" and "situs," and the local rules applied to these terms. Generally, domicile is where you spend 183 or more days per year, and situs means place or location. Usually, tangible property has a tax situs where it is physically located, and intangible property has a tax situs at the domicile of the owner. As you can see from the tax chart, there may be reasons to either carefully document or to change your domicile, and possibly to change the situs of property by utilizing certain trustees. If you have property in two or more states, you want to minimize the possibility of being taxed "both coming and going."

Lastly, if you are considering moving to another state, or choosing between two states where you already own property, please note that the two lefthand columns in the tax chart are not the only pertinent tax factors. Hopefully, you will have many healthy years ahead of you to pay income tax, sales tax, and property tax! Accordingly, the chart also summarizes state income taxes and general sales taxes. Counties and cities often add to the general sales tax, and control property taxes to a degree that the chart cannot capture. For more information on property taxes and the overall state-by-state tax burden, or to check changes in state taxes between future editions of this book, you may find www.retirementliving.com helpful. Bearing in mind that another tax factor in determining the state you choose to live in is how much of each federal tax dollar is returned to that state, you may also wish to track that at www.taxfoundation.com. You should know that thorough research among dozens of Web sites and publications did not yield one single source that was 100% accurate and current regarding all 51 jurisdictions. Thus the caveat above bears repeating: Do consult local counsel in all pertinent states before taking any action.

Jeff Knapp, JD, CLA, Fellow EPI, is the lead attorney at The Knapp Law Firm LLC, which works with families throughout New Jersey. Jeff can be reached at 888-KNAPP-LAW or at jknapp@knapplaw.net.

STATE	ESTATE	INHERITANCE	INCOME	SALES	NOTE
Alabama			2% - 5%	4%	
Alaska					
Arizona			2.59% - 4.54%	5.6% or 6.3%	
Arkansas			1% - 7%	6%	
California			1%-10.3%	7.25%	incl 1% surcharge on income >$1mil
Colorado			4.63%	2.90%	
Connecticut	>$2mil; 5%-16%		3% - 5%	6%	
Delaware			2.2% - 5.95%		
District Columbia	>$1mil; 5.6%-16%		4% - 8.5%	5.75%	
Florida				6%	
Georgia			1% - 6%	4%	
Hawaii			1.4% -8.25%	4%	
Idaho			1.6% - 7.8%	6%	
Illinois	>$2 mil; 7.2%-16%		3%	6.25%	
Indiana		1% - 20%	3.40%	7%	
Iowa		1% - 15%	0.36% - 8.98%	5%	3 yr clawback; gift tax a la Fed
Kansas	>$1mil; 1%-7% 2009		3.5% - 6.45%	5.30%	estate tax ends 12/31/09
Kentucky		4% - 16%	2% - 6%	6%	
Louisiana		2% - 7%	2% - 6%	4%	
Maine	>$1mil; 5.6%-16%		2% - 8.5%	5%	
Maryland	>$1mil; 16%	10%	2% - 4.75%	6%	
Massachusetts	>$1mil; 5.6%-16%		5.3% - 12%	5%	
Michigan			4.35%	6%	inc tax declines 10/1/11
Minnesota	>$1mil; 5.6%-16%		5.35% - 7.85%	6.50%	
Mississippi			3% - 5%	7%	
Missouri			1.5% - 6%	4.23%	
Montana			1% - 6.9%		
Nebraska		1%-18%	2.56% - 6.84%	5.50%	
Nevada				6.50%	
New Hampshire			5% - wages excluded		
New Jersey	>$675K; 4.8%-16%	11% - 16%	1.4% - 8.97%	7%	3 year clawback
New Mexico		may be income	1.7% - 5.3%	5%	inheritance taxed as income
New York	>$1mil; 5.6%-16%		4% - 6.85%	4%	
North Carolina	>$2mil; 7.2%-16%		6% - 8%	7%	July 08 outside RE exempt; has gift tx
North Dakota			2.1% - 5.54%	5%	
Ohio			0.65% - 6.55%	5.50%	
Oklahoma	>$3mil; 8.5%-10%		0.5% - 5.65%	4.50%	3 year clawback
Oregon	>$1mil; 5.6%-16%	see "estate" tax	5% - 9%		*called "inheritance" tax; NO clawback
Pennsylvania		4.5% - 15%	3.07%	6%	
Rhode Island	>$675K; 4.8%-16%		3.75% - 9.9%	7%	
South Carolina			2.5% - 7%	6%	
South Dakota				4%	
Tennessee	>$1mil; 5.5%-9.5%	see "estate" tax	6% - wages excluded	7%	only int. & dividends taxed
Texas				6.25%	
Utah			2.3% - 6.98%	4.65%	
Vermont	>$2mil; 7.2%-16%		3.6% - 9.5%	6%	
Virginia			2% - 5.75%	5%	
Washington	>$3.5mil; 16%-19%			6.50%	
West Virginia			3% - 6.5%	6%	
Wisconsin	0 in 2009-2010		4.6% - 6.75%	5%	resuming 1/1/11 >$1mil
Wyoming				4%	

CHAPTER 86

Pet Trusts – Can You Trust Your Pet?

PEGGY HOYT (Oviedo, Florida)

Surveys report there are more than 140 million dogs and cats sharing our hearts, our homes, and even our beds. These numbers don't include the millions of horses, birds, reptiles, and other pets we call "kids." We treat them like our children, sometimes better. We worry about them when they are not with us and wonder whether they will be properly cared for when we are gone. Our pets love us unconditionally, help reduce stress, and even increase our longevity. They do so much for us, yet few of us have done anything to assure their long-term care in the event we are unable to provide for them personally.

Have you ever wondered what would happen to your pet if something happened to you — a natural disaster, a disability, or even death? Perhaps you are like many people who assume friends or family will step in to care for your beloved pets, much like they would care for an orphaned child. The sad truth is that if you don't take affirmative steps to ensure an enforceable plan for your pets, they may have an uncertain future. In many states, simply making a will or a trust that includes your pets may not be sufficient. Many states do not recognize provisions that provide for pets. Therefore, you need to consider all of your options to provide for the long-term care needs of your "children who wear fur coats."

Planning for your four-legged loved ones can, in many ways, be just as challenging as planning for your two-legged loved ones. A typical question that arises is, "Do I need a will or a trust?" The best answer generally is, "It depends." Factors that have to be addressed when planning for your pets include the following: your goals; wishes and desires for your pets; the number of pets you own; whether any of your pets have unique circumstances necessitating special planning (i.e., health concerns, unusual behaviors, etc.); your financial resources to ensure your pets are provided for adequately; and the identity of one or more caregivers or trustees.

These are just a few of the issues and concerns you must consider to create a comprehensive plan to ensure your pets will be properly cared for when you are unable to do so yourself. No two pet-owners' circumstances are the same, and in each case, your planning goals must be considered so they can be fulfilled.

The first step in planning for your pets, and one of the most crucial, goes beyond the legal design of a pet estate plan. The first step is selecting the caregivers who will have physical custody of your pets and who will provide the home where they will live and the care they will require to thrive. Much like planning for minor children, before any of the financial considerations are addressed, you have to determine and feel comfortable with your choice of caregiver(s). Finding the right person(s) can be a challenge. You may consider family or friends, but what do you do if you don't have anyone suitable for this important role? In this instance, a pet sanctuary or perpetual care facility may be the right choice. Another option is to create an Animal Care Panel — a panel of trusted individuals who will be entrusted with the oversight responsibility for your pets and their caregiver. One client has created her Animal Care Panel from a selection of family, friends, and her veterinarian. Their job is to choose her pet caregiver who will live in her home, care for her pets, and report periodically regarding the health of the pets to the panel, as well as to the trustee, who is responsible for the distribution of her assets for the benefit of her pets.

Selecting a trustee to manage your assets for your pet's care is also a critical part of your plan. Your pet caregiver may act as trustee or you may feel more comfortable if the person caring for your pets doesn't have the dual responsibility of managing the assets for your pets' benefit. Alternate trustee choices may include a trusted friend or family member, or a professional fiduciary such as an attorney, certified public accountant, or trust company specializing in pet trust services. Your trustee will be charged with the responsibility of making sure your wishes regarding the investment and distribution of assets for the care of your pets are followed.

A comprehensive plan for your pets should ideally include a durable power of attorney that includes provisions for the care of your pets, a will or trust, preferably a trust, with specific instructions outlining in detail your wishes for the care of your pets as well as the selection of your pet caregivers and trustees, and appropriate alternates. As discussed above, your plan may also include an Animal Care Panel to provide oversight and guidance to your caregiver and trustee for pet care and asset distribution decisions. All of your legal documents should be supplemented with substantial "baby-sitter" instructions outlining the care requirements for each of your pets, including their daily care, medical history, photographs, and special instructions to meet the unique needs of your pets. Your plan shouldn't stop at your possible disability or death but should also include disaster instructions in the event of a natural disaster or an unexpected evacuation that prevents you from caring for your pets.

In summary, following are the top ten considerations when planning for your pets:

1. Make a notebook with a detailed description and history for each of your pets. Clearly identify your pets for future caregivers with photographs and other identifying information, including unique markings, microchips, and DNA.

2. Post emergency decals at home identifying pets and their locations. Carry a wallet card that advises emergency personnel about the existence of your pets.

3. Seriously consider how you want your pets cared for in the event of a

natural disaster, your disability, and upon your death. What documents have you put in place to accomplish this goal — disaster plan, powers of attorney, wills and/or trust?

4. Analyze the care costs for your pets for planning purposes — how much will be required to provide them with a lifetime of care? Are your resources adequate? Can life insurance assist in meeting this goal?

5. Identify possible caregivers (including perpetual care providers) and their alternates. Will an Animal Care Panel assist in the selection, oversight, and care decisions related to your pets?

6. Determine how your caregivers will be compensated — lump sum, fixed sum, actual expenses, bonus compensation, outright gift of money and pet?

7. Identify your trustee (and alternates) who are charged with the responsibility of administering, investing, and distributing the assets of your estate for the benefit of your pets.

8. Carefully choose your remainder beneficiaries — those who will benefit from your estate plan after your pets.

9. Include pet charities as part of your lifetime and estate plan giving.

10. Choose legal practitioners and trusted advisors who are sensitive to your needs and desires to plan for your pets.

Peggy Hoyt practices in family wealth and legacy counseling, including trust and estate planning and administration, small business creation, succession and exit planning, real estate transactions, and animal law.

CHAPTER 87

The Buildup Equity Retirement Trust or BERT! The Wonder Trust™

CECIL SMITH (Memphis, Tennessee) and CAROL GONNELLA (Jackson, Wyoming)

The Buildup Equity Retirement Trust, or BERT! The Wonder Trust™, is becoming one of the most popular trusts in the practices of many estate planning attorneys. This trust is an irrevocable trust, wherein one spouse (the donor-spouse), makes gifts to the trust using the federal annual gift tax exclusion. The beneficiary of the trust is his or her spouse (the donee-spouse).

BERT takes advantage of several sections of the Internal Revenue Code to keep the assets gift tax-free during life and estate tax-free upon the deaths of both spouses. However, the donee-spouse has access to the assets in the trust for anything he or she needs, based on four standards (the so called ascertainable standards) for the donee-spouse's health, education, maintenance, and support. Based on these standards, the trustee of the trust (who may be the donee-spouse) determines when distributions should be made. This trust can be a haven for retirement savings, without all the onerous requirements imposed upon IRAs and qualified retirement plans, such as 401(k)s.

Generally, the trust is drafted as a "grantor trust." As a grantor trust, the donor-spouse, rather than the trust, is liable for the income tax liability on the income generated by the assets in the trust. Remember, if the trust were not created, the donor-spouse would pay this tax liability anyway. Thus, this is another benefit to the BERT, as the assets within the trust can grow free from income tax.

Because of the flexibility of a BERT, it may hold a multitude of assets, including but not limited to cash, stocks, bonds, real estate, life insurance, annuities, closely held corporate stock, limited partnership units, and limited liability company units. In fact, LLC units are great assets to contribute to a BERT because of the asset protection provided by the LLC and because of the discounts available for gift tax purposes.

Because the income of the BERT is not taxable to the trust, the gifts made into the BERT can grow dramatically over the years. With annual gifting, these trusts can slowly grow to over $1 million within the spouses' lifetimes. The United States

Congress gives every person an exemption from federal estate tax of $2 million (in 2008, and $3.5 million in 2009). This is the amount a person can give away before incurring an estate tax. With a BERT a person can legally create another exemption from estate taxes. However, the assets in the trust are accessible and under the control of the donee-spouse as trustee throughout his or her lifetime.

Husbands and wives (as well as brothers and sisters and domestic partners) can create trusts for one another. Thus, the BERT trusts have the potential to create two additional estate tax exemptions...one for the husband and one for the wife.

With super-funding (gifting more than the annual gift tax exclusion — $12,000 per donee per year in 2008, and $13,000 in 2009), the amount that can pass tax-free to one's children or other loved ones can be several million dollars. The sum of $240,000 is the magic number for superfunding, as 5% of $240,000 is $12,000, the annual gift tax exclusion in 2008. (The annual gift tax exclusion is $13,000 in 2009.) However a donor-spouse may 'superfund' the trust with a lesser amount.

HOW CAN I MAKE GIFTS TO MY SPOUSE DURING MY LIFETIME?

There are several ways to make gifts to your spouse during your lifetime. Most gifting techniques to spouses require that assets be included in the spouse's estate at his or her death. However, there are techniques to keep the gifts free from estate tax liability. Gifts to spouses include the following.

Gifts to spouses who are United States citizens. Gifts to spouses who are United States citizens may be made in unlimited amounts pursuant to the unlimited marital deduction. These gifts may be made outright or in trust. If made in trust, the spouse must receive the income stream from these gifts and the gifts must be included in the donee-spouse's estate.

Gifts to spouses who are not United States citizens. Gifts to spouses who are not United States citizens are limited to $128,000 (2008 figure, as indexed for inflation) per year. They may be given in the same manner as gifts to citizen spouses.

Annual exclusion gifts. Annual exclusion gifts in the amount of $12,000 (the 2008 amount, as indexed for inflation) can be given to any number of people free of tax. A gift must be a gift of a present interest to qualify for this exclusion. For citizen spouses, it makes no sense to use this exclusion, as the donor spouse may make unlimited gifts pursuant to the marital deduction, unless they are given to special trusts, as further discussed below. Non-citizen spouses are not entitled to this annual exclusion gifting.

Gifts to irrevocable life insurance trusts. A spouse may be named as a beneficiary of an irrevocable life insurance trust (ILIT). Gifts of either the annual exclusion amount or of a donor's lifetime unified credit exemption equivalent amount may be used in making gifts to the spouse. However, to keep the gifts out of the donee-spouse's estate, a goal we generally wish to accomplish, care must be taken to insure that if the annual exclusion gifting is used, that two rules are followed:

1) the gift is deemed a present interest gift; and 2) the gift does not violate the 5 & 5 rule. These two requirements are further defined in the next gifting strategy.

Gifts to a BERT. In this trust, we use the donor-spouse's annual gifting exclusion to place gifts into an irrevocable trust that he or she has created for his or her spouse. We must carefully follow two rules if we use gifts of the donor's annual exclusion amount — the present interest rule and the 5 & 5 rule. We insure the gift will be one of a present interest by allowing the donee-spouse a temporary withdrawal right over the property contributed to the trust. In essence, the trustee of the trust must notify the donee-spouse that a gift has been made and that the donee-spouse has a certain limited period of time (30 days, for example) within which to withdraw the gift. If the gift is not withdrawn in that time period, the right to withdraw the gift lapses and the trust assets (including the gift) can only be distributed pursuant to the terms of the trust. Compliance with the 5 & 5 rule requires the following: With annual exclusion gifts placed in trust, the Internal Revenue Code causes a portion of the trust assets to be included in the donee-spouse's estate if the annual exclusion amount is greater than $5,000 per year or 5% of the value of the trust property. So, generally, with a BERT, our goal is to keep all of the trust assets free from estate tax liability upon both the donor-spouse's and donee-spouse's death, and thus if the clients' goal is to avoid any possible gift tax, we take care that the gifts to the trust are no greater than $5,000 per year or that the gift, up to the maximum annual gifting exclusion for that year, does not exceed 5% of the trust assets.

THE ECONOMIC POWER OF BERT! THE WONDER TRUST™

As previously discussed, the annual exclusion from federal gift taxes is currently $12,000 ($13,000 in 2009) per donee. With annual exclusion gifts, if you don't use them, you lose them. In other words, if you do not make an annual exclusion gift to your spouse in any given year, you give it up forever, and you cannot thereafter make that gift without adverse tax consequences. Over time, these annual exclusion gifts can grow remarkably, particularly if the income tax liability of the trust is deflected away from the trust and is instead paid by the donor-spouse, also known as the Grantor. Assume a spouse creates a BERT and funds it initially with some amount between $5,000 and $240,000. The gifts do not have to be cash. They can be stocks, bonds, real estate, business interests, limited liability company interests, family limited partnership interests, annuities, life insurance, etc. In a few states (Tennessee being one of them) a gift in excess of the annual exclusion will be subject to a state gift tax. No federal gift tax will be due. There will be no gift tax on the annual gifts after the first year as these annual gifts are kept under maximum amounts allowed under the gift tax rules so as not to have to pay gift tax.

In the tables below we compare 4%, 6% and 8% growth rates.

> **EXAMPLE 1: INITIAL GIFT OF $5,000.** The tables below reflect the value of the trust assets at the end of various year intervals assuming the BERT is funded initially with $5,000 and annual gifts between $5,000 and $12,000 are made.

4% GROWTH RATE		6% GROWTH RATE		8% GROWTH RATE	
Year 5	$ 28,282	Year 5	$ 29,877	Year 5	$ 31,680
Year 10	$ 62,574	Year 10	$ 69,858	Year 10	$ 78,227
Year 20	$161,950	Year 20	$211,735	Year 20	$ 279,854
Year 30	$373,552	Year 30	$543,948	Year 30	$ 791,930
Year 35	$522,079	Year 35	$799,629	Year 35	$1,239,637

EXAMPLE 2: INITIAL GIFT OF $240,000. The tables below reflect the value of the trust assets at the end of various year intervals assuming the BERT is funded initially with $240,000 worth of ownership interests in an LLC, and annual gifts of LLC interests worth $12,000 (again, not using the full $12,000 annual exclusion amounts) are made in 2008. The LLC interests are illustrated here as having a discount for estate and gift tax purposes of 50%. Actual discounts vary.

4% GROWTH RATE		6% GROWTH RATE		8% GROWTH RATE	
Year 5	$ 344,993	Year 5	$ 376,819	Year 5	$ 411,038
Year 10	$ 487,332	Year 10	$ 575,973	Year 10	$ 679,981
Year 20	$ 871,206	Year 20	$1,199,140	Year 20	$1,655,773
Year 30	$1,439,435	Year 30	$2,315,136	Year 30	$3,762,436
Year 35	$1,818,888	Year 35	$3,169,878	Year 35	$5,604,284

The amounts shown above are protected from lawsuits and creditors of both spouses and will pass free of estate tax to their children when the donee-spouse dies.

It may not be difficult to obtain the growth rates shown above as the BERT trusts do not pay income taxes on their earnings. Instead, the Grantor pays the income taxes, thus allowing the trusts to grow more rapidly. The above gifts are illustrations only. Gifts can actually be any amount between $5,000 and $240,000, and one does not have to make all of the annual gifts. One can skip years and make no gifts at all.

BERT TRUSTS FOR BENEFIT OF HUSBAND & WIFE

These trusts can be funded with any assets other than qualified plans. We like using LLC units to fund the trusts, because the LLC provides asset protection and discounts for gift tax purposes.

If the trusts are funded with gifts under the annual gift tax exclusion (currently $12,000) and within the 5 & 5 rule, the two trusts will likely be worth over $1,500,000 in 30 years, assuming an initial gift of $5,000 and an 8% growth rate. There will be no gift taxes incurred. See the tables above.

However, if H and W are willing to use some of their federal estate tax exemption amount (currently $2,000,000 each) and in some cases pay state gift taxes, these trusts can be super-funded with LLC units that will for example grow in value to over $13,000,000 in 30 years. If the growth rate is 10% the BERTs will likely be worth over $18,000,000 in 30 years. See the tables above.

Achieving the 8% growth rate should not be so difficult since the BERT Trusts are grantor trusts and don't pay income tax.

The BERT ILIT

The only risk of the BERT strategy is that H and W may not live the targeted number of years. So, what do wise people do about risks? They insure those risks. The insurance used in this case doesn't have to be the expensive cash-value type. Instead, the insurance can be an inexpensive tax-free second-to-die policy which is designed to terminate when the BERT trusts reach their targeted values. These types of policies have to be carefully crafted by an experienced life insurance professional.

The BERT ILIT is a Second-to-Die Irrevocable Life Insurance Trust.

The annual gifts to the BERT ILIT as well as the annual gifts to the Bert trusts are all subject to the gift tax rules. Thus, if insurance is implemented, the gifts to cover the annual premiums will reduce the amounts that can be gifted tax-free to the children …birthdays, Christmas presents, anniversary presents, etc.

Note: Some states have a small state gift tax that would be assessed if more than the annual exclusion amount is gifted to the BERT trusts. However, given the growth power of the BERT trusts the state gift tax is pretty cheap insurance.

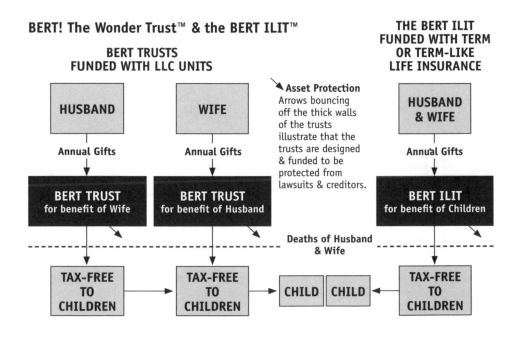

BERT! The Wonder Trust™ & the BERT ILIT™

BERT TRUSTS FUNDED WITH LLC UNITS

THE BERT ILIT FUNDED WITH TERM OR TERM-LIKE LIFE INSURANCE

HUSBAND **WIFE**

Annual Gifts   Annual Gifts

BERT TRUST for benefit of Wife   BERT TRUST for benefit of Husband

Asset Protection Arrows bouncing off the thick walls of the trusts illustrate that the trusts are designed & funded to be protected from lawsuits & creditors.

HUSBAND & WIFE

Annual Gifts

BERT ILIT for benefit of Children

Deaths of Husband & Wife

TAX-FREE TO CHILDREN   TAX-FREE TO CHILDREN   CHILD   CHILD   TAX-FREE TO CHILDREN

Cecil Smith has law offices in Memphis and Nashville, Tennessee. Carol Gonnella has offices in Jackson, Wyoming. Cecil and Carol limit their practices to estate planning, asset protection planning, charitable planning, business planning, and postmortem settlement of trusts and estates.

CHAPTER 88

Beneficiary-Controlled Descendants' Trusts

JAMES N. VOELLER (San Antonio, Texas)

The majority of people who set up wills and revocable trusts leave their assets outright in equal shares to their children when they die. What most people don't realize is that many times by leaving the inheritance outright, they may be unintentionally disinheriting their grandchildren! Suppose you die leaving assets to your son, and shortly after your death, he passes away too. It is likely his will leaves everything to his spouse — who may spend the inheritance on herself, or worse yet, give it to a new spouse — leaving your grandchildren with no part of the inheritance!

Instead of leaving your assets outright to your children, consider the potential advantages of leaving your assets to trusts for the benefit of your children, which you can design and create during your lifetime.

A descendant's trust is created by you, today, within your revocable trust, naming your child as trustee and beneficiary when you die. For example, if your daughter is named Mary Smith, the trust would read "Mary Smith, as Trustee of the Mary Smith Trust."

There are a number of good reasons to leave assets in descendants' trusts you create as a part of your overall estate plan for each of your children. These include the following benefits:

- The assets will be protected from your child's spouse in the event of divorce.

- The assets can be protected from your child's creditors in the event of financial hardship.

- The assets are sheltered from lawsuits of which your child may become a party.

- The assets will not be part of your child's probate estate in the event of the child's incapacity or upon his or her death.

- The assets can be removed from your child's estate so that no further estate taxes will be due when the property passes to the next generation.

- Upon your child's death, the unused assets will go to your blood relatives (such as grandchildren) instead of in-laws or others who are not a part of your plan.

The reality of a descendant's trust is that it is much easier for your child to keep assets separate from a spouse when the assets have been left to the child in trust. At the time of your death, all of your assets are re-titled directly from your trust to your child's trust. There is a world of difference between a child saying to a spouse "my parents left this money to me in a trust" and the alternative of having the child receive the inheritance "in hand," and needing to take active steps to keep those assets separate from a spouse, or trying to shelter them from an unexpected lawsuit.

A descendant's trust may be drafted to provide that during your child's lifetime he or she has complete access to the income and the principal of the trust — so that you are not necessarily giving a "gift with strings attached" or "ruling from the grave." (If circumstances are warranted, however, you may elect to impose tighter control over the assets.) But when your child dies, you can ensure that the unused portion of the inheritance goes to your grandchildren or to a charity you would like to support. The trust can provide that until your grandchild reaches the age where he or she will likely be more responsible, say age 30, someone else will manage the assets, distributing so much of the assets as may be needed for the grandchild's health, education, maintenance, and support. Once the grandchild reaches age 30, you may want the grandchild to be the trustee of his or her own trust. If one of your children dies without leaving children, the assets of that child's trust could go to the trust created for your other children.

The time to design these trusts for your children is now — when you are preparing your own estate plan. Upon your death, your plan will provide this important protection for your children. In the overwhelming number of states, once your children have inherited assets from you, it is too late for them to create their own protective trusts.

If you are going to leave it all to them anyway, consider leaving your children's inheritance to them in a protected trust by doing some additional planning for them today. Your children will greatly appreciate what you have done to put them on the right track to plan for themselves and their families. Talk to your estate planning attorney about how to incorporate these ideas into your trust.

James N. Voeller focuses his practice on helping families structure their affairs to protect their assets from lawsuits and government intervention, and helping families save millions of dollars in estate taxes and probate costs.

Captive Insurance Companies

MARC SELDEN (New York, New York) and BRIAN A. EAGLE (Indianapolis, Indiana)

The captive insurance company strategy is used by privately held businesses desiring to reduce property and casualty insurance costs, control premiums, receive an annual income tax deduction of up to $1,200,000, and have at least $250,000 in excess free cash flow.

A captive insurance company insures all or part of the risks of its parent or the subsidiaries of a parent. This unique company is created when a business, or a group of businesses, form a corporation to insure or reinsure their own risk. These self-insurance vehicles can allow businesses to pay lower premiums, tailor coverage to their specific needs, accumulate investment income to help reduce net losses, access reinsurance markets to transfer risk, and gain greater control over claims as well as their broad risk management operations.

A "pure" captive is owned and controlled by one entity and insures that entity and/or its subsidiaries. A group captive is an insurance company owned and controlled by two or more unaffiliated organizations, which is formed to provide insurance to its group or association of owners. The owners are usually companies from a related business field.

You may form a captive insurance company as a subsidiary or affiliate of a business entity or entities to insure or reinsure the risks of those entities. The premiums paid by the business entities to the captive to insure the risks of the entities are tax deductible. Captive insurance companies are given tax incentives due to provisions in the U.S. Tax Code which allow a captive to accrue reserves against future claims. This tax incentive is only available to insurance companies.

A captive insurance company is an insurance company with claims, policies, policyholders, reserves, and surplus. A captive must be formed as a C corporation in the United States or foreign jurisdiction for the purpose of writing property and casualty insurance to a small and usually related affiliated group of insureds. The main purpose of a captive is to insure the risks of the companies that are also owned by the captive's owner, or parent.

The captive insurance company and the entities it insures should have an arm's-length relationship and should act independently of each other, except for payment of premiums for the risk coverage. In the beginning, a captive is set up to reduce the costs of insurance coverage for the business entities. As the captive grows, it can become a profitable business which enhances the owner's wealth. The captive assumes the risk that is currently self-insured.

With a captive, you can insure deductibles and/or exclusions on existing policies, or you can take on a portion or all of the traditional insurance risk. The profitability of traditional insurance companies, like banks, is tied to its investment income. In strong markets, insurance premiums may be artificially depressed in an effort to raise more dollars. In a weak market, insurance companies will raise premiums to offset its losses. The captive, unlike a traditional insurance company, can charge premiums based on claims history and actuarial predictions rather than on profits and losses.

You can also reserve premium payments when commercial insurance is inexpensive and access those reserves when commercial insurance is expensive. At that time, the captive owner can raise deductibles on existing policies and have the captive insure the deductibles. Alternatively, the owner can refund the premiums which can be used to pay the increased premiums, or explore reinsurance.

The captive can earn investment income on the premiums paid. This investment will allow more funds to be available to pay claims and/or increase profits. The captive will reduce the administrative costs such as agent commissions, compliance with federal and state regulations, office overhead, and salaries inherent in commercial insurance premiums.

With commercial insurance companies, premiums are determined based on the claims experience of other similar businesses. This technique benefits business entities with poor claims experience, but hurts entities with good claims experience. With captive insurance companies, the insured will benefit from good claims experience and the surplus in the captive will be available to the shareholders. The captive determines the terms of coverage, which provides flexibility to tailor the policy to accommodate the specific needs of the entities.

The first step in creating a captive insurance company is a feasibility study to determine whether a captive insurance company is right for a client. This step includes a review of the client's existing liability insurance policies, including workers compensation, general liability, and errors and omissions policies. The captive does not generally replace the existing commercial policies, but is used to provide coverage for policy exclusions and deductibles. The captive has direct access to the reinsurance markets, which allows it to obtain wholesale premium quotes. The captive can also provide coverage for risks for which no insurance is otherwise available, known as naked risk.

Captive insurance companies may be set up in the United States or offshore. Several states have captive insurance statutes, including Arizona, Delaware, Washington, D.C., Hawaii, Kentucky, Montana, Nevada, Utah, and Vermont. Vermont is the largest captive domicile in the United States. Vermont will accept a letter of credit to satisfy the capital requirements. The number of states permitting captive insurance companies is increasing in response to recent IRS "safe harbor" rulings. The most popular offshore domiciles include the British Virgin Island, Bermuda, and the Cayman Islands. Traditionally, offshore domiciles have had lower initial capitalization requirements and set-up costs.

Captives are generally formed by a "turn key" approach. The set-up involves actuaries, attorneys, underwriting, issuance of policies, and a regulatory licensing process. The client will generally work with a team of tax and legal professionals for advice about ownership of the captive for income, estate, and gift tax planning. Formation costs are in the $50,000 to $100,000 range for most simple captives, but more for more complex ones. Turn key administration will cost at least $40,000 per year.

The Regulations provide: "The term 'insurance company' means a company whose primary and predominant business activity during the taxable year is the issuing of insurance or annuity contracts or the reinsuring or risk underwritten by insurance companies." There is no definition for "insurance" or "insurance contracts" in the Internal Revenue Code (IRC) or in the Regulations. However, the Courts have generally held that an insurance contract involves risk shifting and risk distributions.

In 2002, the IRS issued three Revenue Rulings providing "safe harbors" for captives: Revenue Ruling 2002-89 (Third Party Risk), Revenue Ruling 2002-90 (12 Entity), and Revenue Ruling 2002-91, which deals with a group captive arrangement.

The IRC allows property and casualty insurance companies certain deductions against taxable income not allowed for ordinary businesses. This results in minimum or no taxable income on the premiums received. Moreover, Section 831(b) of the IRC sets forth a tremendous tax advantage to captive insurance companies. If the captive's total premiums are less than $1.2 million per year, it may elect to be taxed only on its investment income, and premiums are not taxable income.

You can gain significant income and estate tax advantages if you implement a captive strategy for your privately held business. When the operating business pays premiums to the captive, wealth is transferred from one entity to another tax-free. The premiums paid are deductible by the entity paying the premium and receipt of the premium by the captive is generally tax-free. The monies in the captive will also be protected from the operating business's creditors. If the captive is owned by children or grandchildren, outright or in trust, there will be a transfer without gift, estate, or generation-skipping transfer tax. This type of planning opens up tremendous opportunities for multi-generational planning, including using life insurance to leverage the wealth transferred.

Eagle & Selden, P.C., is a boutique New York City law firm concentrating in Estate Planning, Business Succession Planning, and Asset Protection for families and businesses.

Our philosophy at Eagle & Fein is to make the complex, simple by taking time to understand client concerns, identify potential problems, and seek solutions providing comfort and confidence to clients.

CHAPTER 90

Elder Law Concepts

BRIAN ANDREW TULLY (Huntington, New York)

An old Pennsylvania Dutch proverb says, "We get too soon old and too late smart." Unfortunately this happens to a number of our Nation's senior citizens when it comes to the concept of elder law. Quite frequently, an elder law attorney will be contacted by a child or spouse who is suddenly faced with the reality that their loved one requires some form of skilled nursing or long-term care. Usually, the flood of questions and "what if" scenarios from other family members and health care professionals can start to overwhelm even the strongest of spouses or the most reliable of children.

While much of the emotion and uncertainty in common situations like this cannot be preempted or resolved in advance, some of the most complicated matters, such as establishing who will make the health care decisions, what health insurance coverage exists, and what the best way is to protect the family home can be addressed by an experienced elder law attorney before you get "too soon old." Failure to address these issues in advance of a health care crisis will certainly cost more money and cause more stress, and usually requires court intervention. You can plan ahead to avoid a crisis situation by being armed with accurate knowledge and having in place the necessary tools and mechanisms to help if such a situation arises.

The field of elder law, like estate planning, is not an isolated field of law confined to a single set of statutes and regulations, as you would typically find with other areas of the law. Rather, elder law is defined by the various needs of the client to be served. For example, elder law encompasses most issues a typical senior citizen will face during the second half of his or her life: legal; financial; tax; health insurance; asset protection; housing; and government benefits. Addressing these issues in advance will help you to avoid a crisis situation. While everyone should establish a proper estate plan when we begin our family and/or our careers, a good rule of thumb in establishing our "elder law plan" is to meet with an experienced elder law attorney when you receive your Medicare card at 65 years of age.

A typical elder law plan includes both advice and legal documentation. The advice revolves around achieving the following common goals: maintaining your current standard of living; ensuring all of your hard-earned assets go to your family how and when you choose; reducing or eliminating taxes and administration expenses;

establishing who will handle your financial and health care decisions; and planning for and minimizing the expense of potential long-term health care needs.

The experienced elder law attorney can help you achieve these goals by advising you of the legal and financial strategies available and helping you evaluate the benefits and limitations of the Medicare and Medicaid programs, long-term care insurance and the concept of self-insuring, and by helping you implement a legal elder law plan through documentation that balances these goals and issues. Your elder law plan must be completed before incapacity strikes, as you must have the ability to understand and express your decisions regarding the necessary legal documents such as a Health Care Proxy, Durable Power of Attorney, Living Will, Last Will and Testament and perhaps a Trust, or Family Agreement.

The exorbitant costs of long-term health care are typically the motivator when it comes to addressing the various elder law concerns. Long-term health care, which is usually not paid for by Medicare, is typically required when someone suffers from a chronic or disabling condition that requires either skilled nursing care or custodial assistance with common activities of daily living such as bathing, walking, and toileting. The out-of-pocket costs for these services can range from $2,000 per month up to $25,000 per month depending on the level of care needed and the market rate for the services in your region.

There are only a few payment options when the need for this type of care exists. First, Medicare offers only a limited benefit for those services that are skilled or therapeutic in nature. When Medicare coverage ends, families that have not planned in advance are faced with the extreme costs of paying for the needed care themselves until eligibility for Medicaid is obtained. The eligibility process for this second option can cost upwards of 50% of a single person's assets. If a person is married, eligibility can usually be obtained earlier but there is a very serious risk; the spouse who isn't in need of the long-term care faces the potential of being sued for reimbursement by the local Medicaid agency.

The third, and most recommended option for elder law planning, is to consider long-term health care insurance. A properly placed long-term care insurance policy can help protect the lifestyle of your spouse and/or family from the high cost of long-term care and can help protect your assets for your heirs. Each state is encouraging its residents to consider purchasing this type of health insurance. The New York State Office of the Aging confirms this on their Web site with the following advice: "insurance is an important part of securing your financial goals. Long-term care insurance can help to safeguard your assets and protect your financial stability…[it] is an important tool to help you with the high cost of long-term care services." There are several variables to consider when obtaining this type of health insurance. Your elder law attorney can help you sort through the various options.

While most agree that we do get "too soon old" it is very important to realize we don't also have to be "too late smart." Be encouraged in that there are proactive steps you can take in advance of any long-term health care need that can help you maintain control and security even as you face new challenges.

Brian Andrew Tully, JD, CELA, Law Offices of Brian Andrew Tully, PLLC, located in Huntington, New York, is Certified as an Elder Law Attorney by the National Elder Law Foundation.

CHAPTER 91

Medicaid/Medi-Cal
Preplanning With Trusts

RUSSELL C. MILLER (Visalia, California)

The Issue: If you are worried about the high costs of long-term care and how it will affect your estate, this is the chapter for you. Seniors over the age of 65 have a 50% chance of needing a nursing home someday. The pressing question for most people is: "How can we afford to pay the nursing home without losing everything we own?" The second question is: "What can we do to plan ahead?"

The Problem: In the United States, care in a skilled nursing facility can run from $2,500 to $25,000 per month or more, depending on your location. The average stay in a nursing home is approximately three years. In certain cases, such as dementia, a stay of three to twenty years is not uncommon.

In California, the average cost of care in a nursing home is approximately $5,500 per month, or $66,000 annually. Three years of care is $198,000. The greatest threat to your loved one's hard-earned money is the high cost of nursing home care.

Planning ahead for such costs is prudent and wise. There are only four choices for paying for skilled nursing home care:

1. **Private Pay.** You can privately pay the nursing home by writing them a check once a month.

2. **Long-Term Care Insurance.** It is great if you have long-term care insurance, but even if you do, it does not always cover all your costs and it often has time limits. Moreover, you have to buy it before you need it.

3. **Medicare.** Medicare, in conjunction with your supplement, may pay for up to 100 days of coverage, as long as you continue to improve. If your condition plateaus, or if your health starts deteriorating, Medicare can stop paying for your stay at the nursing home within a week.

4. **The Medicaid/Medi-Cal Program.** Medicaid is a needs-based Federal entitlement program, implemented by the states, which provides funding for medical care for those who qualify. The California version of Medicaid is

called Medi-Cal. The Medicaid Program will pay for your stay in a nursing home and will cover most drug costs for those who qualify.

The Solution: If preservation of assets for your family is your goal, the Medicaid program is the only cost-effective way to pay for nursing home care. There are two important aspects of the Medicaid Program you must know in order to plan properly:

1. **Qualifying for Medicaid/Medi-Cal.** In order to qualify for Medicaid, you must meet a strict asset and income test. The numbers vary from state to state. However, in every state, there are assets that are exempt (not counted) when Medicaid determines whether you qualify. Also, Medicaid will look at the applicant's financial records for the past three to five years to find any "uncompensated transfers" (gifts). If they find gifts, they can calculate a penalty period during which they will not pay for the nursing home. The rules of Medicaid are complex. You need to hire an advocate, such as a qualified Elder Law attorney, who knows the rules and how to formulate a working strategy.

2. **The Medicaid Lien.** If your loved one qualifies for Medicaid, is receiving benefits during a stay in a nursing home, and owns assets that were "exempt" for qualification purposes, such assets may be subject to a Medicaid recovery lien upon his or her death. However, with knowledge of Medicaid rules, your Elder Law Attorney should know how to legally defeat the Medicaid lien and protect the assets from recovery.

THE STAGES OF MEDICAID PLANNING

There are three stages to Medicaid planning:

Stage One: Your Estate Plan

A professionally crafted estate plan is essential for Medicaid planning and should include the following documents:

a. **Revocable Living Trust.** There are myriads of benefits to owning your property in a living trust, but such trusts are especially useful for purposes of Medicaid planning. A properly drafted living trust solves the problem of not being able to manage your assets if you become incapacitated. You can name a person who will act as trustee and manage the assets in the trust if you are unable to do so yourself. In order to be properly drafted, your trust must contain special language granting your trustee the powers necessary to implement Medicaid planning.

b. **Financial Power of Attorney.** Equally important is the financial Power of Attorney, which also requires special language so your agent can implement Medicaid planning along with the trustee of your living trust (typically the same person).

c. **Irrevocable Trust.** In the right circumstances, and in consultation with an Elder Law attorney, families with larger estates and trustworthy adult children may be able to utilize Irrevocable Trusts to achieve Medicaid eligibility.

d. **Other Important Documents Every Estate Plan Should Have.** Every estate plan should also have a Pour Over Will, Advance Health Care Directive or Health Care Power of Attorney (depending on the state), HIPAA Authorization, and a Living Will.

If you have the above documents in place, they are properly drafted, and you keep them current by reviewing them with your attorney every few years, you are ready for Stage Two, if necessary. Suppose you have prepared the above documents and are now faced with a crisis situation where you need to apply for Medicaid.

Stage Two: Spend Down and Application

You will need to consult with an attorney in your state regarding the spend down process and how to fill out the Medicaid application. "Spend down" does not mean spending all your money until you hit the qualification limits. What it does mean is that you implement a plan to reposition assets within the rules of Medicaid in a legal, ethical, and moral manner. The Medicaid rules allow you to spend down your money by paying for any necessary medical needs you may have (i.e., new glasses, hearing aids, etc.). You can also spend money to fix your home. Because the home is exempt, you are turning a non-exempt resource (cash) into an exempt resource, the home. The opportunities for spending down in accordance with Medicaid rules are vast and vary from state to state. One very important purpose behind the rules is to ensure a "well-spouse" is not completely impoverished by spending down the "ill-spouse's" assets.

For example, in California in 2008, the "well-spouse" is allowed to keep $104,400 in assets, and $2,610 in income. John Doe and Mary Doe are a married couple who has $250,000 in assets, and a $250,000 home. John Doe has developed Alzheimer's disease and requires around-the-clock care in a skilled nursing facility. John has $1,200 per month in income and Mary has $700 per month in income. In order to qualify John for Medicaid, his assets must be spent down to $2,000. Mary gets to keep $104,400 in cash assets, plus the house, because it is an exempt asset. Now comes the fun part. John and Mary are "over-property" by $146,000. That amount must be "spent down" or "repositioned" in order for John to qualify for Medicaid. A good attorney will notice that John and Mary's income only totals $1,900 per month. John can only keep $35 per month in income and Mary is entitled to $2,610 in income. Mary's current income is only $1,865 per month. Mary's attorney can go to court and ask the court to increase the amount of assets Mary is allowed to keep from $104,400 to an amount that, if invested conservatively, will produce an income stream that will bring Mary up to the limit of $2,610 per month.

The question then becomes: How much money will it take to produce an income stream for Mary that will produce $745 more in income? Often, the court will award the entire estate to Mary without her having to spend down a dime (except for attorney fees, of course) so she can support herself. This is just one example of a planning opportunity existing within the rules of Medicaid.

Your attorney can fill out your Medicaid application for you and present it to the Medicaid office with evidence attached detailing asset repositioning you have done, along with a copy of the Medicaid rules authorizing such repositioning. A good attorney will determine whether further revocable trust planning is necessary. For example, it is necessary to ensure that the person who is going on Medicaid does not receive an inheritance unless it is in the form of a Special Needs Trust, designed to supplement but not replace Medicaid benefits.

Stage Three: Defeat of the Medicaid Lien

Your attorney will best be able to advise you about how to avoid the Medicaid lien. The issue is very state-specific. If you have done the above planning, defeating the lien should not be a difficult task.

A "Trinity Asset Protection Plan™*" designed by The Disability and Elder Law Firm will relieve your fear and uncertainties regarding disability, the high costs of long-term care, and death.*

CHAPTER 92

Anyone Can Leave Money Directly to Children, but It Is Better to Leave It in Trust – How Not to Make a $250,000 Mistake

ROBERT M. GOLDBERG (Griffin, Georgia)

You don't have to roll the dice when you leave property to your children. Are your kids mature enough to handle new-found wealth? Do they have the knowledge needed to manage money? I think you need to love your children enough to protect them from themselves. Let me tell you my story.

My Mom and Dad were from the old school. My Dad left home when he was 17 to join the Navy. He never finished high school. While he was away fighting in the Pacific during World War II my Mom graduated from beauty school. When Dad returned home from the war, he married my Mom and decided to follow my Mom to beauty school to learn a trade so he could make money and raise a family.

After graduating from beauty school my Dad asked my Mother's father for a loan so he could open his own salon. My Dad was very successful. He ended up owning a string of seven beauty salons. He had a beautiful home in suburbia and an 88-acre horse farm in the Catskill Mountains. He and my Mom also raised me and my three older sisters.

Like I said, my Dad was old school and I became the first person in my family to graduate from college. I remember that day like it was yesterday: May 26, 1982. The day I graduated from West Point.

I am sure almost everyone has seen photos of graduation day at West Point. The Cadets are in their finest full dress grey uniforms. Brass buttons are gleaming over starched white pants. Then, the moment everyone has waited for: "Class dismissed." Thousands of white hats soaring through the air. Then, it was off to Lake Popolopen, at Camp Buckner, to picnic with my relatives.

There we were by the lake enjoying our barbeque — my Mom, my Dad, my sisters, aunts, uncles, and cousins. At some point, my Dad called me away for a private word. He hugged me and told me how proud he was of me. Then he thanked me for going to West Point and saving all that tuition money! Finally, he told me he was going to give me a gift of $20,000 as a graduation present. About a week or two later I received a statement from my new broker letting me know I was the proud owner of $20,000 worth of Exxon stock!

There I was — a freshly minted Second Lieutenant on my way to Fort Rucker, Alabama to attend flight school with all that money in my pocket! What do you think I did? Wrong. I didn't invest it. I didn't save it. After four years without any freedom I spent every penny on wine, women, and song. Irresponsible you say? Your child wouldn't do that? Can you be sure? A West Point education did not make me wise. It took experience.

Now that I am 48 with two children of my own I wish my Dad would have protected me from my youthful foolishness. He could have easily done so by leaving the stock to me in trust rather than giving me his gift immediately. Had he done so, a broker has told me the $20,000 gift would be worth over $250,000 today!

Here's how you should leave gifts to your children. This holds true whether you make the gift during lifetime or at your death. Knowing what I know now, I wish my Dad had left me the Exxon stock in trust. A trust is a separate legal entity requiring three things: a trustee who holds legal title to trust property; a beneficiary who gets to enjoy the property according to the terms of the trust agreement; and the trust property itself. The trust agreement spells out instructions for the orderly distribution of the gift. It is then up to the trustee to invest and distribute the trust property.

Do your children need to be protected from themselves? Are they just too young to handle money? Are they irresponsible? Do they have developmental disabilities? Do they have drinking, drug, or gambling problems? Do they have mental problems impacting their motivation to achieve and succeed? Do they have irresponsible spouses whom you believe married them for your money? The list goes on and on. If you, as a loving parent, are afraid of placing significant amounts of income or property in your children's hands, you should not make direct gifts to them.

Instead, love your children enough to protect them and provide for them during their lifetimes. Your trust agreement will direct your trustee to provide for your child's health, education, maintenance, and support. You could also leave written instructions instructing your trustee to take a look at your child's other sources of income and to decide whether or not the child's income should be supplemented from the trust funds. You can leave instructions for your trustee to help your child start a business or buy a home. This leaves you in control, even after you are gone. This is a loving way to protect your child. Finally, by leaving gifts in trust you can assure there will be something left for your grandchildren because you can decide where you wish your money to go after your child dies.

Trusts are not just for the rich and famous. They should be used by every day people who love their families and want to make sure they are always taken care of.

Robert M. Goldberg's special interest as one of Ed Slott's Elite IRA Advisors is helping clients expand their family wealth through intelligent planning for distribution of qualified retirement plans.

CHAPTER 93

Don't Let the Tax Tail Wag the Dog! Providing Flexibility During Life and After Death Through Disclaimer Planning

PATRICK SHIN (Short Hills, New Jersey) and MICHELLE LEE (Millburn, New Jersey)

"Don't let the tax tail wag the dog." When you begin the estate planning process, your primary focus may be saving on taxes. However, the primary focus should be on you and your spouse's goals and not the "tax tail." If you become so obsessed with saving taxes, you may forget to feed the "dog" and take care of your spouse and family. Although saving on taxes is an important goal, you should not let it become the overriding goal. Other goals may include your spouse's control over monies, asset preservation and protection, and providing for your surviving spouse's lifestyle. One way you can make sure you feed the "dog" is to make sure there is flexibility built into your estate plan. We do this by using a tool called a disclaimer.

By using disclaimers, you may be able to: 1) move inherited monies to the next generation without gift tax implications; 2) fund a bypass trust after the date of death of the first spouse (based on the surviving spouse's situation at that time and the federal estate tax exemption); and 3) alter the distribution of an estate plan after an individual has passed away.

WHAT IS A DISCLAIMER?

Section 2518 of the Internal Revenue Code addresses disclaimers. A qualified disclaimer is an irrevocable and unqualified refusal by a person to accept an interest in property. In other words, a disclaimer cannot later be retracted and cannot be modified by conditions or reservations. In addition, all of the following conditions must also be satisfied:

1. The refusal must be in writing and must identify the property interest disclaimed.

2. The refusal must be received by the transferor of the interest not later than nine months after the later of:

   a. the day on which the transfer creating the interest is made, or

   b. the day on which such person attains the age of 21.

3. Such person has not accepted the interest or any of its benefits.

4. As a result of such refusal, the interest passes without any direction on the part of the person making the disclaimer and passes either:

   a. To the spouse of the decedent, or

   b. To a person other than the person making the disclaimer.

WHAT CAN BE DISCLAIMED?

There are many different types of property that can be disclaimed. Please review the chart below and see how a disclaimer may add flexibility when a beneficiary does not want or need a property interest:

TYPE OF PROPERTY	POTENTIAL BENEFIT & EXAMPLE
Intestate shares (property distributed according to a state's intestacy laws where there is no will or trust)	You and other beneficiaries may wish to disclaim your inheritances so that another beneficiary will receive the inheritance gift tax-free.
	For example, an individual passes away with no surviving spouse. He has only three adult children who have no children of their own. If two of the children decide they do not need the money, they may disclaim their inheritance in order for the third child to receive the property gift tax-free.
Income interests in trusts	You may wish to disclaim your income interest so that the property passes by intestacy to a surviving spouse.
	To illustrate, if A creates a trust for the benefit of his children, with income payable to his spouse during her lifetime, the children may disclaim their interest in the trust, causing the property to pass by intestacy to the surviving spouse.
Remainder interests in trusts (rights to trust principal)	You may wish to disclaim an interest in trust principal while retaining rights to the trust income, as long as you have a separate interest in property that does not merge under state law.
	In other words, if A creates an income interest to A for life, then to B for life with the remainder interest to A's estate, A could make a qualified disclaimer of either the income interest, the remainder, or an undivided portion of either interest.
Nontestamentary property such as life insurance and joint tenancies (property that passes outside of a will by operation of law)	You may wish to disclaim your interest as a named beneficiary so the contingent beneficiary receives the inheritance gift tax-free.
	For example, if A passes away leaving his wife as the primary beneficiary of his life insurance, she may choose to disclaim her interest in the life insurance so that the proceeds pass to the contingent beneficiaries, her children.
Powers held by a beneficiary or trustee (in a fiduciary capacity)	You may be able to disclaim powers while retaining rights to the income from a trust.
	A surviving spouse may disclaim property which then passes to a trust for her benefit and the benefit of her children. To be effective, she must also disclaim any powers she possesses in relation to that trust in order to receive benefits under the trust.
Funding of a bypass trust	The surviving spouse can be given flexibility about whether to fund the bypass trust. Because there is no requirement that the bypass trust be funded, the surviving spouse can determine whether it should be funded based on his or her needs and current tax law. See the example below.

HOW CAN DISCLAIMERS PROVIDE FLEXIBILITY IN ESTATE PLANNING?

Let's take a closer look at how disclaimers are used. In the following example, a disclaimer is used to take advantage of the federal estate tax exemption.

> **EXAMPLE 1:** A husband and wife, A and B, each have $2 million in assets, totaling $4 million. A's trust leaves all of his property to his wife. A provision in his trust states that any property the wife chooses to disclaim will pass to a bypass trust. A dies in 2008 when the federal exemption amount is $2 million. At this point (assuming B has not accepted any of A's $2 million and the nine month time limit has not expired), B may choose to disclaim all or a portion of A's $2 million. If she disclaims all of the $2 million, the money will pass to A's bypass trust. Consequently, the principal will not be not included in her taxable estate. The disclaimer provision gives B the flexibility to evaluate the existing tax law and her financial situation after her husband's death.
>
> Let's say that B chooses to accept her husband's $2 million. Any unspent assets will be included in her taxable estate, but she will have sufficient assets to provide for her family and herself.

In the above scenario, if B is named as trustee or has a power of appointment over the trust, she may have to refuse to act as trustee or attempt to release or restrict her powers as trustee for a disclaimer to be valid. If a surviving spouse has a power of appointment over the corpus of the trust, she will have to disclaim those powers. However, if the surviving spouse has both an interest in the income and a power of appointment over the trust corpus, it is possible to disclaim the powers while retaining the interest in income.

Another scenario in which a disclaimer can be used involves children as the disclaimants. A disclaimer of an interest in trust by a decedent's heirs which causes the property to pass to the surviving spouse by intestacy will qualify for the marital deduction.

> **EXAMPLE 2:** A decedent spouse creates two trusts in his will: Trust 1 for his wife; and Trust 2 for his children. Half of his estate is used to fund Trust 1 and the other half is used to fund Trust 2. His children, along with all the intestate beneficiaries, disclaim their interest in Trust 2. The disclaimer is effective and the property passes to the surviving spouse by intestacy and qualifies for the marital deduction.

Great care must be taken when using disclaimers.

> **EXAMPLE 3:** Assume A dies without a will and the beneficiaries who stand to inherit the estate are his four grown, living children and five grandchildren. They all execute valid disclaimers thinking that the property will pass to B, A's surviving wife, and will qualify for the marital deduction. Under state law, the disclaimants are presumed to have

predeceased A. However, the four living children have children, and those children have children. In other words, A has living great-grandchildren. Instead of the property passing to B by operation of state law, the property passes to the grandchildren and great-grandchildren whose parents attempted to execute the disclaimer. In this instance, the disclaimer is not effective. Therefore, it is important when executing a disclaimer, to be thorough in your understanding of how the property will pass in order to achieve the desired result.

If you do not need money from an inheritance, or when a will or trust does not do what it was supposed to do, consider seeking the advice of a qualified estate planning attorney to consider utilizing disclaimer planning. When property is transferred from one person to another, the IRS imposes a tax on the transfer. However, with the proper use of disclaimers, tax liability may be avoided altogether. This result is based on the theory that the disclaimant never actually received the property and therefore could not be making a transfer by gift for federal gift tax purposes. The disclaimant is deemed to have predeceased the transferor. Because the nine month clock begins on the date of transfer or the date of death, promptly consult with a qualified estate planning attorney if any of the foregoing scenarios apply to you.

Patrick Shin counsels high net worth individuals with entrepreneurial businesses in the use of tax saving vehicles, while implementing the clients' goals. He lectures frequently on new tax developments and strategies.

Michelle Lee is an estate planning attorney in Millburn, New Jersey.

CHAPTER 94

When Should We Do Estate Planning? Make Sure You Plan for Your Disability and Death While You Still Can

TONI DEGASPERIN (Laguna Hills, California)

Clearly, you need to prepare your estate plan before you die. You must also prepare your estate plan before you have lost mental capacity.

As you may have noticed, procrastination with regard to planning and signing your will or trust is something you are likely to do month after month, year after year. It seems to be one of the easiest tasks to put off. Some of you have been diagnosed with a severe medical condition or terminal illness, yet you still delay. Others have minor children for whom you should appoint guardians in the event of your death, incapacity, or for temporary emergencies. Others of you are no doubt thinking, why worry about it? There's always tomorrow, right? Wrong! None of us knows when tragedy will strike or when we will die.

You may be thinking you have already told your loved ones how to implement your desires after you die. But you are operating under an incorrect assumption that your spoken instructions will be enforced. Oral instructions and directions, even from your death bed, are not enforceable for making property distributions after your death. Your will or trust must be written and executed by you.

All states require you to have legal capacity at the time you sign your will, or in other words, to be of "sound and disposing mind."

"Being of sound and disposing mind" means you 1) understand the nature of your testamentary act, 2) understand and know the nature and extent of your property, and 3) remember and understand your relationships to your living relatives — your spouse, descendants, parents, and others who are affected by your will or trust.

Following are a few real life situations provided as examples of what can occur when you delay your written instructions. Without an estate plan, your loved ones may not be taken care of in the way you wish.

EXAMPLE 1: Client came in with his wife to amend his existing trust. They discussed the changes and scheduled an appointment to come back in a couple of days to sign the trust amendment. The next morning, the wife called the attorney to inform her that husband had just suffered a heart attack and died on the golf course. Prior to meeting with the attorney, the client had rendered his primary changes to a typewritten paper which he had signed; other changes were discussed with the attorney and agreed upon. After the death, the Court honored the changes in the signed typewritten version but not the orally agreed-upon changes even though they were verified by an impartial third party and no family member objected to them.

EXAMPLE 2: Wife contacted attorney on behalf of her husband who was terminally ill and asked the attorney to prepare certain documents on behalf of husband who was still cognizant and verbal at the time. Attorney prepared the documents immediately and went to their home to meet with husband. During the time it took to prepare the documents and drive to their home, husband had passed into a state of semi-consciousness and never regained full consciousness. The documents could not be executed.

EXAMPLE 3: Husband and wife were going through a divorce. All decisions concerning the division of their property had been agreed upon by them: All property would go to Spouse A. However, the final divorce decree had not been signed and issued by the court. Spouse A died in an accident without having signed any will. Under the State intestate statutes, all of the property passed to the surviving spouse, Spouse B.

If you elect not to set up your own estate plan, your state's law has a plan for you. If you have no signed will or trust, your state's intestate statutes will dictate to whom your property will be distributed and who will be named to make those distributions. Your state's law also sets forth procedures for selecting guardians for your minor children, if you have not done so before you die or become incapacitated.

Many are in agreement with their state's intestate law because it produces the results they want as to distribution and persons in charge. But you must know your own state's law in order to determine if it actually produces the result you want. There are other reasons, however, why you should consider preparing your own estate plan rather than relying on your state's statutes. For one, you might move to another state with different laws that do not agree with your wishes. A more likely occurrence though, is that by preparing your own estate plan you are likely to avoid probate altogether. Probate in many states can be quite expensive and time-consuming. Relying on a state's intestate laws, or on a will, usually results in probate. Trusts and other estate planning mechanisms can avoid the cost and delay of probate.

Do not delay.

Proper planning now will lead to peace of mind, so you can rest assured that your loved ones will be provided for in the manner you desire.

Toni DeGasperin is a Certified Specialist in Estate Planning, Probate and Trust Law by the State Bar of California Board of Legal Specialization.

CHAPTER 95

The Importance of Keeping Your Estate Plan Updated

BARRY D. SIEGEL (Boca Raton, Florida)

You did a great job! You finally made your appointment to see an experienced estate planning attorney. You did all the necessary planning. You even properly funded your living trust.

Your plan might still not work!

Why? Your estate plan was completed five years ago. Since then, a new grandchild was born, you have divorced and remarried, you reconciled with your son, whom you had disinherited, your health care surrogate has passed away, and you sold the building you had left to your favorite charity. You have placed the proceeds from the building sale in a new bank account you opened in your name, forgetting to title the new account in the name of your living trust. The law also changed. Now your estate plan no longer works as you and your attorney had planned.

Now the people you want in your plan as beneficiaries — your grandchild, your new spouse, and your son are not named beneficiaries, and your ex-spouse is named as a beneficiary. Your charity may not get anything. Your new bank account will go through probate. You also need to name a new health care surrogate to make your medical decisions for you if you are mentally incapacitated. Finally, your entire plan may not work properly depending on the law change and its applicability to your situation.

Nothing stays the same.

Circumstances change. You will experience changes in your family situation. There will be births, deaths, disabilities, illnesses, marriages, divorces, and re-marriages.

You may experience changes in your estate. Your business may take off or go bankrupt. You may win a large sum of money from a lawsuit or you may lose it all from a lawsuit. Fluctuations in the stock market or real estate market may make a major difference in the size of your estate.

Laws will change that affect your estate planning. In 2003, the Health Insurance Portability and Accountability Act (HIPAA) laws, dealing with the privacy of medical records, became effective. These laws had a major impact on everyone's estate plan. In Florida, a completely new set of laws affecting living trusts was adopted in 2007, making changes to living trusts a necessity for most people. The much-discussed federal estate tax laws may change, which would impact many estate plans. Because change is inevitable, part of your estate plan should be a plan or procedure for updating it.

Unfortunately, many people think of estate planning as a one-time event and not as the ongoing lifetime process it is. Remember that the only estate plan that matters is the plan in place at the time it is needed. Keeping your estate plan updated is dependent upon you and your estate planning attorney having a plan in place to maintain a continuing relationship. Your attorney does not have a crystal ball to track the events in your life to know when you need an update based on personal and financial circumstances. Conversely, unless you keep up with estate planning laws and issues on a regular basis, you will not know when it may be time to amend your estate plan. The solution is to have a continuing relationship with your estate planning attorney where the communication channels remain open and there is an updating plan in place.

Many of the top estate planning attorneys today have updating programs, sometimes called maintenance programs, in place. Typically, the client may pay a reasonable annual fee to the law firm for the updating program. The plan may include benefits such as annual reviews, no charge for changes to your estate planning documents, notices of applicable law changes, educational workshops, and other legal services at reduced fees.

If you do not have an updating plan for your estate plan, I highly recommend you discuss this with your attorney immediately. If you are looking for an estate planning attorney, ask him or her about their updating system. Remember, you could follow the advice of the many top attorney-authors in this book and do everything else correctly, but in order to have an estate plan that will work the way you want when you need it, make sure you have a plan for updating your plan.

Barry D. Siegel, P.A. provides comprehensive estate and asset protection planning services. The firm maintains systems for updating and maintaining client plans, assuring the plans work properly when they are needed.

CHAPTER 96

Relationship-Centered Planning

HEINZ BRISSKE (Wheaton, Illinois)

The general public's perception of attorneys is that they "handle files" and "charge fees." The word "relationship" rarely comes to mind when thinking about a lawyer. The WealthCounsel estate planner is a different sort of lawyer.

During the estate planning process, you may feel that we, as estate planning professionals, are getting "too personal." However, the first step in the estate planning process must be to learn about you and what you hope to accomplish through your estate plan, and how we can best help you achieve your goals.

There are a number of steps to a successful estate plan:

- **Objectives:** It is impossible to plan for the transfer of your estate unless we understand you, your family, your goals, your aspirations, your values, and your hopes for your loved ones. The first step in the estate planning process, therefore, involves learning about you and what you expect from the process and how we can best help you achieve that.

- **Education:** The next step involves making sure you understand the process and the issues involved. Often estate planning issues are complex, involving detailed estate, gift, and income tax principles. We make every attempt to explain the issues in a simple and straightforward manner, involving you in the process. We encourage you to ask questions, and to try to make the process as interactive as possible.

- **Design:** Once the legal and tax landscape has been explained and navigated to your satisfaction, we design your plan. The plan design is determined by you, with our guidance. Through our close questioning regarding issues relevant to your personal, family, and financial situation, we are able to craft a plan that accomplishes your objectives, while at the same time incorporating tax minimization and other efficiencies.

- **Drafting:** After the plan has been designed, the process of drafting documents begins. Those documents vary from state to state, but many estate plans include a Living Trust with a companion Pour Over Will, a Durable Power of Attorney for Property Management, a Durable Power of Attorney for Health Care, a Living Will, and a HIPAA Authorization.

Additional planning may involve Irrevocable Life Insurance Trusts, Gift Trusts, Grantor Retained Annuity Trusts, Limited Partnerships or LLCs, Charitable Trusts, and more.

- **Implementation:** Two of the most important and overlooked aspects of estate planning are the processes of asset allocation and funding. Transferring and re-titling assets and designating appropriate beneficiaries are as important to the effectiveness of an estate plan as the documents drafted by the attorney. Failure to make the necessary asset allocations, transfers, and beneficiary designations often results in an estate plan that, although well-drafted, is totally ineffective to accomplish your objectives. We work with you to make sure every estate plan is fully funded. These integrated parts of the plan are critical to an estate plan that works.

- **Follow-Up:** We encourage you to keep your plans current through regular annual meetings to thoroughly review your estate plan. Considering the pace of change in the areas of taxation, IRS rulings, case law, and your personal, financial, and family situation, we feel an annual review is not only wise, but absolutely necessary in most cases.

Our goal is to build a relationship with you that will last a lifetime, and beyond. That relationship will assure an ongoing dialogue over the years that will help us keep your estate plan relevant and current.

Huck & Brisske, LLC's practice concentrates in wealth and estate planning, retirement benefit planning, business succession planning, probate, estate, and trust administration.

CHAPTER 97

Ethics in Estate Planning

MARCELLA DOWNING and ROBERT HOWK (Fresno, California)

The area of estate planning is filled with ethical concerns for the attorney and the client. The ethical issues could fill a book and vary from state to state. We will address some of the common issues that can affect decision-making in your estate planning process and beyond.

Our legal system is an adversarial process; that is, in theory, with zealous representation on both sides of a dispute, the courts will arrive at the correct answer. This works well in many areas but it poses some unique problems in the area of estate planning. Often estate planning is done with a team of people striving to develop the best possible plan for the client. This is a cooperative process, not adversarial. If you understand the ethical rules your attorney is required to follow, it will help you make decisions regarding your team and other important issues. Rules differ from state to state; therefore, the rules discussed here are general and apply to California.

The first question your attorney may ask himself or herself when you contact his or her office is: "Who is my client?" You might think this is obvious; if you walked into the office, you are the client. But this is not always the case. Sometimes a family member will contact the office on behalf of a loved one. This can be for a number of reasons. Some of these reasons may be in the interest of the person for whom an estate plan is being contemplated and some of those reasons may not. It is important for you to know that just because someone pays the bill, it does not mean that he or she is the client or has a right to any information, or to direct the work of the attorney.

One problem estate planning attorneys often see is the personal and financial losses which result when a non-attorney attempts to direct the creation of the estate plan. At its worst, this is done in what is known as trust mills. In such circumstances, typically an insurance salesperson, accountant, or financial planner contacts the client with the intent to sell financial products. The trust is offered as a means of persuading the potential client to reveal his or her financial interests, thereby making it easier for the salesperson to sell products. If there is an attorney involved, the client may never see the attorney and if the client does, the estate planning goals are being driven by the salesperson, not the client. Many of these trusts are done cheaply to attract the client, and at the same time, keep the practice away from the awareness of law enforcement. If an attorney is working for a trust mill, he or she has breached his or her duty of loyalty to the client. Many mills will simply get a plan off the internet or have one created and apply it to all the customers without any legal counseling to assure it is the correct plan for the client. Usually problems with these trusts are only detected when the client dies. In some cases, the family is left to probate an estate because the trust failed, or worse yet, the estate ends up in litigation because the way the trust was created causes conflict or aggravates pre-existing conflict in the family.

Some of these same tactics are being used by those offering to help clients apply for public benefits such as Medicaid or, in California, Medi-Cal. Typically, in this situation, products such as annuities, life insurance and/or long-term care insurance may be sold and, unlike in the case of a sale of a trust, very high fees may be charged for the application with the promise to represent the client in any dispute. Any layperson can represent you in a hearing but only an attorney can represent you in court. Only an attorney can be sure that the qualification and application process does not adversely affect the overall estate plan.

Your attorney has a duty of loyalty to you, the client, not the referral source. This includes your accountant, financial planner, insurance or annuity salesperson, and family members. To protect yourself, first, be sure you see the attorney in person. Second, ask the attorney how many referral sources of this type they have. The more referral sources they have, the less they are dependent on one source for business and the more independent they can be for you.

Your attorney also owes you a duty of confidentiality. You have a right to expect that the confidences you share with your attorney will be kept private. You, not your attorney, are the holder of the attorney/client privilege. For this reason, only you can decide if you want your attorney to share private information with others. Sharing information with reputable professionals of your choice can be a big benefit to you. This creates a team of people who will bring their expertise to solving your unique problems.

However, when the attorney/client privilege is waived by the client, information shared may be accessed in litigation if litigation later occurs. This may or may not be a good thing. It would help to establish your intent if there is any question after you pass away. However, it could mean that information you intended to be kept from the public eye could be revealed. Most estates do not result in litigation after the fact if you create a reliable team and put a good estate plan in place.

Other members of your team may be family members or very close friends, what I will call family of choice. One of the benefits of a trust is that the trust is a private document. However, problems can occur if the person designated to hold your power of attorney or who becomes the successor trustee if you are unable to serve, is not informed concerning the duties he or she has with regard to your estate and personal wishes. Some of this can be spelled out in the estate plan but if your key support people in your family of choice must take on responsibilities and be required to learn what their duties are and how to fulfill them in a time of grief, the responsibility can be overwhelming.

Disclosing your reasoning for your estate plan to family members can help to avoid future litigation that is emotionally driven. Typically, if your family knows in advance why you chose a particular person as a fiduciary, it can reduce conflict later. This is a counseling issue you should discuss with your attorney. Here again, you would be waiving your right to confidentiality if you allow your attorney to work with family members.

Ideally, you will have a lifelong relationship with your estate planning attorney, revising your plan as your situation, goals, or the law changes. This can create some difficult ethical problems for your attorney as you age. Within the confines of the law, your attorney must zealously represent your wishes. Your attorney may not supplant his or her wishes for yours. As we age, it is common for our reasoning abilities to slow down. This can make the older client susceptible to undue influence by unscrupulous people. Sometimes this influence may come from caregivers, family members, or sales people. Financial and physical abuse of the elderly has become such a problem that some states have enacted laws that allow attorneys to receive three times the amount of the money lost and other expenses if they win a case against an abuser. However, by the time the abuse is recognized, the money may no longer be there to retrieve. Worse yet, it can be very embarrassing to admit someone has been able to take advantage of you.

If the client refuses to allow the attorney to report an abuser, either financial or physical, to law enforcement, the attorney may not disclose the information. This is because the law values and protects the special trust that clients place in their attorneys. However, some other professionals, such as bankers and doctors, are actually required to report abuse, with or without the client's permission.

One way to avoid a number of these difficulties is to develop a reliable team in advance. If you begin training your successor trustee to take over the responsibilities of the position while you are still at your peak, mentally and physically, you are more likely to have a trained person you trust in place when the time comes to turn the responsibility over to that person. The problem for an attorney comes when the client is not aware that the time has come to make that transition. Most of us know of situations where family members have driven their car long after they should have given up the keys to the car. This can be true of dealing with financial affairs also. However, if you have trained your successor trustee, the loss of control is not so much of an issue.

Your attorney is faced with an ethical dilemma if you refuse to turn over control and a family member feels, often in your best interest, that it is time. At this point, your attorney must follow your direction, even if he believes it is not in your best interest in his or her opinion. If your attorney has done estate planning for other members of the family involved in the dispute, your attorney will likely be required to remove himself or herself as counsel for all the parties because of a conflict of interest between his or her representation of you and the other family member.

What can you do to be sure you are dealing with a competent and ethical attorney? First, be sure you are dealing with an attorney. Look the attorney up with your state bar. Be sure he or she is licensed and in good standing. Your state bar may tell you if the attorney belongs to any special areas of the state bar or has received any specialized training. Second, keep in mind the issues we have discussed here and ask questions. If you choose to create a team, make sure it is your team. Only you will know whom you trust, and with a little research, you are likely to put together a very good team that will serve you well.

The Law Office of Howk & Downing practices in the area of estate planning, elder law, real estate, and insurance defense.

Index

A

A-B bypass trust — 191

Accounting — ii, vi, x, 45, 69, 101, 102, 211, 212, 213, 222, 223, 225, 291, 298, 314, 324

Administrator — 5, 44, 57, 58, 218, 260, 264

Advance Health Care Directive — 6, 86, 87, 89, 126

Advanced estate planning — 6

Advisory committee — 93

Affidavit of power of attorney — 85

Alaska asset protection trust — 326, 327

Anatomical gift — 88

Annual gift exclusion — 133, 134, 235

Applicable exclusion amount — 11, 15, 136, 234

Ascertainable standard — 203, 212, 346

Asset protection trust — 67, 319, 320, 321, 326, 327, 330, 336

Avoiding probate — 23, 25, 57, 59, 65, 199, 295

B

Basic estate planning — 5, 315

Beneficiary designation — 58, 61, 62, 104, 199, 215, 216, 217, 245, 257, 258, 259, 260, 264, 265, 267, 268, 270, 274, 377

BERT — 346, 347, 348, 349, 350, 351

Blended family — 115

Buildup Equity Retirement Trust — 346, 347, 349, 351

Business planning — viii, 22, 62, 76, 117, 135, 138, 243, 298, 322, 334, 335, 351

Buy-sell agreement — 227, 230, 244, 247, 248, 249, 278, 280

Bypass trust — 66, 67, 78, 79, 80, 119, 191, 198, 199, 200, 274

C

Captive insurance company — 336, 354, 355, 356

Care manager — 93

Charitable deduction — 13, 14, 138, 165, 167, 173, 175, 177, 255, 227

Charitable gift — x, 127, 184

Charitable lead annuity trust — 170

Charitable lead trust — 7, 170, 171, 172, 173

Charitable remainder annuity trust — 166, 175, 177

Charitable remainder trust — x, 7, 165, 167, 169, 174

Charitable remainder unitrust — 166, 168

CLAT — 7, 170, 171, 172

CLUT — 7, 171, 172

Co-trustee — 46, 65, 203, 205, 206, 217

Complex trust — 7, 72

Conservation easement — 178, 179, 180, 181

Conservator — 5, 24, 82, 86, 87, 88, 92, 193

Contingent future interests — 29, 30, 31

Control premium — 291, 354

Corporate trustee — 46, 196, 206

CRAT — 7, 166, 167, 168, 169, 173

Credit shelter trust — 66, 109, 110, 111, 191, 274

Creditor claims — 67, 193, 221, 323, 324

Crummey trust — 131, 138, 145

CRUT — 7, 167, 168, 169, 173

Custodial account — 140, 141, 142, 143, 144, 145, 147

D

DAPT — 321, 322

Designated beneficiary — 215, 254, 258, 262, 263, 264, 265, 267, 268, 272, 273, 274, 275

Disability — 2, 4, 9, 37, 67, 82, 83, 84, 85, 90, 91, 92, 125, 126, 192, 206, 213, 219, 231, 248, 269, 273, 281, 336, 343, 344, 345, 363, 365, 371, 373, 374

Disclaimer — 118, 119, 120, 121, 227, 265, 367, 368, 369, 370

Domestic asset protection trust — 67, 320, 321, 327, 336

Durable power of attorney — 5, 6, 89, 126, 203, 358, 376

Dynasty trust — 67, 74, 75, 76, 285, 286

E

Elder law — 46, 117, 143, 154, 197, 204, 291, 295, 357, 358, 359, 361, 362, 363, 381

Estate Planning Team — 8, 9, 13

Estate tax — 6, 7, 9, 11, 12, 13, 14, 17, 26, 45, 64, 66, 67, 70, 71, 73, 74, 75, 78, 79, 80, 81, 97, 98, 99, 100, 101, 102, 103, 104, 105, 107, 109, 110, 111, 112, 114, 115, 116, 119, 120, 121, 122, 123, 126, 129, 130, 134, 135, 136, 137, 139, 142, 155, 157, 159, 165, 167, 168, 169, 171, 173, 177, 178, 179, 180, 191, 195, 196, 197, 199, 200, 217, 220, 221, 223, 224, 225, 227, 234, 237, 239, 252, 253, 254, 255, 256, 269, 273, 285, 286, 288, 289, 292, 293, 294, 295, 299, 302, 309, 310, 311, 317, 332, 336, 340, 341, 342, 346, 347, 348, 349, 350, 352, 353, 356, 375

Estate tax deduction — 101, 102, 103, 165

Ethics — 378, 379, 381

Executor — 17, 39, 44, 45, 46, 50, 54, 55, 56, 57, 62, 101, 102, 103, 126, 193, 220, 227, 256

Expression of charitable intentions — 182, 183, 184

F

Family Limited Partnership — ix, x, xi, 7, 12, 138, 156, 288, 292, 293, 294, 295, 315, 317, 329

FAPT — 321, 322

Farm — 2, 51, 52, 167, 168, 169, 175, 176, 180, 309, 364

Federal estate and gift tax — 15, 28

Fiduciary — iv, 5, 12, 44, 45, 46, 61, 88, 119, 122, 148, 203, 205, 206, 211, 212, 225, 270, 344, 380

First death planning — 198

Five year rule — 263

FLP — 7, 8, 287, 292, 293, 294, 315, 316, 317, 318, 336, 337

Foreign asset protection trust — 320, 321

Formal probate — 57, 58, 59, 61

Funding — 7, 65, 144, 145, 146, 147, 190, 191, 215, 216, 217, 218, 219, 238, 281, 286, 287, 293, 318, 347, 360, 377

G

Generation-skipping transfer tax — 73, 75, 77, 78, 171, 213, 233, 286, 356

Ghost life expectancy — 263

Gift splitting — 136, 137, 138, 139

Gift tax — viii, 6, 7, 11, 12, 13, 15, 16, 17, 25, 26, 28, 64, 73, 74, 75, 99, 105, 130, 132, 133, 134, 135, 136, 137, 138, 139, 140, 144, 145, 146, 149, 150, 153, 155, 156, 170, 172, 177, 192, 202, 223, 235, 238, 240, 281, 286, 287, 288, 290, 294, 295, 299, 300, 302, 303, 304, 311, 329, 332, 333, 341, 342, 346, 347, 348, 349, 350, 356

Goals of estate planning — vii, 2, 3

Grantor retained annuity trust — 7, 159, 286, 299, 301, 377

Grantor trust — 7, 69, 70, 71, 148, 153, 159, 173, 192, 285, 286, 302, 305, 327, 336, 346, 350

GRAT — 7, 138, 159, 286, 287, 299, 300, 301

Gross estate — 14, 17, 28, 64, 98, 99, 100, 104, 123, 155, 157, 173, 227, 301, 311

H

Health, education, maintenance, or support — 121

Health care durable power of attorney — 89

Health Insurance Portability and Accountability Act — 5, 6, 374

Holographic will — 39, 40

I

ILIT — 6, 8, 67, 237, 238, 239, 347, 350

Incapacity planning — 89, 100

Income in respect of decedent — 252, 253, 255

Independent trustee — 211, 212, 213

Individual retirement account — 61

Informal probate — 57, 58, 59

Inherited IRA — 263, 265, 267, 268, 272, 274

Installment sale — 152, 153, 157

Intangible property — 21, 341

Intentionally Defective Grantor Trust — 7, 70, 71, 153, 159, 285, 305

Intestate succession — 34, 42, 43, 142

Intra-family loan — 149, 151

IRA — 57, 58, 63, 143, 118, 146, 216, 218, 227, 252, 253, 254, 255, 256, 257, 258, 259, 260, 261, 262, 263, 264, 265, 266, 267, 268, 269, 270, 271, 272, 273, 274, 275, 293, 326, 346, 366

IRD — 252, 253, 254, 255, 256

Irrevocable Life Insurance Trust — 6, 137, 168, 227, 237, 239, 316, 336, 347, 350, 377

Irrevocable Trust — viii, ix, 67, 362

Irrevocable trusts — 7, 16, 63, 67, 68, 99, 119, 285, 287, 299, 303, 316, 327, 336, 346, 348, 362

J

Joint tenancy — 23, 24, 25, 26, 27, 63, 64, 108, 113, 126, 198, 199

Joint trust — 51, 66, 196, 197, 217

L

Life insurance — ix, x, 2, 6, 9, 12, 58, 60, 61, 62, 63, 65, 67, 71, 75, 99, 108, 118, 137, 138, 139, 168, 172, 198, 216, 218, 227, 230, 231, 232, 233, 234, 235, 236, 237, 238, 239, 240, 241, 242, 243, 244, 245, 246, 248, 253, 281, 286, 287, 314, 316, 317, 330, 336, 341, 345, 346, 347, 348, 350, 356, 377, 379

Life settlements — 231, 241, 242, 243

Lifetime gift exemption — 130, 134, 136

Limited Liability Company — 7, 156, 172, 216, 218, 248, 288, 292, 296, 297, 298, 315, 319, 321, 324, 327, 329, 336, 346, 348

Liquidity — 4, 6, 227, 233, 244, 295, 316

Living Will — 6, 84, 85, 89, 126, 315, 358, 362, 376

LLC — ii, iv, vi, ix, xi, 7, 13, 49, 77, 123, 249, 253, 256, 284, 288, 289, 290, 291, 294, 296, 297, 298, 315, 316, 319, 320, 321, 322, 324, 325, 329, 330, 331, 332, 333, 336, 337, 341, 346, 349, 350, 377

Long-term care — 90, 91, 343, 357, 358, 360, 363, 379

Lump sum distribution — 255, 259

M

Marital deduction — 12, 64, 99, 102, 103, 104, 105, 106, 107, 108, 109, 114, 115, 116, 119, 121, 122, 123, 126, 191, 237, 255, 295, 347

Marital trust — 66, 109, 110, 111, 112, 116, 119, 123

Marriage — ii, 25, 55, 66, 113, 114, 115, 117, 125, 126, 127, 137, 196, 197, 199, 202, 209, 269, 271, 273, 274, 280, 316, 317, 332, 374

Medicaid — 44, 92, 117, 169, 273, 358, 360, 361, 362, 363, 379

Medicare — 273, 357, 358, 360

Memorandum of Intent — 94

Minor's trust — 131, 145

N

Net Income Makeup Charitable Remainder Unitrust — 168

NIMCRUT — 168

No-contest clause — 50, 51, 52, 193

Non-citizen spouse — 109, 122, 123, 347

Non-grantor trust — 71, 327

Non-probate Assets — 63

Nonspouse beneficiary — 255, 270

Nontraditional relationships — ii, 127

P

Per capita — 47, 48, 49

Per capita at each generation per stirpes — 48, 49

Per stirpes — 47, 48, 49

Personal property — 20, 21, 29, 40, 163, 164, 177, 216

Personal representative — 17, 39, 44, 45, 100, 116, 117, 118, 142, 220, 317

Pet trust — ii, 343, 344, 345

Philanthropy — 75, 182, 183, 184

Physician — 83, 84, 335, 336, 337

Pooled income fund — 177

Postmortem planning — 77

Present interests — 13, 29, 31

Private annuities — 155, 156, 157, 158, 159

Private foundation — ix, x, 180, 185, 187

Probate administration — 57, 59, 222, 226

Probate assets — 60, 61, 63

Probate avoidance — 190, 191, 193

Probate estate — 45, 216, 352

Property interests — 29, 31, 32, 108, 176

Prudent investor rule — 224

Q

QTIP trust — 66, 77, 99, 109, 113, 114, 115, 116, 117, 121, 123, 124, 198, 200, 255

Qualified beneficiary — 222, 223

Qualified conservation contribution — 176

Qualified domestic trust — 108, 122, 123

Qualified Personal Residence Trust — 7, 302, 303

Qualified plan — 174, 261, 262, 263, 264, 265, 266, 269, 270, 336, 349

Qualified terminal interest property trust — 66

R

Real property — 20, 21, 29, 31, 61, 139, 141, 176, 192, 218, 224, 225, 294, 303, 314, 321

Recapitalization — 305, 306, 307, 308

Relationship — iv, 9, 27, 42, 117, 125, 127, 132, 149, 162, 210, 219, 340, 355, 371, 375, 376, 377, 380

Remainder interest — 30, 170, 173, 175, 176, 177, 225, 301

Remarriage — 114, 192, 198, 199, 317

Required minimum distributions — 255, 261, 263, 265, 267, 270, 272, 273

Retirement account — 12, 58, 61, 65, 252, 253, 254, 255, 257, 258, 259, 260, 274, 330

Retirement plan — 2, 57, 60, 61, 62, 125, 168, 215, 216, 218, 227, 254, 255, 257, 258, 259, 260, 279, 282, 326, 346, 366

Revocable living trust — 5, 22, 24, 34, 35, 54, 56, 58, 62, 65, 66, 67, 70, 110, 116, 126, 190, 191, 192, 193, 195, 197, 198, 199, 200, 201, 203, 205, 208, 209, 211, 212, 213, 217, 220, 221, 222, 226, 257, 315, 317, 326, 333, 336, 361

Revocable trust — ix, 51, 63, 64, 68, 101, 102, 103, 111, 195, 196, 221, 352, 363

Roth conversion — 255

Rule against perpetuities — 73, 75, 76, 77, 172, 192

S

Section 529 — 144, 146, 147

Section 6166 — 309, 310, 311

Self-canceling installment note — 152, 153, 155, 285

Separate trust — 16, 66, 196, 274

Simple trust — 69, 71

Special needs trust — 67, 92, 93, 95, 195, 363

Spousal rollover — 264, 265, 267, 268

State death tax — 14, 17, 116, 340, 341

Statutory notice — 221

Statutory will — 40

Stretch — 179, 255, 259, 260, 263, 264, 265, 269, 272, 273, 274

Succession planning — iv, 88, 155, 156, 157, 159, 278, 279, 281, 283, 284, 285, 287, 356

Successor trustee — 5, 46, 62, 65, 89, 190, 191, 192, 195, 205, 207, 211, 220, 221, 222, 238, 318, 379, 380

T

Tangible property — 21, 341

Taxation of trusts — 69, 71

Testamentary capacity — 36, 37, 38

Transfer for value — 235, 236, 244, 245

Trust administration — ix, x, 117, 143, 220, 221, 222, 223, 224, 225, 226, 227, 295, 327, 377

Trust distribution — 66, 210, 223

Trust protector — 94, 211, 212, 213

Trustee distribution powers — 201, 203

Trustee fees — 101, 102, 225

U

UGMA/UTMA — 140

Undue influence — 36, 37, 38, 52, 54, 380

Uniform Gifts to Minors Act — 134, 140

Uniform Transfers to Minors Act — 140

V

Valuation discounts — 138, 156, 172, 227, 288, 289, 291, 293, 294, 307, 336

Vested future interests — 29, 30, 31

Viatical settlement — 231, 242

W

Will substitute — 64, 279

Wyoming LLCs — 329, 331, 333